ANSEL ADAMS

Letters 1916–1984

ANSEL ADAMS

Letters 1916–1984

Edited by Mary Street Alinder
and Andrea Gray Stillman

Foreword by Wallace Stegner

Little, Brown and Company

BOSTON · NEW YORK · LONDON

First trade paperback edition, 2001
This new edition reproduces the entire text of the original book,
as well as a small selection of the photographs.

Library of Congress Cataloging-in-Publication Data

Adams, Ansel, 1902–1984
[Selections. 1988]
Ansel Adams: letters 1916–1984 /
edited by Mary Street Alinder and Andrea Gray Stillman; foreword by Wallace Stegner.
Includes index and chronology.
ISBN 0-8212-1691-0 (cloth) / 0-8212-2682-7 (trade paperback)
1. Adams, Ansel, 1902–1984 — Correspondence. 2. Photography, Artistic. 3. Photographers — United States — Biography. I. Alinder, Mary Street, 1946–   . II. Stillman, Andrea Gray. III. Title.
TR140.A3A4 1988   770'.92'4 — dc 19   [B]   88-1245   CIP

Designed by Dean Bornstein

Printed in the United States of America

Foreword

◦§ ?◦

READING THESE LETTERS, I AM SWEPT BACK IRRESISTIBLY INTO Ansel Adams' hyperactive life. He lived and worked amid swarms of people—his family and assistants, neighbors, friends, conservationists, politicians, other photographers, casual admirers. You never rang his doorbell that his living room and studio did not contain at least four or five people talking to Virginia and waiting for Ansel to come out of the darkroom. When he did come, still in his lab apron and with his glasses on top of his head, there would be a boom and rush of greeting and laughter, a new joke or limerick, a few minutes of impetuous talk, the answering of a question or settling of a problem or determining of a piece of conservation strategy, a regretful admission that he was chained to the darkroom for a while, an admonition to stay—stay to dinner, please—and an apologetic departure through the studio and office on his way back to his trays of hypo.

On the way he would probably pause long enough at the studio table to inspect the work of the assistant spotting prints there; and as he passed through the office you might hear the machine-gun tattoo of the typewriter. That would be Ansel, pausing in transit to add a line or two to the letter rolled into it—perhaps one of these letters I have just been reading, punctuated with multiple exclamation points and asterisks and picturesque misspellings.

Then he would be gone for a while, closeted alone, locked in his wrestle with absolute truth.

The most significant part of Ansel Adams, the spirit that will long outlive the man, has already been well documented. The photographs are what most people know him by; and the photographs, since they are his most profound response to his life on earth, are a form of self-documentation. If we wanted to put the nature images into chronological order, we would have a record of his travels as well as of the places— San Francisco, Yosemite, Carmel—that he called home. If we assembled the notable portraits—Albert Bender, Stieglitz, O'Keeffe, Cedric Wright, Weston, David McAlpin, Nancy and Beaumont Newhall,

Ashkenazy—we would have an anthology of the strongest influences and warmest friendships of his life.

What is more important, those photographs, especially those in which he revealed the grandeur and delicacy of the earth in moments of miraculous weather and light, are intensely personal statements. Whether known through prints, portfolios, screens, posters, or books, they show us the mystical, romantic, larger-than-life Adams who viewed nature with reverence but approached it with such discipline that some critics thought him antihuman.

It is true that his great visual anthems, for example the enlargements that look down from his own studio walls, are devoid of the presence or traces of people. It is just as true that Ansel Adams the artist can never be caught hanging around in or just off the edge of the picture, mugging and hoofing for attention. He submits, he makes himself invisible. That does not mean he is not there.

Distant he could be called. Removed. Objective. Cold or absent he is not. Though the great nature images properly tell us nothing about his external life except that he was there to click the shutter, they tell us everything about his spirit and intentions as an artist. The dawn-struck peaks and shadowed cliffs and piled thunderheads, the black skies in which for his benefit some god has pasted improbable moons, contain and express him. They are, and were intended to be, "equivalents," in the word that Ansel liked and borrowed from Stieglitz, of his own respect and wonder and awe in the face of the world's beauty.

The artist Ansel Adams has been before the public for more than a half century. But the man Ansel Adams, the one his family and friends and associates knew, never hid or withheld himself. Once, oppressed with obligations, commitments, and overwork, he exclaimed to Edwin Land that he wished he could live like Weston, holed up on Wildcat Hill, working only when he pleased and keeping aloof from the rat race. Land said to him, "Weston lives in a shrine. You live in the world."

Precisely. He never lived anywhere else. Withdrawal was antithetical to his gregarious nature. He lived deeply, interestedly, helplessly, in the world. He had a living to make, and so for many years he hung up his shingle and took what came. He had family obligations because he treasured them, hundreds of friends because he welcomed them, thousands of admirers to whom he granted the courtesy of polite attention. He promoted photography as an art and fought to defend the environment against spoliation because he believed deeply in those causes. He was a teacher because, as he confessed, he could never know a thing without wanting to pass it on. As Nancy Newhall's biography *The Eloquent Light* demonstrated, and as his own *An Autobiography* demonstrated even more plainly, the artist who made all those serene, austere, magnificent images lived a life as crowded with people and activity as his art was purged of them.

One motivation for reading the personal letters of artists is a kind of voyeurism, a curiosity about private lives, and especially—since the lives of artists are notoriously messy—the grubby hope of finding something scandalous and titillating. No reader of Ansel Adams' letters is going to have that pleasure, for there is nothing of that sort there. Nevertheless, a mutual friend has said to me that he wonders if these letters should be published at all. Must they mine him like a mineral deposit and then pail his tailings? he asks. Haven't *The Eloquent Light* and *An Autobiography* sufficiently revealed the man behind the camera? Will either a life-in-letters or a career-in-letters much alter our perception of either the life or the career? And isn't it possible that the publication of letters, which are often hasty and in this case are full of clowning and horseplay, jokes, puns, occasional pomposities, doggerel and dog-Latin, asterisks and exclamation marks, cries of *Wow!* and *Ah Wilderness!!,* and unquenchable high spirits that make comedy out of even fatigue and illness, will reduce rather than enlarge the public image of Ansel Adams? Would it increase our appreciation of the Gettysburg Address if a contemporary photograph could be produced showing that Lincoln's shirttail was out when he delivered it?

What happens to Ansel Adams' aloof serenity if we hear him exploding like a firecracker, or see him dirty and dog-tired at the end of a 26-hour day, physically and spiritually disheveled, trying to get enough of a boost from a second or third bourbon so that he can tackle the work that still has to be done that night? ("I can hardly see the keyboard. I have around me piles of letters, bills, etc. to be answered. I have no new jokes. I need—and am taking—a shower.") Is that the man who gave us *Moon and Half Dome?*

Of course it is. Our mutual friend is unduly concerned. For one thing, these letters are not tailings, but various, full expressions of the man. Ansel never adopted a godlike pose with his eyes sternly starward. Seriously as he took his art, and much as he made himself its instrument, he was never precious or pretentious. If there was a touch of theatricality in his public face and costume, it was as good-humored and accessible as the rest of him. It united him with his audience instead of elevating him above it. "Unfortunately," he wrote to Weston, "public presentation is a game, a trick." He played it with his tongue in his cheek and his sense of humor intact, and in fact it matched his private style of ebullience and exaggeration.

One goes to the letters for aspects of the whole man that the art excludes: how he coped with the warring demands of art and commercialism until the art by itself could support him; how his jocular and gregarious temperament at once contradicted and enhanced the high seriousness of the photography. Life-in-letters or career-in-letters (and it is both), it doesn't matter what this selection of his correspondence is called; it enhances both life and career, for they were inseparable. The artist was only the highest stretch of the man.

Art is a by-product of living, not an evasion of it or a substitute for it. Ansel Adams lived amply, warmly, enthusiastically, and well; and the strenuous diversity of his life, however completely the photographs exclude it, is still a part of their context. The photographs give us moments when he held his breath. The letters show him breathing, even panting.

They show him, that is, as his family and friends knew him, in the intimate interchanges of daily life and at the highest reaches of his thinking and feeling. Letters were a tradition and a need for him, the medium of a communion at once more serious and more intimate than conversation provided, and a means of clarifying himself to himself and explaining himself to others. They too, like the photographs, are equivalents.

Look at the earnest, filial, dedicated letters to his father and mother and Aunt Mary. Look at those in which he presents himself, his dreams, and his ambitions to Virginia. Look at the profound, self-searching, sometimes confident, sometimes deeply troubled, letters to close friends such as the Newhalls. Many times, letter writing was a safety valve for Ansel, a release for his enthusiasm or indignation or playfulness. Just about as often, he went to the typewriter as others might go to a chapel.

It should be noted that this is not the collected letters, but a selection. Though Ansel shows himself here as a theorist, a technician, a partisan, a son, father, husband, and friend, Mary Alinder's and Andrea Stillman's editing has cut away much that is merely casual or ephemeral, including many letters to and from some of his closest friends. It must also have cut away some things that, otherwise serious and important, did not contribute to a tracing of the main themes of his life. It is richer for the earlier years than for the later, busier years when it was easier to pick up the telephone than to write a letter.

Nevertheless this is a full and generous offering, all the more satisfying in that it so often provides both sides of a continuing dialogue, and thus reintroduces us not only to Ansel but to Ansel's mentors, friends, and colleagues, many of them major artists and tastemakers in their own right.

Everything central to both life and career is here: Ansel's family relations, first with his parents and Aunt Mary, then with Virginia and their children, Michael and Anne; his dedication to the art of photography, with all the self-examination that that entailed, first in letters to his father, then in correspondence with Stieglitz, Paul Strand, Weston, and others, and finally in the years-long communion with Beaumont and Nancy Newhall; his love affair with grand nature, especially Yosemite, that began at fourteen and continued throughout his life; and his activism in the cause of conservation, from the time when, as caretaker of LeConte Lodge, he led Sierra Club trips into the High Sierra, to his last years, when he let hardly a day go by without a challenge or a rebuke to the environmental policies of the Reagan administration.

Much of the history of photography in the twentieth century went through his house, his darkroom, and his typewriter. He had his favorites, particularly Weston and Strand, and his anathemas, particularly Edward Steichen, "the Antichrist of photography." He did not much like the documentarians, with the exception of Dorothea Lange and Walker Evans, and he liked *them* not because they were documenting social significance but because they were artists.

He resented the pressure of Depression times, and the gang mentality of "proletarian" photographers who used photography for a social or political purpose. Urged to turn his art to social significance, he guessed that a rock had as much social significance as a line of unemployed. Asked why he did not exploit great man-made monuments such as the Bay Bridge and the Golden Gate Bridge, he replied that he would rather work on an old wall with moss on it. By some standards, his artistic principles were conservative, even narrow. He would have replied that they came from his personal conviction, not from a fashion or from social pressures. And it should be noted that what he did has lasted far better than the kind of photography he rejected.

The letters show his early self-questioning solidifying into a set of artistic principles over the years, and those principles rather crossly re-pudiated most modern and abstract art. However much his vision en-larged and glorified his subjects, he was consistently representational. But he never accepted the notion of photography as mere record, and he never submitted to what he called the tyranny of subject. That was precisely what he held against Steichen. Finally, though he was a con-summate technician, capable of instructing even such a master as Wes-ton, he never valued technique for itself. He would have agreed with Weston that it was only a way of seeing.

I have said that the artist is only the furthest stretch of the man. Noth-ing illustrates that continuity so well as the discussions of photography in the letters to Stieglitz, Weston, and the Newhalls. But the letters on conservation are out of the same body of conviction. The man who made unforgettable images out of the grandeur and mystery of nature did so because he could not help doing so, because he loved what he saw. The man who spent his energy defending nature against the careless and greedy also worked from love. His environmentalism was not a side issue, something done with the left hand in spare time. It sprang from the same source as his art, and involved him wholly.

So, to anyone who wonders if Ansel Adams' often hasty, sometimes unguarded, nearly always playful letters should be published, for fear of exposing some "lesser" side of him, I have to repeat: Don't worry. Ansel was not made of pieces or sides, he was all one thing. He had no more sides than a sphere does. And it is only the surface of these letters that is playful. The feelings, the convictions, the concerns, are serious, and the seriousness is somehow not diluted by the playfulness. In some odd way the playfulness is part of his shine, part of the light he shed. It would take a lot of work with prisms to separate his light into different and separate aspects of a spectrum.

I close this book of letters feeling as if I have just had a refreshing visit with a man whose character and attainments I greatly admired and whose company I loved. For the space of this reading, I have been back in the swarming vitality of his life. He has come out of the darkroom and joined those of us still hanging around in his living room. The at-mosphere is jovial, the air is full of talk, our somewhat low-keyed wait-ing has been reanimated.

Outside the windows the hill falls away to the shore, and from the shore the Pacific spreads flat and varnished; at its far edge the sun is about to drown. The sea has the serenity of an Ansel Adams photograph, a glory of light that is in our vision even when we turn away from it.

In a moment, maybe, Ansel will pick up the padded drumstick and knock a deep, throbbing hum out of the Chinese drum on his mantel. He will be laughing at the sound, and at the way it instantly commands our attention. The throb of that drum is so deep it tickles the bottoms of our feet.

"It's an evening for the green flash," he tells us. "Wait. Don't watch the sun, or it will burn its image into your retina and you'll miss everything. Don't look until just at the moment when it disappears below the horizon. There'll be a streak of green light, just for a hundredth of a second."

We wait, wrapped in the geniality and warmth he creates, laughing because he is laughing, but watching sidelong, a little breathlessly, hoping to catch that flash briefer than the wink of a firefly—attending while he teaches us again, as he has taught us so many times before, how to see.

Wallace Stegner
Los Altos Hills, California
November 1987

Editors' Note

ₒ§ ₍₀

ANSEL ADAMS HAD A PASSIONATE NEED TO COMMUNICATE. HE wrote thousands of letters and postcards to family, friends, photographers, environmentalists, and politicians. He began consistently writing letters during his teenage summers in Yosemite. Handwritten, they were difficult to read and laborious to write; he thus quickly adopted the typewriter. He traveled with a portable model so that he could correspond no matter where he might be: at his studios in San Francisco, Yosemite, or Carmel; in cities like New York, Chicago, or Washington; in remote spots like Whites' Cabins outside Carlsbad, New Mexico, or on board a train in Wyoming or a ship to Hawaii; or in any one of more than a dozen national parks as far apart as Maine and Alaska.

Adams' abundant archives of photographs, letters, and related materials are now at the Center for Creative Photography at the University of Arizona in Tucson. The voluminous exchanges between Adams and Beaumont and Nancy Newhall are also at the Center. Adams' letters to Alfred Stieglitz are at the Beinecke Library at Yale University, and his environmental letters are at the Bancroft Library at the University of California, Berkeley. The thirty-five-year interchange between Adams and the Polaroid Corporation, for whom he was a consultant, is at their corporate archives in Cambridge, Massachusetts.

As Adams' assistants in the 1970s and 1980s, we were privileged to work with this prodigious body of correspondence in order to select the letters in this book. Sifting through mountains of papers, we chose those letters that show the development of the artist and the man. We edited some letters; text that was removed is noted with an ellipsis (. . .). We eliminated names and subjects that had no continuous meaning in Adams' life and sections that were repetitive or simply dull and corrected typographical errors and unintentional misspellings that added to the reader's burden and did not enrich the writer's meaning. We offer brief footnotes when necessary and, on occasion, clarification through the use of brackets within the text (e.g., [Sierra] Club).

We are grateful that Ansel entrusted us with this project. We thank his wife, Virginia Adams, who acted as our advisor every step of the way.

Beaumont Newhall, with characteristic generosity, assisted our research. We appreciate the work of James Alinder, who read each draft of our manuscript and offered important comments and counsel, and Phyllis Donohue, Pam Feld, John Breeden, Peter Bunnell, Sarah Greenough, George Kimball, Alan Ross, and John Sexton, who provided important assistance.

Central to this book produced by Bulfinch Press for Little, Brown and Company have been Janet Swan Bush, Amanda Freymann, John Maclaurin, and Elizabeth D. Power. Our editor, Ray Roberts, skillfully guided us through many drafts.

Finally, we would like to thank the trustees of the Ansel Adams Publishing Rights Trust, John P. Schaefer, William A. Turnage, and David H. Vena, who supported our efforts over many years.

Mary Street Alinder
Pebble Beach, California

Andrea Gray Stillman
New York, New York
November 1987

ANSEL ADAMS

Letters 1916–1984

CAMP CURRY

....Yosemite Valley....

DAVID A. CURRY
Proprietor

HAPPY ISLES

Camp Curry, California, June 23 1916.

Dear Aunt Mary,

I am sending you two pictures of Yosemite Valley that I have taken. Films are expensive to develop and I expect to be broke if I keep up the rate I am taking pictures. I have taken 30 alreaddy.

Yesterday I went up to Sierra Point and enjoyed lying on my cheat and looking over the edge - about fifteen-hundred feet down. - perpendicular.

To Mary Bray[1]

Yosemite National Park
June 23, 1916

Dear Aunt Mary,

I am sending you two pictures of Yosemite Valley that I have taken. Films are expensive to develop and I expect to be broke if I keep up the rate I am taking pictures. I have taken 30 already.

Yesterday I went up to Sierra Point and enjoyed lying on my chest and looking over the edge—about fifteen-hundred feet down—perpendicular.

. . . The swimming pool is fine and I am going in today. I expect to go to Glacier Point next week.

Hoping to hear from you soon.

I am,
Ansel Adams

1. Mary Bray, Adams' unmarried maternal aunt, lived with the Adams family in San Francisco.

To Mary Bray

Yosemite National Park
Summer 1917

Dear Aunt Mary,

I would have written sooner but I have not had time. I have walked 175 miles to date and feel fine.

I am sending you a picture of the Mt. Clark Range taken from the Cloud's Rest Trail. I can't seem to get as good finishing done here as in the city. The developing is all right but the printing and enlarging are frightful. I have quite a large number of negatives and most of them are good. I am going to print them as soon as I get home. I went to Glacier Point yesterday for the second time and I hope I got some good photographs. I took enough trouble lugging that camera 12 or 13 miles to get anything but I suppose I loaded the plates upside down or something. I carried it up to North Dome and found I had no plates left. I had a nice 20 mile hike anyway. That $5 you gave me helped me out a great deal. It almost all went for swimming.

Tell Pa I'm going to write to him soon and send him some of my pictures.

Hoping you are well and expecting to hear from you soon.

I am sincerely,
Ansel Adams

To Olive Adams[1]

Camp Curry
Yosemite National Park
May 26, 1918

Dear Ma,

I got your postal, also Pa's. Did Pa get indigestion from S[an].F[rancisco]. lunch? I started out at 5 o'clock this morning with Mr. Holman[2] for Mt. Starr King. There is no trail and it is one of the hardest trips I have ever taken—perfectly safe however. I should not have taken such a trying one the first day but I was surprised how little tired I got. We got to the base of the peak after a long tramp through big snow fields and began to look for a place to start the ascent. The only position was on the north side, intending to follow the line of snow over the summit. It was almost perpendicular for 500 feet and appeared so dangerous that I resolved to turn back. Mr. Holman cut steps in the snow and reached the top, I guess the first man to ever do so as it has been considered unclimbable. If he had slipped once he would have surely been killed. As soon as he got started I went back to some meadows about a mile away and watched him. I could just see him and it took 2 hours to reach the end of the snow bank. There is snow everywhere above 7000 ft. Even if I did not climb the peak the trip was well worthwhile. I promised you I would be careful and I haven't croaked yet. Today was the coldest day in the valley this month, 33 this morning at 5 o'clock. I don't mind it and really enjoy it. The valley was filled with fog this morning, but I don't know how it was the rest of the day. It is chilly tonight and my hands are so cold I can't write good. I would rather have it like this than any other way I know.

When I write again I will put "Dear Ma," but I mean the whole bunch, it saves writing separate letters.

I am going to take Mr. Dittman's camera[3] out tomorrow morning and take a swim in the afternoon. The next day I am going to explore around Half Dome (not on top) with Mr. Holman, saying that he would also be careful himself, the experience today slightly unnerved him. But he said he couldn't rest until he reached the top of Mount Starr King.

I was the first in the swimming tank this season; they were filling it the day I got there. I went in that afternoon.

I hope Gramp feels better.
Will write soon,
Ansel

1. Olive Bray and Charles Hitchcock Adams were married in 1896; their only child, Ansel Easton, was born in San Francisco, February 20, 1902.

2. Francis Holman, an ornithologist and avid mountaineer, whom Adams called "Uncle Frank."

3. Frank Dittman owned a photofinishing business in San Francisco, where in 1917 and 1918 Adams had a part-time job and learned rudimentary darkroom technique.

To Olive and Charles Adams and Mary Bray

Yosemite National Park
April 18, 1920

Dear Ma, Pa, and Aunt Mary,

Arrived safely after a wonderful trip up the Merced Canyon, and am having one grand time cleaning up the Lodge.[1] . . .

It was very cold in Merced, and I think they use the mattresses for battleship construction—excellent steel plate and fine for office building foundation. I unwillingly listened to every train that came within 100 miles of Merced, simply because I couldn't help it.

Left Merced at 8:15 and enjoyed some very wonderful views of the Sierra from the train before we entered the foothills. I noticed particularly a group of snowpeaks that looked much like Mt. Clark, Red and Gray Peaks, but I doubted their identity as I could not believe they were visible from the plains. But as the train changed its course Half Dome and Cloud's Rest were quite clearly seen just a little to the left of the previous mentioned peaks. . . .

The ride up the Merced Canyon was very fine, cold and very clear. Everything is green—such a different aspect from the blast furnace heat and brownness of summer. Arrived at El Portal, attended to my baggage and reached Camp Curry at 2 pm. Snow everywhere, Cloud's Rest one mass of white, Glacier Point, Half Dome, North Dome and Eagle Peak are holding as much snow as the pitch of their slopes will allow. At Camp Curry the tennis court, swimming tank and a large area of the camp is covered with from 6 to 18 inches. I wouldn't have missed this for the world and consider it the finest season I have seen at Yosemite. Of course, it is cold at night but moderate at day time, and the air has more life and snap to it than ever. I do wish you were here —all of you.

Opened the Lodge this afternoon and found things in good condition. Will get settled Monday or Tuesday. Right outside the west window there is a nice pile of snow and I will take a photograph to show you the present aspect of my new mansion.

The wind is quite violent and although the sky is clear, great clouds of snow are blowing from the heights sometimes obliterating the topmost rocks. At present Half Dome looks like a volcano, and little swirls and eddies of snow dust are quite numerous on the cliffs of Glacier Point. I am going to attempt to photograph these snow clouds tomorrow and I do hope they will be successful.

Am feeling fine, and intend to keep so, mainly by diet and sleep.

Hoping all of you are as well as possible and will be careful and will not worry about me.

I am sincerely your son-prodigy-nephew,

Ansel

P.S. I consider myself lucky to be here with the snow. Never saw anything like it before.

Am now going to write to the Sierra Club.

Ansel

1. LeConte Memorial Lodge, the Sierra Club's headquarters in Yosemite, was named for eminent geologist and conservationist Joseph LeConte, who died in Yosemite in 1901. Adams worked as the Lodge's summer custodian for four summers beginning in 1920.

To Charles Adams

Yosemite National Park
April 27, 1920

[Telegram]

CAN BUY BURRO FOR TWENTY INCLUDING OUTFIT. CAN SELL AT END
OF SEASON FOR TEN. FINE INVESTMENT AND USEFUL. WIRE IMMEDI-
ATELY AS OFFER IS FOR TODAY ONLY.

ANSEL

To Charles Adams

Yosemite National Park
June 8, 1920

Dear Pa,

Thanks very much for the $15.00; I was down to $1.29 in the bank and just thinking of getting some photographic paper. I have been very careful and economical with my pictures, only using up film in any quantity when on an unusual trip. Around the valley I study every subject thoroughly and am getting some really encouraging results. You will find enclosed a little view taken in the Little Yosemite a month ago; several feet of snow on the level as you can see. The trees are aspens, of course, not in leaf. In the distance are precipices near Cascade Cliffs, snow clinging to every ledge and crevice and filling all the gullies—a typical winter scene. If I ever get a chance I am coming to the valley at the very earliest time of year as it is then I think it is the most beautiful. The trails are covered, it is true, but that does not make much difference, in fact, I prefer going over snow rather than hot dusty paths—one goes so direct and there is a certain attraction about snow climbing—the steeper the better, as long as one is provided with an ice ax and is careful. . . .

I am more than ever convinced that the only possible way to interpret the scenes hereabout is through an impressionistic vision. A cold material representation gives one no conception whatever of the great size and distances of these mountains. Even in portraying the character and spirit of a little cascade one must rely solely upon *line* and tone. Form, in a material sense is not only unnecessary but sometimes useless and undesirable. I have taken such a photograph and am enclosing it in

[7]

this letter. It is a delicate subject to use and I want to explain the print and my object in taking it thus. In the first place it was taken in the Tenaya Canyon; I waited from 9:00 am until 1 o'clock for the correct lighting. I had the idea all framed several days before undertaking the picture. The idea is as follows—in some way to interpret the power of falling water, the light and airy manner of the spray particles and the glimmer of sunlit water. Very easy to think about but not so simple to do. The power is here expressed by the vigorous triangular composition. . . . As to the character of the water itself and its appearance under varying conditions . . . in the first you will see I have tried to get as delicate a texture as possible in the two streams—always does falling water when examined in detail appear of delicate and airy form; in mass it sometimes assumes great strength and power. The representation of detail and texture here gives the impression of fineness and lightness. As to the portrayal of sunlight on water I have managed that by the lighting—a deep somber background upon which the extreme opposite tone of the water is exaggerated so as to appear almost luminous. Can you see now what I mean when I say the tone and texture of a print has much to do with character and condition? Also the placement of the principal parts are such that the eye cannot follow them without slight *Effort,* adding more to the dynamical portrayal of the scene. I thought I would also have a few sparklings in the pool to suggest that the power has not all been spent in the water's rush down the incline of granite.

The reason for this lengthy explanation is that I want you to see what I am trying to do in pictorial photography—suggestive and impressionistic you may call it—either—it is the representation of material things in the abstract or purely imaginative way. I feel quite happy over this picture, to my mind it is the most satisfactory composition I have yet done. Hope you like it. An artist who is spending the summer here says it's fine and everybody else who see it thinks the same. Of course, before it is disposed of in any way it must be enlarged and manipulated a little, but the basic composition is there and needs but slight elaboration. I feel good after waiting so long and putting so much work on it to have it come out so well. The other print, while nice, cannot compare with it from an artistic standpoint, because there was no basic *Idea* back of it,—just a snap of a nice pleasing view, in other words, a record.

The next attempt will be something different entirely,—trying to give an impression of openness and great spaces, either of sky or valley. Wait and see what I can do with it,—I may fall down completely; photography is limited, you know, but I am hoping for results.

I did not bring any paper to speak of, as I did not know what I would be able to do in my photographic work. But I can get along just as well as at home, although with more inconveniences as there is no running water within the Lodge. All the water has to be brought in in big buckets and the washing requires constant attention. Nevertheless, I get along wonderfully and am mighty glad I brought my outfit. When one gets an inspiration it must be completed at once to hold the thread all through, and a negative taken one day and the print next week is certain to leave a disjointed effect. Of course, I can take as many prints as I want now, but until the first print is made does the above statement hold. I think you will see what I am driving at, to interpret through dynamics of line and tone instead of form. It's all in the head anyway, so why not employ mental effects. . . .

The Graflex[1] has proved to be the most ideal thing for general photography. I never expected, and you know how I anticipate, what I could do with that instrument. It has come up to the wildest dreams I could think of.

. . . Mrs. S.[2] is a wonderful cook; every night when the Lodge closes (at 5 o'clock) we bring in the stove, set the table and get wood, water, and other necessities, and then Mrs. S. cooks dinner. And, oh my, what a dinner that lady can cook—soups, steaks, vegetables, buckwheat cakes, bread and butter and jam and toasted marshmallows and tea. How much more I enjoy this life than going to Curry's.[3] The food we prepare ourselves tastes so much better than any restaurant stuff and we know absolutely that it is the best obtainable and *fresh*.

Ma and Aunt Mary are holding the fort at 305.[4] Aunt Mary has not been feeling well for the last two days, she was quite upset and throwing up her toes yesterday but feels somewhat better today. When asked how she feels and when cautioned to take it easy and rest all I can get out of her is "sugar" or "pshaw" and you know when she goes that far into profanity she means something by it. But I am sure she will be in good condition in a few days, but it is aggravating to be laid up in a place like this. They both send love.

We are going to leave on the afternoon of Friday or Saturday on that five day trip, and will drop a line before we start. Keep well and don't overwork. Best wishes for the Classen.[5]

Excuse me for this terribly long letter.

[9]

Will write soon,

Sincerely,
Ansel

1. The Graflex, an early, large-format, single-lens reflex camera, is believed to be Adams' fourth camera, following a Kodak #1 Box Brownie in 1916, an unknown glass plate camera in 1917, and a Kodak Vest Pocket camera in 1918–1919.

2. Mrs. Stopple, who with her husband was camping next to the LeConte Lodge. The Stopples were ardent Sierra Club members.

3. Camp Curry was the Yosemite tent camp where Adams' family often stayed.

4. Olive Adams and Mary Bray stayed in Tent #305 at Camp Curry.

5. Struggling to achieve a successful business venture, Charles Adams converted the family's ruined sawmill in Hadlock, Washington, into a high-proof methyl alcohol factory called the Classen Chemical Company.

To Virginia Best[1]

Lake Merced[2]
Yosemite National Park
September 5, 1921

Dear Virginia,

You cannot imagine what a really delightful time we are having up here in the wilderness. Excepting a rather severe thunderstorm, the weather has been perfect, and we have done nothing but "loaf" the last three days away.

Tomorrow we start for the Lyell Fork Canyon (of the Merced), and will spend perhaps five days thereabouts. This lofty valley is one of the most remarkable regions of the park, and the grandeur of Rodgers Peak, the ascent of which is our main objective, cannot be described. We are also planning to climb Florence, Electra, and possibly Lyell. The ascent of the latter from the South side is difficult and exhausting, and equally fine views are to be obtained from the crest of Rodgers Peak.

If only I had a piano along! The absurdity of the idea does not prevent me from wishing, however. I certainly do miss the keyboard; as soon as I am back in Yosemite, I shall make a beeline for Best's Studio,[3] and bother your good father with uproarious scales and Debussian dissonances. I certainly appreciate the opportunity offered me this summer to keep up my practice, and I am very grateful to you all indeed. I shall go back to the city feeling that I have lost little in music during the summer. A month, I'll wager, will find me completely caught up.

My aunt sends you her best wishes. Will tell you all about the trip in my next letter, which, I hope, will be a better one than this.

Cordially,
Ansel

1. Virginia Rose Best, Adams' future wife, whom he had met in Yosemite earlier that summer.
2. Lake Merced is in the High Sierra, the mountainous wilderness surrounding Yosemite Valley. On this extended trip, Adams accompanied his Aunt Beth Adams, widow of his uncle, William Adams, and Frank Holman.
3. Best's Studio was the concession in Yosemite Valley established in 1902 by Virginia Best's father, the western landscape painter Harry Cassie Best. The Studio had one of the few pianos in the Valley.

To Charles Adams

Yosemite National Park
June 30, 1922

Dear Pa,

Well, I am going to do my best to make this a real long letter, and to tell you how I am, what I am doing, and how I think my summer in the Sierra is benefiting me. I have not written you a truly confidential letter this year; you must think it strange of me for being apparently so reserved and distant, which I often suspect you must notice in my letters,— for, when I read them over prior to posting, I sense a certain coldness, which I surely do not intend, and which I wish was not present. I cannot seem to express myself as freely, as intimately, as you are capable of doing, even when writing to you or my mother, who are closest to me. With me there seems to be an obstacle to complete expression, which I find difficult to overcome. I cannot explain what this hindrance is, nor why it is present, but I am certain you understand what I mean. Perhaps it is that I have always taken for granted our mutual trust and affection, and have never had the occasion to express my feelings; hence, when I wish to do so, I find myself incapable of setting my mind in words. However, the desire for expression sometimes comes quite strong, as now, and

I intend to take advantage of favorable circumstances, and write you as I truly feel. You will not mind a real lengthy letter in this vein, will you?

It often occurs to me that, in spending the summer in so wonderful a place as this, with everything in my favor, and with comparatively few responsibilities, I am showing an extreme selfishness towards you. I feel that I should be with you,—taking some of your burden, the magnitude of which I now realize more and more,[1]—and doing whatever I could to help you. You see, I am growing up; there is a change in my outlook on life—I think I have become broader, and that I have a greater understanding of what it all means, and how serious it is. Accordingly, my conscience troubles me; I feel I should be with you, no matter how beneficial my summer may be to me. If it were not for you, I would not have been given the wonderful opportunities and advantages I have already had. I do not know how to tell you how I appreciate it; I only hope that someday I may be able to truly *show* it, by coming up to your expectations. These things *are* hard to talk about; I fear that putting them into words may depreciate them in seriousness and importance, but I am talking (or writing) just as I feel.

Another thing I want you to know;—how I appreciate and realize the training and bringing up I have had. You must admit it has not been so much a training by words or conversation, as it has been by *example*, and, in a way, by comparison. The highest ideals have always been instilled in me by the environment I have been raised in; these ideals grow stronger and deeper as I come in contact with other phases of life, and as I observe the principles of others. Do not for a moment think that I feel I am perfect—far from it,—only that I am trying my best to be and live as you would wish me to. This much I will say for myself. I have been given a strong will, I know, for I am able to resist the usual common temptations—I have never done anything to be truly ashamed of, and I trust I never shall. I am only too well aware of the fact that I have a very slight knowledge of life, but I daresay I know more than you think I do. I have met a lot of people of all types and grades, I have been thrown more or less upon my own responsibility up here, I have had occasion to use what will and judgement I have in important things directly affecting me, and I know I have conducted myself in such a manner as to satisfy you in every way. Do not think me conceited—I am writing you as I would like to talk to you—in a candid way.

I am well aware that I have reached the age when you may, not without reason, worry about me. If I felt for one moment that I needed support, I would certainly let you know. By "support" I do not mean advice—I want all of that I can get—I need it. What I mean is that I feel capable of properly carrying myself through this formulative time. What surprises me most is the unprincipled life of so many people I have met or known of—people of whom one would expect ideal lives. They are not the few,—it seems the majority come within this class. Those who deride and laugh at the principles I have been taught to consider sacred and fundamental, those who have no self-control, and who think that money is the only wealth, the hypocritical, dishonest, and the cold-blooded wretches, such as you have known in the business world; they seem to be all about us in multitudes. There are very few of the right kind, it seems to me. Perhaps I exaggerate; but such seems the case to me. Do you think I can ever forget for a moment the reputation and name which you hold and which my grandfather[2] held before you? I have made a positive and final promise to myself that I shall never let down knowingly one point the high standards I have been taught to follow, and which you and my mother have always maintained. Should I happen to receive no material gain by following these principles, I shall receive something far more precious: the knowledge of having done as you would wish me to do. I am sure you know what I am talking about—I have done lots of thinking lately. It is about time that I should get hold of myself—think—I am old enough to vote next year. I have come to the conclusion that I have often been a real D-fool, and I freely admit it now. Music and the Sierra have certainly worked an effect—for the good I hope.

You certainly cannot imagine what a relief it is to me to get this out of my mind and to tell you what I feel, and how selfish I think I must be. This vein of thought has undoubtedly been developing gradually, but only recently have I come into a full realization of it. I feared that you would think I was not progressing, and still wandering in the clouds (which I *may* be doing yet, to a certain extent), so I have been intending to write you for a little time, but could not do it until now. You may take this letter seriously, or you may laugh at it, but I have been strictly sincere in everything I have set down in it. Needless to say, I nervously await your opinion.

Everything is going well with us here—I had hoped to include the print of an Azalea photograph I took, which seems excellent, but I have not had the opportunity to make the print. Will send it very soon, however. Glad you liked the other photographs. Was so sorry to hear you had a bilious attack, do be careful. I hope you are all over it now. . . . Give my best regards to all.

Aunt Beth is fine and sends her love. She will write you soon. We *did* enjoy the delicious box of fruits—thank Ma for the $1, I appreciate it. I am trying to be economical this year. Wish you could all be here.

With love,
Ansel

1. Charles Adams was desperately working to make the Classen Chemical Company a success.

2. William James Adams was a successful lumberman until a series of catastrophes decimated his properties shortly before his death in 1907.

From Charles Adams

San Francisco
July 5, 1922

My Dear Ansel:

Mr. Miller, the auditor, is working on my books today and I therefore have to sit around and wait till he is through before much office work can be done, and think it a good time to write you a letter which, in a measure, will be a reply to your fine one of the 30th.

In the first place, Ansel, I am very glad you wrote as you did, for, while you and I have always been very close, it is not often that opportunity affords a good heart to heart talk, and we have just drifted along from day to day and from year to year; knowing that a perfect understanding existed, but really never trying it out.

It was not the place for either your Mother or for me to write you or to talk with you along the lines you have written, for you have not sought advice such as this calls for, and have given us no cause to worry; no regrets because of your acts. It was your place to bring the subject to us, and this you have done in such a fine spirit that both your Mother and I have been made happy and we truly appreciate what you have done.

There are some things perhaps which only belong to the individual in this world. They pertain to him alone, but they do not affect his life or welfare. In other words they are matters of small import. On everything pertaining to your life, your welfare, your hopes and plans, we want to share with you (if you can let us), for you are all we have, and perhaps you do not know yet that you are a very important individual in this world through the eyes of your Mother and through mine. Of truly great importance, for your life and happiness are ours, and your troubles, sorrows and burdens (should they come to you) will be ours also.

So, as I said above, I am glad you wrote, for you have broken the ice and you find beneath, not the cold waters of the River of Life, but a warm stream of sympathy and understanding that will always flow from our hearts to yours.

Whenever you feel the need, do not hesitate to come to us. We can always understand you and perhaps can give you the help you crave.

I am going to take your letter as you have written it and answer it as each different subject calls for an answer.

You speak of your inability to set down in writing the thoughts that you wish to express and fear that your letters have been cold. We have not found them so at all. You must remember that you have been faithful in writing us; sending a line or two at least, almost every day. Unless important things are happening every minute of the days up there, we realize that really there is little to write about, and that except occasionally we can only expect short notes. These are most welcome for they tell us that your thoughts have been of us, and that you are well and evidently happy. Every week or so a good long interesting letter has come, and we have found them *good* letters too and not at all cold and distant as you fear. So don't worry on *that* score.

Now, to go on to your idea that you are selfish; that you should be here sharing my burdens and helping to carry the load which has been imposed upon me. While I appreciate the thought and the consideration you have shown, I would most certainly deplore your being forced into the grind of work of this character. No, Ansel, don't feel selfish. Just feel that by going into the Sierra each year, you are doing what we want you to do. You are laying strong foundations for I hope a very long, happy, useful life. You are building in the right way, for without the foundation of good health, it is not possible to do much in this world.

Then, you are meeting and forming friends who will, in future years, mean much to you perhaps. Even though they do not remain with you in later years, their acquaintance has left a mark which may be beneficial to you. Then too, you are rubbing up against all sorts and conditions of beings; some good; some otherwise, and from each you are learning your lesson, and I thank God you are showing strength of character for you are evidently choosing the good from the evil. This training oneself to make the choice is, in itself, a mighty good schooling and in your case I am not afraid that you will make the wrong choice.

Ansel, there is one thing I want to speak of at this point, and that is: many is the young man who lives a straight, upright life during all his younger years; whose actual experience with the wrongs of life is nil. Suddenly, after all his young years following the straight and narrow path of rectitude, he meets with some character or, under some extraordinary circumstance, he falls from grace, and great is the fall thereof. Had he been one who had not lived so carefully all his younger life, he would not have suffered so great a shock perhaps, for he would have been more or less hardened. It seems strange, but this happens in many cases, and I am giving you a strong warning now, old man. Never deviate from the path you have blazed out for yourself at this time. It is a noble path and if you follow it strictly, you cannot make any mistake. Your life is a successful, happy life; no matter what hardships you may have to endure.

Don't think I am fearing for you at all Ansel, for I know you have a strong will and a character above reproach, but from your Dad you can take a little warning. He has seen men fall—and good men too, and so knows whereof he speaks.

Now to get back to your wonderful summers in Yosemite, as I said above, you are doing what we wish you to do. You are not idle, for even though you do not appear to be doing such a wonderful lot in your music, your reading etc., you are unconsciously laying up a store of natural knowledge and of valuable experiences, and so we will say you are busy in the extreme. Then too, you *are* keeping up in your reading some I know and you are practicing and keeping your fingers from growing indolent so that when you get back to the city you can be ready for a good winter of serious music work.

You don't know how glad your Mother and I are because of the final promise you have made that you will "never let down one point the high standards" you have been taught to follow. I think you realize now of what high character your Mother's life is formed, and I can see where it is reflected in you. It is indeed a very grave responsibility you have to assume; the maintenance of such a standard as she has handed down to you. You can do it though—never fear, for you are strong as she is. Then her happiness and her memory will force you to carry out her heart's desire, i.e., an honorable career for her boy; a career she may be proud of.

I am glad you appreciate too the high standards of your grandfather who struggled through years of trouble, carrying burdens that would have killed most men at once, and yet he carried them cheerfully, always maintaining his honesty of purpose and his strength of character.

[Next 26 lines of this letter are missing.]

. . . So, Ansel, keep up your music. Live as you are whenever you can, in touch with the finer things of life and close to nature and you cannot go wrong.

Your letter enclosing the photo of the Azalea came this morning. It is FINE. Couldn't be better, no matter how much you tried. The final one will certainly be a wonderful addition to our collection. . . .

Love to Beth; remembrances to all my friends and lots of love to you. Keep well and write when you can.

Your
Dad

To Charles Adams

Yosemite National Park
July 7, 1922

Dear Pa,

Such a wonderful letter as the one I received yesterday from you is certainly something to be most thankful for, and to treasure in a very high degree. It is an expression of trust, confidence, and hopes, that I shall do my utmost to live up to. There is no need to say more—I am supremely happy to know our intimacy is established so securely that I have not the least hesitancy in coming to you and telling you both *everything* about myself and my thoughts, hopes, and ideals. It *is* strange that there should have been a restraint of expression with my father and mother—who are closest to me—but that, happily exists no longer.

I am sure you will not mind—I *know* you will not—when I tell you I have met someone, of whom I have grown very fond of indeed.[1] A very lovely character—one whose affection is a privilege to possess. She constantly reminds me of my mother—more so every day—by her kindness, gentleness, and good level head. Pa, I have been hit very hard, and I make no pretense of denying it—for I am proud of it—but I do not want you to worry about it—I shall always be prudent and rest upon your advice. Remember this—my first duty is to you and my mother. I fully realize it, and always shall wish it so. I do not think the other attachment will disturb you; it is a very wonderful thing to me to have so pure an ideal to look forward to at some distant time. You appreciate the difficulty I was under to tell you of this; not bashfulness—I am far past that age—but the thought of this—that you might consider me selfish and forgetful of you in caring for someone else. It was rather a heavy load on my mind until my good Aunt Beth sagaciously maneuvered the cat out of the bag by writing you and then letting me know. She is a wonder— understood exactly what I was up against, and took it upon herself to help me out.

The world seems fuller, more beautiful,—there is something in it now that was not there before, something I did not dream would come so soon. I am beginning to realize what real life is—life of the loftiest kind.

Well, I have told you everything—you know who it is—I do not think you will worry about me. I shall not mar this letter with everyday facts and conventional phrases, so I will close what seems to me to be a very important communication. I will write you and Ma soon again. Keep well. And that letter of yours!

My love to you and Ma—this is addressed to both of you.

Ansel

1. Virginia Best.

To Virginia Best

Moraine Lake
Yosemite National Park
July 17, 1922

[Postcard]

A placid lake, rimmed with a rich evergreen forest, beyond which rise tremendous mountains, snowy and still—such is our home for four days—a period of rest and relaxation after strenuous miles on steep Sierra trails. The remoteness of these lovely places—the leisure of toll behind us as the even greater beauty to come as we approach the climax of the great range and the spirit of comradeship and sympathy of ideals among the members of this party—the simple food and the glorious pagan activity—it is all a delicious procession of unearthly experiences discounting civilization and chronological time.

Precious beyond telling are these crystal days—they form great foundation domes firmly supporting our ideal lives and filling us to the depths with their qualities of stable, permanent beauty.

"Are they not mine, sayeth the Lord, the everlasting hills!!"

Any "news" in the ordinary sense would be an insipid blur of thought—I would much rather send you some little hint of *mood*—something that echos, though ever so slightly, the primal song of the wilderness—the whisper of silver winds in the lonely forest—the hollow chant of falling waters.

AA

To Virginia Best

San Francisco
September 28, 1923

My Dearest Virginia,

Just a little more than a fortnight separating us! How happy I shall be to have you near again. I have missed you terribly, in spite of the fact that I have kept very busy, but I have tried to look at the matter sensibly—we must wait a little while—and the best way to pass the interval is to work hard and not spend the time regretting the necessary delay. So I have been anything but lazy this summer after my return from Yosemite. I am now doing a little teaching [piano]—most excellent for me, as it will help my getting established. I will not go into small details now, for I shall see you so soon. But it is a beginning, and brings us closer to the happy day. I will continue my photographic work as a means of incidental income until I find my music is filling my time; thereafter the photography will become a hobby only. I cannot let anything interfere with my music, which is my life work. I have definitely made up my mind about photography. From now on I will only do special work—that is, work of the highest quality that I am capable of. I want to establish a reputation for artistic work, and I have not the time to devote to lesser quality production. That means that the finest of my negatives will be used without exception; that the finest materials I can get be put into my work; that I will take the utmost care in the making of the prints; and that my photographs will always be purely photographic—not for coloring, not for reproduction in books . . . without proper remuneration and the understanding that the original quality be retained: I almost think I shall cancel all business of this kind, and sell none for reproduction. I want my work to reach really high standards of art; if I can do such work as I hope to hereafter produce I am sure I will be able to take in quite a little revenue from the type of people who admire that kind of work. This will help me considerably; if on the other hand I were to do what pictures I could for no other thought but to sell them, I would find that I could not keep the quality, and the time spent in making such prints could be used to better advantage by applying it to my music. So, you see, I will be a little "independent," and will sell what I can at a good price—always doing my best to keep the quality as high as I can. I have taken up the Bromoil[1] process, and individual prints in this medium sell for $10 to $50 each. I will show you the method when you are here—it is hard and long and difficult, but it is worth it. From now on I shall eliminate from my selling subjects all but a very few of the very best. . . .

Well, what do you think of those plans? You see, what work I do will be profitable, and, what is very good, I shall not be swamped with so much work. I must devote all my time now—all the best time—to my music so that later I can provide you with all that I want you to have.

I want to make my home my studio—the simpler the better. The way it is now is lovely, and I am sure that those that came to me would enjoy the home atmosphere. What do you think? A pretty garden, a cozy home, a friendly fireplace, and a restful atmosphere,—how is that for a studio? And then we will never be so very far away from each other, as would be the case should I go to a downtown studio. They are too cold and formal. I think people appreciate and enjoy that "homey" atmosphere. Tell me how it strikes you.

Went to a wedding—made me envious—but I don't see how I could stand the ordeal of a big church "hitch." The poor groom was a nervous wreck. He certainly has a lovely wife. So will I have, happy *me!* I hope I will make a good husband. But really, would you not rather have a *simple* ceremony? Tell me. Admiration and hatred both reign in the neighborhood regarding my "musent touch it."[2] Ma and Auntie openly despise it—Pa is indifferent, and most of my friends like it. Such is life!

Well, my dear, I think I have made this letter too long and unwieldy— and perhaps you do not yet understand about my pictures—but you will be here so soon that I can then explain matters so that you will know what I mean. You see, I must now think of the *practical* side of life; how to acquire the wherewithall to make *you* happy and comfortable. And I want to bring happiness to you as soon as I can. So I am to be as economical as I can. We want you to stay here just as long as you possibly can—I will practice just as hard as I am now—I will not gad about as much as I did—I must keep at work. But it will be heavenly to have you near. My regards to Dad—tell him I would like to show him the Bromoil Process.

Love from us all,
Your own,
Ansel [X]

Don't tell Dad that I don't like colored photographs.
I like either a painting or a straight monotone photograph. The picture he gave me a copy of for my father is a wonder, and I like the black and white photographic copy very much indeed—but would not care for it colored. Monotone is the domain of photography! That's my opinion. What's yours? Tell Dad everyone admires his Mt. Rainier painting. It is a beauty. Forgive this long letter.

1. The bromoil process, popular with pictorial photographers, produced a print of reduced optical sharpness with a softer quality than a silver chloride print made from the same negative.

2. During his Yosemite summer Adams had grown a mustache, which he here refers to as "my musent touch it."

To Virginia Best

San Francisco
November 15, 1923

My Dearest,

You must think me anything but thoughtful of you by the manner in which I write you, but there has been so much to do that I know if you were present you would understand and in every way forgive me.

This is a very crucial time in my father's business career; all that he has so diligently worked for during so many years, hangs delicately on the verge, and every moment must be utilized to bring his affairs to a proper issue. You see, he is and has been, perfectly straightforward and honest—and in all ways most considerate of others in his business dealings. What he has received in turn for these principles is this; he has, in many ways been the victim of modern grasping business; business that is absolutely cold-blooded and selfish. People he has most sincerely trusted have tricked him and those he is associated with, an attempt by a big concern to freeze us out[1]—by methods too complicated to detail here, is the latest struggle, and it's hard to say just what will be the outcome. We hope for the best. If he does lose out financially in the long run he has gained something more vital than money: a reputation for perfectly honest and square methods, like his father had before him. I say all this in no spirit of boasting, it is the plain fact. I only hope I shall have the opportunity to show that I can do business of any kind under the same principles. I am sure it wins out in the end.

While all this intense work is going on it is my duty to help my father all that I possibly can, for it is he that has given me everything. Everything except you. I even think that he, by his example, taught me to appreciate and love such a character and type as you. Remember, I live for you and look forward to your having the best in life in every way.

As soon as things get settled I shall go at the piano again, but until Pa no longer requires relief and help I shall do all I can to make things easier for him.

Remember me to Dad. How does he like the pictures? We all send our love and I hope that soon I shall have some good news for you. Write him when you can. He is so happy to hear from you.

With Love,
Your Own
Ansel

1. Betrayed by both his brother-in-law and his attorney, Charles Adams attempted to recoup the family fortune but ultimately failed.

To Virginia Best

San Francisco
October 20, 1924

My Dearest Virginia,

. . . I am so happy that Dad decided not to make the [Grand] Canyon trip with the car in its rather uncertain condition. I was greatly worried when you left, and had a vague premonition that something was to occur of a nature not exactly welcome. I am very happy you ended your trip at San Diego. I admit that I believe in "premonitions"—so many in my experience have actually "worked out," that it would be difficult to discredit them.

Promise me, dear, that you will work with all your heart and soul with your voice, and that you will devote much of your spare time to cultural subjects—read and study, and bring into your heart as much of the nobility of true art as you can. I trust you to do this—it is of greater importance to you than you realize. I know you will forgive me when I say that the realization of your need for this mental application at this time gives me great concern—please—in the name of our love—bring the qualities of your mind equal to the qualities of your heart and soul. I never have written you this way before; it is not criticism, but purely an observation on my part that I hope you shall understand. Remember, one cannot live on love alone—the soul hungers for expression and ceaselessly strives for an understanding of all that comprises the cosmos. The more of beauty in the mind, the more of peace in the spirit. Time is a definite and moving quantity—conserve it!

Devote certain hours to singing and other musical work—certain hours to reading—and good reading at that, and take some exercise each day. And try, please try, to make each and every minute count for something. Young as I am, I look back with regret at the time I have wasted through lack of purpose, weakness of will, and very often just pure laziness. We are living in an age that fosters idleness of mind if we remain passive. Where would my father be today had he not kept alive his interest in mental things. The depressing luck he suffered in business would have made him ten times as miserable had he not had the recourse of study and of interest of purely cultural subjects. Contrast with him, the rather nervous and unhappy state of mind that my mother is in, had she now the old-time hobbies and interests she, too, would be a little happier, I am sure. She says so herself. The life of my teacher, Miss Butler,[1] has been, in the main, one of distraction and sacrifice. Yet her profound interest in music and literature has held her up through many years of worry and responsibility. I cannot recall who sang that,

> "Life is a dome of many-colored glass, ringing the radiance of Eternity."

The structure of life we build for ourselves determines the color of our soul. It is very simple after all. Simple if we have the will to do! Think more of yourself, realize your duty to yourself, and your duty to those who shall come after you, who shall shape their lives on your influence. Develop the sense of the inner beauty and majesty of Nature; realize that Art in all its forms is but an attempt to interpret the Divine in Nature. Study technique—the *means*—but always relegate it to its true place;—the works of Liszt exhibit the worship of the false God.

Will you forgive me for this all too long letter? I am merely speaking my heart to you, and I hope you will understand what I have said. I shall make some suggestions for your reading, and you may take them for what you think they are worth. My dear, remember that when we are married we must help each other, mentally and spiritually, and we must have many things in common to achieve the greatest happiness. I know we shall be wondrously happy in our own home.

I have been very busy since you left, but I found several hours of spare time in which I made a Bromoil. It is a scene near Muir Woods—one that I took when we made the trip in the car. It is my masterpiece to date. I am anxious that you see it. I would like to show it to you at Christmas time. . . .

I am working hard and will try to save a little money. I always have the great event in mind, and I pray that it will soon come to pass. . . .

We all send our love. How happy I should be to have you here now.

With the deepest love
Ansel [X]

1. Marie Butler was Adams' piano teacher.

To Virginia Best

Marion Lake[1]
Sunday, August 3, 1925

My Dear Virginia,

This lake is the most beautiful I have ever seen: it cannot be described. The several days we shall pass here will be a fitting climax to a wonderful trip. It is my hope that my pictures will give a little of the beauty and atmosphere of this delightful place. . . .

I have never felt that I would find a *religion;* but I have done so. The Carpenter book[2] has established a real religion within me. I think it the grandest thing written. Read it, live it, absorb it, and you will be raised spiritually to the heights. Reading it, as I have been, in the mountains, has greatly aided my understanding of it, and I cannot tell you of the great joy and peace it has given me. It is so broad, so inclusive, so reasonable, so lofty, and so magnificently written! "It is all straightforward."

My deepest love to you and to all,
Your Own
Ansel

1. Marion Lake is located in the region which became Kings Canyon National Park in 1940, thanks in part to the testimony of Adams' photographs and writings on the area. On this trip, Adams accompanied Professor Joseph LeConte II (son of the revered early environmentalist), his son Joe, and daughter Helen.

2. Edward Carpenter. *Towards Democracy*, London: George Allen & Co., Ltd., 1912.

To Virginia Best

San Francisco
September 22, 1925

My Dear Virginia,

I began a letter to you the other day, but it did not go as I wished, and I am rewriting it. I have played so much today that my hand is tired and I cannot produce intelligible writing with a pen; hence the typewriter. . . .

I hope you had a most delightful trip in the High Country, and that you were benefited in mind and soul and body by the divine influence of the mountains. I think nothing can be compared to the Hills for the elevation of spirit, and peace of mind, which they produce in man when he lives intelligently among them. All aspects of nature lead to elevation and knowledge when you once have the idea. The commonplace growth of weeds beneath a pile of refuse appear to shine with the divine light when you know the meaning of the world and sense the unity of all things. In a great city the buildings, the machinery, the works of art, everything produced by man, are naught but the material expression of ideas. We look on lines and forms and masses of what we call matter, and we know these things existed in the mind of man in the form of ideas before they were expressed in the physical world in the form of matter. I look on the lines and forms of the mountains and all other aspects of nature as if they were but the vast expression of ideas within the Cosmic Mind, if such it can be called. With that outlook, I am assured there is nothing in the Universe that is not the expression of mind or of life. The sense of unity is enormously increased. How could I ever describe what the mountains meant to me this summer; what they did for me, and how strongly this new sense has grown within me. My dear, I am an entirely different person. I know that better than anyone, for I feel my reaction on other people to be quite different. In other words, I know that people know me to have changed, and changed in the depths.

It is almost a rebirth; I sense another and a much deeper personality within me, a greatly extended perception and appreciation. Alas, I cannot put in words what comes into my mind regarding this subject. I hope this does not seem all foolish prattle to you, for I MUST have it out of my system. If you only knew what perplexity of mind I am at present entertaining in attempting to adjust myself and consider my future! I feel so much bigger; I feel so much more the duty of life, and the necessity of improving myself and my Art to the last peak of my ability. The world has suddenly opened up to me with tremendous and dazzling effect and I am having the very deuce of a time to realize it all. New personalities, new outlooks, new ideas, new possibilities, all crowding into my consciousness, and above all the nameless dread of having to continue under this life, and the dread also of separating myself from it. Can you understand what I mean? This is very vague. It can be much better expressed in *tone*, now much more so than at the time you were here. "Supreme Music is heard only by the Soul"[1] and "Music is a flame of Love mounting to the Skies." Tone in itself is spiritual, and speaks spiritual messages. The soul can float to undreamed of heights of expression on the luminous wings of tone. I find in old compositions that I have played new meanings and marvelous beauty that I did not comprehend before. The quality of Scriabin's music cannot be told in words nor the vast thunders of Beethoven. Great Art—"It is all straightforward."

"For the mind has many lips
That kiss you with their thought
When that mind is a soul which embraces yours."

The world distracts me from my purpose; I know I am not understood. The thousand little things compel me into a tension, mental and physical, as if I were threatened with myriads of relentless darts, which would torture me were I to dare a single motion while surrounded with them. "Freedom, the Deep Breath!!"

"The sincere soul utilizes the Universe for a brain." and,
"A thing is never great in itself, only its emanations."

I wish to "be quiet long enough to hear what Nature has to say." (I seem to express myself much better through the use of quotations.)

"Love life so much that you cannot divine what is most beautiful in
    it, all life being beautiful."
"Genius is the accumulated experience of the Soul."
"Some questions are too great for argument."
"Every genius is a reincarnation."
"The Strongest things are the most fluid, Witness the Ocean."

These things I wish to write of are well expressed in the above quotations, if even in a vague suggestive way.

Life is before me, what shall I make of it?

So now, after this long and I suppose, tiresome, letter, I shall close and write you again soon. I have so much to do that sometimes I think I shall explode unless I eliminate a considerable amount. Again, "Freedom, the DEEP BREATH."

Remember me to your father. I am happy that he enjoyed the trip and give my regards to all my friends. We all send our love to you all. Tell my Aunt Beth I will be so glad to see her. And I will write to Mr. Holman. I think of him often.

With Love,
Ansel

1. All quotes in this letter are from Carpenter, *Towards Democracy*.

To Virginia Best

San Francisco
September 30, 1925

My Dear Virginia,

During the last few weeks I have been thinking and thinking mighty hard. I have thought of my music and what I am to make of it; I have thought of my future life, and what it will amount to; I have thought of present conditions and circumstances and of future ones as well. I have tried to work everything out with a reasonable mind, and with a fair appreciation of "values." I have arrived at some rather tremendous conclusions. Here they are:

I. It will require six to ten years to complete my musical education, or rather, to bring it to a point where I may call myself an *Artist*. I am just beginning to realize this. You know, I have done very few years of serious musical work, and there is *so much* to be done.

II. If I come forward at this time as a teacher and enter into the work with the seriousness required to handle responsibilities, my musical study will be almost entirely arrested. To undertake my profession at this early stage would mean that I would be but a neighborhood teacher—nothing more. I would earn a precarious and uncertain living, and I would be filled with sorrow and bitterness that I had not perfected my Art to the limit of my ability. And this condition of heart and finances would bring naught but misery on those dependent on me.

III. I know above almost all things that a fine instrument is essential to my artistic development. None that I had were of sufficient quality for my work.

IV. I know that if I teach, I must have a proper studio—an impossibility at the present time especially in view of all the other considerations.

V. I know that God has bestowed upon me a great gift, which in itself is a most tremendous responsibility. To neglect it would be criminal indeed.

VI. I know that for the last several years I have been entirely unaware of, and passive towards, my abilities; I was living in a dream world, no real plans, ideas or objects to work for.

VII. I realize now more than ever before my duty to my mother and father. They have given me everything—I have returned nothing. I must present them with *accomplishment*. I must prove worthy of them.

These are conclusions based on deep and earnest thought. Carpenter says, "It is all straightforward." That is what I wish this letter to be. I have put all the energies of my mind into these thoughts; I have weighed advice; I have called pure reason to the fore. I feel deep in my heart that what I have written here is a correct expression of a sincere and reasonable line of thought, and that it is *righteous*. I say this in justice to you, to my parents, to the world, and to myself. My life now unfolds before me. What do I see? Years of painstaking work—patient plodding, towards the perfection of my music. Fulfillment of my life's duty. For if I do not carry my Art to the crest of my ability, my life shall be blasted and the

lives of all dependent upon me. "To thine own self be true."—I dedicate
my life to my Art.

I have taken the first step on the new road: I have purchased a Mason and Hamlin Grand Piano, the finest instrument that money can buy.
So confident was I of the righteousness of my new resolve that I ordered
the piano into the home with almost religious awe and reverence, as a
symbol of my new life. I shall put all my heart into my work: some day
I shall be an *artist*. Stretching far into the great, mysterious future, I see—

"The path that God would send me shining fair."

I know you are sensible, and will understand all that I have written
here. It has been a tremendous thing for me to do, but I have done it,
and I give myself unto the mercy of God, with the prayer that He will,
in His perfect understanding, direct and use my life for the good of all
the world.

I trust that I shall hear from you soon.

With love,
Ansel

To Virginia Best

San Francisco
June 6, 1926

My Dear Virginia,

So sorry to go away for the summer without seeing you; but I will
write you as often as I can.

Tomorrow I am off for the High Mountains—back to my paradise for
a good, long soul-building rest. I go with the most delightful mood in my
heart—and the most wonderful hopes for the future. In the last month I
have become someone very much bigger and better than I was before.
So many lovely things have happened—so many friends—some very
dear ones—have come into my life,—so much has developed with my
music,—so much bright enthusiasm and warm, spiritual energy has
come about me. I am in a new world,—and now, the climax, this wonderful trip:[1]—well, next year I will really accomplish something—something big—I feel it. (I figure my year from the summer trip.)

And the sweet knowledge of our friendship—perhaps, of a quality
equally beautiful as our love. I seem now to stand in a shining world of

love and beauty—what have I done to deserve such glories? I cannot write of even a little of how I feel, and make sense of it. I know you understand. Perhaps I have grown up.

I hope you will be happy this summer, Virginia, and not work too hard. Try to absorb the wonderful Spirit of the Mountains, and enjoy them as much as you can, despite the tourists. Yosemite is very beautiful.

My regards to all, especially to your Dad.

My love to you always,

Ansel

1. Adams was once again invited to accompany the LeConte family into the Kings Canyon region.

From Virginia Best

Yosemite National Park

[Christmas, 1926]

Dear Ansel,

Just a line or two to let you know that the lamp arrived quite safely and we are all delighted with it.

I enjoyed the symphony immensely. It was dear of you to think of me and now I have another lovely memory stored away to keep me from being lonesome so far away from the music of the world. We're more apt to have the "music of the spheres" in Yosemite. At least, our thoughts should turn in that direction.

Today I walked in the woods, and gathered fir and cedar branches that I might send my friends a bit of the fragrance of the mountains. I wish I might also imprison in a box the clear, crisp air and the clouds that hang low, over the Cathedral Rocks at sunset.

You would love it here now. It is utterly different from the smiling, placid meadowy place you know. Not only do we lack the tourists and the green grass and trees, but the haze of summer, and the dusty smoky atmosphere of fall. Clear, cold moonlit nights, with the stars as bright as though they'd just been polished and hung up and days with blue sky and sunshine on the white-topped cliffs, when you're glad of a coat and gloves, but feel that there's nothing too hard for you to conquer. Oh, I *can't* find words for it, Ansel, but there's more the *feel* of the Minarets[1] in the air. If you ever need a tonic like that in winter, you'll find Yosemite waiting for you and it will be the old Yosemite that we used to know, and now can't find in summer.

It's raining now but will probably turn to snow by morning, and then there'll be ice all over everything.

I'm sending you some green branches and will mark them, so don't mix them up with the Christmas presents.

Love,
Virginia

1. The Minarets, rocky crags, their name suggesting their form, are in the Sierra Nevada to the southeast of Yosemite, in the Ansel Adams Wilderness Area, established shortly after Adams' death in 1984.

To Cedric Wright [1]

San Francisco
February 17, 1927

Dear Cedric,

Goddam it Wright! You and I am in der same boat an der same deck—I guess its der Steerage. If your violin sounds like mildewed cheeze, my piano sounds like a Septic Tank mit der lid off. Cheezeus, ve got to do something—nottible! I repeat you *are* a Redwood in der mountains, only you sound like a kaktus. But der kaktus has got lots of pricks, (unless it's spineless) so *you* should worry about it.

Read, in Carpenter,[2] der following p. 27—XVII.

"These waves of your great heart."

It is just the thing that this picture I send you here represents, that keeps me going from year to year. That and a dream of a perfect love that waits somewhere for me. All else can slide to Hell. The shams of the world are too much for me, I guess. We will have to get the best of them. Let's try for a short spring trip in der Sierra. Will see you soon as possible. Remember, you *are* a Redwood.

Ansel

1. Cedric Wright, photographer, violinist, and mountaineer was for many years Adams' best friend. It was Wright who introduced Adams to the writings of Carpenter.

2. Carpenter, *Towards Democracy*.

To Virginia Best

San Francisco
March 11, 1927

My Dear Virginia,

Your sweet letter came yesterday, and I was so happy to get it. Mumps themselves are not so bad, but the enforced inactivity is terrible! Added misery developed this morning, when I picked up some *Sierra Club Bulletins*[1] and got the mountain fever with a bang! And I have to stay in this miserable pile of bricks and bootleg—the city—for some time to come. If you only knew the yearning to get into the mountains that fills me these days!—that has tortured me for months. I feel I would give up everything to be once more in the hills. . . . how I envy *you*, up there in that marvelous valley! Music is wonderful—but the musical world is the *bunk!* So much petty doings—so much pose and insincerity and distorted values. Something in me revolts to all that, and, lying here in bed has given me many hours of thought and it seems very clear to me now that unless I get more of the outdoors, I will blow up. Oh, for the sleek, self-assured conceit and bull of some of our musicians! I am disgusted: but what to do.

For some reason or other, I find myself looking back on the Golden Days in Yosemite with supreme envy. I think I came closer to really living then than at any other time of my life, because I was closer to elemental things—was not so introspective, so damned sensitive, so infernally discriminative. How I long to get back to it all—to feel the contact of everyday, commonplace, material, primitive things—Rock—Water—Wood—and *unanalyzed* love and friendship (the only satisfactory kind). I want to write. I want to take pictures. I am tired of moving my fingers up and down under smug rules of past ages and evoking series of tones that are supposed to represent emotion. 1/100,000,000 of them do! I have become too well aware of the ever-changing conventional standards, and I want to express myself freely, individually. . . .

There's something about *You*—damned if I know what it is—that is so refreshingly *natural* and *un*complex. . . . *No,* I am not delirious—I am perfectly sane, only a little hot under the collar. I think you understand. . . .

Nothing else to write down now. Hope you can read this—my pen is bum and writing in bed is the bunk. But I shall be up in a few days.

I love you *immensely* at this moment—and all others, too, and will be so glad to see you again. . . .

I am coming to Yosemite sometime in Spring—or bust!

> Regards to Dad,
> Always yours,
> Ansel

1. The Sierra Club journal, now titled *Sierra*.

To Virginia Best

> San Francisco
> April 25, 1927

My Dearest Virginia,

I have been so very busy and I have so many new ideas. I feel now I am more or less settled on something definite. Your wonderful self—your spirit of kindness and love—returns to me now with hundred-fold force. My excursions into experience have brought me to stern realizations of fact—and, to be frank, I find the world more solidly beautiful than when clothed in glittering fancy.

There is little use of my writing my heart out to you—you know it already—it cannot be explained; it must be lived. Know that I love you—know that I always shall love you, beyond the powers of my telling. I want a little studio—acoustically correct, and with wall space for my prints. And a suitable workroom as well. And you must have your room—as you want it—and it will be yours in every way. And I want friends about me and green things—and the air of the hills.

My photographs have now reached a stage when they are worthy of the world's critical examination. I have suddenly come upon a new style which I believe will place my work equal to anything of its kind. I have always favored the effect of engravings—the neat, clean, clear-cut technique fascinates me. In this new effect I will try to combine the two processes of photography and the press into a result that will be exceptionally beautiful and unique. A print will be made on Parchment Paper,[1] enclosed by a small, delicate black line, engraved directly upon its edge, leaving a spacious white margin. The title will also be engraved in very small and light letters near its lower edge, and the folder will be also engraved with the title and my name. The whole effect will be one of exquisite beauty.

[33]

This will precede the issue of the complete portfolio[2] which will appear before the winter months. I would like to put out about 150 prints of this order and I figure it shall cost me $75.00. Selling each for $3.00 will result to me (less the conventional third deducted) a sum of $2.00. Not all at once but there in value, nevertheless. I will *make* over $200.00. The portfolio will be very much more, of course.[3]

I think these prints will exceed in beauty anything I have ever done. But if you think best I will also make up a set of my prints in the regular style—mounted, and on Bromide. Tell me what you think. . . .

I must come up soon again—especially to see you—and get some pictures of the Falls to complete my set. And what pictures I shall get this summer!

My Love to You Always. May the Spirits of great Souls infuse our lives with beauty and truth. Read much, think much, do much, be one of the new world.

Yours always,
Ansel

1. Vitava Athena Grade T. Parchment Paper, a matte-surfaced photographic paper, produced by Kodak 1925–1928.
2. *Parmelian Prints of the High Sierras* [*sic*], San Francisco: Jean Chambers Moore, 1927; Adams' first portfolio, which included the photograph *Monolith, The Face of Half Dome*.
3. Each portfolio of 18 prints originally sold for $50.

To Albert Bender[1]

Sierra Club Camp[2]
Junction Meadow
Kern River Canyon
July 25, 1927

Dear Albert—

I wish I could set out to tell you of this marvelous summer, but I shall have to let my pictures do that. If nothing unfavorable happens to the plates[3]—and I hope nothing does—I will have to show you the best set of mountain pictures I have ever had. But the pressure of my work has allowed me little time for rest and writing. Up at 4 or 5 in the morning— rushed breakfast—then off on the trail with 30 pounds on my back and a tripod in my hand—and by the time I return I feel like doing "just nothing" until the next morning.

Yesterday I climbed Milestone Mountain—13,600 feet—and hauled my camera to the craggy top. The peak is about the most majestic I have ever seen—and the view incomprehensible. We have been favored with wonderful rolling clouds that have blanketed the entire Sierra.

I have been reading a good deal of Jeffers[4] whenever I have the chance, and he grows on me constantly. The power and vitality of his verse blends so perfectly with the rugged mountains. I think he is *great*.

I will be home somewhere around the tenth of August and wish I could tell you how glad I will be to see you again. I have missed you a very great deal. As I said, I regretted leaving the city for the first time on account of the new lease on life your interest and friendship have given me. I shall return with unbounded enthusiasm for work.

Cedric Wright sends his best wishes.

Virginia Best   "   her   "   "

and I   send my   "   " and lots of affection besides—just oodles of it.

Remember me to all my friends and take care of yourself. "Don't eat from cans." That's what I have been doing for 4 weeks.

Yours always,
Ansel

Sold a portfolio to the president[5] of the Sierra Club.

1. Albert M. Bender, Irish-born philanthropist and collector, was Adams' first patron and the sponsor of the Parmelian portfolio.

2. This was the first of many summers that Adams participated in the Sierra Club's annual outing in the High Sierra.

3. Most of Adams' negatives at this time were made on glass plates, with the inevitable hazard of breakage.

4. Bender introduced Adams to the poet Robinson Jeffers earlier that year.

5. Aurelia S. Harwood.

To Virginia Best

San Francisco
Tuesday, December 21, 1927

My Dearest Virginia –

If I come up on the 26th and bring Ernst Bacon[1] and 2 sleeping bags and a promise to eat at the cafeteria, can I sleep on your porch, or under your piano, or down the chimney, and play for you and walk with you to some dear old places?

This week has been a fright, and there is no one more ready for a change than myself, and when the change means seeing you, it is just marvelous. Can we scramble up to the Diving Board?[2] I have a mania for that place.

. . . I have felt for the last two months that we were destined for one another, and that some strange barrier was restraining us; if we could pierce that barrier, establish our true relations with life, have life to ourselves: it would be wonderful.[3] I visualize a studio—and just "us" in it— and our friends. Not "us" mixed up and overseasoned with negative environments.

Well, there is some great power beyond all our decisions, and we follow its force, even without realizing it. . . . My love to you *always*—loads of it –

Ansel X^2

1. Ernst Bacon, pianist and composer.
2. The Diving Board is the granite projection at the base of Half Dome from which Adams made his seminal photograph, *Monolith, the Face of Half Dome.*
3. Adams and Virginia Best were married on January 2, 1928, in Best's Studio, Yosemite National Park.

From Charles Adams

San Francisco
January 30, 1928

My Dear Ansel:

This letter is for you and Virginia and not for another soul. Your mother will know of it. In other words it is just for us!

Do not think, in reading this, that I am ill, or that I am going to die, or even that I am depressed and blue and unhappy. Far from it, for I am happier than I have been in many a year. Happy because you have Virginia and because *we* have her too, for through you, we have taken into our home and our hearts one of the finest girls in the whole world. So, how can I be unhappy? As I told you a few evenings ago, when you two were at home with us I was almost afraid and could not understand why so much happiness had come to me. Everything in my life during the past twenty-five years has brought nothing to cheer, nothing to hope for, and much responsibility. A future which is at times as black as a ton of coal. You know how fond I am of our dear Ollie;[1] you know her life is mine; that her happiness, her sorrows and her cares are mine, and so, when one disappointment after another came to me; when one mistake after another brought to me the conclusion that my life had been a failure, my journey has been a rather up-hill one. However, I am not one to lie down, to give up, to grovel. I have fought a fair, honest fight and am not ashamed. Further, I am still fighting and working and hoping and aiming at success ahead and will win out yet, so that I may leave dear old Ollie provided for and free from cares and worries, and that I might leave you and Virginia so that you may have your lives full of the joys of living. I don't care to make enough to leave you *rich,* even if that were possible, for that would only weaken your chances for happiness. I want you to have enough so that your high ideals may be realized; so that you, of whom I am so proud, shall fulfill a destiny as great as I dream of. I want Virginia to share with you a full, happy life, for God knows she deserves all there is in this world that is good and kind and true.

Now, before going any farther with this I want to tell you one very important thing. Don't think I have worried and suffered alone. Your mother has gone through it all with me. She has suffered far more than I, for I have been on the "firing line;" fighting and having all the excitement, the rough and tumble of a man's life. It was only when I stopped and rested that worry and care strode in. On the other hand, your mother has sat at home, alone in her thoughts, hoping for my success and finding naught but failure and disappointment. She could not get the stimulus of the fight, but must wait alone and bear the burden in silence and stand by my side to cheer me up, when her own heart was torn. She has never faltered, never was she impatient with me; always giving me her heart and her hand to lift me up and strengthen me! Ansel, always be gentle with her. Be gentle with [Aunt] Mary, for she too loves you and hopes for you, and while it may seem hard at times to over-look "things," you will do it for me, I know.

Here endeth a rambling prelude, but it had to come out before I could go ahead with the rest of this letter.

In the first place, the human being is a very peculiar little atom in this interesting universe of ours. He rushes about, through the years, often blindly, striving for something and always striving in his own way. For some reason or other, he never profits by the experience of those who have gone before him. Individuals and races are alike in this. They come into being, live a life which is perhaps successful, perhaps not, but gen-erally a life of their own making, and then comes the end. Whatever they do, they do *not* take advantage of the experience of others. Experi-ences which have brought failure or brought success. If they would only stop once in a while and think of what certain things brought to certain people or peoples, perhaps much trouble could be avoided and much happiness assured.

As you read along, you will better understand what I ask of you and why.

Twenty-six years old! Just beginning your life. What an opportunity lies ahead of you, Ansel, if you but truly shape your course. You have strength and energy and high ideals, and aims that are worth working for and worth realizing. Life to you now is like a wonderful sunrise in your beloved Mountains. I am so glad for you.

Later in life, there will come a time when things will change. High noon will have passed and the afternoon shadows will come and will fall upon you and Virginia with a softness and kindness that will bring a lus-tre of gold to your hearts and minds and you will want to set aside the heavy cares of life and to sit down for a while and look back through the years that have passed and into the time which is yet to come. When comes this autumn of life, a little peace, a little quiet and rest is so good, so good. I want your lives to be so planned that you may together have these happy years, free from the burdens of worry and care.

With your youth, strength and power to work and with your wonder-ful gifts, you have a capital which is invaluable. I believe your ideals and your character to be so high that none of the human weaknesses will turn you aside in your career. I say these things, Ansel, because I know them to be true, and I know too that you will so live that my estimation of you will not be shaken.

Great is your responsibility! When you were alone it was very important that you maintain these high standards, but now that another very dear life is in your hands, it is obligatory. What a wonderful thing is life! And what a terrible thing that in our hands is given the power of making a life a heaven on earth or of bringing unhappiness and misery, though ever so unwittingly to one whom we love.

I can see in the years to come, when you will have worked hard and faithfully, there will come a day when you will wish to rest, when you will wish to give to her whom you love and whom you will love the more as the years pass, your own time, your own self, that you two may go hand in hand into the winter, unafraid and unburdened by cares and sorrows.

The twenty years to come are your best working years. Try and plan so that at the end of each month something may be set aside to provide for this later time. Let Virginia be your guide in this. She can see that the idea is carried out better than you and your time will be free to work.

This I ask, Ansel, that you may have no regrets, and that this wonderful girl who is yours will not have to worry later in life. That she and you may have those golden years as I would wish.

I love you so much that I cannot help but write this letter and tell you. I love you *both* so much that I can look ahead through the time to come and offer a suggestion and ask that you follow it, that the setting sun of your lives may be as glorious as is now the dawn.

Dad

1. The nickname for Olive Adams.

To Cedric Wright

Yosemite National Park
1928

Dear Cedric—

While I am exposing a picture that takes 30 minutes, I will try a letter to you that will be more than a postcard squawk. I have never been in Yosemite when I felt the real mountain spirit as I do now: it is very quiet and we have taken several hikes in fresh, new places. Today the great cliffs are wreathed in steel-gray vapors: their vastness is revealed in the strange intimate glimpses through rolling clouds of crags and pines and snow. They are very kind and very real. The complexities of the modern world, of art striving for so-called "realities" through a process made up of self-deception and bunk, is supremely foolish in the face of the eternal openness and beauty of these mountains. Here, I am at home. I can forget the people, the studios, the gasoline and wander off into the oak shaded rocks and be happy.

Virginia is a perpetual surprise—I am beginning to think I have never known anyone to understand these things as much as she. She keeps very quiet, and I have, for a long time, judged people by what they do and say on the surface. Some of us are gifted with facile expression— and show their entire spirit at once. She is not one of those, and in many ways I am thankful. There are more enduring things than temperament.

I eagerly await some good news from you. I can picture the relief that the finishing of this show will be to you. I don't know what else to say— except that we are with you in every hope for your happiness. Don't be scared about my music—it will be better for the things I am working on now.

Jezus Kriste—be careful and don't worry—wish you could roll up your sleeping bag and come to the valley.

Ansel

To Virginia Adams

Sierra Club Outing
Canada
July 1928

My Dearest,

Every time I think of you and of what you represent to me in so many varied and beautiful ways, I reproach myself heartily for harping so much upon certain things affecting your life. After all, they are of minimum importance compared with all the very wonderful things that make up the essential You. But the essential You would blossom forth more freely, more intensely, were your attitude of life and living more in your command.

You have a most lovely voice, a most lovable personality, brains, and heart and grace of manner. Give all these more light and freedom. Place your singing foremost of all, and put every ounce of energy (always within reason) to the perfecting of your voice. We will have a home—

one you desire so much, and it will be more than an indulgent shell; it shall be a suitable setting for the things we live and work for.

Living for me is creative action; I am unsatisfied with simply existing. I can't help it—it is part of my make-up. I want to know every moment how I can refine and intensify my relation with the world, and every moment make some definite contribution—some crystallization of a perception—some actual golden experience. That's my idea; I don't want you to copy it, or reflect me, but I do want you to be yourself—I mean truly YOURself.

Finding the little box of candy gave me quite a thrill—for it came from you! Will write soon. Comfortable trip so far. Love to Aunt Mary. Take care of yourself.

Loads of love,
Ansel

To Charles Adams

Santa Fe, New Mexico[1]
April 4, 1929

Dear Pop,

Today there is a thick black sky and snow is falling in the hills. Tomorrow it may be a crystal clear day; the changes of the weather are always startling. The night we went hunting the Penitentes the stars were more brilliant than I have ever seen them—I could really see the shape of the Orion Nebula. And the sunrise over the Sangre de Cristo mountains was most extraordinary.

Mary Austin[2] gets back in a day or so. We are enjoying every minute of the time, and the people are all so good to us that we feel quite at home. There is unfolding a perspective of work that seems much, much more than I had ever hoped for. Everyone agrees that I am the only photographer that has come here really equipped to handle the country (pardon my vanity). But it is always good to look things square in the face; if I was not able to manage it, I would freely admit it. The opportunity is so apparent that I would be a complete chump to disregard it. I am certain that New Mexico will keep me half the year at least (in the future—not this year) and I shall meet with a great success. The wealth of material is beyond belief.

I hope Ma is all right now, nothing you said indicated anything serious, so we have not worried. But she must not over-do. And you must not either. How is the oil flowing?[3] Am thrilled that the prediction was fulfilled. Await all developments with the greatest interest.

If we do not write everyday, do not think we have forgotten you. We think of you all constantly, and hope that some day we can persuade you to visit New Mexico.

Love from us both to all,
Ansel

1. This was Adams' fourth trip to New Mexico and Virginia's first; Adams' first had been with Albert Bender in 1927.
2. Mary Austin, writer.
3. Following a dowser's prediction, Charles Adams had invested in an oil exploration venture in a South San Francisco cabbage field. No oil was found.

To Cedric and Rhea[1] Wright

Los Gallos,[2] Taos, NM
April 1929
Monday

Dear Cedric and Rhea –

Lookee! Roosters! Jezuz Krize but this is a great place. Such MOUNTAINS!!!! Peaks are 13000 feet high—MIT SNOW!!!!
Pines Aspins Snow Klouds Burros Swell People Injuns No photographers but me.
You gotta see this place before you die. Excuse my raving but it is now 12 midnight and I was up at 5am.

Just to keep in touch with you,
Ansel
Back in Santa Fe Wednesday

1. Rhea Wright, second wife of Cedric.
2. Los Gallos was the home of Mabel Dodge Luhan, heiress and patron of the arts; there she entertained artists, poets, and musicians. Her striking letterhead featured roosters and the surrounding Taos mountains.

To Albert Bender

Taos, New Mexico
April 1929
Thursday

Dear Albert,

We have finally decided on the subject of the Portfolio. It will be the Pueblo of Taos.[1] Through Tony Lujan,[2] the Governor of Taos was approached "with velvet"—a Council Meeting was held, and the next morning I was granted permission to photograph the Pueblo. It is a stunning thing—the great pile of adobe five stories high with the Taos peaks rising a tremendous way behind. And the Indians are really majestic, wearing as they do their blankets as Arabs. I think it will be the most effective subject to work with—and I have every hope of creating something really finc. With Mary Austin writing the text, and Nash[3] printing the book, I have a grand task to come up to it with the pictures. But I am sure I can do it. Dear Albert—look what you started when you brought me to Santa Fe!

Your letters have come as bright lights from California—I am really homesick for you all, but it will not be long now before we are together again! I should be home about the end of June. I have four weeks with the Sierra Club,[4] and then will be set firm and adamant in the splendid city of San Francisco for all Fall and Winter. . . .

Gawd bless you Albert—for a million glorious things.

Love from us both—always,
Ansel

1. *Taos Pueblo*, San Francisco: privately published, 1930; an edition of 108 with text by Mary Austin and 12 original photographs by Adams bound into each volume.
2. Tony Lujan, Taos Indian, husband of Mabel Dodge Luhan.
3. John Henry Nash, San Francisco book designer.
4. Annual outing into the High Sierra.

To Virginia Adams

My Dearest,

Thanks for the letters. The reason I have not written you is that I have been awaiting news from Don[1]—he gets back late today from Snow Creek. I shall send you a card just when I leave.

You may bill that lady $5.00 for the *Monolith*—she saw it at the Sierra Club party, so put down, "Sierra Club Rate."

. . . About your singing—I think the committee is the *bunk*. Your diction has always been most clear; I remember many compliments to you on that. Personally, I think they just wanted something to say.

Granted that you need more study—yet I do not think you should focus your study around that particular church work. You should study for the benefit of your general musicianship: when Miss Anderson[2] comes up, you should, I would think, work hard with her, but in a normal way. It seems foolish to work strenuously just to develop a certain phase of your singing to satisfy an arbitrary church committee. It would be a limitation self-imposed and ridiculous.

While I think it would be nice for you to have some regular singing work, I would never care to consider it other than a *secondary* thing. The main thing is to perfect your voice and your musicianship to the utmost— then you shall find many things will come to you. By keeping your independence you will be better off.

The time you have wasted is most distressing to me—not for any reason other than that it has retarded your development. If you had a second-rate voice I would not even think about it—but your voice is so fine, and your gifts so complete that it cuts like a knife to think of your neglecting it.

Now, you have your house[3]—a fine stage is set. Only one thing remains unfinished—that is yourself. I will get a job as an elevator man or anything if it is necessary for your musical development. But you must work—and work hard.

Two years have elapsed—the original agreement remains unfilled. I will do all I can to help you fill it—but the time is getting short.

Perhaps you are not entirely aware of the importance of this statement—it is by no means a passing fancy of mine. My love for you is directly proportional to your creative work—proportional to the extent which you become a real person. Character is to me an empty shell when it is not filled with vital intention and accomplishment—rather, accomplishment of the beautiful creates character.

But I believe in you—as I imagine you believe in me. There is too much to be done in life—and too little time to count on. Every minute is precious; and how I regret my own wasted time!!

I shall be greatly disturbed if our new place becomes your master. I would rather burn it up than have that occur. A certain amount of housekeeping is fine,—but too much!!! "Domesticity is the thief of time."

Please do not wait for Miss Anderson to show up. Start right off with your practicing—and steep yourself in your work. For the next week or two you should have a delightful lack of interruption. I will give you 100 hugs for each song—*new* song—that you will sing, completely memorized, and polished.

Forgive this sermon-like letter—but I could not help it. Especially when I thought of you sitting around this place in a most depressing and stagnant atmosphere. It has been particularly depressing to me this time—I shall be glad to be finished with the work and home again. I feel better when I am actually working—but the weather is not favorable—I have had two days of successful work—chiefly ski touring.[4]

The new camera[5] is *swell!*

This last page I should make less belligerent and more affectionate. But there is an enormous lot of affection hidden in the preceding hard words.

I love you and miss you tremendously. I cannot say anything that would carry my thoughts for you—so I will let it go at that and trust you can enlarge it to its proper dimensions.

Love to all—tell Pop to take care of himself. I look forward to coming back HOME!

Love always,
Ansel

A "semi-epigram":

Stone is not less serene when clothed in ice and cold
Than when bright-garmented in sun, and the warm glance of Spring.
But he who boasts of his enduring weight
May break in frost, and shrivel in the sun.

1. Donald Tressider, president of the Yosemite Park and Curry Company (YPCCO), who commissioned Adams to photograph Yosemite for advertising purposes.

2. Miss Anderson, Virginia Adams' vocal coach.

3. In 1930 Ansel and Virginia Adams built a house at 131 24th Avenue, next to his parents' house, in space formerly used as his mother's garden.

4. YPCCO wanted pictures of skiing to promote winter visits to Yosemite.

5. From about 1923 until 1930, Adams' primary camera was a 6½ x 8½-inch Korona view camera, which utilized glass plates. The new camera was a 4 x 5-inch view camera that used sheet film.

To Cedric Wright

Yosemite National Park
July 1930
Sunday

Dear Cedric,

I am having a ghastly time trying to sit painlessly after a 90 mile riding trip. It's fierce!

We went to Pate Valley, then up the Tuolumne Canyon to Glen Aulin. The Tuolumne Canyon is a tremendous place above the Muir Gorge, it's kind of Cosmic.

I got 20 dozen pictures. Jezuz!!

How is der brat?[1]

And how is der Brat's Mommer and Poppa?

We are going on the first of July over to Bishop. Meet the [Sierra] Club there. Then pick up der car there and go on to Tuolumne Meadows after the club trip for ten days. Then home for a week and then off to New Mexico for ten days, then home for a considerable time, thank God!!

I am getting kind of tired running away from my new place.

It is hotter than an embarrassing situation here now and I drag around like a fly in an oven. No new poems or anything. I can hardly wait for the Sierra trip. I get kind of weary of "$2.00 each, three for $5.00,[2] etc. etc." I only got one regret—that you will only be with us for two weeks. . . .

Goddam Mule did a jig on my good tripod and it's all over the Muir Gorge. I salvaged three screws. Lost my lens shade. Laughed so hard at a joke I fell off a log and scratched my hand. Shutter went to hell.

Film pack stuck on the best picture of the trip. Hit my knee on a snag after dark and said GDSB-*H to the packer, but he turned out to be a lady.

Love to you and Rhea and Joanne and your garden,

Ansel

1. Joanne, Cedric and Rhea Wright's daughter.
2. The selling price of his photographs.

To Virginia Adams

Santa Fe, New Mexico

[Late August 1930]

My Dearest,

I thought I would be able to write you yesterday, but Mary Austin asked me to supper and I stayed quite late. And I was working in the Old Museum the entire day.

Everything is going splendidly. I accomplished a lot at Taos, in spite of Mabel, and made some very good friends. Paul and Becky Strand[1] are in one of Mabel's houses. The transformation in Becky from last year is amazing—she was terribly nice to me and we had a lot of fun. Paul Strand is a peach. O'Keeffe[2] was there also, breezing around in a rather cool way—but not as frigid as last year. They hardly ever see Mabel, and the entire situation is too funny for words. Will tell you all. . . .

But the one gorgeous thing in Taos is the painter, Marin.[3] We had a morning with him. His work is a revelation. They are all acknowledging that Marin is doing things in watercolor that puts him at the top of American painters. Intuitively, I feel something very great indeed about the man, and, as all of that type, he is about as simple as a baby, and terribly funny. It was refreshing to punctuate sophisticated arguments with a few hours with Marin.

In the last two weeks something has clicked inside me and I have an entirely new perspective on many things concerning my work. I can't write it out—I just will have to do it.[4]

. . . Tell Pop and Ma and Aunt Mary that I think of them a lot, but have not enough to say to write them about. But I wish you could all come down, just to see the gardens. Much love to everybody. . . .

Just oodles of love to you. I will be very glad indeed to get close to you again.

Yours, lonesomely—
Ansel

Say hello to Albert for me. All here send love to him. How is he?

1. Paul Strand, photographer, and his first wife, Rebecca.
2. Georgia O'Keeffe, painter and wife of Alfred Stieglitz.
3. John Marin, painter.
4. Adams returned to San Francisco with the resolve that photography, not music, would be his career. He soon opened a professional photography studio in his new home.

To Albert Bender

San Francisco
January 15, 1931

Dear Albert,

I promised you a letter and it seemed necessary to wait until I was in bed with a cold to write it. And I do not know how much I shall be able to convey of what I want to say, but I will try to make it clear and not too long.

In the perspective of the past several years I am aware of a very even and well-ordered development of my work—almost a routine development which seems beyond the play of chance. From the first evening that I knew you, when I showed you some miserable prints in Berkeley, until now, when I have the completed Taos Book before me, I have figuratively had my breath taken away by trying to keep even with my evolution.

The Taos Book sums up all the elements of my progress in a most satisfying way; the quality of the pictures, the association with Mary Austin, the combination of my work with other graphic arts, and the ever-extending circle of contacts and patrons. But, "underneath and after all" it is you who have made all this possible, it is you that succored a poor artistic fish from the dry land of moronic isolation, it is you that cleared the way for the individualistic expression of a highly technical art. It is not the pecuniary phase of this assistance that requires the most difficult expression of gratitude, although the good Gawd knows this is a material world. But I am helpless to discover some means of properly indicating just what I feel about your amazingly generous and kindly attitude towards me and my work. Perhaps the only fitting expression of my gratitude would be that which is implied by a constant perfection and refinement of my work, to arrive sometime at a position that will in part justify all you have done for me.

The Taos Book represents much more than an effort of fine book-making; it reflects the thoughtfulness and generosity of a dear friend. In type it is dedicated to the Indians—but in spirit it is inscribed to you.

Affectionately,
Ansel

From Edward Weston[1]

Carmel-by-the-Sea
January 28, 1932

Dear Ansel—

I have not written to thank you for the Xmas greeting,—which I am very glad to add to my collection of fine photographs: nor have I acknowledged the magazine with your article[2] on my exhibit, because I am in the midst of printing my New York exhibit which opens February 29—to March 13.[3]

Your article I appreciated fully, it was an intelligent consideration, by far more so than most I get because it was a subject close to your own heart.

The discussion of phallic symbolism should at least clear me of intention, though the disciples of Freud will not be convinced, they are as fanatically religious as Methodists!

The part you devoted to my vegetables provoked a trend of thought which I will try to put into words. You are not the first to object to them: my good friend Charlot,[4] whose opinion I value highly, also cared less for them than my rocks, thought they resembled sculpture too much or held other implications. Others have had similar reactions.

I think first of all we must understand that Whistler (or was it Wilde?) was wrong, that nature does not imitate art, but the artist continually imitates nature *even when he thinks* he is being "abstract." Of course Whistler was playing with words, but this thought will lead us to a consideration of an abused word, "abstract."

No painter or sculptor can be wholly abstract. We cannot imagine forms not already existing in nature,—we know nothing else. Take the extreme abstractions of Brancusi: they are all based upon natural forms. I have often been accused of imitating his work,—and I most assuredly admire, and may have been "inspired" by it,—which really means I have the same kind of (inner) eye, otherwise Rodin or Paul Manship[5] might have influenced me! Actually, I have proved, through photography, that Nature has all the "abstract" (simplified) forms Brancusi or any other artist can imagine. With my camera I go direct to Brancusi's *source*. I find *ready to use*, select and isolate, what he has to "create." One might as well say that Brancusi imitates nature as to accuse me of imitating Brancusi, "Negro sculpture," or what not,—just because I found these forms first hand.

Now I am not a missionary, I will not try to convert you into liking my peppers or cabbages! Please consider what I have to say as a broad discussion, rather than argument. I have no unalterable theories, nor dogmatic beliefs to defend. I am trying to clear myself of another intention, that of making a pepper something it is not. I choose my peppers for comment, because they have been most often discussed.

I have on occasion used the expression, "to make a pepper more than a pepper." I now realize that it is a carelessly worded phrase. I did not mean "different" than a pepper, but a pepper *plus*,—seeing it more definitely than does the casual observer, presenting it so that the importance of form and texture is intensified.

Did you interchange the words "seeing" and "perception" in your analysis of photography? Well no matter,—I will use "seeing" for further discussion.

Photography as a creative expression—or what you will—must be "seeing" plus: seeing alone would mean factual recording,—the illustrator of catalogues does that. The "plus" is the basis of all arguments on "what is art."

But photography is not at all seeing in the sense that the eyes see. Our vision, a binocular one, is in a continuous state of flux, while the camera captures and fixes forever (unless the damn prints fade!) a single, isolated, condition of the moment. Besides, we use lenses of various focal lengths to purposely exaggerate actual seeing, and we often "overcorrect" color for the same reason. In printing we carry on our willful distortion of fact by using contrasty papers which give results quite different from the scene or object as it was in nature.

This, we must agree, is all legitimate procedure—but it is not "seeing" literally, it is done with a reason, with creative imagination.

No—I don't want just seeing—but a presentation of the significance of facts, so that they are transformed from things (factually) *seen,* to things *known:* a revelation, so presented—wisdom controlling the means, the camera—that the spectator participates in the revelation.

An idea just as abstract as could be conceived by the sculptor or painter can be expressed through objective recording with the camera, because, as I have already noted, nature has everything that can possibly be imagined by the artist and the camera has possibilities beyond factual recording.

But after all, Ansel, I never try to limit myself by theories. I do not question right or wrong approach when I am interested or amazed,— impelled to work. I do not fear logic, I dare to be irrational, or really never consider whether I am or not. This keeps me fluid, open to fresh impulse, free from formulae: and precisely because I have not formulae—the public who know my work is often surprised, the critics, who all, or most of them, have their pet formulae are disturbed, and my friends distressed.

I would say to any artist,—don't be repressed in your work—dare to experiment—consider any urge—if in a new direction all the better—as a gift from the Gods not to be lightly denied by convention or *a priori* concepts. Our time is becoming more and more bound by logic, absolute rationalism: this is a straitjacket!—it is the boredom and narrowness which rises directly from mediocre mass thinking.

The great scientist dares to differ from accepted "facts,"—thinks irrationally—let the artist do likewise. And photographers, even those, or *especially* those, taking new or different paths should never become crystallized in the theories through which they advance. Let the eyes work from inside out—do not imitate "photographic painting," in a desire to be photographic! (This latter is not an original thought with me. More, in detail later.)

Has this sounded like a sermon? I despise sermons, preachers—so I hope not. Perhaps I am really talking to myself. I have done some dangerous reasoning at times, but fortunately something beyond reason steps in to save me—

Greetings to you and Virginia.

Your friend
Edward Weston

I have been reprinting everything for N. York (opens Feb. 29) on "Velour Black"![6]—and getting prints incomparably finer than those you saw in San Francisco—Edward.

1. Edward Weston, photographer.
2. "Photography," *The Fortnightly*, December 4, 1931, p. 25.
3. Weston's photographs were shown at the Delphic Studio, New York City.
4. Jean Charlot, painter.
5. Paul Manship, sculptor.
6. Velour Black, a photographic printing paper made by DuPont.

To Alfred Stieglitz[1]

San Francisco
June 22, 1933

Dear Alfred Stieglitz,

I have planned to write you ever since my return to San Francisco.[2] I wanted to tell you a little of what my talks with you have meant to me. But the words will not come out as I want them to. So I will not try to write anything new—I trust you will believe me when I say that my meetings with you touched and clarified many deep elements within me. It has been a great experience to know you.

I am writing to tell you of an experiment I am undertaking. I have secured an admirable location downtown in San Francisco as a studio for my work. In conjunction with this studio is a gallery—very simple, fairly spacious, and well-lighted. I am planning to operate this gallery as a center for photography.[3] There is nothing of its kind out here, and, in view of the great interest in photography in San Francisco, I feel it will prove successful. I want to show the best photographic exhibits I am able to obtain—local, eastern, and foreign. I am anxious to present within a year a cross-section of present day photography—also some early photography if I can obtain it. Selections will be made with the greatest thought and care. Only the most important and significant phases of photography will be shown; I will certainly not include any "Salon" work. I know it will be difficult to get what I would like to have—but if I have only two shows the first year, the selection must be right to the limit of my ability to define what *is* right. My venture is not an attempt to imitate what you have done at An American Place—not an imitation of what Julien Levy[4] is doing. It is an attempt to experiment with the public response to fine photography. The support of the project so far has been more than encouraging. I may go down to ignominious defeat, but I am willing to take the chance. Someone here has to take the first step, and I have chosen to do so. Pray for me.

I plan to open about September first. Would you be willing to cooperate in this experiment and send me about twenty-five prints for my first show? (Exclusively a Stieglitz show, of course.) I know this is a tremendous thing to ask, but I ask it with a deep confidence in what it will mean to many of us here. I feel you would be surprised if you knew the interest in photography that exists here. One gentleman (not a person of means) said to me, "If you can ever secure a Stieglitz show, I will designate a print—I can stand up to one hundred dollars." I feel that others would respond in the same way—to say nothing of those who would consider a Stieglitz show in San Francisco a great personal experience. Furthermore, I will guarantee expenses of shipping, full insurance and the necessary announcements, and will take no commission on the sale of any of your prints. The prints would be hung under glass and fully protected.

I am, as it were, embarking on this experiment on a shoe-string. I am counting on my own work to pay the rent and expenses. I have raised a few hundred dollars with which to paint, clean up, buy glass for exhibits, etc. I am paying that money back in photographic work in the future. I expect to derive a little additional income from the sale of prints in the routine shows, and from lectures, etc.

I have put my cards on the table. I ask for a Stieglitz show—reverentially—in the hope that many people here who are unable to travel to New York will be offered the great experience of seeing your work and absorbing what they may of its extraordinary quality and spirit. If this request is refused, I will take it philosophically—knowing that your work is your life, and that no one must question the directions of the spirit.

Sometime I will write you at length on my reactions to our talks, and on what I am trying to do with my photography. The *Letters of John Marin*,[5] and the copies of *Camera Work*[6] which I brought back with me, have meant a great deal. I am looking forward to the time when I can afford the entire set of *Camera Work*.

I hope that Georgia O'Keeffe is improving in health, and that you have a fine summer at Lake George.[7]

With all good wishes,
Ansel Adams

1. Alfred Stieglitz, influential photographer, editor, and gallery owner. His gallery at this time was called An American Place.

2. Adams and Virginia made their first trip to New York City in March 1933 with the purpose of meeting Stieglitz.

3. The Ansel Adams Gallery opened September 1, 1933.

4. Julien Levy Gallery of modern art in New York City.

5. *The Letters of John Marin,* edited and with an introduction by Herbert Seligmann, New York: privately published for An American Place, 1931.

6. Stieglitz published a photographic journal, *Camera Work,* from 1903 to 1917.

7. Stieglitz spent his summers at a family enclave on Lake George, New York.

From Alfred Stieglitz

Lake George
June 28, 1933

My dear Ansel Easton[1] Adams:

I have often had you in mind & frequently regretted that I was unable to show you really a good lot of my work.—But I knew you understood. It was a tough siege not only for O'Keeffe but for me with "everything" up to me.—Had I had your address I would have sent you a few copies of *Camera Work* with my compliments. Let me know what you have so that I don't duplicate—Well I'm very glad to have your letter. I came up here 10 days ago—The Place is really in shape for the coming season.— I was about all in when I did get away finally. The Metropolitan Museum has *that* collection[2] officially under its roof. It was not a gift. The museum salvaged it. That's all there is to it. There is nothing like it in the world whether one likes it or not—I have had your own work in my mind too. Been thinking quite a lot about it. Now as for your letter & the request. Here I am up here & won't get into town until late in September. So sending you anything for the present is out of the question. But even if I were in town I don't know whether I could respond to your request—You see I am a stickler in the presentation of everything. My work would have to be framed. I have the frames. There would be glass, etc.—But the main thing is that of the things I'd want the world to see there are rarely "duplicates" & the "prints" I keep together & at home even if I never show them. It's just a feeling.—The things in the Metropolitan & Boston Museum happened to exist in duplicate—even some in triplicate—Some day I'd like to send you a good print of mine

[54]

for yourself as a token of appreciation of your purpose.[3] I know you won't misunderstand me—I hope to print here. Whether with O'Keeffe still very low I'll ever get up enough energy remains to be seen—I'm a pretty tired man.—Much more tired than I show. –

I know your "Experiment" will be a good one. I know well it won't be an imitation of anything else—I wish you every success in your own work & with the Gallery.

My cordial greetings to you & your wife,
Sincerely,
Alfred Stieglitz

1. Adams stopped using his middle name, Easton, around 1932.

2. Stieglitz gave his collection of photographs (including both his own work and that of other photographers) to the Metropolitan Museum of Art.

3. After Stieglitz's death in 1946, O'Keeffe gave Adams an original Stieglitz photograph, *The City at Night*.

From Virginia Adams

Yosemite National Park
August 2, 1933
Wednesday Noon

My Dear,

Just to think it's all over, and we have a son! He's really very cute, + I can't look at him enough. I mean, so far they've only brought him in to eat twice, + he is too sleepy to try—they leave him a few minutes but he's still asleep all the time. He's hardly cried yet—they say he will when he gets hungry. I'm *quite* thrilled. More than I thought I'd be—He has lovely long hands + beautiful nails. I really feel proud of our new possession. . . .—the baby was born at quarter of nine, + by 9:20 I was back in my bed in my room + had a little visit with Dad. He had come to see me about 7:30 + waited around. I certainly didn't need an anesthetic + Dr. Dewey said it was one of the easiest 1st births he'd had. Once he said, "You're entitled to holler"—but I didn't have the inclination. I'm so anxious for you to get here, dear—I think you'll be as enchanted as I am. And by the time you come, I'll probably be dying to get up, so I'll need some company to keep me settled. . . .

A letter came from Stieglitz, + one from Albert with a check for

$50.00. I'm not sending them + may not write you again—unless I just have to "express myself"—So much love, darling,

Your,
Virginia

When anyone asks the baby's name I say Michael Adams.[1]

1. Michael Adams was Adams' first child, born August 1, 1933, in Yosemite Valley, while Adams was on the annual Sierra Club outing.

From Charles Adams

San Francisco
August 2, 1933

Dear Boy of mine:

I can picture you, way off in the high country, hearing the call from Yosemite, which by this time has probably reached you and which will bring you the good news from Virginia.

A boy! Well, you and Virginia are now given a very great happiness and I know it will be a lasting blessing to you both. These events put a different meaning on Life. This boy of yours will reach down into the depths of your hearts and touch the strings there, to sound such rich chords of music as cannot be comprehended by us, for they come from another world, but they touch the soul as nothing else can. These chords will fill your being with a joy unknown before and a happiness, which we cannot define, through many, many years.

God Bless you and Virginia! With love from us all, and with blessings on your boy.

Affectionately your
Pop

To Cedric and Rhea Wright

Yosemite National Park
Saturday, August 5, 1933

Dear Cedric and Rhea,

It is a boy with swell violin fingers. You have a new pupil for der future!

It is now 4 days out.

I missed the coming out party by two days, but everything went slick. I left Palisade Creek Thursday morning, hiked out over Bishop Pass (18m) drove from Parchers Camp to Yosemite that night at one helluva rate.

Feel tired but elated. Will call you when I get back on Monday to S.F.

Virginia and I say thanks for all der swell letters. Will try and tell you how much we liked them when we recover.

Alberta[1] was swell. Trip was good. Lots of pictures.

See you later,
Ansel

1. Alberta Wright, Cedric Wright's daughter from his first marriage.

To Paul Strand

San Francisco
September 12, 1933

Dear Paul Strand,

You may remember me and you may not. I had a few days with you and your wife and O'Keeffe at Mabel's at Taos [in 1930]. We motored down to Santa Fe together and shot at tin cans with a revolver on the way. If the last mentioned event has slipped your mind perhaps you will recall that we had a wonderful morning with Marin at Taos; seeing his things remains for me my most immense experience in art.

I have been working hard with the camera since that time; I have suffered the inevitable change that several years can bring at a critical time. My work might interest you at this time—Stieglitz, with whom I had many fine hours in New York this spring, was very helpful and encouraging. I am perplexed, amazed, and touched at the impact of his force on my own spirit. I would not believe before I met him that a man could be so psychically and emotionally powerful. Among the treasures at "An American Place" I saw some very beautiful things of yours. In Santa Fe, a month later, I saw quite a few more. I do not forget them.

Since my return I have attempted a new venture; I desired something that would touch more deeply the general current of art than my own local attempts with the camera. I have opened a small gallery. My own work continues in a much freer mood, and I feel, for the first time, a bit more functional as a human organism. My place is most decidedly not an imitation of Stieglitz'; I wrote him at great length and outlined my plans—I told him I was going to alternate my exhibits between photography and painting or graphic arts, that I was not a missionary or a promoter, and that I did not care if I made anything out of the gallery or not—I only hoped it would pay its own rent. I am trying to bring things to San Francisco that should have come many years ago. Despite a certain sneering attitude in the East about California I can truthfully say to you that I would rather live here and work here than in any other American city I have seen—and I have seen most of them. There *is* a vitality and a purpose, and a magnificent landscape (Hollywood, etc. has ruined the reputation of all California). There are some of the good qualities of New York here, and few of the bad ones. It was refreshing to me to come back to it, even after weeks in New Mexico. To get back to the gallery: I have been fortunate in getting a very good schedule for the season. The present show is of photographs by Group f/64.[1] Then comes Charlot, Bruehl, Zorach, Weston, Stackpole, Berlandina,[2] etc.

I would like to have a show of your photographs—25 to 40 things. I do not know your attitude towards exhibits, but I can assure you there is enough interest in photography in San Francisco to provide a large and grateful attendance to a Strand show. Within eight days about 500 people have come to the f/64 show, and I am gratified that most of them evidenced a real interest and understanding in what the group is trying to do. A show of your things in the spring would be an event of major importance here.

I am certain you would like the gallery—it is simple, well lighted, and in no way smells of that baleful quality of pseudo-bohemianism or over-plucked modernism that so many show places of art possess.

I would appreciate hearing from you at your convenience. Much good news has come to me about your success in Mexico. Write me about that, too. I have always regretted the shortness of our contact.

Yours,
Ansel Adams

1. Group f/64, founded in 1932, was a loose organization of northern California photographers who championed straight photography; they opposed the work of the pictorialists who made photographs that often imitated other art forms through various techniques such as soft-focus lenses and manipulation of the print surface. The name

Group *f*/64 refers to the aperture setting of a camera lens, commonly used by the Group members, that yields maximum sharpness and image definition. The most influential members of the group included Adams, Imogen Cunningham, Willard Van Dyke, Edward Weston, and Weston's son Brett.

2. The painters Jane Berlandina, Jean Charlot, and William Zorach, the sculptor Ralph Stackpole, and the photographers Anton Bruehl and Edward Weston.

To Alfred Stieglitz

San Francisco
October 9, 1933

Dear Alfred Stieglitz,

. . . I still have faith in my gallery—the Charlot show went over big. Strange, precious little paintings in a nightmare idiom of Maya-Peon un-Riveraesque derivation (yet not derived obviously or trickily) caused an astonishing flood of enthusiasm and a few Spartan sales. I will not forget the color for a long time—it is like a strident, twanging chord on a harpsichord. I now have Anton Bruehl's Mexico photographs on the walls—most of them are of tired, simple people, unmindful of sun and flies. Bruehl has caught the hot bright sun in hard deep blacks; his pictures give us quite a little jolt—we are fussing over his technique and turning over in our graves about the way he looks through his finder. I say *finder* for all these pictures of his are glorified snap-shots. My goddam ideas of purity of technique suffered a sort of sea-change after seeing your things, and an added slight disturbance after seeing Bruehl's. I still hold forth for good technique—perfect technique—but there are so many other things for good besides. I will always remember what you said about the quality of *tenderness* (it's a rotten word for a deep cosmic quality) in things of art. Tenderness—a sort of elastic appropriation of the essence of things into the essence of yourself, without asking too many intellectual questions, and the giving of yourself to the resultant combination of essences. The soup stirs the cook—perhaps that's what happens in Art.

I wish to issue a manifesto—a manifesto to you, 3000 miles away, from me, 3000 miles away from you. It's a manifesto in the form of a grouch (a grouch is wrath without guts, I have to save the guts for things here). It's this—I hereby object to trying to support myself, my photography, my gallery with such a prostration of spirit as the following example indicates.

[59]

A man who owns 3,000,000 $'s and has a Responsible Position in the Community tells me he likes my pictures and wants a portrait[1]—tells me he wants me to avoid making his head look like a species of fruit—tells me to show only one ear—tells me to be sure and make him look at the camera—tells me, moreover, he understands ART—and I am a big enough jackass to try it, needing the cash—then he didn't like it—then I tell him for God's sake how can I get him to look at the camera and not show his two ears when he won't turn his eyes sidewise—and he says never mind I don't know my business—and I say Right!! I don't know that part of it—and he sails out like a clipper ship in a riptide (and I hope he flounders on a good muddy oyster-bed) and I am left Alone kicking myself in the pants every time I remember that I tried to make that picture, which was just a collapse of moral stamina. Hell!

The high priest of commercialism bellows from the tower of necessity the call to prayer, and the faithful bend and sprawl and grovel at the ghost of the Almighty $—rents have to be paid, food bills have to be paid, shoe-shines and clean shirts have to be bought,—so that the smirk of ideals compensating with existence is given a proper setting. Hereafter, I do only what I want, in the manner I want, and if at the middle of next year I find myself on the municipal relief list it will be with a clear conscience.

But there are better phases of the work here to tell you of than the kind of thing above—I just had to get it off my chest. I have had some very interesting work to do—and am always more and more amazed at the interest in decent photography out here.

I find myself brooding over rocks and clouds and Things of No Value that would make good pictures. I remember campfires, a few gigantic mountains to inflate my ego—and a few very long miles to deflate it again. It's funny—I have had lots of that kind of life; I didn't know what it was all about when I had it. Why is it that Things of No Value make the best pictures, and that a stomachache becomes interesting when remembered. I had appendicitis at Taos and enjoy looking back on it with the rapture of a physical martyrdom endured and escaped. . . .

I remember New York: subtracting you and a few other people, your work and very little other work, what is there in that memory but a vision of a slowly dissolving inferno? Migraine from looking up—Nausea from looking down—Total jitters from looking sidewise. Noise, sweat, stink, more noise—this is the Center of Civilization (God help Civilization)—no Earth in sight—the City is sitting on its chest with a strangle hold—even the clouds look like they were intruding. Chicago, the same. Detroit, the same. San Francisco, not quite the same, some stinks, some noise, but Earth is in sight—sand dunes, hills, long moor-like solemn stretches of windy seafront, ocean, fortunate fog. And, not very far away there is a land and sky that would be heroic if given the chance. Here, there is some beauty within reach—in New York you have to stretch for it. I wish you could come out here sometime—without telling anyone where you were going—anyone there or here except a few people you could trust. We would help you to experience what we have, and try to keep you from what we have not. This part of the earth cannot help it if they call it California.

I remember my mountains, my old clothes, my pack-donkeys, my first funny plate camera (6½ x 8½ with glass plates)[2] that I animal-packed and back-packed over unimaginable miles of rocks and roughness and pointed at amazed landscapes. The results, photographically, were terrible, but the life bent and tempered something that I can never unbend and untemper in this existence—even if I wanted to. There is too much clear sky and clean rock in my memory to wholly fall into self-illusion. I wonder—as I pick this out on the typewriter to you—I wonder if I can bring anything of that absolute honesty into my work and into this experiment of a gallery? If I can make something or show something that will be as inviolate as a piece of Sierra Granite. You have weathered storms that would put me on the bottom with the old bottles in a week, but I don't think the public will beat me after-all. You face the winds like a rock, and I have to stream-line my front. But thank God, there are some people here who understand a little about it—who forget that it's Art and know it for Something Said about Something Felt.

This is certainly a strange letter—I confess I send it to you with the complete assurance that you will understand it—that you will read between the lines that somebody out here remembers you and would want to talk with you were there not 3,000 miles of Moronia Gigantica separating us. I hope O'Keeffe is progressing and that you are in good shape for the coming season in New York.

Yours ever,
Ansel Adams

1. In the early 1930s Adams made many portraits on commission.
2. A Korona view camera, probably Adams' sixth camera.

From Paul Strand

Mexico
October 14, 1933

Dear Adams—

Please excuse my delay in answering your very nice note. The past few weeks full of things that demanded a great deal of me—

Of course I remember the summer you came to Taos—remember your staying with us—the pleasure of having you play at the hotel, in spite of those surroundings and your hesitancy after so long a time away from a piano—In short my memories of meeting you are all pleasant ones—

I am glad you saw Stieglitz last winter and that he encouraged you— I have no doubt your new work is a development over the things I have seen—probably more direct, a simpler approach to the object—truer to the real qualities of photography—Yes these are critical years for anyone who is alive—aware—has not insulated himself in some "esthetic" rut—away from the world—The world itself in profound process of change—social change, as it appears to me—

Your new venture of a gallery in San Francisco—does interest me— for I feel whatever you try to do will be in an honest and un-arty way— Nevertheless I cannot say yes to an exhibition of my things at the present time—Actually I have little interest in exhibitions—because at the basis they seem to be un-American—just a mean and meaningless affair; mean in that they exploit the artist to entertain the public free of charge—meaningless in that they seldom establish any standards—

I turned down three museums last year in just the above terms— Their impudence and complete ignorance of what they are doing is just disgusting—They think that flattery is a substitute—but they can all go to hell as far as I am concerned—for I refuse to be part of that racket— That is my general feeling about exhibitions—I can never get used to the idea that pictures are free entertainment in the U.S., elsewhere too, that the people who claim to enjoy a thing never support the individual who makes what gives them pleasure—However this isn't a specific answer to your question. First the difficulty of sending anything out of Mexico— which is considerable—and I have most of my work here—The balance is in storage in New York—But in addition I don't like to let these prints go out of my hands (they exist for the most part in only one example), to be handled by express or mail carriers—customs inspectors, etc. They

[62]

are not the usual tough gaslight print and a scratch means ruination—
So for the present it doesn't seem feasible. Perhaps some day I will get to
Frisco again and that would be different—All this I hope you will un-
derstand and not feel me to be merely uncooperative—

Last February I did have a show here under the auspices of the Government. The best part of it was the democratic character of the people who came. Some 3,000 in 10 days—The Gallery opens onto a main
street, so that all sorts came in—middle class—workmen in blue jeans,
soldiers, Indians—many children—How much or how little the things
meant to these simpler people, I cannot know—But to see them entertained me—and it is seldom one gets any pleasure out of one's own exhibitions.

I have worked hard here—started new problems—and have taken up
lines of work started way back in 1915. Now I have been made director
of motion picture work in connection with the Department of Fine
Arts Secretaria of Education and that offers the greatest problems to
solve—We hope to begin work soon –

Thanks for what you say about the prints you saw in New York and
Santa Fe. I wonder what things you saw at Stieglitz for I didn't know he
had anything around. Also where and what you saw in Santa Fe.

I would always be glad to hear from you—and about you—both your
own work and the gallery—In both, my best wishes—

Greetings—
Paul Strand

From Alfred Stieglitz

New York City
October 20, 1933

My Dear Ansel Adams:

I'll make one more attempt to write to you. Since I received your letter
in Lake George on Sept. 25th I have made four distinct attempts to write
—that is, have started four letters. But every time I was taken away. It's
one hell of a time I have been going through. Everything seems to be
piling up like the straws on the proverbial camel's back. . . . Well I got
down here to the Place on Oct. 1st & single handed . . . I have whipped
The Place into shape & it was never quite so magnificent. The Marin

Exhibition is a very grand affair. It will be neglected I know. But that makes no difference. So was the Cézanne Show in 1911 at "291."[1] This Exhibition is perhaps the apex of my lifework.—One can't tell about it. It must be seen. In the meantime the racketeering in the so-called world of art becomes more & more brazen & engulfing.—The sordidness of it all is appalling & every one coming into touch with Art is more or less contaminated by it & perfectly unaware of that fact. That's really my fight & has been all these years.—Integrity of endeavor means nothing to the American people. Nothing whatever. Still I fight on & shall till I drop.—O'Keeffe is still at the Lake—& still a very sick woman. She is well out of this all for it is very terrible in spite of the outward calm & peace which seems to reign here. As for your idea about an O'Keeffe-Stieglitz Show my dear man I understand only too well about the starved souls in San Francisco as well as elsewhere.—But what you ask for is absolutely impossible—physically impossible as well as otherwise impossible. The O'Keeffes are needed here. I dare not risk them out. She is not painting. May never paint again. As I know what they do here primarily to the Europeans that come here they are amazed. Marin amazes them too. And so do my photographs. As for the latter they hardly exist for me. No I cannot spare the energy to go through them & send you a lot for exhibition even at your place. You know I hate the very idea of all exhibitions for exhibitions as such are rarely true.—Have no fundamental significance.—Are "entertainers" & not enlighteners. I know whereof I speak. I know my America & know the American character. It's very hard for me to write you in the spirit in which I do but I cannot do otherwise. And I know altho' you'll be disappointed you'll not feel hurt nor will you think I "might" if I had any good will. It's all a long long story which never will be told & if told but few, if any, would understand.

My greetings to you & your wife. I hope the latter & child are thriving & that you are a happy husband & happy father

Stieglitz

1. Stieglitz directed The Little Galleries of the Photo Secession (nicknamed "291") at 291 Fifth Avenue, New York City, from 1905 to 1917, where Paul Cézanne had his first American exhibition in 1911.

To Alfred Stieglitz

San Francisco
October 23, 1933

Dear Alfred Stieglitz,

Your good letter of Oct. 20th came this morning. I hope you did not feel worried about any delay in answering my letters—I fully understand the difficulties of your life at present, and I am more than grateful that you write me at all. . . .

Yes, I do understand your attitude about sending exhibits of yours and O'Keeffe's work out here. Perhaps I have been too forward in asking you for them, but I felt that you would interpret my request for what it was—a sincere reflection of the desire of many of us to see those marvelous things. However, they will exist in New York, and it is some comfort to know that.

I would like to write you at some length sometime about your attitude. I am wondering, and it may be presumptuous to say it, if you have not been bitten so severely during your life that you present an all-enfolding armor to the world which keeps both the good and bad from you; or rather, which protects and prohibits at the same time. After all, there is only a handful of souls that care and know—in all the world there is only a handful. But they—that handful—are not all tagged so that we can perceive them at a glance. They are hidden away in the vast pile of humanity, and we can't see in and they can't always see out. If you bring a light close enough they may be able to see it and respond. . . . I am with you in spirit—had I the means I would contribute to the limit to what you are doing; I would buy O'Keeffes, Marins, your things. I would do what else I could to support the most remarkable institution in America—I think you and your place is just that.

There may be obscure people in obscure places that need but the touch of a rare beauty to awaken them to the highest things. And what is the function of great art but to do just that—to kindle something of a flame in the human material that is ready to burn? I am one of the thousands that have come to your place—perhaps I am one of the very few that went away with even a fragmentary understanding of the great thing you are doing. But it is just a fortunate series of circumstances that permitted my visit to New York.

I am not complaining about your attitude, nor am I indicating that I do not agree and understand. The situation, as it exists, is more than

[65]

hard—is more than discouraging. But has the actual existence of art ever been otherwise? Or of creative thought? There has been more than one crucifixion.

I got a very cordial letter from Paul Strand from Mexico. Same ideas. Exhibitions are free entertainment. Beauty and wonder and magnificence for only *the walking into* a gallery—for only the simple physical effort of transporting the corporeal carcass so that the more corporeal mind can collect a few thrills and have something to talk about.

Right—99%. What about the other 1%? or the remaining $1/10$ of 1%? What is it all about anyhow?

What is to be the solution of the question? Would an enlightened proletariat bring art into its own? Or does it require a super-cultured and wealthy aristocracy to support the phosphorescent glows of surface-civilization? Is the whole thing a surface, two-dimensional shadow, or does it go deep after all? Does it probe deep like a needle in the flesh of humanity—at isolated spots, or is it some sort of a rash on the outer skin?

Are you breaking your spiritual and physical neck to both present and preserve your art in the face of a huge indifference? Frankly, it isn't worth your neck. It is not so much the art as what you have expressed through it—I refer to Marins, O'Keeffes, Doves,[1] Stieglitzes—all together. I should not be surprised if the future histories of Art will define you and your group with equal significance to the post-Renaissance high-spots; perhaps of more importance. But that's the future. *Now*— you are still a living, breathing human being who deserves at least a little peace, a little relaxation. You have done enormous things, but for God's sake don't forget that your own self—your own spirit—is more important. Without *you* these things would not exist. Without your vision— God knows where photography would be.

No matter how hard you toil and fight—you cannot make a Moron understand a Marin. What I am trying to get at is this—why not let yourself ease up a bit now and trust the slight residuum (Humanity minus the morons) to come as they will. Let them do a little of the work. I am doing my little bit for you here—I wish I could do more. But I remember you—and I read into your letters—as a swift vortex of defensive energy, which, after all, has done its work these many years, and now deserves a little peace. I think there is a small army of people who would hasten to support your standards were they only reached. They extend over the world. All that is needed is an organization—a sort of brotherhood. I don't mean charity—I mean understanding. . . .

I am continuing this on Nov. 6th: things have been so rushed that I have not had the chance to finish it before this.

My god!! I sent off my New York show[2] yesterday morning. It goes with two or three prayers and a certain off-hand mood that amuses me with myself. Most of the things you have seen—I have been so swamped with the place here and commercial tasks that I have done very little new stuff.

A few of the things I feel hit the mark. And that gets me into the mood of despair about my own work—is this set-up here I have started going to make my own personal photography impossible for me? I see things with a new perspective now—creative work is one thing and "commissions" are another. I have so much I want to do; I want to take the technique I now have and turn it into more expressive channels. My meeting with you gave me confidence in my technique and *photographic* methods, and made me feel a great urge to do things. But all this detailed business I have put on my shoulders looks like it is impossible to do very much other than just attend to it.

The commercial work is sometimes interesting—most often not. Were it not for the inherent dishonesty of most advertising the commercial field might be a fine functional thing. I did one job for a linen concern which I sent on to Alma Reed. If you call to see my show ask to see that picture; it is not on the wall. It was the most pleasant task I have had of its type. There was something real about all the things in the set-up, and something real in the way they wanted it to look and something real in the fact that they wanted as good a photograph as they could get.

But—to make a living out of commercial things is certainly a multiple crucifixion.

I imagine you will be displeased at the way I have mounted the prints. I thought a lot about what you said regarding the presentation; I know it is not adequate, but I cannot seem to determine a better way at present. I suppose I shall wake up some morning with a clear idea about it. I made lots of experiments, but nothing seemed adequate. So I just proceeded with the theory that the mount served to isolate the print from its environment and let it go at that. Everything else I tried seemed forced and not "felt." . . .

With all good wishes to you and O'Keeffe, and trusting things will go better for you this season,

Yours ever,
Ansel Adams

1. Arthur Dove, painter.

2. Adams' first exhibit in New York City was at the Delphic Studio, owned by Alma Reed.

To Paul Strand

San Francisco
October 31, 1933

Dear Paul Strand,

Many thanks for your very cordial letter. I read between the lines that you have found an environment and work that is fluently favorable to you. Not many of us can say that. Open war or shallow compromise seems the lot of most of us. I certainly wish I could see what you are doing in Mexico. I have always had things happen to me—psychologically, even physically,—when I have seen your things. I believe you have made the one perfect and complete definition of photography. Stieglitz is to me the great catalyst; he has taken rare mental and emotional material and turned it into creative channels. He has turned himself also into these channels; I cannot think of Stieglitz apart from his group, but I can think of Marin and you apart from the group. Perhaps I make myself too thick in trying to put this in words, but I hope you get what I mean. I have often wondered what Stieglitz would have been had he concentrated entirely on his own work.

I saw a rock and a wood detail photograph of yours at Stieglitz', and quite a number of your things at Santa Fe. . . . The prints were of New Mexican buildings, Colorado mining towns, and a few child portraits. They were very fine indeed.

I understand perfectly your refusal to send an exhibit to me. You have many good and sufficient reasons. I must admit that I do not fully understand your attitude (and Stieglitz' attitude) about exhibitions in general. I think there are always a few people in any part of the land that would react completely to truly fine things—that would make those things functional in a social sense. After all, should we not be resigned to the naked fact that there is (as there ever has been) only a very very small real audience for anything worth while? And should we not trust that in almost any group there will be a few—perhaps only one—who will perceive the significance of a great expression? And if there is only one, wouldn't that justify an exhibit? I don't think there is anyone who detests the average American attitude towards Art more than I—but if there wasn't *anyone* who understands I think I would go jump in the Ocean.

The country is raw, uncouth. It seemed to me that New York was the rawest place of all. I cannot tell you what a dismal reaction the place gave me; everything decent seemed to be having such a hell of a time to breathe. I think I felt the lack of earth—the few pitiful rocks in Central Park were orphaned by all the square miles of structure.

[Remainder of letter is missing.]

From Alfred Stieglitz

New York City
December 7, 1933

My dear Ansel Adams:

It has been impossible to go into your lengthy & most interesting letter. I have been at my post daily but with a mean attack of sinusitis & laryngitis & the overwhelming demands made upon me to write to anyone at length has been humanly impossible. You ask what my attitude is. Man can't you figure it out for yourself. I am trying to sustain life at its highest—to sustain a *Living* standard. To let every moment *actually live* without any ism or any fashion or cult attached to it. The Place is a Living Center even if deserted. Everything connected with it or found in it is rooted in its vital center—There are no exhibitions in the sense of exhibitions elsewhere. There are no pictures just because of pictures. Don't you realize I hate the very idea of what's called Exhibition. Don't you know I hate the very idea of what's called a Picture.—Is there no idea of nobility left in the world or does our Country not recognize that there is such a thing. Of course you have tackled an impossible problem. You must realize that. But that doesn't mean that you must give up. No it's your problem. You have a family to support. That's the rub. The clash of the ideal with the commercial—for you cannot escape the latter unless you are ready to starve & have your family starve—I chose my road years ago—and my road has become a jealous guardian of me. That's all there is to it. –

I hate all sham & half-business of any kind as I told you. But I refuse to sit in judgment. Everyone is his own judge as far as I am concerned. I have only a certain amount of energy to expend—remember I am 70—altho' I am lavish with it I cannot as yet move mountains by addressing them with beautiful words. I have hoped to get at printing since I'm back—Oct. 1st—but it has been impossible. I have been wanting to go to the Bank seven blocks away to attend to very important personal affairs & yet I haven't had a chance. This is literal. Two weeks ago I should have gone to bed but if I'm not here the Place might as well be sealed up.—The Marins are a grand affair & there have been about 5000 visitors or so since the opening. But Art Directors & Collectors & all that ilk seem to steer clear of 509[1] as if it were the devil's own resort. Or perhaps because they don't know is it that or God's.—So they play safe. If ever there was a genius Marin is one. As for San Francisco over 20 years ago—or about 20 years ago—I gave the San Francisco Museum a Marin & a beautiful impression of Cézanne's "Bathers." No acknowledgement was ever received. . . . So you can see I did do something for California. As for the set of *Camera Work* the Library you speak of was one of *Camera Work*'s original subscribers. When the earthquake took place *Camera Work* was destroyed. The Library at once ordered a set to replace the old one!!—& paid handsomely for it altho' I quoted it a relatively low figure at the time. You must remember that the first 39 numbers were bought by the Berlin Museum for $600!!—Only a year ago the Chief of the Congressional Library wrote me he considered $1000 a very low sum for a complete set of *Camera Work*. So it goes. Actually *complete* sets are very scarce.

I hope you are at work & making two ends meet & that the Boy & the Mother & Father are all thriving. –

As ever,
Cordially,
Stieglitz

1. An American Place was on the 17th floor (Room 1710) of an office building at 509 Madison Avenue, New York City.

To Alfred Stieglitz

San Francisco
May 20, 1934

Dear Alfred Stieglitz,

Here I am installed once again in a simpler environment and quite contented and busy. I could not operate both my photography and an art gallery and do them both well. I was losing out painfully in the photography and wearing myself out in the bargain. So—I have turned the operation of the Gallery over to Mr. Joseph Danysh, who, by virtue of 15 hours a day hard work, will undoubtedly make it go. I am still associated with it in spirit but quite divorced from it in the material sense. It is a relief to be entirely free of weighty responsibilities and see a clear road ahead for my photographic work.

You may be at Lake George by now, with a happy and peaceful summer before you. I hope that the season has been good in every way—I have heard great things about the exhibits you have held. I also hope Georgia O'Keeffe's health is improved.

I entertain a gradually growing disgust on the way the Delphic Studio handled my exhibit. I received many fine letters about the exhibit, and, what press releases I saw were cheerfully favorable. But I am convinced that no effort was made to really put my stuff to the attention of the public; I did not give my New York show to sell prints, but to adequately show them and get much needed criticism. I did sell about eight prints—and have heard nothing "material" from the Gallery concerning them. So, you can see, I am not too happy about any future association with the Delphic Studio.

I have been doing some new things—several I think are quite acceptable. I want to give another and more alive exhibit in New York in order that my work can have the advantages of decent presentation, at least. Where to go? I am not insinuating that I would want you to show my things—wonderful as it would be for me—for I know that if you wanted to show them you would tell me so. But I am frankly perplexed as to where I could give a decent, simple, dignified exhibit of my work, and feel that I had shown what I am trying to do (without ballyhoo or bloated sales-intention). Julien Levy is out completely—I told you how depressed I was at what I saw there. And I frankly cannot afford to pay for a gallery—although I am willing to forego any collection on what is sold. I do not want a large show—twelve to twenty-five prints is an adequate number to show my new photographic intentions.

My gallery experience has been very beneficial, if wearing. I have seen a fair cross-section of the ridiculous mania for sophistication which is unsupported by anything generous or real. I realize that the artist's job is to produce—not to sell his own productions, but there does not seem to be more than a handful of trustworthy agents in the country. It's not that they steal—they are merely ruthless in "getting the stuff over." Pictures may sell, but the artist's sensibilities are put in the dog house. How you have kept going in the strain of it all for so long is totally beyond me.

The PWAP[1] work here is fair—that in Los Angeles is much better. But all through it one can smell a self-conscious striving to be "contemporary." Soap-box art in the main. I am getting dreadfully tired of being used as a tool for radical interests—artists in the main are asked to do "Proletarian" work, photographers are asked to photograph May Day celebrations, old human derelicts in a dingy doorway, evictions, underpaid workers, etc. etc. I grant that the times are portentous, but I'll be damned if I see the real *rightness* of being expected to mix political economy and emotion *for a purpose.* I am ready at any time to offer my services to any constructive government—Right or Left, but I do not like being *expected* to produce propaganda. Half my friends here have gone frantic Red and the other half have gone frantic NRA.[2] The artist occupies a sort of No-Man's-Land. I can imagine it is much worse in New York.

My wife sends you kindest regards. I have thought very often of our visits in New York. I may be along again in the Fall—if I can get the trip subsidized.

With all good wishes,
Ansel Adams

1. The U.S. Government Public Works of Art Project (PWAP) provided employment to artists and craftsmen during the Depression.

2. The NRA (National Recovery Administration) was instituted by Congress and President Franklin Delano Roosevelt in 1933 as the umbrella agency to deal with the nation's financial and industrial recovery from the Depression.

From Alfred Stieglitz

New York City
June 9, 1934

Dear Ansel Adams:

Of course I frequently wondered how long you could manage a Gallery *and* photograph at the same time. Your letter therefore didn't come as a surprise.—Of course the experience is invaluable—I remember how Picabia[1] & his wife after having spent months at 291 in 1913 were so enamored of their experience that forthwith they decided Paris must have a 291. And when they arrived there they made the attempt.

Inside of 4 weeks they realized to run a 291 meant a lifework—a cutting out everything not pertaining to it.—So the Parisian 291 came to an end quickly. Picabia was wealthy so the experience meant no "sacrifices"—on his part or his wife's.—It has been a very hard season for me. Since Oct. 1 last I have been at The Place daily excepting the 4 times I visited O'Keeffe in Lake George & spent a day or two with her. Many a day I should have been in bed nursing this or that but I had no choice. I had *no one* to take care of the Place. My not being there meant it was closed. As it was when I visited O'Keeffe.

—The Marin & O'Keeffe shows were grand ones.—Dove's was very good.—I had 2 Marin shows—a retrospective & then all new work. O'Keeffe was retrospective—& chiefly abstract.—She is still not painting. Looks well enough but has no vitality. And without that it is impossible for her to paint or really do much of anything.

I do hope she'll gain strength eventually. It is a trying siege for her. And it is heart-breaking to watch.—Her show was a very grand one—& was visited by nearly 9000 people. Fashionables don't frequent The Place. They visit modern art in the shape of Whistler's mother at the Museum of Modern Art[2]—Poor Whistler if he could know what happened. A more vulgar performance in the art line I never heard of. I suppose you have seen Craven's book *Modern Art*[3]—that's common enough entertainment as it may be—but that Modern Museum stunt makes Craven's performance the quintessence of refinement by comparison.— I haven't made a photograph since I left Lake George. It's the first time in 50 years that a winter has passed by without my making a single exposure. And there was no printing either. I leave for Lake George in about 10 days. Maybe there I'll begin afresh.

—I'm a tired, very tired, person.

O'Keeffe has left for New Mexico to see what that will do for her. So I'll be alone, on the Hill.—I do hope New Mexico will restore her health somewhat—& that maybe she will feel impelled to paint a little.—

—I hope you are doing some work that satisfies you & that you & yours are thriving. My cordial greetings to you all.

Stieglitz

1. Francis Picabia, painter.

2. Museum of Modern Art, 11 West 53rd Street, New York City, founded in 1929.

3. Thomas Craven. *Modern Art: The Men, The Movements, The Meaning*, New York: Simon & Schuster, 1934.

[73]

To Edward Weston

San Francisco
November 29, 1934

Dear Edward,

I gather that things are not entirely smooth with you in Carmel, and I have been intending to write for several weeks and just think out loud to you. What I say may mean nothing to you at all, or it may be of some little help in aiding you to organize yourself out of the dumps. I may be presumptuous in writing you at all, but I know what just such letters have meant to me when I have been "down" and in an indefinite state of mind and spirit.

First, suppose you take stock of yourself—that is, I am taking stock of you as I know you and your work. You have made a definite contribution to photography that puts you on the immortal shelf along with [David Octavius] Hill, [Eugène] Atget, Stieglitz. Your influence is far-reaching. You have crystallized your work in Carmel; the sea, rocks, trees, and the mood of that coast has grown into you and you into it. You are *not* (thank God) a metropolitan person. Commercial and advertising work as it is inflicted today is not your line. It isn't mine, either, and I suffer the pangs of Hell with some of it. But as long as I am here I will have to do it. At the same time I have wires and strings out for very different work which may take me away for most of the time. But to get back to you:—that which you have done is monumental. People should and will come to you—not you to them.

You have had a slack period. But that doesn't mean it will always be so from now on. I have periods when I am scared to death—and then something always turns up to clear the air and the bills, and the mood is regained.

Now, I may be wrong, but here is what I would do if I were in your particular boots:

1. Simplify your Carmel set-up as much as possible.

2. Investigate the possibilities of various cities for exhibits and periods of work therein. That is, if you arranged for an exhibit in Portland and announced that you would be there for a month for sittings, etc. during the exhibit, you would undoubtedly get lots of work. But a real manager is needed. Witness the "Musical Masterclass" idea; it is generally more lucrative than continued work in one place.

3. Suppose you were able to find a manager who would place exhibits

and make all arrangements for you—would you not be relieved of a great amount of routine work, and would you not also profit thereby? The trick is to get the proper manager.

4. If you undertook such a program, you should not give up Carmel as your headquarters; it has a glamour and character which is very favorable to your work and to the *presentation of your work*. Edward Weston, Carmel, California, is a very logical and incisive address. Edward Weston, San Francisco, Los Angeles, Chicago, etc. is something quite different. People will come to you at Carmel quicker than they will to their own city spots; I find they come to my house just as quickly and as easily as they came to me downtown—and there is more "flair" in coming to my house than to 166 Geary Street.[1] Unfortunately public presentation is a game—a trick—and none of us can neglect that attitude towards it.

5. As I see it, your chief danger (a danger to which all of us are vulnerable) is in being submerged in society, becoming a metropolitan "fixture," being taken-for-granted. We all should keep alive by keeping just a little remote; by establishing an environment that is not of *every-day*.

There is nothing I would like better personally than to have you come here permanently. I never think of competition with you, and such competition which would obtain would be stimulating and helpful to all of us. But I do think you would be unhappy—in yourself and in your work—in any metropolitan environment. I am not happy here—I find little that urges me to work creatively. I am definitely naturalistic; were I free of all responsibilities I would live in the mountains—I would rather chop wood for a living than do most of the trips I have to do in commercial photography. You would undoubtedly profit in the immediate sense—if such available work may be termed profitable—but what would be the result in *yourself*. I never think of Strand as of New York—he is always in my mind as associated with diverse environments—New Mexico, Maine coast, Mexico, etc.

Both you and I are incapable of devoting ourselves to contemporary social significances in our work; Willard [Van Dyke] is gifted in this respect. I come to think of him more as a sociologist than a photographer. His photography seems to be turning into a means to a social end, rather than something in itself I will regret it if it becomes that entirely, for he is too damn good a photographer to submerge it in anything else. I still believe there is a real social significance in a rock—a more important significance therein than in a line of unemployed. For that opinion I am charged with inhumanity, unawareness—I am dead, through, finished, a social liability, one who will be "liquidated" when the "great day" comes. Let it come; I will try to adapt myself. But, Goddamnittohell, I refuse to liquidate myself in advance!

I think it is up to such as you and I to maintain our conception of art as expressed through our medium. You and I differ considerably in our theory of approach, but our objective is about the same—to express with our cameras what cannot be expressed in other ways—to trust our intuition in respect to what is beautiful and significant—to believe that humanity needs the purely aesthetic just as much as it needs the purely material.

Stieglitz has dynamically maintained this point of view. Your shells will be remembered long after [Walker] Evans' picture of two destitutes in a doorway. Dorothea Lange strikes the middle road—she takes contemporary material and always sees it emotionally—there is always something beyond the subject in her things.

All this is hardly related to your immediate problem, but I had to get it off my chest.

Anyway, let me know if there is anything I can do to help clear things up for you. I wish I could order $1000 worth of prints from you, but I am looking around for someone to order just that from me. But, if there is anything I can do, let me know. I am still hoping I can get away for a few days and come down to see you.

Yours ever,
Ansel

1. The address in San Francisco of the short-lived Ansel Adams Gallery.

From Edward Weston

Carmel
December 3, 1934

Dear Ansel –

What a grand letter you wrote me! Really, I am profoundly grateful,— more so than I can easily express.

I find nothing to disagree with in your philosophy, nor in your analysis of me,—my needs. I am not metropolitan, left S.F. because I was unhappy, wanted to get my feet on the soil, to get away from canned people. I will return to city life only as a last resort. I am glad to be able to tell you that the economic pressure has lifted. But I really was not worried in the usual sense. In fact I am not often bothered, because, as you know, when things seem impossible something always happens to save the situation. I will never make money because I don't care enough about it; but I always keep one jump ahead of the wolf, and ask no more!

You are absolutely right about keeping remote. I have done this for years, in Los Angeles, in Mexico, in Carmel—yes in S.F. too, out near the Presidio. Our kind of work cannot be done on "Main Street." Increased overhead means hiring cheap help and probably a manager. I can't be bothered.

The economic problem is a perennial one which I accept because I made my own choice many years ago. I could have spent time and effort making money; I chose to spend it on my work. My real problem is a more personal one,—the need of being alone. I am not anti-social; I have a deep affection for my friends and family, feel deeply for suffering humanity (also for suffering animals!) but at times I have a desperate need to be absolutely alone. This desire is all bound up in my work. You can understand. This subject might not be exhausted in a week's discussion. Let us continue it in Carmel. I still have hope that you will escape someday and find yourself here.

I am glad you feel that I have made some contribution to photography. I should blush over your good words. I really am discriminating, and appreciate the source. Such words mean more to me than a lot of gush and ballyhoo.

I agree with you that there is just as much "social significance in a rock" as in "a line of unemployed." All depends on the *seeing*. I must do the work that I am best suited for. If I have in some way awakened others to a broader conception of life—added significance and beauty to their lives—and I know that I have—then I have functioned, and am satisfied. Not satisfied with my work as it is, understand. Thank the gods we never achieve complete satisfaction. How terrible to contemplate Utopia: Contented Cows.

There is so much talk of the artist getting down to the realities of life. But who is to say which are the realities? Obviously they cannot be the same to everyone. All arguments are futile which do not take into consideration the fact—(fact for me at least) that persons differ in *kind*, not just in degree; differ just as horses and elephants do.

[77]

But we all have our place, and should function together as a great fugue. And the tension between opposites is necessary; the two poles, feminine-masculine, radical-conservative, etc. What would the poor red do without his conservative to play with! He would *have* to invent one. Likewise the conservative.

I have the greatest sympathy, even understanding, for those who have gone sociological (politically). They had to—granted they are honest. If I saw an interesting battle between strikers and police I might be tempted to photograph it—if aesthetically moved. But I would record the fight as a commentator regardless of which side was getting licked.

Random thoughts, these, and rather disconnected. Do your best with them until we meet.

Again, your letter meant a lot to me.

> Always your friend,
> Edward

To Virginia Adams

> Yosemite National Park
> March 9, 1935

[Telegram]

ANNE[1] PUT ONE OVER ON ME AFTER ALL STOP I EXPECTED IT WOULD BE SIMPLE AS USUAL BUT I WAS WAITING FOR A WIRE OR CARD AND WAS ALL READY TO RUSH DOWN STOP EVERYONE SENDS LOVE AND CONGRATULATIONS STOP ARE YOU ALL RIGHT STOP SHALL I COME RIGHT DOWN OR SHALL I STAY HERE UNTIL MONDAY AND FINISH IMPORTANT WINTER PICTURES STOP WHATEVER YOU WANT ME TO DO I WILL DO GLADLY LET ME KNOW HOW YOU ARE AT ANY EVENT STOP LOVE TO ALL AND AN ESPECIAL LOT FOR YOU AND ANNE

> ANSEL ADAMS

1. Anne Adams was born in San Francisco on March 8, 1935, while Adams was in Yosemite on a commercial photography assignment.

From Alfred Stieglitz

New York City
May 13, 1935

My dear Ansel Adams:

I have often had you in mind. But as I am literally alone holding the bridge—An American Place—single-handed letter writing has become really impossible for me. But somehow I must let you know what a great pleasure your book[1] has given me. It's so straight and intelligent and heaven knows the world of photography isn't any too intelligent—nor straight either. But why single out photography? Another year is nearly gone. My years begin in October and end June 15th for at least as long as the Place exists.

O'Keeffe was about ready to leave for New Mexico when laid low with appendicitis. She is convalescing. She has been very frail for 3 years. I hope the turn has come for her—so for me. And you? What are you doing? How is the kid[2] and the wife[1]? Once more my congratulations to the book. I have bought a copy & recommend it.

With heartiest greetings,
Alfred Stieglitz

1. *Making a Photograph: An Introduction to Photography*, London: The Studio Publications, 1935.

To Alfred Stieglitz

San Francisco
May 16, 1935

Dear Alfred Stieglitz,

Nothing could have made me happier than the letter I received from you today. It was wonderful to hear from you and to know that you approve of the book.

Frankly, I was doubtful that you would like the book. Not that I did not have faith in what I was writing about, or faith in you that your criticism would be just. I felt that you might react to it as just more *writing* and not enough *doing*. I hesitated when asked to write the book; I thought, "It is comparatively easy to write about photography—there is too much written already—and not so easy to make good photographs. Should I spend the time and energy required on the book in making photographs?" And then I figured that someone should write on photography in a simple and direct way and try to give some conception of the straight simple photographic approach. So I tried it. I know I could have done much better if I had not been distracted with many things to do. But the book is released and I am more than pleased at its reception. And I am *most* pleased that you like it. When I get my second shipment of author's copies (I only got six copies at first) I would like to send you one suitably inscribed.

Incidentally, I would like to get your opinion on the reproductions. I think they are stunning in that they reproduce the surface aspect of the prints. They are quite different than *Camera Work* plates, but they are representing the aspects of glossy prints.[1] How do you like the plate of Dorothea Lange's photograph? I think it is a grand photo-document. She has done beautiful stuff; you should see it. I would like to follow this book with another—a compilation of 25 fine prints from the best photographers of the day. No, it would NOT be an Annual—I certainly am disgusted with the Annuals. If they only had proper advisors! It would be wonderful if you could direct the selection of prints, or at least pass on them, for such a book.

Am terribly sorry to hear that O'Keeffe has been ill. Perhaps her appendix has been the cause of her former troubles. Mine certainly kept me down for a long time before I knew I had one. I hope she progresses rapidly to health. My kindest regards to her.

I wish I could get east and see you again. My visits with you at An American Place remain my greatest experiences in art—they opened wide and clear horizons. When times were flush and there were lots of people with warm pocketbooks, spare time, and 70% intelligences I suppose you had adequate material and nervous support of the Place. But these times are the test of anything's endurance. It is wonderful that you have kept the Place going—kept it alive and vital—by yourself. One thing I am certain of—as long as you are the Place will be. I wish I could come and be your janitor!

With a family—two babies now—my nose heats the grindstone. I am doing as well as can be expected, keeping a little less than even. But that is better than not keeping at all! I could let down the bars of conscience and make lots of money (I guess) photographing Paris hats and undies, but photography means too much to me to do that without pain. I do lots of things I am ashamed of—have to do them to pay the bills—but, thank God, I *know* when they are not good and that's something, I hope.

A good friend of mine, Willard Van Dyke, is in New York (or will be presently) and will undoubtedly call on you. He is VERY talented in photography, and I am sure you will be glad to see him.

My wife and I send most affectionate greetings. We wish you could jump on the train and spend a few weeks with us here in relative tranquility. Our door is always open to you.

Thanks again for your benediction of approval.

Yours ever,
Ansel Adams

1. *Making a Photograph* was illustrated with tipped-in halftone photographic reproductions printed on heavy glossy stock; a coat of varnish added brilliance and depth. In contrast, the highly regarded reproductions in Stieglitz's *Camera Work* had effectively used the gravure printing process on matte-surfaced paper.

To Edward Weston

Ten Lakes
Sierra Club Outing
Yosemite National Park
August 6, 1935

Dear Edward,

I have been thinking a lot of your attitude towards the people who expect you to be a good Bolshevik and photograph all the plants in the vestibule of Revolution.

Goddam.

I am getting very tired of just the same thing—of being called "dead" because I do not include "social" material and subjects of "class-significance."

I want to tell you I feel as you do about it—I am sore all over at what I consider to be a major example of "duping." The "intelligentsia" have proven a swell tool for "left" political activity—and swallow the thing whole. I think we have to stand up for the rights of the *artist* and condemn the real exploitation of the artist by political and social powers. It is not that we would refuse to apply our work to the general good—but I feel that the work of the creative artist—the free and intimate expression—is much more important than any phase of direct propaganda or an artistic medium.

I hate to see so many good artists going goofy over the vaguely understood future "order." If it's Communism—or Fascism—I am ready for it, but Jezuz Kriste!!!!!—I want to keep the work *clean*.

I don't know what the [labor] *strike* situation will lead to (we know very little about it up here in the wilderness), but at all events, let us keep the integrity of the work in mind. I feel that all *propaganda-expression* is transitory, anyway. But a rock seems to last some little time!

Wish you were up here with us.

Yours,
Ansel

To Virginia Adams

New York City[1]
January 17, 1936

My Dearest,

Everything seems to come to him who waits!!! The net result of two full days in N.Y. is as follows:

I am to have a show at Stieglitz in the Fall. Jesus!!! He is exceedingly pleased with the pictures.

Have made a wonderful contact with Zeiss. Dr. Bauer the head of the U.S. Branch has been more than kind. I emerge with another lens for the Contax,[2] a new case, a new developing tank, AND, believe it or not, a Zeiss "Juwell" $3^{1}/4$ x $4^{1}/4$ with a real Zeiss Double Protar lens. It's the best in the world. . . .

Am seeing Paul Strand tonight. That's good too. . . .

Tell Albert all this (the Zeiss matter is confidential except to him), and tell him I have just begun what seems to be a really grand trip. Tell Francis[3] I shall write to him at the first chance. I have done a lot of heavy research on the Kings' matter.[4] Will stay with George Wright[5] in Washington for a few days at least. Will leave here Sunday night or Monday at the latest but I may come back for a few days.

Much love to ALL and loads of it to you.

I miss you!!!
Ansel

1. This was Adams' second trip to New York City.

2. The Contax was Adams' first 35mm camera.

3. Francis Farquhar, president of the Sierra Club and editor of the *Sierra Club Bulletin*.

4. In 1934 Adams was elected a member of the Board of Directors of the Sierra Club. On the Club's behalf he lobbied Congress for the establishment of Kings Canyon National Park.

5. George Wright was an active conservationist.

To Virginia Adams

New York City
January 1936
Monday

My Dearest,

Here I am back in N.Y. . . . I expect a wire at any time to come back to Washington for a conference with Congressmen on the Kings River. The National Park Service is trying to arrange one either Tuesday or Wednesday. However, I will be in Chicago on Thursday and leave there on Friday at the latest. I should arrive in L.A. Monday morning and will be home Tuesday morning at the latest.

The conference was very successful. I am sure it was worthwhile. But Washington is a funny place. So is this, but this is more interesting. However, I shall be immensely pleased to be home.

I wish you would tell Francis [Farquhar] about the possible conference. Tell him that all I plan to do is to make a presentation of our side of the matter, avoiding any belligerent attitude towards the opposition. Senator Johnson[1] was quite interested; he did not know there were such mountains in the Kings—he thought it was just a Canyon! And Eugene Meyer [publisher] of *The Washington Post* wants an article and pictures of the Kings region; he will give it editorial notice. The conference, by the way, will be only with the Congressmen from the districts related to the Kings River territory.

I love you and miss you and Anne and Michael. I hope everyone is well and happy. Love to all

Yours ever,
Ansel

Did you send in the Auto License fees?

1. Senator Hiram Johnson of California.

To Alfred Stieglitz

San Francisco
March 15, 1936

Dear Stieglitz,

I have been very lax in writing you since my return to California for the simple reason that I have had very little to say. I have had rather a ghastly time with a bad dose of flu which put me back in my bread and butter work so far that I have been working day and night to catch up with it.

However, I am getting things organized now and will prepare some new things for you. I have some rather interesting pictures of you and O'Keeffe which I shall print at the first opportunity I have and send to you. It takes time to do things well, and the flu knocked me out for nearly a month.

I hope the elevator strike did not reach your building. The papers here gave very dramatic reports. We are certainly existing in a strange time.

I have done one good photograph since my return which I think you will like. It is a rather static picture of a fence—the pickets covered with moss and dark rolling hills moving beyond it. The Protar lens has an amazing quality—I seem to get more light—more glow in the images although I feel it is not quite as hard and sharp as a Tessar. My visit with you provoked a sort of revolution in my point of view—perhaps the word simplification would be better. Also, I can't get the O'Keeffes out of my head. I do hope the show has been successful.

As I sit writing you I see out of my window the two enormous towers of the Golden Gate Bridge and I can visualize the still larger Bay Bridge going up to the east. I am wondering what these bridges will do to our local civilization. They will open up a vast territory in which all the miserable fungus of "development" will flourish. And yet, the bridges are magnificent in themselves; they are potential instruments for good but they won't be used that way. And the funny thing is that I don't want to photograph them—I would rather work on an old fence with moss on it. Do I live in the past—or in the future? Beethoven, living today, might have written, "The Glory of God in Engineering." Don't eat too many gumdrops!!

Yours, and with good wishes to O'Keeffe,
Ansel Adams

From Alfred Stieglitz

Lake George
July 30, 1936

Dear Ansel Adams:

I had just been remarking "I wonder how Ansel Adams is faring" when your letter was handed to me. So you can imagine how glad I was to hear from you.—

I haven't been well. Heart. Damn it.—Am about but doing virtually nothing. The years are beginning to tell more & more.—But there is much still to be done & I must be ready to do it.—

Did you hear Marin is to have a one-man show in the Museum of Modern Art Oct. 12—Nov. 18th. I'm in charge of it.—It's really ready except for the hanging.—Got all done before leaving town.—Invitation came as a great surprise. Impulse was to turn it down. But I had to think of Marin & family & not my own feelings about Institutions, etc.—I may have written to you about this. If so pardon repetition. My memory isn't what it was. It's like the heart. A bit on the blink.—

—I'm still counting on a show of yours if you can make it. But remember if you can't just say so. Outside of it I have no "plans."— O'Keeffe reports she is very happy in New Mexico & that is wonderful for me. She did a marvelous painting as a sort of mural for Elizabeth Arden.—6 x 7 feet—Pardon these disjointed lines.—

My bestest to you & yours—
Stieglitz

The bit of Green from The Peaks—many many thanks for it.

To Alfred Stieglitz

San Francisco
October 11, 1936

Dear Stieglitz,

The photographs have been expressed today direct to you at 509 Madison Avenue, New York City. . . . I only hope you will like them. I feel quite happy about the prints, but I have been working on them for so long that I am slightly etherized.

[85]

One thing in particular; when I made the final selection of prints, I tried to recreate the experience of making the negative. The pictures seemed to become more intense and more accurate in tone and detailed proportions. I was surprised how some of them looked much better than the first prints I made of them. Usually it is the other way. I think I have a consistent quality throughout the show.

On an enclosed sheet you will find a list of the prints and my tentative prices.[1] As I said, if you feel any alteration of prices advisable, please change them. On another enclosed sheet is an attempt at a statement about photography. If you can use it—fine. If you don't like it—tear it up. I have a fierce time stating what I feel about anything in words. On another enclosed sheet you will find a rough list of the technical data of the prints; there may be some curious photographers who think the work is more complicated than it is.

I certainly hope they arrive in good condition. And I hope you will not find the show less than your expectations. I will, of course, await news of the response with great eagerness; I will bet that $\frac{1}{3}$ of the spectators will like them, $\frac{1}{3}$ will be noncommittal and the other $\frac{1}{3}$ will heartily dislike them. As for the critics—I expect 90% slams, 9% milky comment and 1% approval. However, I want to know everything—even the worst.

With all good wishes to you and O'Keeffe,

Yours,
Ansel Adams

1. Adams suggested prices of $15 to $25 for each of the 45 photographs exhibited.

To Virginia Adams

New York City
November 16, 1936

My Dearest,

The show at Stieglitz is extraordinary—not only are they hung with the utmost style and selection, but the relation of prints to room, and the combination in relation to Stieglitz himself, are things which only happen once in a lifetime. He has already sold seven of them—one (The White Tombstone) for $100.00. The others for an average of over $30.00

each. He is more than pleased with the show. I am now definitely one of the Stieglitz Group. You can imagine what this means to me. The numbers of people that have visited the Place and the type of response is gratifying. In other words, the show is quite successful!!!

. . . I have seen about 100 other people and am going from morning to midnight steadily and exhilarating. . . . Had a swell dinner with Stieglitz and O'Keeffe last night. She has a very beautiful new studio in which Stieglitz wanders around like a lost sheep. Her things are wonderful.

But what is probably the most impressive thing that has happened here for many years is the Marin exhibit at the Museum of Modern Art. It cannot be described in any fashion. I am photographing the walls and arrangements this afternoon for Stieglitz.

How did the color picture come out? And how is everybody and everything in general? I wish I were a better letter writer. I will have so very much to tell you when we meet in L.A. . . . Tell Francis and Albert I am thinking about them. Love to the family. And loads of love to *you* and *Michael* and *Anne,*

Ansel

To Alfred Stieglitz

El Paso, Texas
November 27, 1936

Dear Stieglitz,

Here I am writing in a funny but surprisingly nice hotel room overlooking an extremely desolate city and desert that is almost obscured by a dust storm, waiting for a phone call from the possibly more desolate town of Carlsbad,[1] about 160 miles away. The only available entertainment is a radio blasting forth U.S. jazz alternating with Mexican advertising lectures appassionata. Such is America.

I find myself thinking constantly of you, the Place, Marin, O'Keeffe, the Marin show, and my own emotional and intellectual reactions.

These reactions are exceedingly strong; they are not clearly defined as yet. This I know positively—the Place, and all that goes on within it is like coming across a deep pool of clear water in a desert. This would be a trite statement if I were referring to an ordinary sentimental pool in an ordinary desert, but it is the only metaphor I can lean on now. Whoever drinks from this pool will never be thirsty.

My own work has suddenly become something new to me—new, and exciting as never before. The praise you give never nourishes conceit—it reveals too much of the future for that. And your criticism is never disintegrating. The entire experience *evaluates* much more than it *defines*, and the joy with which I will attack my problems from now on will be a joy that has nothing to do with conquest, superior accomplishment, fashionable fame and all the other transparent gewgaws that ornament the garment of social intercourse. I can see only one thing to do—make the photography as clean, as decisive, and as honest as possible. It will find its own level.

In Chicago my exhibit[2] had all sorts of commercial results; the kind of results that enable one to eat and keep warm—in other words the results were "successful." But it did not do anything for the essences—for the perceptions, for the development, and for the Thing itself. All I will get out of the Chicago show will be necessary materialities. What came to me through your show was something that cannot be measured, classified, or compared to anything else. Not that the sale of the seven pictures was not very nice in a practical way, but the fact that they were purchased by people to whom they will mean something for themselves is the important thing.

Here I am experiencing America. I am held over in this exotic burg due to the failure of the baggage system of the great Rock Island Line; my trunk has gone on to California! Evidently it was deposited, with the tag underneath, in the far corner of the baggage car. It will return in due time. I wait.

Next day—Whites' Cabins [Carlsbad, New Mexico]

This letter looks like a diary; it may be better for all that. Whites'—a typical auto camp (I came by stage). White shacks heralded for thirty miles with white road signs that appear, over ten miles of desert, like a number of static gulls. Samples:
WHITES'—GOOD EATS
WHITES'—WHAT LITTLE BIRD TOLD ME ABOUT
      WHITES'?
WHITES'—WHERE LIFE IS BETTER
WHITES'—LET'S HAVE SOMETHING TO EAT AT
      WHITES'

WHITES' — HERE'S WHERE THE ROAD DIVIDES —
WON'T YOU STAY AT WHITES'?

All this going on shriekingly in front of a great bronze and green rolling desert with incredible rolling bronze mountains peeking out of the horizon—hills Marin would pile with his little finger. Adams and Adams' trunk are installed in a room with one single bed and one double bed, oil heater, boiler, dressing table, wash table, toilet, shower (exactly 4 feet 3 inches high), two rugs and a calendar (1936, by Gawd). The cultural center comprises a cafe, office, curio counter, and a museum (containing the mummy of a man 6,000 years old and other questionable articles of wonderment). In this cosmic setting I await the auto to take me to Carlsbad Caverns. Beyond and above lie a sad infinity of desert and an enormous cloud-filled sky. Nobody pays the slightest attention to either.

later—after the Caverns –

I feel like a bat. I have just been 800 feet underground—transported thereto by an office building elevator, guarded by rangers, guided by paths. I have just gone through something that should not exist in relation to human beings. Something that is as remote as the galaxy, incomprehensible as a nightmare, and beautiful in spite of everything. I will attempt to describe to you what I have seen:

Something underground that was conceived in absolute darkness illumined by electricity in the best Wagnerian Tradition. Fafnirs might emerge anywhere. The hell of it is, they do not. (The illumination is cut off in sections as you pass through the God of Economy inhabits the bowels of the earth.) Here the mountains are turned inside out—where there should be mass there is space, where things should grow there are phallic stalagmites and stalactites, reaching and meeting, boiling and dripping, hard, crystalline, and terribly silent. The lighting is grottoesque; darkness would be grateful. Things are seen (which never should be seen) in light consistently from the wrong direction (but I cannot think of any *right* direction). Can you imagine an illuminated stomach? The tour (three miles by my estimate, seven by the guide's) culminates at a point of public rest. Here we are admonished to sit and remain silent SILENT S I L E N T. The Superintendent speaks. HE tells us of—and directs –

THE ENORMOUS AGE OF THE CAVERNS
THE DISCOVERY AND EXPLORATION THEREOF
THE MYSTERY

THE BEAUTY

THE FACT THAT WE ARE SITTING CLOSE TO "THE ROCK OF AGES"—SIX MILLION YEARS OLD—(the logical result of inhuman drippings)—THE LIGHTS ARE TO GO OUT—ALL OF THEM—WE ARE TO EXPERIENCE ABSOLUTE DARKNESS AND SILENCE (Tourist #486579 sneezes) AND WE ARE TO CONTEMPLATE GOD. GOD IS DULY CONTEMPLATED FOR THIRTY SECONDS. A MALE TRIO SINGS "ROCK OF AGES." THE LIGHTS GO ON—SECTION BY SECTION—AS "ROCK OF AGES" IS DIMINUENDO POCO A POCO. AT THE FINAL STANZA ALL THE LIGHTS ARE ON, THE BOWELS MOVE AGAIN AND THE CROWD IS ELEVATED TO THE SUN VIA TWO ELECTRIC ELEVATORS. (We can walk up and save fifty cents.)

Back at Whites' (traversing six miles of excellently paved roads), I write you this. The sun sprays a blowtorch of bloody fire over unimagined miles of desert and the clouds echo the light on the earth. The string of colored lights are turned on over the service station, a radio is blasting, cars spin on the road and Tourist #486583 clears his throat.

This I must photograph—pray for me.

It is good now to remember you, the Place, and the solitude of clouds drifting over the desert.

Yours,
Ansel Adams

1. The National Park Service commissioned Adams to photograph Carlsbad Caverns National Park, New Mexico.

2. Adams had an exhibit at The Katherine Kuh Gallery in Chicago in November 1936.

From Alfred Stieglitz

New York City
December 16, 1936

My dear Ansel Adams:

I have been very delinquent in letting you hear from me. I offer no excuses. You know the constant pressure I'm usually under. And it has been more so. And the heart is apt to kick up. And I cuss it for there is no time to pay much attention to it.

Of course I received your delightful letter from Whites', etc. I read it to McAlpin[1] and [Paul] Rosenfeld, to O'Keeffe and [William] Einstein and others interested. All enjoyed greatly. And now for some good news. I enclose it. McAlpin has taken three more large ones and one of the small ones.[2] I "priced" the small one somewhat lower than the large ones. So I enclose check. He gave Dorothy Norman[3] $49.00 for the Place. So you see you are helping pay rent for the Place. Works all around. I hope you are pleased as well as surprised. I am. It's all too wonderful. But Lord you deserve it. I know your head won't be turned. And remember just go your own way. Don't let the Place become a will-o'-the-wisp. So many have done that. And that's awful all around. Destructive in the worst sense. Of the four additional pictures McAlpin bought two for friends of his as Xmas gifts. Beautiful people. And two he keeps.

I have been so busy I haven't had a chance to take a look at the Protar.[4] Nor at any of my own work. Will I ever get at my own photography again? I wonder. Well Adams it has been a great experience for me to have had your prints here and to have you here. A great one truly. Oh yes there are ten of your prints on exhibition at the J. Walter Thompson Co. I rush this off to you. It's hardly a letter. But it carries with it the best of wishes for time to come. This holds good for your family as well as for you.

Your old
Alfred Stieglitz

1. David Hunter McAlpin, businessman, art collector, and Adams' patron.
2. McAlpin purchased eight photographs from Adams' show.
3. Dorothy Norman, Stieglitz's friend and associate, helped run An American Place.
4. Adams gave Stieglitz the Zeiss Double Protar lens described in his letter to Virginia dated January 17, 1936.

To Alfred Stieglitz

San Francisco
December 22, 1936

Dear Stieglitz,

I hope this will be a better piece of writing than that scrappy note I wrote you a few days ago from the hospital. But there is something about a hospital that might be good for the body but it's hell on the mind. Everything goes dead and the expense is terrible.

Anyway, what happened to me is very hard to describe. For years I have been driving myself beyond reason, assuming responsibilities which, in the light of common sense, I never should have undertaken. The gradual nervous and physical pileup of exhaustion had to be accounted for. The last trip to New York was a frantic attempt to keep the wheels spinning—and when I arrived home I felt at the breaking-point. And add to this an extremely intense emotional experience developing over the last five months—it is little wonder to me now that I contracted a chest infection. I went under in a big way. I have the doctor literally on my neck now and have made a series of uncomfortable, irrevocable and expensive promises to him. I fully realize how important it is to return to full health, and how very far I am from it now.

However, do not be alarmed that your show was my swan-song or anything like that. In fact, I feel I am only beginning. I cannot do any work for several months. I have to take a long easy trip, on a boat if possible. Virginia and I will probably train or boat to N.Y. in January. To see you again will do us a tremendous amount of good. We then will probably sail to Europe and back just for an easy trip. And then, be it or not in the "pattern," this event has made a great decision for me. I am ceasing any and all photographic work of a purely "commercial" nature. I am going to concentrate on honest things—a book on San Francisco, fine Industrial work, etc. for the bread and butter. That will give me time to do some of the things I really want to do. I will only do such advertising work that I know is honest and real as possible. I would like to say with Robinson Jeffers:

"A little too abstract, a little too wise,
It is time for us to kiss the earth again,
It is time to let the leaves rain from the skies,
Let the rich life run to the roots again."[1]

That's it—I have a hard time accurately remembering the words of any poem. Incidentally, have you read much of Jeffers? There are certain poems that never should be read except after a long steeping in his style and thought—and those are the ones people usually read first and get a poor opinion from. But there are any number of short poems and quite a few long ones that sound more music and pile more mountains in the spirit than almost anything I know of. There is something colossal in Jeffers' mind that can encompass something like the following in a relatively rigid style:

"Does it matter whether you hate your
    self? At least
Love your eyes that can see, your mind that can
Hear the music, the thunder of the wings"[2]

It seems to be a phase of critical excellence to interpret Jeffers on a Freudian basis—but they are all wrong who do so. I wish you could see him and talk to him in his stone house at Carmel; I think you would find greatness there.

The news in your last letter seems to be still an incredible horn-blast from the Milky Way—it's too good to be true. I wish I could express to Mr. McAlpin what I feel about it all. I know it has given you great joy to have things come to pass like this in your Place and I am glad for you and very proud to have had anything to do with it. I wonder if you can ever know what the showing of my work has done for my whole direction in life? Or what the influence of you and your work, and of Marin, O'Keeffe, etc.? And I am only one of thousands; with a little closer touch perhaps through the exhibit.

When I get to N.Y. we can have a continuation of conversation. I will have many regrets that the Marin show will be down but I know you will have something in your Place to soften the loss. . . . The color-roll will go off to you in a few days; I want to study it and find out what I can from it about the color-reproduction of paintings. I think I wrote you about it—that I used a special type of Kodachrome for artificial light, but that the "daylight" globes caused an over-stress of the blue-green. I think you will get a lot of excitement over some of the pictures anyway. Let me assure you I did *not* get the Yellow of the Yellow Room; that had to do with something other than sensitometry.

Wednesday

Your last letter just arrived; I am completely overpowered. There is no use my trying to write any thing I feel about it all now. Will send you a long letter soon. I am very humble before you and all you have done.

A very happy time for all of you!!!

Ansel Adams

The Color Film goes off today.

1. Robinson Jeffers. *Solstice and Other Poems,* New York: Random House, 1935. From the poem "Return," p. 145.

2. Jeffers, *Solstice and Other Poems.* From the poem "Love the Wild Swan," p. 146.

To Cedric Wright

San Francisco
[Late December 1936]

Saturday
Dear Cedric,

I am so sorry I could not and did not come over to the party and see you and Ernst [Bacon] and have a good schmooze. I missed it a lot, but things were too hot or cold to permit it. Michael did not feel good yesterday, with a temperature of 103, and I feel a bit rotten myself.

The truth of the matter is that I am so goddam low emotionally that nothing has any meaning or significance at all. I *know* what I should do and feel—I *know* I should go off on a swell easy desert trip, I *know* I should try and make a new life for myself. But the matter is simply this—I am not physically in good shape and I am very bad off emotionally. Everything is dead—flat—without reason or purpose. I have said my say in photography and have reached the top with Stieglitz. Only the emotional stimulus that you know about enabled me to get that Stieglitz show ready; I could not do another one now if my life depended on it. I know that if I was in better physical shape I could meet the problems with comparative ease—but I do not seem to know how to get in that good condition. There are so many responsibilities—the kids, the Yosemite concession,[1] the family next door[2]—all of which could probably get along perfectly all right without me.

Seeing you is perhaps the best thing that has happened to me for a long time. The only thing wrong with it is the mood I must have drooled all over your place. I am going to Carmel with Albert Bender in the morning, and will, at least, keep my mind busy talking about books and pictures. Will see the Jeffers and take a good big bite of granite. The poem I wrote you—I guess I was kidding myself all right—it was just a mood of what I would *like* to be able to write in reality. And to live in a sort of emotional sunlight—in a tent—in anything. Where there is less of matter and more of spirit.

Will see you soon anyway. May take you up on trip with you and Albert to desert or mountains or someplace. Virginia now does not want to go anywhere. Oy!!

Ansel

1. Upon her father's death in 1936, Virginia Adams inherited Best's Studio in Yosemite.
2. Adams' parents and Aunt Mary.

From Edward Weston

Los Angeles
[Late May or early June 1937]

Dear Ansel—

No word as to your proposed Sierra trip. Is it off, or still too early?

I have made the last desert expedition of the year, or season. Getting too warm. We went across the Colorado desert taking the old stage route from near Julian to near Coyote Wells. A very exciting adventure too long to be written. Will tell you. Got a beautiful negative of a fresh corpse. Part of the tale.

One reason I write you at this time is for opinions and information on lenses. I'm sure you have 10x my knowledge at your finger tips.

My Turner-Reich, 12-21-28, which I bought because it was a good bargain, has proved quite satisfactory under most conditions. I had the diaphragm fixed so that it stops down 3 extra notches after the $f/64$ it came with. The single elements have all the definition I demand when used at smallest apertures except when I use the 21 inch with bellows completely extended. I can't work close, of course, with 28 inch. 90% of my present work is done with 21 inch. I could swear that I focus carefully, but when I develop find that I'm off. This only happens when I work close. Of course I can't see what happens on ground glass when I get beyond $f/64$ or so. I tried a newspaper in brilliant sun to see if focus changed, and I tried light bulbs placed so I would have to use swings, but discovered nothing. I must admit my eyes are not what they were but I can't believe I'm so far off.

All this has led me to believe that I would like a doublet of not less than 19 in. not more than 22 in; 20 or 21 would be perfect. I would want up to date color correction. I would prefer a slow lens because I don't want to pay too much and because it would be lighter, less bulky.

[95]

Nichols has a 19-inch Goerz doublet f/6.8, but it's so heavy and he wants 150.00

In looking through B & J catalogue I notice a Kodak Anas-Process lens f/10, 19 in., if I remember, for 60 odd dollars. I understand this is color corrected, and it should not be bulky at f/10. But what do you say? Have you any ideas knowing my needs? To recapitulate: a 20 inch lens (more or less), slow, cheap, color corrected. It does not need to be convertible. Thanks!

Affectuosamente (and to V——)

Edward—

Are you completely recovered?

To Edward Weston

Yosemite National Park

June 3, 1937

Dear Edward,

It was swell to hear from you—I look forward to the picture of the corpse. My only regret is that the identity of said corpse is not our Laguna Beach colleague.[1] I am convinced there are several stages of decay.

By no means is the Sierra trip off. Only—what with mosquitoes and high water—the season is not just right for a high country trip. Nevertheless, the Yosemite Valley is wonderful at this time of year and if you can come up here any time now we could have a swell time. In July—or the end of June—I will make the first high country excursions.

Incidentally—did I loan you my Pola-screen?[2] I know I loaned it to someone, and I can't remember who.

As for the lens trouble you write about, I am not an optical expert. I only know some of the causes and effects. I will try to explain your troubles, but I am not certain that the diagnosis will be correct. Here goes: –

1. Any good modern lens is corrected for maximum definition at the larger stops. Using a small stop only increases depth; beyond a certain point definition is actually impaired.

2. Perhaps your lens will not stand the very small diaphragms; or, if it takes it OK at normal extension (inf.) it might break down at greater extensions. This is very easily accounted for in optical mathematics. All

corrections are compromises—change of stop, change of extension, chromatic correction, etc. and balanced out to a satisfactory practical degree in universal lenses. If a lens was to be used at only one focal setting the degree of definition which could be obtained would surprise you. I believe that the chromatic corrections are about the first to break down in erratic use.

3. *Visually* you may focus with the greatest accuracy; *chemically,* the negative may have an entirely different opinion about it. The visual and actinic rays match in a lens which is working under normal conditions; alter the relationships of focal-length, stops, etc., and you may throw the entire lens system out of balance.

4. I think what you want for your best solution to the problem is a Zeiss Protar No.6 19 in.[3] This lens can be combined at any time with a 14", 16", 19", 25", or 27" Protar to make an effective combination of $9\frac{1}{4}$, $10\frac{1}{2}$, 11, $12\frac{1}{2}$ or 13" focal length. The 19" Protar works at $f/32.5$ and I believe it can be stopped down to a greater extent than any other lens made and still keep its quality. It is, of course, fully corrected. It is a single-cell lens of four glass elements and is designed to work back of the shutter diaphragm. It comes in a Compur shutter and lists at \$150.00 complete. We would, of course, see what we could do about the latter statement.[4] The lens is quite light in weight. You could always add the second element to it (or have a set of elements to use singly or in combination). The Protar gives the most beautiful "breathing" image of all lenses—you cannot enlarge as many times as you can with the Dagor, but for contact work and moderate enlargement it cannot be excelled. I would like to show you some of the stuff I have made with my $5\frac{1}{2}$ inch Protar.

5. A Process is corrected principally for copying; the corrections often break down badly when the lens is used for even moderately distant objects. Also, the definition is very wiry, and the depth of focus apparently at a minimum. That is because the critical plane of focus is so exceedingly sharp—it is an illusion. The Protar "breathes" off the critical plane.

I am feeling much better. We look forward to seeing you very soon. Let me know what I can do for you—if anything. I hope you are getting some swell stuff.

Yours ever,

Ansel

1. William Mortensen, pictorialist photographer, who represented all that Adams, Weston, and Group f/64 opposed.

2. Pola-screen, a polarizing lens filter.

3. The Protar No. 6, a 19-inch lens, was one of Adams' favorites.

4. Best's Studio sold photographic equipment and often supplied Edward Weston.

To Cedric Wright

Yosemite National Park
June 10, 1937

Dear Cedric,

A strange thing happened to me today. I saw a big thundercloud move down over Half Dome, and it was so big and clear and brilliant that it made me see many things that were drifting around inside of me; things that related to those who are loved and those who are real friends.

For the first time I *know* what love is; what friends are; and what art should be.

Love is a seeking for a way of life; the way that cannot be followed alone; the resonance of all spiritual and physical things. Children are not only of flesh and blood—children may be ideas, thoughts, emotions. The person of the one who is loved is a form composed of a myriad mirrors reflecting and illuminating the powers and the thoughts and the emotions that are within you, and flashing another kind of light from within. No words or deeds may encompass it.

Friendship is another form of love—more passive perhaps, but full of the transmitting and acceptances of things like thunderclouds and grass and the clean reality of granite.

Art is both love and friendship, and understanding; the desire to give. It is not charity, which is the giving of Things, it is more than kindness which is the giving of self. It is both the taking and giving of beauty, the turning out to the light the inner folds of the awareness of the spirit. It is the recreation on another plane of the realities of the world; the tragic and wonderful realities of earth and men, and of all the inter-relations of these.

I wish the thundercloud had moved up over Tahoe and let loose on you; I could wish you nothing finer.

Ansel

To Alfred Stieglitz

Yosemite National Park
July 29, 1937

Dear Stieglitz,

I have been thinking of you a lot, but have had so much to do that I have written very few letters. I hope all is well with you and O'Keeffe and that you have some opportunity to photograph.

The season here has been very hectic—I have few good negatives. On top of a rather jittery state of mind we had the misfortune to suffer a fire which consumed half of our new darkroom and burned up a lot of my good negatives. Insurance covers material loss—but the negatives!! However, the negatives that burned had the highest commercial and lowest aesthetic value of the lot. Practically all the prints shown at "An American Place" can be made again. And the Sierra negatives for my forthcoming book *Sierra Nevada*[1] are almost entirely intact. It was luck, in a way. One fortunate thing—I lost many inferior negatives, and can start the slate clean in several directions.

Edward Weston and I had just returned a half hour before the fire from a fine trip in the high mountains; it was a spectacular sight to see four photographers[2] toil into the dawn removing films from soaked envelopes and pouring them into a bathtub full of water. In this way we saved many films that would have been hopelessly spoiled.

Edward Weston just bought a 19" Protar and has made some swell stuff with it. It is most interesting to me how his work has developed. I think you would like some of his clean, objective pictures of clouds and rocks. It is quite different from the Shell and Pepper period.

There is little news to tell you other than the above. The world moves in strange and perplexing tracks. I am 35 years old, and feel a deep growing urge for some sort of change—to simplify and enrich my life and work. I feel I have a lot to do and my energies will be taxed to the utmost to do it. If I can cook up a practical reason for coming to NY in the Fall I will do so; I feel it is important to see you and talk with you— just to look around the Place and see a few real pictures.

Let me know how you are when you feel like writing.

Yours ever,
Ansel Adams

1. *Sierra Nevada: The John Muir Trail*, Berkeley: Archetype Press, 1938, illustrated with tipped-in halftone plates.

2. Adams, Edward and Charis Weston, and Rondal Partridge (son of Imogen Cunningham).

To Alfred Stieglitz

Ghost Ranch[1]
Abiquiu, NM
September 21, 1937

Dear Stieglitz,

By a miraculous sequence of circumstances and the kindness of David McAlpin I am in New Mexico with three cameras, a case of films, a big appetite, and a vigorous feeling of accomplishment.

It is all very beautiful and magical here—a quality which cannot be described. You have to live it and breathe it, let the sun bake it into you. The skies and land are so enormous, and the detail so precise and exquisite that wherever you are you are isolated in a glowing world between the macro and the micro, where everything is sidewise under you and over you, and the clocks stopped long ago.

O'Keeffe is supremely happy and painting, as usual, supremely swell things. When she goes out riding with a blue shirt, black vest and black hat, and scampers around against the thunderclouds—I tell you, it's something—all that is needed to complete the picture is to have you out in the gardens at six am in your green cape. I am quite certain you would like it here. But it is a long way from New York, especially for a person with your kind of schedules to fill.

I think I am getting some very good things—quite different, I believe. I like to think of my present stuff as more subtle, more lifting-up-the-lid, if you know what I mean. I did some new things in the Owens Valley in California that I want you to see; I hope I will have things from here that I would want you to see, too.

Nothing important has happened to me, except a glimmering of wondering what it is all about—work, and living in general. Perhaps I am on the edge of making a really good photograph. I hope so. I have a growing awareness of the insufficiencies of my work. I hope it's a good sign.

O'Keeffe tells me you are in good shape and have had a bearable

GHOST RANCH
ABIQUIU, NEW MEXICO
Telegraph: Espanola, N. M.

September 21st, 1937

Dear Stieglitz,

By a miraculous sequences of circumstances and the kindness of
David McAlpin I am in New Mexico with three cameras, a case of films, a big
appitite, and a vigorous feeling of accomplishment.

It is all very beautiful and magical here- a quality which can
not be described. You have to live it and breath it, let the sun bake it into
you. The skies and land are so enormous, and the detail so precise and exquisite
that wherever you are you are isolated in a glowing world between the macro-
and the micro-, where everything is sidewise under you and over you, and the
clocks stopped long ago.

O'Keeffe is supremely happy and painting, as usual, supremely
swell things. When she goes out riding with a blue shirt, black vest and black
hat, and scampers around against the thunderclouds - I tell you, its something!
All that is needed to complete the picture is to have you out in the gardens at
six AM in your green cape. I am quite certain you would like it here. But it is
a long way from New York, especially for a person of your kind of schedules to
fill.

I think I am getting some very good things - quite different, I
believe. I like to think of my present stuff as more subtle, more lifting-up-the-
lid, if you know what I mean. I did some new things in the Owen's Valley in
California that I want you to see; I hope I will have things from here that I
would want you to see, too.

Nothing important has happened to me, except a glimmering of
wondering what it is all about - work, and living in general. Perhaps I am on
the edge of making a really good photograph. I hope so. I have a growing
awareness of the insufficiencies of my work. I hope its a good sign.

O'Keeffe tells me you are in good shape and have had a bearable
summer. I am glad - you deserve the best of good health and peace of mind. A
season such as yours in New York must be a very wearing thing for the strongest
person.

Its trite to say it, but I wish you were here. Gawd knows when I
will get to New York again - but I hope it will not be in the too distant future.
McAlpin send you his very best. He is a good man, with a precious mixture of
caution and enthusiasm.

all good wishes to you

summer. I am glad—you deserve the best of good health and peace of mind. A season such as yours in New York must be a very wearing thing for the strongest person.

It's trite to say it, but I wish you were here. Gawd knows when I will get to New York again—but I hope it will not be in the too distant future. McAlpin sends you his very best. He is a good man, with a precious mixture of caution and enthusiasm.

All good wishes to you,
Ansel Adams

1. The Ghost Ranch was Georgia O'Keeffe's home and studio near Abiquiu, New Mexico.

To Francis Farquhar

Yosemite National Park
November 8, 1937

Dear Francis,

. . . I had quite a blow today—totally unexpected. The Lakeside Press fizzled on the reproductions—they are not acceptable. That means the Book [*Sierra Nevada: The John Muir Trail*] will not be out until April. Mr. Starr[1] and I agreed (by phone) that the delay is unavoidable, and the book may be a better production for the postponement. But I had everything ready to go into production and it would have been distributed by December 10th had not the Lakeside Press balled things up. As it must be a perfect job in every way, I must resign myself to the postponement.

About Dave Brower[2]—we are interested in him and his future and I feel he deserves all the advice and help we can give him. The several suggestions which were made seem to have bugs in them: (except the last)

1. Mesa Verde. The job would be somewhat along the lines of the job he has just left,[3] he would be isolated from the world a good part of the year, Ansel Hall[4] is not too easy to work with, and the variety of things he would have to do might restrict his development along the path he would like to go.

2. Forest Service. Dangerously political, and unstable as far as a secure position is concerned. Possible combination of National Park Service and Forest Service in one Dept. would cause considerable weeding out of personnel.

3. Sierra Club. This to me is the ideal situation.[5] I know it would be a problem to put it through, but I feel it is an immensely important chance for the Club and for Dave. It has always bothered me that there has been no one in the Club management who was a true assistant secretary. What we have now is a competent stenographer. We need someone basically interested in the mountains and in the work and possibilities of the Club; to do the secretarial work, dispense accurate information, arrange activities of the right kind, engage in proper promotion work to increase membership, and generally tie things together and hold things together in the right direction. This work would be exactly in line with what he wants to do, and, besides, it would give him the chance to develop as he should; to write and illustrate articles, and to assist you in a very important way with the Bulletin. The routine work in volume should be farmed out. I feel that Dave would more than pay for himself in a very short time, and his association with the Club would be of the utmost value to all concerned. He is not afraid of work and would attack the problems with the utmost efficiency and spirit. I most strongly urge that this be considered and given every bit of attention possible now. It is a wonderful chance and it would be too bad if it dragged out and faded. Sometimes startling decisions and changes are healthy and I think this is one of them.

I am tickled purple with pleasure over the good family news.[6] All good wishes to you and Marge.

Cordially,
Ansel

1. Walter Starr financed the publication of *Sierra Nevada: The John Muir Trail* in memory of his son Peter, who was killed in 1933 in a mountaineering accident in Yosemite.

2. David Brower was an active member of the Sierra Club.

3. Brower had worked in the publicity department of the Yosemite Park and Curry Company.

4. A former National Park Service employee in Yosemite, Ansel Hall was now the concessionaire at Mesa Verde National Monument, Colorado.

5. Brower was not hired until 1952, when he was appointed the first executive director of the Sierra Club.

6. The Farquhars were expecting the birth of their first child.

To Alfred Stieglitz

Yosemite National Park
November 12, 1937

Dear Stieglitz,

The O'Keeffe Portfolio[1] arrived two days ago. I have looked at it under all conditions of light, digestion, freshness and fatigue. It is one of those rare and stimulating things that completely holds its own irrespective of external conditions. As I wrote O'Keeffe, it is not only a superb job of reproduction, it is something that recreates the O'Keeffe aspect of the world; I have the feeling that O'Keeffe is in the room with the reproductions. This may seem a bit vague—but, having had the company of O'Keeffe on an intense and very stimulating trip, I feel that I sense her quality of perception and expression to a high degree, and these plates actually convey that mood.

It is a wonderful job.

I proofed all of my 5 x 7 Southwest negatives today. Tomorrow I do the 4 x 5s and the Contax pictures the next day. Then I will be able to take stock and throw most of them away. The residue will be about the best things I have ever done. I am anxious for you to see them when finished. Incidentally, I have some color pictures of the Autumn Coloring in Colorado that make me feel that Color photography has possibilities for me. I want you to see these, too.

Adams is in a hell of a state. The goddam work here in Yosemite is pulling me down—terribly. Big Business had taken my work and prostituted it without regard for ethics, personal feelings, or anything.[2] I am blowing up in a style that befits a hot-water geyser in Yellowstone Park. Let the spray fall where it may.

Why I should write you and burden you with my troubles when you already have a world of your own on your shoulders may be a problem—but, it may please you to know that I am undergoing a major scrap of my own for my photography and I am really enjoying it (in a sadistic sort of way).

Business (with a capital "B") proceeds along a path of logic that is most certainly one of the great jokes of the ages. Businessmen hide behind rows of stenographers, adding machines, production charts, profit-and-loss statements, glass-top desks and baloney. If the financial report is in the black—they are successful; if in the red the administration is to blame—or the sunspots, or supply and demand, or the war in Borneo. And Advertising, the skin of the baloney, smirks with self-satisfied conceit either way. And Advertising tells the artist "we want your interpretation, we want Good Stuff" and then proceeds to take your interpretation and rape it. You protest—but you are advised that you do not know anything of Advertising. Besides, you have a CONTRACT. And then the artist, who is also a human being, has to think of his family and the high cost of Grape-nuts, and grin and bear it. Only, the Grin may turn into Lock-jaw and the fists will clench someday with a nasty rigor.

The picture here is amusing—if it were not tragic. Yosemite is one of the great gestures of the Earth. It isn't that it is merely big—it is also beautiful, with a beauty that is as solid and apparent as the granite rock in which it is carved. The U.S. owns it and administers it; a Public service, the Company [YPCCO] makes it possible for you and me to eat and sleep in it. This Company, with the steam-roller momentum of Big Business, needs to "bring people" to it. In order to achieve this end, it proceeds to approach the People in typical resort style; the quality of Yosemite is completely forgotten in the competitive urge to get the best of its banal competitors in Los Angeles, Santa Cruz and other "vacation areas." It is just like jazzing up the "Poem D'Ecstase" of Scriabin—a little hot rhythm, and there you are. I shall not go on, you can complete the picture as well as I. The fact remains that Adams has to take a break. Otherwise Adams will crack up. Adams remembers how his prints looked on your walls and he is very humble before you and those walls. Adams has had to make a living. He has tried to make it with what he had to offer—which was considerable in this place. It is the same old story. You can expect anything to happen to Adams in the near future—except Homicide, Suicide, Grand Larceny and arson. Please forgive this growling letter.

I have to blow off steam to someone.

Yours always,
Ansel Adams

1. *The Work of Georgia O'Keeffe: A Portfolio of Twelve Paintings*, New York, 1937.

2. The Yosemite Park and Curry Company published *The Four Seasons in Yosemite National Park* in 1936, using Adams' photographs but without asking his permission.

From Alfred Stieglitz

New York City
December 25, 1937

Dear Adams:

Of course I received your letters. And I have seen proofs of many of the shots you made on that trip with McAlpin & Georgia & others. All interested me greatly—letters & photographs. Great. I can see you tearing away at a great rate. Can follow your feelings. I hope 1938 will be a great year for you. Above all that your health will not betray you.—That right all else will be right.

The Place becomes a greater & greater responsibility & I'm virtually carrying it single-handed—Georgia's Show is hung.—It's "different"— Very extraordinary. I hope she gets some support. Everything becomes more & more precarious & more & more a gamble. My own photography is virtually completely sidetracked. The spirit is more than willing but the flesh—ye gods! That becomes more & more a drag. You know the feeling when physically handicapped—Still the Place is very alive & as ever goes its own way—never flinching—I sent you Georgia's Catalogue. I assume you received it.—

Officially the Show opens tomorrow. The last Show was a grand & very important one. Didn't receive the recognition due it. But so it goes. —My cordialest Greetings.—

Your old
Stieglitz

From Edward Weston

Carmel
[1937]

Dear Ansel –

You, and *your work*, mean a lot to me. Realize that I have almost no one who speaks my language. And those new N. Mexico landscapes,— superb! I know the mood you are in, but don't undervalue them. Your problems must, and will work out. Sounds like a cheap optimist!

Convira[1] tests interesting. M H[2] *is* too cold,—contrasty, but no depth. I have yet to get a stain in Amidol,[3] developing up to $3\frac{1}{2}$ min. I believe you will eventually arrive at a combination of chemicals, time & temp. that will give you the best prints you have ever had.

Our new home growing. We should be able to move in before long.[4] Then I will start printing! I seem to be always asking you questions. This time because your name is mentioned as a contributor. Knight Publisher's Inc. have asked me to write a booklet. No mention of my "percentage," or any other conditions. Their prospectus sounds pretty bad; "The Art of Retouching," "The Lighting of Nudes," "Composition," "Big Prints xxx"—Any advice? No hurry. Let them worry.

I have not developed yet. No place.

Thank you, Virginia . . . for royal welcome,—and love to all—

Edward—Charis

1. Convira, a photographic printing paper.
2. Metol-hydroquinone, a fine-grain print developer.
3. Amidol, print developer favored by Weston.
4. Weston is soon to marry Charis Wilson. His son Neil built a simple house for them in the Carmel Highlands, south of Carmel, which they named Wildcat Hill.

To David McAlpin

Yosemite National Park
July 11, 1938

Dear Dave,

Your letter arrived fifteen minutes ago, and I hasten to reply. I might sound silly in a way to express so much enthusiasm on a typewriter—but I want you to know how much pep your letters give me. You are enthusiastic—and few people are; you like the outdoors, you like photography, and you have a grand human point of view. All of which distills a cheerful, cooperative and constructive mood in people, and certainly must make life happier for you.

September 4th is not so far off. I can't help shouting for joy that you will be here WHOOPEE!!!! whoopee (echo). I shall be terribly disappointed if Godfrey and the Mrs. (I don't know her directly, so maybe I shouldn't call her Helen until I meet her)[1] do not show up. I guarantee them the trip of their lives. I really think the Sierra will be a revelation for you. And, of course, if O'Keeffe comes the party will be extraordinary—never was there such a collection of personalities in the Sierra all at once! Please don't think that I mean that the party would only be extraordinary if O'Keeffe were along—but there is something about the lady that is dynamic, to say the least. . . . You can assure O'Keeffe that we will take her to the most beautiful parts of the mountains, that we will do everything we can to make things "fluent" for her. . . . I will meet you in San Francisco, take you for a day's trip around there and drive you to Yosemite. The next day I will drive you to Glacier Point and the Mariposa Big Trees. The next day we can leave for the High Country! I may change the itinerary a bit to include the Mount Ritter region, but conditions will determine that. Apart from the obvious personal equipment, here is what you will need:

1. Good walking boots. I think you better get a pair in New York that you know will fit; I would be afraid of our local supply.
2. A couple of pairs of Keds (basketball shoes).[2] Good for climbing around smooth granite and for resting in camp.
3. A small, comfortable knapsack for cameras, etc.
4. A couple of pairs of bluejeans (Levis) and a light camp outfit.
5. One warm coat or jacket and one light sweater.
6. Plenty of socks.
7. A good pair of dark glasses. The light is strong at 11,000 feet.
8. A light waterproof box for films (we might get a day or so of rain).
9. An ice-ax (climbers). This is a great help in walking (as a cane) and climbing around (I am *not* going to take you on dangerous climbs!!!)

As there will be no mosquitoes, you will not need netting or lotions. Fishing is in order, but as I know very little about fishing I cannot advise you—but I can send you all the information you want from local experts. Of course, there is no hunting in a national park. Tents and waterproof tarpaulins are provided. Also sleeping bags, and slickers. I will see to it that you get a good horse. . . .

Tell O'Keeffe, (she probably will bring it up) that I will do everything I can to assure safe and convenient transportation of her sketching and painting materials. I plan to keep you all several days in camp in various places, and she will have a multitude of subjects that will excite her. During those stay-overs, the photographers will go berserk—why not O'Keeffe?? I think I can get the packer or the cook to help Godfrey pack his 8 x 10 around.

Now, we *could* do away with the cook. But I do not advise it. The best time to photograph is in the early morning and evening, and, if we do our own cooking we will find that that duty will cut into valuable photographic time. Powerful gas lamps are provided and I suggest that you set the dinner hour for late dusk and thereby keep the shutters clicking up to the last light. . . .

You know how crazy I am about the Southwest. But I tell you, that for sheer beauty, there is nothing like the Sierra. And I will get you into the best parts of the region hereabouts—parts that very few people ever see. I know it all just like I do my own backyard. Wait until you see the Lyell Fork of the Merced.

Impress on O'Keeffe that she will see things she has never seen before, and see them under conditions that are rare. Any ordinary trip through this region would not include many of the swell things we are to experience. This is really important. There is no human element in the High Sierra—nothing like New Mexico. But there is an extraordinary and sculptural natural beauty that is unexcelled anywhere in the world. . . .

What you write about Stieglitz is most heartening; he apparently is all right. I guess he had a tough time of it. I have always felt he is sympathetic to my work, and I always appreciated the brow-beatings. But there is a considerable gap between the attainments of Stieglitz and Adams. What I will be at sixty, seventy and eighty remains to be seen. Probably I will be a photographer!!

. . . I am concerned about my work, of course. I feel a certain responsibility in carrying it out; the purely personal advantages do not seem to count for much. A lot of people think I am crazy because I do not "cash in" on commercial photography. As I do not like it or believe it is important I would make a failure of it. It *would* be important if it were *honest,* but the requirements of the Advertising racket prevent the application of much integrity. But I can't neglect the practical altogether—so the problem is both simple and complex. I am also concerned about Stieglitz and what he represents. Not so much as far as he is concerned personally, for his life has been a rich one indeed, but for the idea of photography. I suppose, had I the means and temperament, I would proceed somewhat along the line of Stieglitz; at least I would take an active interest in the association of photography with the other arts as a major expression. But 1938 is not the same as 1898 or 1908. Stieglitz, starting today would be confronted with a quite different set of problems. In the terrific mass of photography pouring out of the darkrooms today there will be found very few good things—things that are truly expressive of our times, or things that are timeless. Somebody has to gather the good things together—not in just a museum way, but in a way that is emotionally stimulating and which will evaluate, on a clear-cut basis, the powers of the medium.

But I suppose nothing worthwhile comes easy. Here I am writing about photography when I should be out in the darkroom making prints! However—it doesn't work that way. Putting down ideas in writing can help out the photographic mood to an unbelievable extent. And the mood is so exceedingly important; extraordinary how it is reflected in even the physical aspect of prints.

Stieglitz certainly flatters me when he feels his mantle falls on me. I wish I could be half as good as that would deserve. However, I do feel I am one of the very few that feel about photography as he does. What will probably happen is that our group will continue to make photographs as best we can, and the "leadership" will precipitate itself out of the general solution as a natural and inherent effect of the formula. . . .

Have not forgotten about your prints. Your letter boosted up the productive mood, and I think I can get at them very soon. All good wishes to you, O'Keeffe, Godfrey, et al. I will write Stieglitz.

Remember September!!

Yours ever,
Ansel Adams

1. Godfrey Rockefeller, cousin of David McAlpin, and Godfrey's wife, Helen.

2. Adams wore Keds basketball shoes for hiking and believed they were superior to leather boots.

To Alfred Stieglitz

Yosemite National Park
September 10, 1938

Dear Stieglitz,

The gang is here!—O'Keeffe, Dave, the Rockefellers! We leave tomorrow morning for the high mountains—about fourteen mules, guide, packer, cook, much food, warm bedding, photographic equipment, and great expectations in general.

I met O'Keeffe at Merced and drove her in to Yosemite Tuesday. She liked our country, and immediately began picking out white barns, golden hills, oak trees. As we climbed through the mountains the scene rapidly changes and as we entered Yosemite she was practically raving—"Well,—Really, this is too wonderful!!!" We came into Yosemite at dusk—a very favorable hour, and the first impression will not be forgotten.

On Thursday I met Dave and the Rockefellers and drove them in— via Hornitos, an old mining town near Yosemite. They, too, seemed quite touched by the scene. Yesterday we drove to the Big Trees, and had lunch there; later we drove to Glacier Point, where we had supper. O'Keeffe had told you of what we did there, I am sure. It was an incredible moonlight night.

Dave got a little worried over the apparent bleakness of peaks and canyons as seen from Glacier Point in the afternoon with a bleak back-sun and a dismal kind of haze over everything. It was rather sad and desolate, and there was a cold wind blowing, and Dave got a little forlorn. But at sunset—a rare one—the mist gave up, and the contours of the [Sierra Nevada] Range came to life. It looked more like it will look when we are in the midst of it.

Today we are packing, sorting, eliminating, and generally hard at fussing with fussable things. Tomorrow we start, and for fifteen days many of the fussy things will become simple and many of the simple things will be fussy, but we will have a grand time.

The only regrettable thing is that you are not out here seeing all this with us. I know you would like many of our places—not the kind of place you have to ride a mule to—but just warm, rich places along the road, or as seen from the porch chair.

To see O'Keeffe in Yosemite is a revelation; for a while I was in a daze. Her mood and the mood of the place—not a conflict, but a strange, new mixture for me. She actually stirred me up to photograph Yosemite all over again—to cut all the advertising rot and see things for myself once more.

She says very little, but she looks, and once in a while something is said that sums everything up in a crystal, inevitable clarity.

This quality you perhaps have seen a million times to my once or twice, but it explains a lot—everything, in fact.

And I am pleased to tell you that she looks better than I have ever seen her, she is in excellent spirits, and the trip will be beneficial to her in many ways.

I have planned the trip to assure easy marches, and plenty of time for rest and relaxation. She will be taken the best care of possible.

We think and speak of you constantly. Take good care of yourself, and know that we all wish you were right out here with us.

Greetings from us all,
Ansel A.

To David McAlpin

Yosemite National Park
November 4, 1938

Dear Dave,

. . . Arrived here last night after ten days of busyness in San Francisco. Am feeling swell—slightly tired, but on the up-and-up. The trip started the rise!!

Have finally achieved a print quality which is most gratifying to me. The Southwest prints I am to make for you will be of that type—you can see for yourself. I have always felt unhappy over a cold black-and-white print no matter how good it was. It so often takes full scale tonal range to carry at all, and, as I said before, one does not always play *all* the 88 notes of the piano. What really counts to my mind is the luminous relationships of the tones—not their physical range. Well, I think I have it now, and I feel swell about it.

The Sierra Book [*Sierra Nevada: The John Muir Trail*] is practically printed and the engravings should arrive from Chicago very soon. They have worked hard on them and I think have achieved a wonderful result. The next step will be for them to match the color of the new kind of prints!

For the first time in a long time I feel happy and healthy and damned enthusiastic. And you and your encouragement have started it all. Actually, the trip was wonderful and opened all sorts of new vistas. . . .

I have the Walker Evans book[1] at hand, and have studied it most carefully. I think I wrote you about it from San Francisco. There are some really swell photographs in the set. . . . But these are lost in the matrix of the book and its apparent purpose. A picture stands by itself, but it can fall when standing against another, and bring the other down with it. I have no idea but what Evans had a conception that was very subtle about the whole thing, but it does not come through. America is not that way; some of it is, but not all of it. And this "some of it" loses impact when separated from its whole. Had the title been *Photo-Documents of*

Some Phases of the American Scene, it all would have been more logical. But so few of the pictures are good photographs in any qualification that I do not believe the book should be called *American Photographs* and put out by an art organization. One could logically expect, by comparison, the Mount Wilson Observatory to put out a portfolio of forms and designs derived from the Spiral Nebula. And I would certainly not expect the Museum of Modern Art to sponsor my Sierra book because the subject is limited and a large percentage of the content is representational. But see what happens—the "esthetes" who are mostly pink because they lack the guts to be truly red, build up a good bit of smoke about a rather damp fire. Afraid of honest sunlight, they stay in dusky alleys of thought—return to the past and the unargumentative Dead—and draw comparative conclusions on the art value of document and the documentary value of art, and indirectly and vicariously take their petulant jabs at the social order. The result is that true documentation suffers by an anemic plaster of art, and true art gets all mixed up with doctrine and examples and "facts." If you remember Stieglitz' early street scenes of New York—they were, first of all fine photographs—they were so fine that the "third dimension" of mood vibrated in them. Conclusions on the part of the spectator are inevitable. Hence, they are infinitely better propaganda documents than some self-conscious messenger of decay. I would rather see a perfectly regular edition of the *Daily Worker* than all the socio-esthetic productions under the banner of "profound expression." Dorothea Lange's work starts out to tell a story with no esthetic undertones. First it tells the story. Then the miracle of the creative personality appears—they are very swell photographs. But still, there is never a self-conscious attempt to make them "art." She merely does the work as well as she can, and the results are most impressive. And I certainly do not like [Lincoln] Kirstein's article in the book in question. So glib and so limited: Oh, well. But I still think Evans has made some beautiful pictures.

I repeat, America is a land of joy—more than any other land. With all the misery, all the economic troubles, and the crack-pot politicians, we are still the most liberal, the best off, and the most beautiful country in the world. I am very far from being "Patriotic," but I do resent untruths, exaggerations, false colors in relation to the land in which I work and live. Let us show everything that is false and inhuman, sordid and without hope, without alleviation of the larger fact and our infection can only widen and deepen and eventually consume us. But, as Dorothea has done with her Farm Security photographs[2]—showing a magnificent moment in the plowing of the land in one picture, and in the next showing a pitiful shack of a migrant family—we can show the good along with the evil—making the good more desirable, and the evil more detestable.

If I feel I have any niche at all in the photographic presentation of America, I think it would be chiefly to show the land and the sky as the settings for human activity. And it would be showing also how men could be related to this magnificent setting, and how foolish it is that we have the disorganization and misery that we have. I, too, could go back into the past for comparisons of points of view. Much of the art of the Renaissance gave man his "setting;" recall the magnificent bits of landscapes in Italian religious paintings. Again, in Durer, both the exalted and sordid subjects are shown against the earth and the sky. These are "keyed" to reality. The Hegelian theory of opposites certainly has greater significance than the accidental juxtaposition of a "For Sale" sign on a delicate pillar. The sign may have been there along with the pillar, but the true significance of it is exactly what you choose to make of it.

They are tearing down the old Sentinel Hotel here in Yosemite. It was a swell old building with a wonderful mood about it. The delicate pillars are shattered, a pile of junk is on the porch, a big "Keep Out" sign is plastered on the wall. I can photograph it to represent the pitiful dissolution of a sound culture, as an example of the final wrecking of a run-down shack, as a mere record of work-progress for the engineers, or as a step towards improvement of Yosemite. It actually happens to be a good thing it is coming out.

But I cite the above just to indicate how very false photography *can* be—false intentionally or unintentionally as the case may be. A picture such as above could be placed in a collection such as Evans' and the intentional story would be quite obvious—we are falling to pieces!! As it happens I made some pictures just before it was wrecked just to give a little of the mood and preserve a suggestion of the architecture. I am amazed at the comment on those pictures—I never expected them. Chiefly, the beauty of the California colonial architecture is perceived; there is regret that more of it is not maintained and that more new architecture is not based upon it. . . .

You may wonder why I am blowing up so much about this, and I can only answer by saying that I get annoyed when things go off at tangents.

I spend a lot of time being annoyed at myself for the same reason! It's just mussy thinking and decadent perceptions.

You will hear from me soon again. Hope all is well with you.

Affectionate greetings from us both, as always,

Ansel

1. Walker Evans. *American Photographs,* New York: Museum of Modern Art, 1938.

2. To document rural America during the Depression, the Farm Security Administration (FSA) commissioned photographers to depict American life. Dorothea Lange worked extensively for the FSA during the 1930s.

From Alfred Stieglitz

New York City
December 21, 1938

My dear Adams:

You have literally taken my breath away. The book [*Sierra Nevada: The John Muir Trail*] arrived an hour ago. Such a grand surprise. O'Keeffe rushed over to see it. I had phoned her at once.

—Congratulations is a dumb word on an occasion like this. What perfect photography. Yours. And how perfectly preserved in the "reproductions."—I'm glad to have lived to see this happen. And here in America. All American. And I'm not a nationalist. I am an idolator of perfect workmanship of any kind. And this is truly perfect workmanship. I am elated— So is O'Keeffe. Many many thanks from both of us for the magnificent gift & the thought of us.

Our deepfelt affection,
Stieglitz

Do have your publishers ship the book in boards. My copy arrived with corners damaged—both cover & individual pages. The U.S. Mail is a pretty terrible & heartless affair.

From Harold Ickes

Washington, DC
January 28, 1939

My dear Mr. Adams:

I am enthusiastic about the book—*The John Muir Trail*—which you were so generous as to send me. The pictures are extraordinarily fine and impressive. I hope that before this session of Congress adjourns the John Muir National Park in the King's Canyon area will be a legal fact.[1] Then we can be sure that your descendents and mine will be able to take as beautiful pictures as you have taken—that is, provided they have your skill and artistry.

Sincerely yours,
Harold L. Ickes
Secretary of the Interior

1. Congress established Kings Canyon National Park in 1940.

From Beaumont Newhall[1]

New York City
February 7, 1939

Dear Ansel Adams:

Enclosed please find our check for $20. to cover your expenses in printing *Pine Cone and Eucalyptus Leaves*. I am sorry that we could not get this to you sooner.

As you probably know, your friend David McAlpin has just given us a copy of your "Sierra Nevada" book. This is a handsome job, and I compliment you upon it. As you wrote me some time ago, the reproductions are remarkable, and the invariable reaction of those who have looked at it casually has been, "Oh! These are real prints!"

Mr. McAlpin has also given us a very handsome contribution to found a photographic division of the museum.[2] We are indeed indebted to you for putting Mr. McAlpin on our track. He is a delightful man, and I look forward to getting to know him better. . . .

You have heard, I am sure, about the Eliot Porter[3] show at Stieglitz' gallery. It was a splendid group of photographs, displaying a warm and nature-loving personality, with an excellent technique.

I hope that I shall hear from you soon.

Cordially,
Beaumont Newhall

1. Beaumont Newhall, librarian at New York's Museum of Modern Art.

2. David McAlpin funded the Department of Photography at the Museum of Modern Art, the first such department in any museum.

3. Eliot Porter had an exhibit of black-and-white photographs at An American Place in 1938–1939.

To David McAlpin

San Francisco
February 14, 1939

Dear Dave,

I received a letter from Newhall of the Modern Museum in which he tells me of the wonderful thing you have done.

It is not necessary for me to say what I feel personally about it—I am sure you know how deeply your gift to the Museum thrills me—but I think that, in the "official" sense, you should receive the grateful acclaim of all serious photographers. You have done the most important thing that anyone could do for Photography in the larger sense—you have made it possible for a large and very potent museum to incorporate photography in the presentation of the Fine Arts.

I wonder if you yourself fully realize the truly grand elements of your gift? Probably not, because people like you can't do big things based on detailed detached thought. You did it because you wanted to do it, and I am sure you had a bright intuitive flash of the potentials. You knew that if the larger aspects of the project were sound, the details would fall into line. It is especially touching to me insofar as I wrote quite strongly about the need of just such a foundation in my book.[1] My only hope is that the museum will manage the project well, keep the standards high and selective, and make a sharp discrimination between functional and experimental work. The greatest menace to photographic development—as far as the basic lay appreciation goes today—lies in the confusion of the Expressive, the Documentary, and the Socio-Economic functions. All these phases are essential, but they do not mix as well as they should. Anyway, I am sure you will keep a paternal eye on it and that all will be well.

[117]

I am anxious to know what Stieglitz thinks of it!! I will be disappointed if he does not bestow upon it his patriarchal blessings!

My work is almost finished—just one or two days more! Then I will write you and send you some new examples of new prints, etc.

Again—I think you have done a magnificent thing for photography; I am certain it marks a milestone, and a very important one, in the history of the art.

Cordial greetings, always,
Ansel

1. *Making a Photograph*, p. 14.

To Alfred Stieglitz

Yosemite National Park
June 16, 1939

Dear Stieglitz,

Home again and ten million little things to do. But just wanted to drop you a line and tell you how much the trip meant to me, and how happy I am that we had so many good visits together.

Seeing you and your work acts on me just like touching the Earth reacted on Atlas! (I *think* it was Atlas.) And, in truth, I find that my work of the last month has taken on a much more subtle quality, and seems to mean more than ever to me.

I developed the films of the Place pictures; they look *good*. I will get them to you as soon as I can (the prints). As soon as I arrive home I get a telegram from *Fortune* magazine asking me to do a job for them.[1] As the job will pay quite well, and as I can use the cash to VERY good advantage, I accepted.

All good wishes to O'Keeffe; I hope she is getting better. You all live a pretty hectic life! But you have no idea how gratifying it was for me to see you in such splendid condition after your siege.

Keep well. Don't work too hard. Remember, you have people that will always help you in any way they can—but you just have to say the word. Save yourself the details—it's the details that take it out of you.

Good wishes, always,
Ansel Adams

1. Adams photographed the Pacific Gas and Electric Company for a story in *Fortune*, September 1939.

To Alfred Stieglitz

San Francisco
May 27, 1940

Dear Stieglitz,

The show[1] is up, and—except for a few changes and perfections—I am very much pleased with it. . . . It's been a big job—but I am pleased to say that a lot of people out here will see some good photography!

I am sending you today a set of photographs by Brett Weston; I think you should see them. He is, as you know, the son of Edward Weston. A good amount of his earlier work was definitely tinged with his father's approach and technical quality. But it seems to me now that he has overcome a definite influence, and—while his technique is not strikingly different—his message is certainly his own. I told him to send me some prints and I would ship them on to you, for I felt you should see them. He is quite a grand person— hale and breezy—and exceedingly simple and direct. It is my opinion that he is one of the best—or will be as time enriches his reactions. . . .

. . . It was certainly strange to attend a brilliant exposition opening (very good and very gay) while so many terrible things were going on in other parts of the world. But I do not see that it would do any good to sit and gloom about it all. Things have to go on.

Keep well and save yourself as much as you can. The Place means more than anything else in photography. Some of us have to be out on the front line, but it is always wonderful to know that the pattern of perfection exists somewhere.

Affectionate greetings,

Yours, always,
Ansel Adams

1. Adams organized the exhibit and edited the catalogue for "The Pageant of Photography" held at the Palace of Fine Arts, San Francisco, as part of the Golden Gate Exposition. It included a historical view of creative photography, starting with nineteenth-century daguerreotypes and ending with work by Adams and his contemporaries.

To Cedric Wright

Dear Cedric,

Your letter was very moving; also a bit perplexing because of its nostalgic mood. Not exactly like you. What's the matter? Tell papa. Maybe it is because you *did* pass certain little nooks where you *would* like to be with certain people. Almost any nook in a storm! I understand perfectly. In fact, it's like this—first catch the person, and let the nook take care of itself. For me, there is a certain nook at about 9000 feet on a windy day with a big thundercloud muttering in the east. And the light that always reflects from muttering thunderclouds seems so damn much in key with the mood of what it is reflecting upon—you see, I really envy you at the moment, and I sorely miss the thunderclouds and the things they are muttering over.

But I do think that a full awareness of the world comes from inside and not necessarily from a crowd of things and people outside. There is something very satisfying about the thought that within ten feet of you at any given time lies enough material to keep you busy a lifetime learning to understand it. And I don't mean *interpretations* of things, or predetermined convictions about things. I really feel like Stieglitz who would lie against a rock all day and photograph the clouds that came overhead with a small Graflex. He did hundreds of them—calls them "Equivalents"—and they are swell. They are all small contact prints and have tremendous impact. He called them "Equivalents" because, for him, they represented moods—they were *equivalent* to something felt deep within. Really now—isn't practically everything that we react to just that?

When I read the stuff I used to write I feel very strange. The true meanings of the words and the collective syntax were then just "equivalents." I can't say they *mean* much to me now—but they still *feel* good. I wonder what they can possibly mean to anyone else other than those who feel the same about things and can sniff out the same emotional fragrances.

The world is in a terrible mess, but I feel that we have more of a job than we ever had. . . . And don't for a minute think that the people will stand for the pomposity and the brutality for long. As soon as a stable economic pattern is established, you will find the things of the spirit peeping out of their holes again. We have to keep going with the ideas and the imagination; but we might have to keep our mouths shut for a little while. Cheer up! Peoples are more important than States.

Just take the mountains for all the radiance they mean for you; chew the grass, wallow in the cool waters, make nice fiddle music, and TAKE GOOD PICTURES. Don't forget I got to have a good show.[1] And I also got to have some pictures and an article for *U.S. Camera* Magazine (I am now an Editor)!!!

Love to you and the others I like!!

And regards to the remainder, including the mules!!

Ansel

The next time you see a muttering thundercloud, give it my greetings. I got a new Pontiac station wagon with an air conditioner—wonderful machine!

1. "The Pageant of Photography" exhibit included changing one-man shows.

From Alfred Stieglitz

Lake George
July 25, 1940

Dear Ansel Adams –

Your letter of the 23rd just to hand—It seems my letter to you about Brett Weston's photographs never reached you.—I wonder about the loss of letters—yours to me mine to you. How many more to each of us?

As for Brett Weston's photographs what am I to say? They are naturally "perfect" technically. No wonder as the son of his father & having seen your work & so many other fine photographs. Whether he has a vision of his own I couldn't tell. Here & there I liked to believe I saw potentials peeping through. I couldn't say from these photographs, "Here is a man I believe in." You know what I think about virtuosity. I am always a bit suspicious of it. And BW shows signs of virtuosity. But I'm probably all wrong in my intuitions this time. At any rate I am glad you gave me a chance to see those prints. He is certainly far above the usual in some cases.

And you and Weston have been teaching.[1] I'm sure the classes you have had have been given rare opportunities by both of you. And now

Newhall is with you for a few days in Yosemite.[2] I had a fine letter from him this morning. I hope you received my wire and letter sent off day before yesterday. It will be good to see you in New York when you come East in October.

My most cordial greetings,
As ever your old
Stieglitz

1. Adams taught his first Yosemite workshop, the U.S. Camera Photographic Forum, with Edward Weston in the summer of 1940.

2. Beaumont Newhall and his wife, Nancy, accepted Adams' invitation to visit northern California, where he introduced them to Edward Weston and showed them the California coast and the mountains of Yosemite.

From Brett Weston

San Francisco
1940

My Dear Ansel—

Many thanks for forwarding the Stieglitz letter. It was very interesting to hear what the old boy had to say though in stating that my work is perfect technically he revealed a fading vision.

Perhaps if I knew Stieglitz personally—his conversations—and was more familiar with his work I might have been more deeply moved by his analysis.

Will certainly have a *couple* of well-rounded bitches on hand for your arrival Ansel—only give a few days notice!

Warmly—
Brett

From David McAlpin

New York City
September 7, 1940

Dear Adams—

Newhall and I both feel it essential for you to be here for six months to a year as a member of the committee and special adviser in launching the Photo Dept.

The catch of course about getting it started is to raise the cash. The trustees have asked me to be chairman of the committee. . . .

I have accepted the chairmanship *provided* you would come and stay here and devote as much time as necessary and serve as advisor, organizer and policy director. And I have offered to underwrite your retainer. So it's in the bag if you can be induced. And I don't know what "if" or "no" mean! I realize it's a big thing to ask but there would be many pleasant sides to it—Stieglitz & O'Keeffe. A real visit to N.Y.C. New faces—a bit of opera and music on the side. New scenes to interpret, etc., etc. And, of course, I intend that there should be no financial sacrifice. What do you suppose it would come to—what you would expect to produce in the time if you didn't come plus added expenses? It's hard for me to arrive at any estimate. Could you make a guess? Somewhere between x & y? When can you get here? October 15th? Let me have your reactions, as they say! . . .

All best wishes,
McA.

To David McAlpin

San Francisco
September 9, 1940

Dear Dave,

As I wired you, I am overcome with your letter and its implications, and I will say YES!!! It all seems too swell to believe—that the idea is coming to a head. I think you are brave in these times to foster it, but I think that if we are to keep on in a civilized way of life that all the top cultural things must never be neglected. Bravo McAlpin!! . . .

It seems that the numerous discussions with you and Newhall, and the rather detailed observations I have been making in the past two years, have given me a rather good idea of what this idea is all about, and has suggested implications of the responsibility as well. I would like to go on record here that I think Newhall is the most valuable force photography has had in our immediate time. I also want to go on record here that I feel my position in this idea is one of assistance and cooperation with you and Newhall. I am a photographer; as such I can help. I have no desire, or capacity, to assume the task that you, as instigator, or

Newhall, as integrator, can effect with great efficiency and dispatch. I have the capacity to correlate photography in the creative aspects—critical or selective—with the desire you have to develop it as a form—an important form, of art—and with the critical capacity of Newhall to *place* it as an art-form. This is, of course, a limited expression of a much more fluent situation. All of us have our definite contributions to make, and our contributions will assume the proper complexions as the idea develops. . . .

I think one of the real tasks of this program will be to make a thorough investigation of American photography; I am certain there must be lots of magnificent work hiding in obscurity. And I believe that wherever we find a suggestion of good work we should function as a stimulant thereto. . . .

Ansel Adams

From Beaumont Newhall

New York City
September 17, 1940

Dear Ansel:

Things have been happening during the last few days! The creation of a Department of Photography is a fact; the Trustees have approved of the plans I submitted to them last July, and have appointed me Curator. Dave McA has accepted chairmanship of the Committee. . . .

We are very excited that you are able to come on. Dave gave me the facts in your letter, and it seems to us ideal to have you come on for the six weeks beginning October 15. . . . We were delighted with your cooperative and enthusiastic attitude as outlined in your letter to Dave, and await your arrival eagerly. It seems hardly worthwhile going into all the details of what we can do in this letter—I think that you have a good idea of my attitude from our California conversations, and I hope that you have the same of mine. Isn't it swell of Dave to get the thing started? . . .

It's grand that things are at last moving in the direction of an important center for photography. I know that we can work together admirably, and that we can make a really vital thing of this project.

Please give our very best to Virginia and the children. . . .

With all best wishes,
Beaumont

PS I have written Stieglitz about the plans in general, and have appealed to him for advice and counsel. I want him to feel that he is *in* on the work from the very foundation.

To Virginia Adams, Charles and Olive Adams, and Mary Bray

New York City
October 21, 1940

Dear Everybody,

. . . My position is Vice Chairman of the Committee of the Department of Photography, and I am supposed to represent Dave and put tacks under the seats of the museum staff.

Have seen a lot of people for just one week. Have a lecture on Nov. 6th; go to Dayton, Nov. 7th and 8th, have another lecture towards the end of the month, etc. etc. . . .

Take care of yourselves,
Much love to you all,
Ansel

From Beaumont Newhall

New York City
New Year's Day 1941

Dear Ansel:

The opening¹ was a great success, and we all wished that you could have been with us. . . . About 500 people showed up—which was very good considering that the exhibition was not a major one and that it occupied only one gallery. The room was crowded from 5 to 7 with people eager to see, not one another, but the pictures. They actually formed a queue right around the wall which slowly progressed from picture to picture; seldom have I seen such interest in the pictures at an opening. It was, I think, a good sign for the future. . . .

The show looks beautiful, if I do say so myself. Clean, precise, and striking.

Stieglitz came to see the show yesterday morning with Dave, and spent about half an hour in the gallery, looking at every print. What he had to say was most interesting. He liked the [P. H.] Emerson very much—the best Emerson print he had seen. Next he singled out the [Luke] Swank footprint as especially fine. Even more surprising was the good he had to say about the Westons—*Lettuce Ranch, Tide Pool,* and *Melting Ice* he thought were all Edward at his best. He said he had a personal prejudice against Moholy[-Nagy], and would refrain from commenting. [Man] Ray's *Schoenberg* he liked. The [Edward] Steichen *Morgan* he thought unfair to Steichen, as it was a photogravure, and did not hold up to the [D.O.] Hills beside it. This was his chief criticism of the show— an unfairness to Steichen. "I don't like much of his work, but he is a force, and you should have gotten more and finer things. You'll be criticized for this. Even if I'd let you take the big *Morgan* you couldn't have shown it here; it would have been out of keeping, because it dominates so. And the gravure is badly presented. It should have been drymounted, so that all could tell that it was a gravure. It tries to be something else; it demands comparison with the originals beside it." We had put the O'Keeffe *Hands* beside [Eliot] Porter's *Baby,* a juxtaposition which he liked. The [Lisette] Model he didn't seem to like; the [Walker] Evans *Legionnaire* he thought revealed Evans' weakness, a completely meaningless handling of the background. But the Evans interior he thought fine. The [Berenice] Abbott *Foundation* he disliked: "the work of an unsure person." The [Charles] Sheeler *White Barn* was one of the finest things in the show; the *Ford Plant* not so surely seen. Ending the panel on the south wall—I am following him around the gallery, clockwise—were the three big photogravures, looking simply magnificent in newly sanded and varnished frames. Clean, beautifully matted, and well lighted, they are superb—the best and most striking group in the whole exhibition, I think. And he was very much pleased that we had put them together with a certain isolation, and was pleased that we had cleaned up so well the frames. Then, on the end wall, he liked the [Henri] Le Secq greatly; your *Gravestone:* "I still think that's the best our friend has done: magnificent." The [Eugène] Atget Paris view he very much liked, and wished that [Berenice] Abbott did nothing else but print those negatives. The [D. O.] Hills: no comment. The [Timothy] O'Sullivan: "Nothing better has been done." And finally the hanging panel, with his *Poplars.* "Perfectly presented; just the kind of lighting it needs. Only I would have put the print higher, for it sweeps upward."

Then we went up to the library, and I showed him where I worked.

He was impressed by the atmosphere of light, and sat down in my office with Dave and myself. . . . He thought that we had made a beginning, a fine beginning. "Mistakes, yes; not the way I would have done it, but sincere and fine. What Barr[2] has written is very important. He has committed the museum to photography. More important than he knows, or you. You have a lot to fight for. So long as you do the things you believe in, so long as you can please yourself, all will be well. You'll be criticized. Correct only the misstatements, the falsifications."

. . . Here was praise more generous than I had hoped for. And I wished that you could have been present to hear it. These words don't begin to convey that feeling of sincerity, that placing of confidence, that belief, which passed between us. Dave was delighted, and, I think, as surprised as I that Stieglitz was so very pleased and so very cordial and receptive.

Hope you had a fine Christmas, and thank you for the wire. Phoenix[3] is definitely in the family way, so when you come on there'll be a menagerie here. With every wish for a most successful New Year to you and Virginia,

Beaumont

1. The new Department of Photography at the Museum of Modern Art opened its first exhibit, "Sixty Photographs," on December 31, 1940. The show was a survey of highlights from the history of photography curated by Adams and Beaumont Newhall.

2. Alfred Barr, director of the Museum of Modern Art.

3. Phoenix was the Newhalls' cat.

To David McAlpin

San Francisco
February 3, 1941

Dear Dave,

Thanks very much indeed for your letters. . . .

I appreciate, more than I can say, your comments on my work. Your comments are always valid because, first, you speak up what you think (a rare quality), and, second, you have the taste and intelligence to back up what you feel and think. So, after those bouquets—which are very real—I can proceed to say:

1. I realize, and have realized for a long time, that the presentation of myself and my work is very poor—grossly incomplete.

2. You would be surprised, Stieglitz would be surprised, I am surprised myself, at the variety of my work. The cataloging of my negatives has convinced me that I have been guilty of obscuring all but a fraction of what I do. This may sound conceited, but no one could have been more surprised than I to get a rough survey of ten years' work (in the negative) and realize it was *theirs*. I have done advertising. Commercial, Portrait, Architectural, Illustrative, Reproductions of works of art, Photo-Micrographs, even made a picture of an Eclipse of the sun, color photography, landscape, naturalistic details, cities, people, animals, clouds, news, nostalgics—the list is tremendous. I have made Bromoils, Carbons, Gums,[1] transparencies, murals, screens, fine books, ordinary books, folders. I have written one textbook and perhaps fifty to sixty articles. I have taught, talked, demonstrated, exhibited, managed a little gallery in San Francisco, and put on the big show at the SF Fair. 95% of this has been done since 1930; the remainder in 1926 to 1929. In addition, I have had to make my living at it—without any backlog.

3. I don't think I entertain any missionary complex, but Weston and myself (and Group *f*/64) made a tremendous contribution of photographic technique—especially in the west where it was exceptionally bad in 1930. Collectively, we defined the meaning of technical clarity; our influence spread all over the country. We did not intend this—it just happened. In the working-out of our problems we naturally concentrated on the type of subject-matter most favorable to our demonstrations. This, I believe, is the chief justification for criticism by Stieglitz and others. But it must be remembered that we were intent on clearing the fogs of procedure; we wanted to make sharp, clean photographs as a counterbalance to the sticky muck that was going on about us. The technical standards we established have not been exceeded anywhere— not even by Stieglitz himself. With the exception of Anton Bruehl, no commercial photographer has matched them. And all we desired to do was to show that a clean print was possible without muss or fuss!

4. Weston has gone very far—is considered by many as the top man today. In some ways I think this may be so, although I distrust "top ratings." Weston would be the last one to care about being "tops." But Weston is far more limited in the scope of his work than I am, with the exception of his portraits (which are really many variations on about six themes) he is far more "static" than I am. His book[2] contains only one

"human" picture—the picture of Charis. And my picture of Edward on the jacket. The text is complementary to the pictures—completely different in mood and approach. I bring this up merely in reference to the Sierra Book—I know that book is static—but it is not a "Book" in the true sense—it is a memorial, and its program was just to give an impression of the landscape and the landscape details of the Sierra. This it does, and it also hits tops in the reproduction field. But its 500 copies makes no pretense to compete with the 5000–10000 copies of the Weston book. . . .

6. Both Edward Weston and I have certain feelings about the Natural Scene—which we both arrived at independently, and which we express differently. The whole world is, to me, very much "alive"—all the little growing things, even the rocks. I can't look at a swell bit of grass and earth, for instance, without feeling the essential life—the things going on—within them. The same goes for a mountain, or a bit of the ocean, or a magnificent piece of old wood. Tombstones are magnificent photogenic things because they contain "photographicable" textures and nostalgic connotations—not necessarily of Death—but of a certain ceremonial quality apart from ordinary things of life.

7. Whether any form of photography is an Art Form or not makes little difference to me. I feel that if someone feels and says something through any medium of expression, and if this is communicated to others—to some others—not necessarily the majority—we have the basis of art. I think fine photography is not dissimilar to the spirit of the old Madrigals—a group would sit around and sing. They were not virtuosi. They just sang. But there is a way of seeing—more than the superficials—and a way of saying, that distinguishes true beauty from banality.

8. Stieglitz' remarks about my needing a "terrible experience" is the corniest thing I have ever heard him say!! Every once in a while he comes out with something like that, and I wonder about it. It's just like saying the artist should starve, live in a garret, be disappointed in love over and over again. Good old Bohemian stuff!!! How can he possibly know what experiences I have, or have not had? What my every day state of mind is? Why I did this and why I did not do that? Stieglitz never had any real economic pressure as far as I can make out. I don't think that had any particular effect on his work except to condition his appraisal of others' work who developed under different conditions

9. Stieglitz says there is "no leadership today." He wants to climb

down in his cyclone cellar with photography under his arm and close the door after him. I say there IS leadership—and it's not going to be found by denying it. As far as others are concerned, Stieglitz and O'Keeffe live in a negative world—all, except their own, exists as that which others have not accomplished. Those are hard words, but they are perfectly true as far as I'm concerned. There is a strange esoteric quality about it all which is both stimulating and extremely depressing. Stieglitz' *standards* are superb; the thing he fights for is supremely worthy, his own contribution is tremendous. But he is wrong when he says "no one has gone beyond me." It isn't a matter of *beyond*, it's just a matter of progression along the individual line. He has no idea how much his nudes influenced Weston's nudes—yet Weston's are totally different in their present form. The same goes for Strand and Steichen. Strand is very positive in what he does—Steichen is really unsure. Bruehl is magnificent—knows his limits and stays in them. Sheeler is a fine artist, but limits himself in photography by self-imposed mechanical equipment. Weston is perfectly sure, competent, free, simple, and doesn't give a damn. He records what he sees and reacts to. He has no fixations, not a single phobia, not rationalizing mysticism (except a personal fatalistic and semi-mystical concept of the world and himself in relation to it).

10. We all have our *stresses*—with me it happens to be technique. It's a sort of stock in trade; it really does not relate to what happens inside of me—except to help me to say things a little clearer. I wrote in a recent article for Morgan[3] that, "Technique (in relation to a fine print) may be likened to 'touch' as a quality of a fine musician." The number of good prints in the world are very few—just like the number of fine etchings. There are millions of almost good prints. I think it's a definite emotional and esthetic achievement to produce a truly fine print.

11. I think Paul Strand has made the most beautiful photographic prints—excepting nobody living or dead.

12. I think many people confuse *subject* with statement. I like Stieglitz' *Poplar Tree* better than the *Cloud at Lake George* in terms of *subject*—or, in terms of a picture of a subject. But I think that perhaps I like the *Cloud* better as a statement. These things cannot be defined. You like the *Wave Sequence*[4] of mine better than the *River*—is that a preference of subject, or of statement? I can't answer my own preferences, so I shouldn't ask. Many things of Stieglitz I do not understand at all—many things are blank to me. But for that reason I cannot say they are superficial—they do not have inner meaning. All I can say is, they very well may for him,

or for others, possess deep meaning. The more esoteric, the more lonesome one gets, and the more acute the struggle for position.

13. On the other hand, we are going to be weakened if we listen to too broad criticism and take it for anything more than what it really is—opinion. I sense, in regard to the exhibit at the MoMA, that the reaction has been to public opinion in terms of an *inclusive* exhibit of photography. It wasn't that at all—it was a selection of sixty prints which gave an indication of the camera's capacity to look into the world and state what it says. It was clearly out in the catalog that there were other agencies to provide a knowledge of the progress of the art in various fields. I think the Museum of Modern Art is perfectly ready to show anything that comes its way—Stieglitz included!! After all, it would be His show—put up the way he wanted it. Maybe he isn't ready (this apart from health).

14. I am just thinking out loud. I don't like to see things get involved. The world is simple—the sunlight is simple, photography is simple. Fine artists have shown this to be true. Why all the poker playing?

15. So, finally, to get back to me—Stieglitz has seen only three sets of my pictures since I have known him (excluding the first meeting)—the Exhibit, a set two years ago, the large prints (about twenty of them) I had with me this time. It's up to me to show him more; it's entirely my fault that I have failed to pull my stuff together to make a decent group. Your letters have stimulated me no end in this regard—but I can't put up anything as a fine photograph that is not also a fine technical job.

Please continue to write as you have—it makes me itch to get to work!! Hope you don't mind my long-winded conversations!!

Yours ever,
Ansel

Feb 7th

. . . Don't know just what to say in addition to what I have said above and before. Fine prints are nothing in themselves—they are only conveyances. A fine print of a documentary photograph might be a very different thing from a fine print of a rock detail. If the print was the best possible expression of the photograph—then, and then only, it would be a fine print.

Most photography today, in superficial aspect, is just like calendar art, postcards and advertising sketches. In other words, it is entirely apart from any profound experience. A fine commercial photograph is just as good and just as important as a fine expressive picture of a cloud or a figure.

Again, most "documents" are not casual snapshots. Good documentary photography depends on a long, solid program. So does sports photography. I have made comparatively few skiing photographs because I do not understand skiing; I might get some swell spectacular compositions—but I do not get them at the "expert's" chosen moment. I suppose I have discarded at least 250 swell photographs of skiing for that reason—swell pictures, but inaccurate as skiing documents. . . .

Fine print standards are, fortunately, not fixed. Stieglitz' prints are fine because they convey his ideas; they would be completely out of line for Edward or myself. I was making "fine prints" before I ever saw a Stieglitz print. His influence has been along the lines of making people "see" things, rather than stimulating "fine printing." It's all very mixed up.

I am doing an article for *Magazine of Art,*[5] and I intend to stress just this point of argument—the meaning of "esthetics" in photography. This implies the futility of misapplied esthetics, and the tremendous importance of clear statement. Old man [William Henry] Jackson, for instance, is a wonderful person, and one of the swell old photographers. But his work is not creative in the sense that Weston's is. It's good straight stuff, that's all. And there's no scorn in that. It has about the same place in American culture that the old steel engravings had—excellent craftmanship, charm, accuracy. But there is something else—something that comes in Stieglitz' *Hands of O'Keeffe,* Atget's Paris scenes, Weston's *Tide Pool*—perhaps in my *Tombstone,* and perhaps in some funny little print that some obscure sincere person made in the throes of amateur experiment. We can sense it when it's there. But it certainly is obvious when it isn't there.

I am interested in Stieglitz—and O'Keeffe—because I am only beginning to put together in my mind what they are and what they represent. I can't define them yet—perhaps never will be able to—but I am trying. I am trying to judge "experience" in terms of something universal, and again, in terms of an individual. Dorothea Lange, for instance, has a logical progression in her life from a student at the Clarence White School, through a long career as a portrait photographer, and into a phase of work in the documentary fields which is absolutely tops. It combines sensitivity, extreme devotion to expressive qualities, adequate technique. Stieglitz has, by example, preached extreme sensitivity, understanding of the little things, grasp of the big things. He has fought most of the phases of the material world; has maintained a little "court" of sympathetic spirits, and has given extreme encouragement to those who came to him with something sincere to say. He claims to have "anticipated" many of the points of modern photography. It is amusing, but it seems that Clarence White used to get a bit mad at this, claiming that HE did certain things first! (I got that from a friend out here.) There seemed to be a sort of gladiator complex going on for years.

It is unfortunate that their personal relationships with most people are so strained. . . . It is also unfortunate that S. has most of the younger people absolutely against him. I have known this for years, and have been unable to do anything about it. What I think is back of it is this: S. and O'K have a strange intellectual Feudalism—something belonging to two generations ago—and it just doesn't sit today with the people who have tragic responsibilities and face a tragic future. To me, S. has always been marvelous—I have no complaint. But I am just trying to understand him—and it's a hard job, I assure you.

Someday I want a show at the Museum—just a little room—with about twelve pictures in it. There will be a little grass in the sun, a piece of rock with water flowing over it, a juicy thundercloud. And then there will be three or four of people—simple people doing simple things, or maybe just simply doing nothing—and I will have a city and a farm, and maybe a boat—and a street scene and maybe something spectacular as a condiment. And I know that through these pictures, important or secondary as they may be, a little fresh air will blow through those chromium halls—and Gawd knows they need it!! Forgive this long letter. 2800 prints may have affected my logic!!

Affectionately,
Ansel

1. Carbon and gum bichromate prints, both non-silver photographic processes, were popular at the turn of the century.

2. Charis Wilson Weston and Edward Weston. *California and the West,* New York: Duell, Sloan & Pearce, 1940.

3. Willard (Herc) Morgan, who later published Adams' books under the imprint Morgan & Morgan.

4. *Surf Sequence, San Mateo County Coast, California, 1940.* (See *An Autobiography,* pp. 198–199.)

5. Unidentified article, probably never written.

To Alfred Stieglitz

New York City
Sunday, May 4, 1941

Dear Stieglitz,

It seems funny to write you a letter when I am right here in New York, but for some reason I want to. I don't think I will be able to be any more coherent than when I come to see you. I want to say things—many things—and there are never words available. Your photographs fertilize something which is hard to define—to say they are stimulating is just silly. I remember them with a mood of *recognition*. That is probably the closest I can come to a definition of what I feel.

Something else happens: irritations I have about things and people suddenly become inconsequential. Those photographs give you strength. I can't get the Lake George storm sequence out of my mind. Everything is there; every mood is echoed in some part of those pictures. I usually fight subjective definitions and interpretations as final things. Those photographs *are* final things, and there isn't any fight or rational search possible. What you said about my surf sequence pleased me no end—gave me a real lift. It was exactly what I felt about them myself—and yet people think they are wonderful! I don't. I think they are good, provocative, and damned decorative. But wait until I get at the same subject again!!

The little snaps I made of you the other day are really swell. I made some proofs, and am quite excited.

Whatever you do, spare yourself as much as possible. Hope the cold is better by the time you get this.

Affectionately,
Ansel

To Alfred Stieglitz

San Francisco
June 8, 1941
Saturday a.m.

Dear Stieglitz,

Well, Adams is home again!! What used to be a vast journey is now just an excursion. You ride on feathers at 90 miles an hour, and the earth just slips away from under you. If you went in a plane it would be 200 miles an hour, and the slipping away would be just that much worse. I got thinking about America on the way out—how can anyone feel defensive about earth that slips away from under you so easily? I live in mountains and I know the solid earth doesn't slip away from you there. But for millions of people the earth is just something to evade. Perhaps, in order to make the people feel really conscious about their land, we should make everyone cross the continent on foot or in a wagon. It's a funny mood— to have been in New York Wednesday, terrible Chicago Thursday, San Francisco Saturday. It's a bit like coming out of an anesthetic.

But it smells good out here—I had forgotten how good the earth can smell—grass and miles of empty space. West Virginia would smell good too if they gave it a chance—but the hills there are obscured with continual industrial haze. I think the Eastern haze, being largely superimposed on the land by industry, seems to permeate the spirits of many eastern people. Most easterners seem to be frantically putting out a cold light like a fire-fly just to be seen through the haze.

I enclose a little leaf or two from our garden in San Francisco; maybe the smell will last long enough to reach you.

But let me assure you there is no haze in [Room] 1710, 509 Madison Avenue!![1]

Affectionate regards, as always,
Ansel

P.S. It's no use for me to try to tell you about what you and the Place signify to me; I can best tell you by making some kind of photograph that you might like.

1. An American Place.

To Beaumont and Nancy Newhall

Mesa Verde Nat'l Park[1]
Colorado
October 26, 1941

Dear Beaumont and Nancy,

. . . We[2] have had a spectacular and dangerous trip. All went well through Death Valley, Boulder Dam, Zion, North Rim, South Rim,

Cameron. Then we spent the night on Walpi Mesa, proceeded to Chinle, and had two spectacular stormy days at Canyon de Chelly. I photographed the White House Ruins from almost the identical spot and time of the O'Sullivan picture!! Can't wait until I see what I got.[3] Then our troubles began. They have had the worst rainy season in twenty-five years and the roads through the Indian Country are unbelievable. The road from Chinle to Kayenta was so terrible that it took us fifteen hours to go sixty miles; then we ended up at midnight flat on our chassis in the worst mud hole you ever saw—with lightning and thunder and rain roaring on us. We slept in the car that night and worked from 5 AM till noon getting the old bus rolling again. Then, after Kayenta and Monument Valley, we struck a very tough road in Utah—Snake Canyon is just the rocky bottom of a rugged gorge and is also the road, and that is something fierce; you feel as if the car is to turn over any time or get impaled on rocks. Then, in short order, we had the terrible hill— so steep a car can just make it in low. It was muddy; we could not keep on the crowns—chiefly because I did not want to drive closer than two feet from the precipitous edge on the right—and four times we slid off into the mud ruts on the inside. That meant backing down over 1000 feet of road and starting off again. Finally, we unloaded the car—1500 pounds of stuff, finally made the grade and then had to carry all the stuff up by hand. After recuperating from that little exertion, we proceeded a few miles and encountered the Butler Wash. It was running fifteen inches deep, so we thought it was safe. I set the car in low and proceeded to barge through as I have many such affairs. When the front wheels touched the far bank the motor stopped—water was thrown on the block by the fan belt. I should have removed it first. Well, there we were with the backside of the car actually under water. In a moment of panic I decided to reverse and get out of it all; I could not budge the car ahead after getting it started because the rear wheels had ground a hole and no advance was possible. I put it in reverse, gunned it, got half way across, and the entire ignition passed out! Here I was, with the muddy water running over the floor board and within two inches of cameras and films in the back. A storm was coming up; things looked black indeed because those washes can rise five feet in fifteen minutes. We stripped and moved everything out of the car onto a high bank. It was seven miles from the nearest town, Cedric Wright started out to walk for help while I finished unpacking and covering stuff against the coming rain. The water was coming up, and the car looked done for. Cedric met a car about three miles out, and they tried to pull us out. No luck; practically burned out their own clutch. Water still sneaking up; storm looking bad. Car took me to next town—Bluff, Utah,—and I got the state road man to come out and try to save us. Even with a large truck, the mud, water, soft wet sand, etc. made it necessary to remove us by a system of shattering jerks. We just did get the car out; the storm broke, and the wash went up. We were so completely lucky—timed almost to ten minutes! We then had a tough tow for seven miles, and spent the night getting mud and sand out of brakes, axles, etc. Got to Monticello and had to have the clutch done over. Breathed a vast sigh of relief when we struck the pavement in Colorado. Never such a trip. We have only 4000 more miles to go!!

So much for that. Give my best to E[dward] and C[haris] when they arrive. And to all the others. . . .

Affectionately yours,
Ansel A.

1. The Department of the Interior commissioned Adams to photograph national parks and monuments with the purpose of making gigantic murals of the images for their Washington offices.

2. Adams, Cedric Wright, and eight-year-old Michael Adams.

3. *White House Ruin, Canyon de Chelly National Monument, Arizona, 1941.* (See *An Autobiography*, p. 220.)

From Beaumont Newhall

New York City
June 3, 1942

Dear Ansel:

. . . Well the Steichen shebang[1] got up on the walls in time for the opening by nothing short of a miracle. Everybody pitched in and with one grand spurt of activity we finished the job. The public finds the show very exciting, and we have been showered with praise about it. Between you and me the show, for all its spectacular timeliness, has nothing whatever to do with photography, and may be more harmful than good. It's like a Stokowski orchestration of a Bach fugue: very spectacular, very tuneful, very popular but it ain't Bach and it ain't good taste. Perhaps I'm a chamber music photographer, but somehow the ten Stieglitz photos that we are acquiring seem to me more important than the entire "Road to Victory." They will last, and the show will not—physically as well as spiritually, as the enlargements came in stinking of hypo![2] But this criticism is mighty personal, and so many people have fallen for the show that I am beginning to wonder if my opinion is a correct one.

Alas, alas. It seems now quite improbable that we shall be on to work up a Weston show. My draft number is in the works, and while I shall probably be able to appeal the case and be deferred for a while, the process of doing same will prevent me from leaving town. Anyway I have definitely decided to find, if I possibly can, some kind of commission, preferably one which will enable me to stay with Nancy, but if necessary anything that will make real use of my talents. It seems foolish to find one's self in the draftee mill when there must be places where I can be of real service and hold a more attractive position than that of a private. . . .

With all best wishes and lots of luck from both of us,
Beaumont

1. "Road to Victory: A Procession of Photographs of the Nation at War," an exhibit at the Museum of Modern Art, directed by Edward Steichen, with text by Carl Sandburg.

2. Steichen insisted on having photographers' negatives printed by a laboratory, rather than by the photographers themselves.

To Nancy Newhall

en route, Wyoming
June 11, 1942

Dear Nancy,

It just occurred to me that I have been a very inconsiderate guest; I have never written you at all and told you what a swell time I had at 25 W. 54th!! So, you can tell your old man to go feed the cat—this is just a letter to you. Of course, you CAN read it to him if you want to, but I don't give a damn if he gets jealous. I am way off in the wilds and try and catch me if he can!!

It's been a hectic period since I returned. Got the work done, and also got orders to march on this parks job. Well, it's all over June 30th.[1] . . . Sometimes I wonder how I keep driving the way I do, but it seems to agree with me. Only I don't get essential things done as I should. I hope people understand—partially, at least. The wolf growls accompaniment to a whole flock of squawking problems. But I am really not any different from most people I know; life is easy for only a very few—and maybe it isn't worthwhile for them at that.

Well, I think of the fine days with you and Beaumont; the peace and decent tempo, and the fine friendship. I had almost forgotten how to live; you people gave a swell demonstration for me! Someday I will do something for you. Wish you were right here on this train, going north through a very beautiful, but very arid country. Will arrive at Billings, Montana, tonight; then to Yellowstone, then to Glacier, then on west to Rainier and Crater Lake, then home. Have been getting some perfectly swell negatives; developing them in National Park Service darkrooms, and am immensely pleased. Got a superb picture of the Never-Summer Range west of Rocky Mountain National Park—great snow-covered mountains with shaded snow-covered hills in the foreground and a very nostalgic sky. Well, wait and see!! I will send some on.

We are roughing it through a deep canyon, can just see the tops of the walls from the Pullman window. Green grassy slopes, yellow-cream rocks, sagebrush. Just passed about fifty miles of snowy mountains—so many mountains here there is no chance to remember what they are.

They take off the Pullman soon; then in a day coach to Billings, Montana; arrive at 6—take coach at 11 p.m., get off at Livingston at 2:15 a.m. Wait for stage to Gardiner; then take government car from Gardiner to Yellowstone. Tell old [William Henry] Jackson I will be thinking of him. He might have had a portable darkroom and a 57 x 1118 camera, but I got 280 pounds of baggage and cameras and tripods and typewriters and am having a hell of a time without the old station wagon!!

How is Stieglitz? I have tried to write him for weeks, but have not gotten down to it. Give him my warmest greetings. And how is the manuscript[2] progressing? You have a tough job with that. You must know, no one can ever question your complete integrity, so I don't think you should be too influenced over what Stieglitz thinks of your writings and statements. A very large part of S's technique is making it just about impossible for any force or influence or condition of the outside world to get to first base. I get a strange mood when I am away from N.Y.—a mood of living in a tremendous land—fresh, endless and friendly—and looking in on a literal tempest in a hall bedroom. All that intense, burning fencing with life and people doesn't seem to make sense from the Wyoming mesas.

I often wonder about you two—you are both much bigger in spirit than the world you have chosen to live in. Your world (basically yours) seems to relate more to the sarabande, and some fresh air, and some space under the sky, than to the esthetic chess games of people . . . or the witch's cauldron of the museum melange, or to the burning, feverish struggle of Stieglitz. It's funny what the Wyoming plains and mountains do to Fifth Avenue and 53rd Street![3]

Come out west soon—come and take a real simple trip in the Sierra; I can show you places near at hand that would make you both feel like the shipmates of Ulysses. You just saw the worst aspect of Yosemite—it's all going to be quiet this year (thank God). But there are some crags and meadows in Echo Creek that would resound beautifully to the Newhalls!!

Just passed an acre of blue lupine, with snow peaks in the distance— it's almost too much.

Thanks again for a swell time at your home—and keep the torch burning with the same old glimmer.

If your old man has come back from feeding the cat (or worse) give him my best. Same to you.

Yours ever,
Ansel

Next address: c/o Superintendent, Glacier National Park, Montana.

1. Adams' Department of the Interior mural project ended June 30, 1942, as a result of America's entry into World War II.
2. Nancy Newhall was working on a biography of Stieglitz that was never completed.
3. The Museum of Modern Art is on 53rd Street, just west of Fifth Avenue.

To Nancy Newhall

Los Angeles
September 14, 1942

Dear Nancy,

. . . There is nothing as important to you as Beaumont;[1] photography (and what we can do with it) may be of supreme importance—OUT-SIDE that first consideration, which is Beaumont. And it's the same thing for him—you are the point around which everything revolves for him. I sense you have a struggle in your mind (not in your heart); you want to be with him, yet you feel the deep obligation to the department. I say to hell with the department, with the museum, with anything, if it's going to keep you away from Beaumont! It's the old New England conscience creeping out and sunning itself. I know. I put the conscience in the sun and lost something of inestimable spirit and power. You do not have the same problem, thank goodness, but you do feel the obligation of the museum, and you are torn between doing the job and Beaumont. . . . I repeat, put everything else aside and go to him, and if the museum cannot understand the museum is not worthy of further attention.

I am a congenital optimist; I feel we are coming out of this mess earlier than most people think; and that the world will be a better place for it. But that does not mean you should not act and think realistically; you would never forgive yourself the loss of days with Beaumont which you might have had should things go the other way. If such were to come to pass, the museum would be a shallow compensation. Forgive me for speaking this way, but I am so anxious to stand behind you in this and urge you not to be over-concerned with the museum now. The time will come when all the threads can be resumed. If it is a true thing it will live. And do not forget there is great support of the idea—more than you perhaps believe now.

I am just a bit worried about you; I know what you are going through. It isn't only being with Beaumont in Harrisburg; it's being there *completely*, without obligations, and concerns, and attentions, except for *him*. Do you understand what I mean?

As far as the museum is concerned . . . it can all go splash in the Hudson; the *Idea* of the museum is something that will continue. The building has imposed a mood of power: the staff are so very professional that they have forgotten that art, after all, relates to something which goes on inside people, and isn't, after all, a stately ballet of hung pictures. There is something morose and sad about that kind of people and mood—especially so now when realities are making a fearful din. I find it hard to think about esoteric presentations when I hear about Stalingrad. I am anxious to get going—anything—to teach photography to the army, to make up pictures of America to send to England, to do anything which will help solve the terrible problem. I would prefer to drop bombs where they would do the most good, but I fear, for a while at least, the army wants younger people for that! . . . Beaumont is fortunate; he is *in*, and will have an important work cut out for him . . . . Please get me

[141]

straight—there is more need for real art now than ever before; I refer to that sticky, intellectualized, unreal mood that thwarts us so often at 11 West 53rd. . . .

Whenever you feel like "letting go," just drop me a line. I will do the same with you. That is a true privilege of friends. . . .

Will send some more little prints, but have none here just now. Am touched that they mean something to you both. Whenever I get a bit down I think of the mountains and of people like you two, and then everything is OK, OK, OK!

Yours ever,
Ansel

1. Newhall had enlisted in the air corps.

To Edward Weston

Yosemite National Park
1943
Tuesday—by Gawd!

Dear Edward,

Vell, today comes a package from Carmel—OY OY OY !!! I open it—what a shame to disrupt such a swell piece of packing!! But what is inside—OY OY OY OY OY! Magnificent prints!

The Louisiana Bayou one is just tops.

Modesty prevents my uninhibited comment of the other two.[1] They are wonderful pictures; you got a quality in the prints I think is marvelous.

Apart from the photography, I think I should grow a beard! But you can't help that; Gawd hath made mountains but he did a louzy job on my nose. Maybe the kind of beard I should grow would be one that looks like one of those Scotch Scurriers—those Dawgs that look like (and through) a section of a hair mattress.

Vell, my little girl says, "The boats and lake are just swell, and the funny one of daddy is AWFUL funny, but the other one is too grave, too sad, far off!" See—SOMEBODY likes Daddy!!

As far as I am concerned I like them tremendously; it's the first time anyone ever got a true mood through my face. The only thing is that the mood that was there was one of fatigue, disgust with the Art Center experience, and a couple of sore eyes from all the formaldehyde I was dosed with at the L.A. morgue the night before.[2] However, there is a glimmer of the fine mood I was getting into with you and Charis—but Jeez, I was pooped that day. The gesture of supporting the cross—or have I just descended??—has a connotation all its own.

Now, what can I do for you for these swell pictures? I am really touched a hell of a lot with them. I have had no chance to get any work done at all—it's just been a madhouse here, but in a worthy cause. I do have some swell new negatives—but no prints! I hope to come down to San Francisco very soon—perhaps drive, and, if so, I *shall* go by Carmel. We are doing very well here this summer in spite of everything, and I have decided that the best thing I can do is to accomplish as much bread-and-butter work as possible during the coming six weeks and have something in reserve for the lean and fallow months—in which I can do a lot for myself. One moment I feel utterly useless—the next moment I feel I am filling a niche quite adequately.

How is it with you and Charis? And news? And new work? Still wardens and spotters?[3] Feel OK? Any trouble getting materials, etc? How is the Acrol [Amidol]? What's the Pyro[4] stock? Who goosed your Grandma? Any more cats? Need any film?

Jeez, I wish I could see you soon.

Vell, maybe it *will* be soon.

Anyway, write and let me know how you are.

I have VERY affectionate feelings for E and C.

Love,
Ansel

Virginia sends her love to you both but she said that if she saw the man portrayed in the "sad" picture—saw him especially on a dark lonely street—she would scream and await the attack. Hmmmm. Not so bad!!

PS My article, severely deprecating the Pictorial point of view and the Salon lads, etc. accepted by the *American Annual of Photography!!*[5] Whadayouknow!!

PPS Several fine letters from Nancy; did you know Beaumont was a Captain?

PPPSS Looks like the Museum of Modern Art Dept. of Photography is zooming along the path of expansion in a big way. Nancy is doing a fine job. Herc Morgan is Director of the Dept.; Nancy acting curator.

For me, I would prefer it more simple, but the MoMA is Big business and I guess they must do it that way!!

pppssspsps Got a pretty good one of you, but, Goddamn it, have had no chance to print it!!

1. Portraits of Adams by Weston.

2. Adams taught at the Art Center School in Los Angeles in 1941 and 1942, but he left in 1943, disgruntled with the school's politics and bickering. One assignment Adams gave students was to photograph bodies at the Los Angeles morgue.

3. Edward and Charis Weston kept watch for the enemy off the coast of Carmel, California.

4. Pyro, a photographic developer.

5. "Personal Credo—1943," *American Annual of Photography*, 1944.

To David McAlpin

Los Angeles
January 10, 1943

Dear Dave,

It was certainly good to hear from you. In these times a word or two from friends helps more than anything else. At the same time, one cannot be expected to write conventional or frequent letters.

I may be wrong—guilty of wishful thinking—but I cannot be really pessimistic about our times. I know we are going to win—even at tremendous costs—but I know every one of us is going to be hardened and tempered and far more realistic than ever before. This will reflect to the good of art and to the good of human relationships. We were all soft; living in a sort of gentle oxygen tent of superficialities. I like to think of the trips we had together—we shall have more—they were perfectly swell, and reflected a beautiful and intense awareness of the world. The Sierra, the Southwest, the east coast, Cape Cod; I look back now and derive as much or more from the memory than I did from the actuality. The War can't prevent Man from returning to Nature, because Nature can be found everywhere about us. We might not be able to go so far with such ease, but there will always be the stars and the wind and the clouds and growing things. Someday I am going to really print up the pictures we have made together—print them up in the right way—and then the memories will take a much more poignant form of sublimated actuality.

That brings me to the picture of the *Moonrise at Hernandez.* Sure you saw it at the museum; Steichen picked it out there for *U.S. Camera.*[1] I think it one of my best. The reproduction is not good—none of the rich velvet blacks of the original come through properly, but it is still not bad. I will certainly make you up one of the best possible prints of that picture at the earliest possible time. I shall have to go to San Francisco to do it because my machine [enlarger] there will take the 8 x 10 film. I expect to go soon, so you will get a copy in a month or so. I have hundreds of pictures—good ones like that—which have never been printed, or merely proofed, which I MUST finish someday. But it takes time, and a certain mental and spiritual poise, and both those elements have been scarce for me of late. I have a storm sequence of the Grand Tetons, a sequence of the Yellowstone geysers,[2] and many other new things made prior to June 30th, 1942, which you have not seen. Maybe I can send you a set just to look at, if it will give you pleasure. I have some real swell things.

Nature, for me, is alive—just as alive as people. But my next phase will be *people in relation to Nature;* I feel it coming. At present, I am engulfed in teaching, but this, too, is a phase. I cannot force myself into subject matter which is not perfectly clear and justified; every time I have done so I have produced inferior work. But I still have more pictures of people than I have seen myself! . . .

My very best to you and yours, and all kinds of good wishes.

As ever,
Ansel

1. *Moonrise, Hernandez, New Mexico, 1941* was first reproduced in *U.S. Camera 1943,* pp. 88–89.

2. *Old Faithful Geyser, Yellowstone National Park, Wyoming, 1942.* (See *An Autobiography,* pp. 278–279.)

To Nancy Newhall

Yosemite National Park
1943

<u>Personal</u>

My Dear Nancy,

Certainly wish I could see you. Certainly wish Beaumont could get home for a while[1] and that we all could be together for a little while in New York—or out here! I have missed you all tremendously, but have not had you out of mind. But the mood of your letters is cheerful, and I gather things are progressing well with you—in spite of Beau's long absence. As for me, I have been keeping my nose close to the whirling grindstone. We have actually "madeuhbituhmoney" this season to help us over the fallow winter months, so I do not have the usual tension of immediate wolves gnawing at thin doors. The kids are growing up swell, and I am pleased that things are smooth and well in hand.

My history of recent months is both simple and complex. I have been doing bread-and-butter work for the Dept. of the Interior here; photographing Army convoys that visit Yosemite. There have been thousands of soldiers visit the place, and now we have a large Naval convalescent hospital (formerly the Ahwahnee Hotel). In addition, I have worked with Dorothea Lange on Office of War Information jobs relating to both the Italian and Spanish people in this part of the country. It was quite exciting. Then I contributed two weeks to the teaching of photographers in an ordnance battalion at Fort Ord, and did some work for the Army in San Francisco. I have also been taking Navy patients out for photographic sessions here in the valley. I did a small *Fortune* job and a few other commercial tasks. Also, I have written a good part of a book on landscape photography in Yosemite,[2] have made corrections and additions to our Yosemite guidebook,[3] and have done some articles for Herc [Morgan] and the *American Annual of Photography*. And I have made a few good negatives on my own. And there has been a lot of little things for our place here.

But the most important job I have done this year is politically "hot" and, therefore, *confidential*. Dorothea Lange and Dorothy Norman know about it, because I have just written them for some advice, and I am anxious that you know about it, too. I was asked to do some pictures at the Manzanar Relocation Center (where the loyal Japanese-American citi-

Album page of Ansel Adams' first photographs, Yosemite National Park, 1916. (Titles are in his mother's hand.)

Ansel Adams holding his Box Brownie camera, Yosemite National Park, c. 1918

Charles Hitchcock Adams,
San Francisco, c. 1922

Aunt Beth Adams, Uncle
Frank Holman, Ansel
Adams, and Virginia Best at
Merced Lake Camp, Yosemite
National Park, c. 1922

Ansel Adams and view camera,
Yosemite National Park, c. 1920
(by Arnold Williams)

Ansel Adams on Sierra
Club outing, c. 1933

35mm proof sheet from Canyon de Chelly National Monument, Arizona, 1937.
(Included are Georgia O'Keeffe, Orville Cox, David McAlpin, and Godfrey Rockefeller.)

Ansel Adams cooking on the tailgate of Helios IV, June 1949 (by Cedric Wright)

From left: David McAlpin, camp cook, Helen and Godfrey Rockefeller, and Georgia O'Keeffe around campfire, High Sierra, Yosemite National Park, 1938

Alfred Stieglitz at An American Place, New York City, 1944

Ansel Adams, Wildcat Hill, Carmel Highlands, 1943 (by Edward Weston)

Edward Weston, 1945

Beaumont and Nancy Newhall, Westport, California, 1960

Ansel and Virginia Adams at the exhibition "Ansel Adams and the West," MoMA, 1979 (by John Sexton)

zens are, pending their relocation throughout the country).[4] The object of the pictures is to clarify the distinction of the loyal citizens of Japanese ancestry, and the dis-loyal Japanese citizens and aliens (I might say Japanese-loyal aliens) that are stationed mostly in internment camps. There is great opposition out here to all Japanese, citizens or not, loyal or otherwise, chiefly coming from reactionary groups with racial phobias and commercial interests. Of course, the fact remains that an American citizen of assured loyalty has all the rights under the Constitution that you or I have, but the big-business boys have the unfortunate gift of vaporizing the Constitution when their selfish interests are concerned. Well, it seems that the pictures have turned out so well that a book is being contemplated—a semi-picture book with short but adequate texts.[5] To me, the job is about as constructive a thing as anyone could do—and strictly American. It was a great experience for me and I have a striking series of direct portraits and other pictures that are intensely human and real. Through the pictures the reader will be introduced to perhaps twenty individuals in as many branches of trades and professions—journalists, farmers, garment workers, scientists, mechanics, etc.—loyal American citizens who are anxious to get back into the stream of life and contribute to our victory. Thousands of loyal Japanese-Americans are in the armed forces, and making a very fine showing. As I said, a book is contemplated, and if it goes through, I shall probably come east to promote it. But you can understand how important it is to have everything completely in hand—to allow no opportunity for anyone to accuse us of any production detrimental to the war effort. Hence, the distinction between the loyal and dis-loyal elements must be made crystal-clear, and the emphasis on the Constitutional rights of loyal minorities placed thereon to support one of the things for which this war is all about. The War Relocation Authority is doing a magnificent job, and is firm and ruthless in their definitions of true loyalty. In effect these pictures imply a test of true Americanism, and suggest an approach to treatments of other minority groups. I may be wrong, but I feel I have material of tremendous value. But the presentation must be adequate and appropriate. Any ideas that come into your capable head would be greatly appreciated. I am still putting it together so have nothing I can show you now. . . .

I have tried unsuccessfully to get into some work relating to the war effort. Perhaps, as Stieglitz wrote me about himself, I am a "man of peace." But I certainly would like to be of use. So many things are at stake. We will undoubtedly win a complete military victory soon—but then what? Big business seems crouched and ready to spring as soon as the guns stop booming. I refuse to think that the fruits of this terrible war will be plastic bobbypins, streamlined bathrooms, aluminum summer houses, the ability to get nowhere faster than ever before, and televised soap operas. It's our job to do what we can to destroy the foundations of the next war which seem to me to be in the "form" stage—all ready for the concrete of greed and exploitation. Well, I suppose if I can be of any real use I will discover the way. In the meantime, I am continuing much as before, but anxious to keep producing something.

Write when you can. Tell Beaumont I think of him a very great deal, envy him the contribution he is making, but will be *damn* glad to see him home again. Tell Dave I am writing him a letter now, and the same to Stieglitz.

Good luck and good health,
Affectionately
Ansel

1. Newhall was stationed successively in Cairo, Tunis, and finally Italy.

2. Never published.

3. Ansel and Virginia Adams. *Illustrated Guide to Yosemite Valley,* San Francisco: H. S. Crocker, 1946.

4. Adams photographed at Manzanar on the east side of the Sierra in the Owens Valley in 1943 and 1944.

5. *Born Free and Equal,* New York: U.S. Camera, 1944.

From Alfred Stieglitz

Lake George
August 8, 1943

Dear Adams:

For months my intention & desire was a Hello to you. But somehow between heart attacks & very down feeling chronically I kept postponing & postponing, living in a state of indecision which is purgatory for certain. Running The Place virtually single-handed has been a terrific ordeal. An impossible one. That's why you haven't heard from me. How often you have been, & are, in my mind.—I wonder tho have I such a thing left. My correspondence has all but ceased to exist.—The Place should be called The Sarcophagus wherein I lie entombed with the glory of the Marins, O'Keeffes, Doves, your photographs as well as mine & what else—A part picture of the age! –

I finally came up here on the 4th. & have been lying here instead of lying about at the Place.—Here at least I breathe no soot. And there is supreme quiet –

The painting of The Place is what finally drove me here.

I hope you haven't misunderstood my long silence. You are ever one of my pleasant thoughts. Yes Adams that is true.—

I suppose you are not having an easy time.—If you are well—& I hope you are—you have the supreme asset in this world of ours.—

With most cordial greetings
Ever your friend
Stieglitz

To Alfred Stieglitz

Yosemite National Park
August 22, 1943

My Dear Stieglitz,

Your letter was like a big gust of clean wind in the pine trees—timed exactly right as far as my receptive mood was concerned. In fact, I had been worrying about you—it's not that I expect letters, but I do like to know if you are all right. I just feel that way about it, and, while I do not want to inflict my concern upon you, I admit selfishness in wanting to know if you are all right or if you are not. Not much that I can do about it, of course, 3000 miles away! But perhaps thoughts do get around, and help or hinder.

What a time in the history of predatory man!! I have come to the conclusion it is not a war of this or that country against another country, or one "system" against another—it's just a decisive fight between the predatory spirit and the generous spirit. Of course, the generous spirit will win—and then become predatory!! Seriously, I have been able to boil down everyone I know into these two groups—those who take and those who give. Am I right or wrong? Are there other compromising classifications? I don't think so. The wolf can put on the generous act but he still remains the wolf. The sheep can back up against a rock and BAA in bass clef, but it's still a sheep. . . .

I am, however, personally fed up with the self-conscious [Carl] Sandburg Americanism; the paeanic glorification of *what is,* instead of what might be. The only true thing is the poor wretch on the firing line—not the expansive poems, texts, and pictures which depict him. I don't like [Norman] Rockwell's posters, Hollywood war movies, Roads to Victory, Free verse in Praise of Sacrifice, etc. I have talked to a lot of the men who have been in the middle of it—the fighting—and what *they* say rings true—not what the professional "social chanter" constructs. . . .

I think of Marin's work—the sharp accent of inner realities so simply set forth. And your photographs of the essential things that are so big in their potency. All such things, and the things they represent, are worth fighting for. But the bathetic world of advertising is not worth the powder to blow it all to Hell; and those advertising boys are in the saddle it seems—at least with most phases of our daily lives. They seem to honestly believe that a streamlined icebox is worth a battle. I got such a dose of that way of thinking when in Los Angeles that I feel competent to speak violently about it. . . .

Well, Adams is therefore hibernating as it were. But Adams is disturbed, not at the immediate condition of his photography, but at the appalling accumulation of work which is still in a negative stage. I have scores and hundreds of negatives—equal to my best finished work, such as it is—that are unprinted. I don't know what to do about it. If I could weigh out time like Sodium Sulphite[1] I suppose I could get the printing done "in my spare time." . . . I have many things which I am sure you would class as equal to the White Tombstone. What to do? . . . Edward Weston seems always caught up with his work—but he does relatively little work (in volume), has relatively small requirements in a material sense, and in many ways is a recluse. You know me—I was born to be gregarious, and my life is a continual round of experiences with people. It's sometimes wonderful and sometimes terrible. But, I seem to thrive, although often wishing from the depths of my being for a little lonesomeness. But nature has been very generous and given me wonderful views from my windows, and I have perfect health, and can still climb 3000 feet with a forty-pound pack and enjoy it. There are few people who can leave their homes, walk a quarter mile, and spend a whole day rock climbing in the midst of incredible cliffs and spires and domes of clean granite. The little proof attached is a sample of "what goes on" on a good rock climb—it is of the base of the great Half Dome Cliff—

2000 feet sheer. The tree on the skyline is about 150 feet high. Size is nothing in itself, but these mountains and rocks add up into something tremendous. To get to the point from where this picture was taken required 36 rope belays—well, I'll explain it to you in person. It's like chess or pinochle—emotional besides!!

I also enclose a snap of my son—aged 10—on the way down from Cockscomb Crest. The snow fields are normal for July 1st—this was July 15th of this year. Just proofs—but I will make some decent prints for you someday. These just represent clean air and clean stone and snow. It's a far cry from the booze-soaked, smoke-cured Spirit of Broadway (a symbol, thank God) infested with Oscar Levants and Irving Berlins and George Gershwins, studio photographers, columnists, agents, Dalis and Dilettantes. Why I am in this nasty mood I don't exactly know, but I am enjoying it—in a grim sort of way.

Dave [McAlpin] in the Navy—Beaumont in the Air Force—me doing nothing in particular—the Museum of Modern Art expanding—the Museum of tolerance contracting—bugles and boleros, bonds and bombasts, vice and victories—you are undoubtedly carrying on with the least dislocation. . . .

Places that are naturally horizontal in mood—the desert, perhaps Lake George,—give one a chance to be isolated by the simple expedient of a hedge or a wall, or by the sheer inertia of being at a distance on level ground. But in the mountains there is no such isolation; the vertical aspects of the earth tower over the entire herd, bell-mares and burros alike. Streams flow down and converge, mountains slope down into canyons, everything funnels into a few places of possible habitation. There is no escape—other than climbing out on the cliffs—from which sooner or later, one must return. . . .

I hope Nancy will be able to hold the fort until Beaumont returns. I feel she has a real and alert interest in photography and is exceedingly capable. She has an adoration for you which is balanced and very deep. I feel that nothing but good can come from her interest and association in photography and all of us should back her to the limit. . . .

Edward Weston is still in Carmel; he and Charis serve as airplane watchers. Do not know what he is doing at the moment, but the last I saw of him a little while ago indicated all is well—he was busy printing up some negatives, making some portraits, chopping wood, and living a simple life. . . .

Well, enough for the present. It's just grand, as I said, to know you are all right, and I must repeat I don't expect you to write any answers to my safety-valve letters.

My affectionate greetings and thoughts for you always,

Ansel

1. Sodium sulphite, used as a preservative in developing agents.

From Alfred Stieglitz

New York City
November 5, 1943

Dear Adams:

I don't know have I, or have I not, acknowledged the receipt of your long & grand letter? My memory has become a curious affair—rather old & rickety. The Place continues but is pretty much neglected by all but myself. Every one is hyperbusy & rushed, "young." So The Place becomes more & more wonderful. You ought to see it. The Whiteness of the Walls. And now the new Marins up. Oils & watercolors. An amazing output. 1943. What a giant that modest American. Really incredible that human. The truth that is Marin!

And a few days ago O'Keeffe returned. Bronzed & fit. She pitched in at once, & hung the Marins.

And her new work. Well as there is but one Marin there is but one O'Keeffe. Two Americans—male & female.

The Place. Yes I can say there is but one Place. Has it anything to do with the madness called the World—Has it? If there be such a thing as peace,—the Place is that. Yes you'd love it if you could walk in just now.

And I'd love it if you could –

As it is you are much in my mind—You. Your photographs. All you mean to me.

Yes I know what you are up against. And most others too. Should I say *all* others.

This is just a greeting and a very warm thank you.

Your old
Stieglitz

Italy
February 27, 1944

Dear Ansel,

. . . Yes, the more I think of creative photography, the more I realize how true it is that what counts in art is what is inside of us. That is what separates the artist from the layman—the ability to recognize and the skill to transmit to others those observations and feelings. How much we have to do when all of this is over! A fight for the real recognition of photography, not the intellectual acceptance of it which, I am afraid, is as far as we have gotten. There's no formula, no secret—it either happens or it doesn't. It is shameful that a man cannot photograph as he can paint—that it is almost impossible for a creative photographer to make a living through his creative photographs—that from the sale of a dozen fine prints he cannot live comfortably for a year. Surely it is possible for a painter to do so. Yet photographs are still mechanical pictures, and those who are willing to reward the original artist are few in number.

. . . As you remark, it is a godsend that Nancy has the job while I'm away. She has plunged into it hard, and it keeps her so busy that the pangs of separation are somewhat lessened. And the continuity is being maintained—all the spade work and contacts which you and I did. Our fight for photography will be a hell of a lot easier for this.

How I long for a weak, very weak, bourbon and water, a few Bach partita records, and a cozy room with you and Nancy! So much to talk about! Letters are unsatisfactory, being one way.

All my best to you, Ansel.

Yours as ever,
Beau.

To Alfred Stieglitz

[on the train]
June 11, 1944

Dear Stieglitz,

We come to foggy Californie with a grapefruit on our knee!! Nancy and I have been writing and talking and eating and looking out of windows, and wishing you were with us. The real fun starts today when we get out of this comet and settle back in a good old rough station wagon.

Will write soon,
Ansel

Here's Nancy—

Hello, darling!

Nothing like a three thousand mile perspective, through mountains and deserts and sunsets and dawns. The Museum is a nasty spot but you look even bigger and better than you do from 54th Street.[1] And to think I'm going to get my hands in hypo again and breathe photography along with mountain air, unperturbed by being busy with being busy or interoffice memos or phone calls or committee meetings. Last night we went through what looked like the first pale intimations of O'Keeffe's country. Hope I shall come back to you with photographs.

Affectionately,
Nancy

1. The Newhalls' apartment was on West 54th Street, opposite the Museum of Modern Art.

From Alfred Stieglitz

New York City
July 4, 1944

Dear Adams:

I received your & Nancy's letter. I hope you are both having a great time. I'm struggling along. It's tough going. It was very good to see you.

If I could only make one more print. Just one. But it seems as if that is not to be. As little chance as having a new heart –

It's July 4. Andrew[1] is here. So am I. No one else. Not even a phone ring. Why should there be?

I often think of your new prints. It wasn't fair to either you or myself to look at them as hastily & under the conditions as I did. I know they are very good –

Love to you & Nancy & the family.
Stieglitz

1. Andrew Droth was the caretaker at An American Place.

To Nancy Newhall

Yosemite National Park

July 15, 1944

My Dear Nancy,

Nice letter from the Overland Limited. Nice you saw Dorothea [Lange] and Imogen [Cunningham]. Sorry you missed [Cedric] Wright. Hope you get home not too exhausted. Hope things are right for you there. Let me know everything that happens. Am terribly interested, as you know.

Did not really do much for you—not nearly what I had hoped to do.[1] I think that we will get a perspective on lots of problems one of these days. You really worked hard most of the time.

I have always been talked about; in grammar school, as a kid, I was considered "unusual"—not in my right mind, so to speak. Then, I lived "north of Lake St." which automatically made me an aristocrat in relation to those who lived "south of Lake." This distinction seemed to be based on the fact of two hideous stone pillars, or pylons, which the real-estate development company set up to mark a perfectly ordinary area as "exclusive"; the only sad gap in their logic is that the pylons were built about eight years after my father "moved out there in the country." Hence, my snootiness was thrust upon me. But I went through Hell at that time; was sent to a private school for "adjustment," and otherwise enjoyed a rather irregular youth. Of course, I was always aware that people talked about me. The fact that I could do many things deftly and never was a "bad little boy" was not sufficient to overcome the stronger fact that I was "different."

My father had a series of business misfortunes and things were not so hot for quite a few years. As my father was about played out an old friend insisted he take us to Yosemite for a vacation. This was in 1916. From that time on, things became crystallized in a far more healthy way. In making the choice between music and college, I still think I did the right thing, but others seem not to think so. Anyway, here I am in photography; most of my friends of earlier days keep stressing their regret I did not stay in music! My family said, "What!! you don't want to be anything else but a photographer!!" That helped, of course. I was talked about because:

I could play AND photograph (something immoral about that!!)

I wore a beard

[155]

I knew a lot of artists
I did not dance
I dared to question the status-quo
I became engaged to Virginia
I became dis-engaged to Virginia
I had too many girlfriends
I did not have enough girlfriends (something funny there, YES sir!!)
I married Virginia
I did not live in a garret
I moved to Yosemite
I liked Modern Art
I charged too much
I charged too little
I always did like women
Virginia should not have been so lenient
Virginia should have "understood" (think she has done a very good
    job of that kind of "understanding")
I drink too much
I can't follow the Commie line
I think expression is something in addition to politics and vice-versa
I'm a radical
I like to be reasonably precise (this seems to create immense
    annoyance)
I read PM^2
I know Ickes
I should be free
I should have some real responsibilities
I live in an ivory tower
I am complex
I am simple
I am rich as all get-out
I live off my wife
I live off my father
My work should be in line with my Tempo
I don't like people
I don't understand the BIG social problems of today
I'm precious
Nobody seems to inquire if I am actually any more or less happy than
the average Homo sapien, any more or less adjusted to conditions, or

figure out some objective appraisal. I have an answer which I think may suffice—perhaps it's just a rationalization, but here goes:

I know what I have in photography—what I have done, and what I believe I can do. In relation to most of my friends I have made a rather obvious success. Very few of my friends have made that kind of success. They fundamentally, subconsciously resent it. They would like to uncover the weak spots; set me up as they think I should be—put me in my place, in other words. Well, perhaps I am not ideally situated, personally, financially, creatively. But I am definitely NOT unhappy. In fact, just about now I am happier than almost anyone I know. I would feel very bad to think I were not man enough to assume the normal responsibilities without adversely affecting my work. I am always violently in love with something—an idea, a person, a job. I am actually quite *un-moral;* my restraint in certain cases is not based on any personal moral inhibition, but on an objective appraisal of potential harm to the other, or others, concerned. I can't think of much I wouldn't do if it would not hurt anyone else. I think I have been most fortunate; after quite a few years of adjustments I find myself stable emotionally—to all outward appearances—fairly well set in a routine of daily life—terribly fond of my environment, terribly fond of my family. I have a huge program laid out, material obligations fairly well under control, hundreds and hundreds of friends. I do have distractions, worries, disappointments. But am I unique in that? I do not envy Stieglitz his life; it seems tragic to me—much more so than anything I have had to contend with. The fact that he has accomplished what he has is a miracle—the evidence of strength and clarity of purpose. Think how much more he gets talked about than I.

. . . If the above sounds hopeless to you, write me what YOU think!!

Love and cheer!!

Ansel

Still in bed with the goddamn flu—but getting a lot done.

1. Nancy Newhall was beginning research for her biography of Adams for the years 1902–1939: *The Eloquent Light,* San Francisco: Sierra Club, 1963.

2. *PM,* a liberal newspaper.

To Alfred Stieglitz

My Dear Stieglitz,

Things went off the beam this season; I have been away for weeks doing bread and butter jobs for *Fortune*,[1] and giving a series of lectures in San Francisco. Just got back home. Am sitting here in a warm room with a lot of cold outside—beautiful snow-peaks against a pure sky—and listening to the "Art of the Fugue" of Bach's. Am writing you and Dave today, and my thoughts have been filled with both of you.

As the war moves to a climax, the only enduring things seem to be the aspect of Nature—and its reciprocal, the creative spirit. I have just had a few tremendously moving experiences. I will tell you about them, because they, too, are reciprocals—of many dreary months of hoping and waiting and doing much-but-little. The first experience was the re-emergence of an emotional stimulus—the same stimulus that motivated the making of my exhibit for An American Place. It defies description, and it is modulated now by all the intervening years. It is "like the flash of a meteor" moving in a vast space. I see clearly once again, and anew.

The second experience was getting at the heart of some tragic human problems; one, the loyal Japanese-Americans at Manzanar Relocation Center; the other, the flux of mixed humanity in the great shipyards at Richmond, California.[2] Nancy has probably told you all about the first—the exhibition, the book, the struggles against weakness, divergent concepts, poor quality of printing (book). God bless Nancy for her solidity of spirit. In relation to the Museum she stands out as a glowing and beautiful light. She and Beaumont—the future rests with people such as they.

At Richmond I was exposed to a cross-section of sheer brutal life that exceeded anything in my experience. Dorothea Lange and I worked on the interpretive problems for *Fortune*. Dorothea is a superb person and a great photographer in her particular field. Only through the pictures can I tell you what I saw and felt. I would like to print up about 12 of them as well as I can and show them to you. They comprise a new phase of Adams! I think you would approve.

The third experience was the response to my lectures. About twenty-five people came for six evenings; many were professional photographers—some were just salon pictorialists. It was obvious that for the first time they saw examples of resonant creative work. The Museum *(Nancy)* sent out a group of prints from their collection. Among this set was one of your Equivalents. A girl stood in front of this bit of you, and with tears in her eyes, said, "Now I know what you are talking about!" God knows how many there are in this world who should know what *you* have been "talking" about. As a bitter obverse of the course, the biggest commercial photographer in San Francisco frowned upon an employee attending the lectures because he might get "artiste" ideas!! (pronounced ARTEEST!) . . .

The "Art of the Fugue" progresses, and the sun is creeping with inquisitive clarity into my room. I think of the winter sun flowing into your Place, of the incredible living color of the Marins and the O'Keeffes, the tranquility of your prints. I think of the Place as a great thought arrested in time. Now the organ is playing one of the "Mirror Fugues"— as intricate and scintillating as sunlight on shining rocks. But it is organized—Gothic, flowing in a strong and rippling line to its own divine close. It is a Pattern for Life, and its resonances are of both the soil and the stars.

Tell O'Keeffe I am thinking of her. A certain acidity of mood which has enveloped our relationship in the past several years served somewhat as a reagent, revealing, I hope, the basic elements of our spirits. I feel that way—maybe she does, too. Tell her I want to have good long talks with her when I come east in February—if she wants to. Tell Marin *he* should illustrate the "Art of the Fugue"!! Tell Andrew—thanks for all his patience and devotion. Tell all my other friends I am thinking of them. And I tell you I am thinking of you—now more than ever before.

Affectionate greetings always,
Ansel

1. Adams photographed a ranch in California's San Joaquin Valley for an article entitled "The El Solyo Deal," *Fortune,* February 1945.

2. The Office of War Information hired Adams and Dorothea Lange to photograph the Richmond, California, shipyards.

To Edward Weston

Yosemite National Park
January 5th, 1945 by gum!!

Dear Edward,

Just as I was sitting down for a three weeks period of rest, recupera-
tion, sin and animalistic delights I get a phone from New York and I
have to go East on the 15th and do an industrial job in Ohio, Penn. and
way points[1]—ending up at the Museum of Modern Art about Feb. 1st.

So—it's the same old story—no Pt. Lobos until spring!!! Jezuz Kriste!
Well, I can't turn down $1000.00 in these times, can I?? (Maybe I could,
non-financially speaking!!)

I will carefully pack your prints and express them to you. I will wait a
day or so because I might be able to come via Carmel. I'll try, anyhow.

Something bothers me a lot. I did not know of it until just recently. It
seems that *Fortune* is using one of MY Death Valley pictures instead of
yours!![2] I told them they should use yours as you are identified with the
place; but they said they had a lot of yours and it would look like
padding if they used another.

They selected about 100 of my things when they were here, including
that vertical shot of D.V. from Zabriskie Pt. I never doubted they would
use yours of that place. I really feel bad about it, and I want you to know
I told them so. I am more than adequately represented, and that picture
should have been yours.

Well, wait until next time! Hope they send you a big check. They were
crazy about your stuff, and I have no doubt you will hear from them
about other work.

I talked to Nancy on the phone yesterday, and she sends love and
kisses. Gather Charis is still in Washington. Hope I see her while east.

Best to you and the cats. Is the little lady from Black Mountain [Col-
lege] still with you?

Have some new jokes,

Best ever,
As ever,
Ansel

1. Adams had a variety of commercial jobs, which included a huge bakery, a U.S. Navy
chain and shell factory, and bronze and aluminum manufacturing, all in Ohio; in Pitts-
burgh he photographed the building of huge crankshafts and propellers for ships.

2. *Death Valley*, by Adams, was reproduced in *Fortune*, February 1945, in a story entitled "The Grandeur that is Home."

From Edward Weston

Carmel Highlands
January 9, 1945

Adams, I'm *sure* you're going East to find my *wife*. Well, tell V. I am alone (for the moment). Death V. episode doesn't bother me! For a price I'll give you a lesson on how to live without working. Funny, I thought that *Fortune* was taking mounted prints to *order from*. Same to me—Black *Mountains* gone. E.

To David McAlpin

New York City
[1945]
Monday

My Dear Dave,

. . . I was touched by your interest in my new things. The sum you mention is over-generous. You selected about 28 prints. I am anxious that you allow me to supplement this selection with certain additions that I feel you should have and which you have not seen as yet. Some of the selections you made are top-quality prints, and I shall send those to Washington[1] as soon as I complete spotting. Some of the others I think I can improve; I will either send you the prints you saw and follow up with better prints—or just send you the better prints as soon as I can make them. I have had serious trouble with paper—it is hard to get the full deep tones that we like, and some of these prints seem a little weak in comparison to what they could be. However, I shall get you the prints as *soon* as possible—*all* the satisfactory ones immediately.

After you left Stieglitz' I told him I had some prints to show and that I could leave them for his convenient examination. He wanted to look at them then and there. Apart from a few interruptions of minor nature, he spent about two hours looking and talking and I went away much refreshed. He has a rather uncanny way of saying exactly the pointed thing at exactly the right time for maximum effect. I believe he recog-

[161]

nized what I was trying to do in these new prints, and I am sure he realized they were only a fragment of what I could show if I had the time to prepare prints from all my negatives.

I feel he is getting old and tired, and while "well" in a comparative sense, I am aware of a gradual withdrawal from activity. I did not expect him to ask to show the prints, but I was surprised how close he seemed to come to saying he would. I agree with him that my first show sounded the Adams note, and that there is no justification to show repetitions of that note no matter how much more in pitch it happens to be now. When the new note is sounded a new show would be in order. I feel I am just about on the edge of tooting this new honk. The prints you get may be the last of an era! If so, I want them to be the finest possible examples. . . .

I feel things are going better at the Museum and that Nancy is doing a perfectly grand job of it. The Strand show[2] and book[3] are to be both knockouts. I do feel, however, that if the Dept. is going to function in the expressive fields that we must clarify the whole emphasis; the committee seems to have a big general uplift complex about photographs in general—the photography-in-particular (the expressive phase) is not enough in evidence in the agenda. Someday we may have a little room somewhere—about the size of the little room at Stieglitz'—show just the cream of the idea—and publish a journal that will speak the truth. I tremble to think of the postwar bombast; the expansion of the industry and the magazines will be terrific. I can talk for hours on that but won't bother you now with it.

Best to you and yours, and thanks again. See you soon.

As ever,
Ansel

. . .

1. Still serving in the armed forces, McAlpin was stationed in Washington, D.C.
2. "Paul Strand: Photographs 1915–1945," curated by Nancy Newhall, Museum of Modern Art, 1945.
3. Nancy Newhall. *Paul Strand Photographs 1915–1945*, New York: The Museum of Modern Art, 1945.

To Alfred Stieglitz

St. Louis
April 15, 1945

Stieglitz,

Thinking of the Place, of you. No space makes any difference; it's there, inside, getting more clear every day. There is only one way—the way of the truth. You and the Place have shown people that Way and, for that reason, you and the Place are perpetual.

I get worried about you—both for the way you feel and for the way you are depressed. I am not depressed; I can't believe you should be. The Place and all that it is is a wonderful thing; you have made a tremendous and enduring contribution to life. Long after you are gone the impact of the Place and of you will continue to grow and expand all over the world.

I will be back soon, I hope. Things are moving fast for me now. Hope I can manage them.

Most affectionate thoughts, always,
Ansel

I leave here next Sunday for the West.

From Alfred Stieglitz

Lake George
July 23, 1945

Dear Adams:

What a beautiful surprise. A few days ago a package came from the Museum of Modern Art. No other identification. I wondered what catalogue it might be. So imagine my surprise on finding instead prints of yours. And what beautiful pictures. I feel a note running thru them. A great tenderness. A lovely tenderness. Really I was bowled over & deeply moved. So my thanks dear Adams.

I'm up here since the 12th. The pure air is a godsend. I'm pretty much alone low in spirits a tired old man. Taking inventory of self—not in an introverted sense but as objectively as human can be. It's

—Later: I was interrupted. And now I have lost thread of what I was about to say. You see that's what's happening to me. To the remnant of mind left me. Well Adams you are super-active & that is good. I say it's good as those prints before me prove.

Andrew will be delighted with the prints for him. He is certainly Old Faithful—A most essential at the Place.

Here's to you Adams. Warmest Greetings.

Your old
Stieglitz

The portrait of Nancy & myself is a rare piece. All of it. And the portrait of me with the O'Keeffe[1]—the Lachaise also there, very, very fine. The Dove—the Marin beautiful—all like good music. Again thanks Adams.

1. *Alfred Stieglitz and Painting by Georgia O'Keeffe, An American Place, New York City, 1944.* (See *Classic Images,* plate 18.)

To Alfred Stieglitz

August 12, 1945

Dear Stieglitz,

I guess this is it: we have 'won' another war—

I think of the Place; of you and Marin and O'Keeffe; of the wonderful days I have had there, the wonderful things I have seen, and the wonderful happenings within me.

The prints you received were just pictures; but the fact that they reflected what you called 'tenderness' is stimulating to me. It is just that quality of the cooperative as against the quality of the Predatory that is going to set the patterns of the world to come. I am doing books on photography now—one book for the London Studio which will expand *Making a Photograph,*[1] and a series of 6 books on technique for Morgan and Lester.[2] In all of these, I am going to strike at the damn fool *U.S. Camera, Popular Photography, Minicam* patterns; I am going to do my best to call attention to the simplicities of environment and method; to "the enormous beauty of the world," as Jeffers writes. Pray for me. The Place must live forever.

Ansel

1. Never published.

2. *The Basic Photo Series* (a series of six books on the technique of photography), Hastings-on-Hudson, N.Y.: Morgan & Morgan, 1948 to 1956.

To Nancy Newhall

Carmel Highlands
September 18, 1945

Dear Nancy:

We are having an incredibly swell time at the Westons' what with Charis racketing on the re-corder and Edward negating my unprintable negatives, getting even with me—and the world is rosy!

It seems that I must bother you with one more little thing. I have written that recording outfit to send out all the extra recordings that are left[1] and I haven't heard from them, so I am wondering if you can get on the 'phone and find out how much I have coming to me in return for the hard-earned wealth I have diverted to their profit.

Edward says, "Jeez, that's one hell of a sentence" to which I agree. I have had four bourbons, two brandies, six cups of coffee and three sandwiches since 9:00 this morning. The little gray home in the West-ons is wracked with sin and Sinegaglia. Edward says, "Wicked old man, isn't he—son of a bitch!" Edward hasn't done a lick of work since we have arrived or for two months previous, to be truthful about it—not since the Newhalls left. Charis says I must admit the Gounod was "rather lovely" but I swear there must be crickets in the recorder—they produce all the harmonies. Ever since the Newhalls left Wildcat Hill has been tamed.

Just a friendly letter without rhyme or reason, like Lewis Carroll's "Hiawatha, the Photographer." I think Edward is still the sexiest son of a bitch I ever knew in my life, including myself.

Love from everybody!
Ansel

1. While he was in New York City in 1945, Adams had a recording made of himself playing the piano, including pieces by Beethoven and Chopin.

To Edward Weston

My dear Edward:

Now that we have left you it has occurred to me what a great opportunity I lost in not leaving Miss Benedict[1] with you, and it is only my high
regard for you, my sympathy and understanding for the already great
burdens which weigh upon your soul that I simply didn't sneak out when
she was talking to Charis. The world would have been a much brighter
place for me.

To see you two both dancing in the exuberance of uninhibited youth
with that glint, that glint, my dear Edward, which I have not seen for
a long time, not seen titillating in those wide and understanding orbs
which have looked through so many 8x10 lenses and at so many women.

It really hurts me to feel my impotence, my inadequacy, my sheer
dullness, my hypocrisy, my all pervading and destructive sin. For you,
my dear Edward, reflect the light of Mexico and not the spine of the
cactus, the surge of the ocean and not the unholy stink of the fish
beach, the simplicity of pyro and none of the confusion of pyrocate-
chin.

It is only the complete consuming loyalty of Miss Benedict that suffers her to stay with me during these trying literary times and what I am
really getting at is—how about a little deal, Edward? I am sure a change
would do Charis a great amount of good. What verve! What form!
What patience! What a chess player! I think to understand your work
better I should have a month or two with Charis and during that time
Miss Benedict could take down your memoirs.

Having nothing further to say on the subject, I await advice from you
at your early convenience.

Hopefully,
Ansel

1. Lee Benedict was Adams' secretary in the mid-1940s.

From Edward Weston

Carmel Highlands
September 1945

Dear Ansel,

A million thanks for all—Package not here yet, but I'm in no hurry. Check enclosed. You overpaid me for the 8x10's used.

I have no E[astman] K[odak] catalogue—So maybe you could tell me if K2 gelatin comes in sheets large enough to use for printing through? I don't want to change from chloride paper while winding up the work on shows.[1] It is now due "whenever convenient." A shock to me!

What is Weston rating on XXX?

I don't feel *too* guilty asking questions since you have "stenog."

I always "glint," by the way, when I dance. Dancing is one of few pleasures I have left in life. Of course I admit needing someone to take down my memoirs, especially a last chapter. But you must admit my dear Adams that a mere male has little to say on *some* subjects.

Love to you—all —
Edward

1. Weston had a major retrospective at the Museum of Modern Art in 1946.

To Edward Weston

Yosemite National Park
September 28, 1945

Dear Edward:

Thanks for letter and check. Insist that the check relates only to 4x5 film. The 8x10 film is exchanged for photo services rendered.

The speed of Tri-X Pan is Weston 160, daylight and Weston 125, tungsten. With your development, proportionate change in speed will apply.

In regard to the Wratten filter you ask about, the largest listed size is a 5-inch square which lists for $2.48; the same in square B glass would be $9.42. I am writing to ask if a sheet of K2 in 8x10 would be available, in gelatin form, of course. The only thing I can see against using a large sheet of gelatin would be that dust and abrasions would accumulate. My suggestion would be that you get the new Eastman Kodak darkroom lamp, a cone-shaped device which hangs down vertically, holding a 5½" diameter safelight. This costs $3, including one Wratten safelight.

My recommendation would be either the Series 6B or Series oo; then if you used a 200 Watt lamp you would have a powerful amber printing light which should work well on Chloride.

Always happy to answer questions if I can do so. Here's to completely frank autobiographies—long may they sizzle!

Ansel

From Edward Weston

Carmel Highlands
October 1945

Ansel, Old Top,

. . . Am on *last* day of signing and spotting show. Many thoughts come to me as I see myself in review; the age-old (my personal age) struggle between mass-production-in-seeing, and the desire for best possible prints—my "precious" side. But more of this via conversation one day. You, with 1000 negs to print will face this same issue! Probably have. . . .

Love all around –

Yrs,
Edward

To Edward Weston

Yosemite National Park
October 14, 1945

Dear Edward:

Congratulations on the completion of the show! It is my problem too—balancing one best possible print against many for distribution. I do think that if the concept is clear and the technique adequate that duplication and superior quality are possible to combine. The more I work with photography, techniques, teaching, lecturing, the more I am impressed with the fundamental fact that what we see is all that really matters. The technical perfection merely conveys what is seen with maximum clarity. It is usually a matter of putting cart before ass.

Glad the pictures arrived okay. If you ever want any of yours—that is, any of you, please do not hesitate to ask for them. I think it was a pretty good showing for Adams during a hectic Carmelite episode.

Best to all,
Ansel

From Edward Weston

Carmel Highlands
November 1945

Dear AA Thanks for writing. And I will be *here* for at least awhile. You will never again see Charis *and* Edward together on Wildcat Hill. Divorce. I must relocate. If you see an old farm-house for sale let me know—E

To Edward Weston

[Late November, 1945]

Dear Edward,

Am hearing some Wagner on the radio; tremendous shapes and tone. Can't help thinking of you at this time. Appreciate your letter; don't expect you to write. Just want you to know that I am here on earth and sympathetic.

I am saying this in all sincerity—not just because I want to speak platitudes. I just thought about some people I know who string platitudes in a glittering chain on the harlot bosom of convention. People who can "feel sorry," or who (with internal moral effort) are "sympathetic." Frankly, I don't feel sorry for you or Charis at all in the deepest sense. I have complete faith that you both would take the appropriate action for the particular circumstance, and who could feel really sorry for that? I do regret the *surface* effects—Carmel, the sea, rocks, the little house with the big mood. But I know that there will be other and more wonderful things and moods—that's why I don't feel basically too bad.

I believe you to be one of the greatest artists of our time—certainly the top man in photography. I mean that in every way. I am proud to

[169]

Sunday

Dear Edward,

Am hearing some Wagner on the radio; tremendous shapes and tone. Cant help thinking of you at this time. Appreciate your letter; don't expect you to write. Just want you to know that I am here on earth and sympathetic.

I am saying this in all sincerity - not just because I want to speak platitudes. I just thought about some people I know who string platitudes in a glittering chain on the harlot bosom of convention. People who can "feel sorry", or who (with internal moral effort) are "sympathetic". Frankly, I dont feel sorry for you or Charis at all in the deepest sense. I have complete faith that you both would take the appropriate action for the particular circumstance, and who could feel really sorry for that? I do regret the surface effects - Carmel, the sea, rocks, the little house with the big mood. But I know that there will be other and more wonderful things and moods - thats why I dont feel basically too bad.

I believe you to be one of the greatest artists of our time - certainly the top man in photography. I mean that in every way. I am proud to know you, to know you are my friend. I am doing what I can in photography; I am doing some real good in my way. But you, in the production of your photographs, your statement of the real vital world, do a hundred times as much as I can ever do. You have been going through a relatively thin phase; I have the feeling now that a new world is opening up for you; a new vision. Hope you understand my temerity to talk about you to you this way. Please get in physical good shape without delay. The sun is shining on all sorts of wonderful things. I wish I could go with you out into the world just as we went to Tenaya. Wonderful for me. See, I'm selfish after all! But I cant go; I have the big problem here. Luck to you, and a real glory.

as ever

know you, to know you are my friend. I am doing what I can in photography; I am doing some real good in my way. But you, in the production of your photographs, your statement of the real vital world, do a hundred times as much as I can ever do. You have been going through a relatively thin phase; I have the feeling now that a new world is opening up for you; a new vision. I hope you understand my temerity to talk about you to you this way. Please get in physical good shape without delay. The sun is shining on all sorts of wonderful things. I wish I could go with you out into the world just as we went to Tenaya. Wonderful for me. See, I'm selfish after all! But I can't go; I have the big problem here. Luck to you, and a real glory.

As ever,
Ansel

From Edward Weston

Carmel Highlands
December 1, 1945

Dear Ansel,

I have read your letter over and over. It moved me deeply. Men should retain the right to weep when occasion demands.

I will not protest your appraisal of me, my work; I *want* to believe everything you say!—even though I don't think *there is ever a "greatest."*

You are right, neither Charis nor I want or need sympathy. We remain to each other best friends.

The present plan is for me to return, take over W. C. Hill, until I can find another location, make an unhurried decision. This is no time to change without much consideration. I hope this will be my last change.

A good Mex. Abrazo—
Edward

—Obviously pen and paper don't match!

[171]

To Nancy Newhall

Dear Nancy,

What a swell letter! Things ARE popping—that's all too apparent. The class opened today at the Art School[1]—more than full! About ten people want it continued as is until the main department opens for the summer session. Ouch! How I am going to do my work and keep my promises is a question that is beginning to trouble me. I find myself a wee bit tired. Getting old? Perhaps. Any loss of enthusiasm? NO!! All in all, I am doing OK. Books are coming along;[2] it's a terrific job—the work is somewhat like a rock-climb; Class three and briskly simple up to the last short, but steep pitch. Then it's Class Six requiring artificial aid, and a night's bivouac. But it's a grand roping down!! I hope Herc is not getting impatient; I want the books to be concise and a real contribution. I also have to make a living while preparing them. It's really quite nice being back in the SF house—my own big piano, the Chinese Drum, the big darkroom, friends, et al. But I do get homesick for the valley, and am distressed to think I will not be there much of the time. Well, so much for me! NOW for N and B!

I wrote Dave a few days ago; he had confidentially sent me the reports, etc.[3] I spared no words in regard to Steichen. I said as far as I am concerned he is the anti-Christ of Photography. I said other things, too.

You know, I feel somewhat as Stieglitz does; I would rather have my prints destroyed than allow them to fall under Steichen's control. I CAN make other, and better, prints; Stieglitz' prints will not be made again. But I wish you could convey to Dick[4] that I seriously desire my prints destroyed—or given to some other institution—rather than have them tainted by that Goddamned advertising scheme set-up. As far as I am concerned, there is NO COMPROMISE!! SO!!!!

I cannot think of anything WORSE than either you or Beaumont staying on under the Steichen-Maloney set-up.[5] No matter what was promised, you should know what the end result would be; unhappiness, frustration, disaster. We can fight the dragons of ignorance, bad taste, pictorialism, and so on—and win out—but we can't fight $100,000.00 and an institutional tidal-wave. Our defeat would be their gain. Better withdraw and maintain dignity. AND WITHDRAW UNDER GREAT AND WIDESPREAD PROTEST. In other words, make it very clear to the world WHY you are withdrawing. You take the most precious thing with you—integrity. . . .

Seriously, you and Beaumont are about the most important focus of creative photography there is today. That's what *I* think! . . .

More soon.

Best from us all,
Ansel

. . .

1. Adams founded and taught at the Department of Photography, California School of Fine Arts, in San Francisco (later the San Francisco Art Institute).

2. *The Basic Photo Series.*

3. Edward Steichen was to become the director of the Department of Photography at the Museum of Modern Art and Newhall was to remain as curator under him.

4. John E. Abbott (Dick), director of the Museum of Modern Art.

5. Steichen counted on the help of Thomas J. Maloney, advertising man and publisher of *U.S. Camera* magazine, who promised to raise $100,000 a year from industry to support the Department of Photography.

From Beaumont Newhall

New York City
March 7, 1946

Dear Ansel:

The Rubicon is passed. The die is cast.

I enclose a copy of my letter of resignation to be effective 30 days after Steichen comes in.

After these months of indecision, after Nancy and I had talked ourselves out about the whole matter, I have at last come to a final and irrevocable decision. The Museum cannot have me if they have Steichen.

There is no need of explaining things to you, for you have urged me very strongly to get out. I think that to temporize and go on half heartedly would be a great mistake. The only possibility that tempted me to give the proposal a trial was that the thing might work. But it won't. Nothing founded on mutual suspicion and distrust will work. I got a good line on Steichen when he came to the Museum, saw Edward's show, and told Edward that he was "taking over." The matter has not been settled except in Steichen's mind. He has not made the slightest effort to find out what we are doing, what the collection is like, what I have in mind doing. The one time we have met during this whole business, apart from chance encounters, was when I asked him to lunch. He wouldn't let me set the date. No. He would call me. The talk was vague and elusive, with much emphasis upon my war work. Not once has he gone out of his way to talk to me. Even at the beginning of the scheme he had two boxes of photos sent to himself at the Museum! Imagine if I were to send a box of prints to the Chicago Art Institute addressed to me, with no word of explanation! No, no. No amount of intellectual rationalization will allow me to bridge that emotional gap.

I feel a hell of a lot better now that the matter is decided. I have a clean feeling inside, while at the same time I regret all that I shall be leaving behind. But there's no reason why we can't build anew, why we can't make a real photo center. One without compromise and without all the petty problems which absorb so much time and energy.

I am returning all the letters which good friends wrote on our behalf. Yours is enclosed. It was a good fight but a hopeless one, because the decision had already been made before Dave or I heard about it. Dave has been swell, and so also has Jim Soby.[1] They see my point and I am sure that they will back whatever we do next.

Future plans. Not to rush into anything. I hope that we can take advantage of your hospitality and that we can work in the school this summer. That depends on Nancy's book and, of course, on just exactly when the resignation will take place. (If the cash is not raised it is not inconceivable that the whole bubble will burst.) So I can't make any definite plans now. I certainly plan to spend a good bit of time *photographing.* I need to get a lot out of my system.

Will write more soon. Your wires were wonderful. You are a grand friend, Ansel, and your support throughout this winter of indecision has been marvelous. Today is a spring day. There is a freshness in the air. I think that the day reflects my decision. It's been a tough winter for both of us spiritually, with this damn reorganization casting a shadow. Now I'm free, and perhaps in a little while I shall be able to create and to work with the directness of purpose the lack of which has bothered me more than I can tell.

Yours as ever,
Beau

1. James Thrall Soby, critic, art collector, and trustee of the Museum of Modern Art.

To Alfred Stieglitz

San Francisco
March 15, 1946

My Dear Stieglitz,

. . . I often wonder just what the devil is the use of anything with the world in such a mess. But then, it would be in a worse mess if we did not try to keep things really alive.

I guess Newhall has given you the news.

I am glad in a way that I am not in New York at the moment, because I am sure I would go on a window breaking spree at the Museum. What a bunch of stupid fools they are. Dave and Beaumont and Nancy have put up a fine fight. But they did a tremendous lot of good, and it is definitely not wasted.

The domination of ego and of Subject seems to be growing; I often think what a thin shallow play the world must appear to those bloated egotistic militaristic predatory bastards that run things. It's the glorification of the *empty*, the crowing over the sterile egg, a blast of trumpets muchly off key.

Well, there is You, and the Place and O'Keeffe and Marin and Dove, and the Idea. Maybe it's more than the world deserves!

I think of you a lot. Please know that.

Wish I could see you
Affectionately,
Ansel

From Edward Weston

Carmel Highlands
[March or April 1946]

Dear Ansel,

Your letter to New York was too important to try an answer there. Even now I don't feel equal to it.

You are now 44—your best, your great, years are to come. Mine did not start until just about 44, after Mexico.

But I learned earlier than you have that too much can't come out of the old engine. You must save it for your creative work.

In fact, dear Sir, as one of the few important photographers of all time, you owe a lot to posterity. Come down and let me tell you more on this important subject, and give you that kick on the old tocus.

I flew back on "Constellation." All about it, about Beau and Nancy, about big party when next we meet –

Love,
Edward

To Edward Weston

April 1946
Wednesday

My Dear Edward,

Just after mailing my first letter to you today I got some exciting news.

It's confidential until April 15th, but I wanted you to know among the very first.

I got the Guggenheim Fellowship! Yep! At last! Generous project—interpretation of the Natural Scene—National Parks and Monuments! Two years—perhaps three.

It's the turning point in Adams Creative work, I am sure.

You and your spirit have had much to do with the direction of things for me. An intangible urge and support. Hope someday to express what I feel.

Best to Brett. Tell him, of course.

Affectionately,
Ansel

From Edward Weston

Carmel Highlands
April 12, 1946

Dear Ansel,

I rejoice with you. This must be a, or the, turning point in your life & work. And you are ripe for it. With you and Brett both having Guggenheims I'm stirred with memories and desires.

I'll be in better shape next time we meet. My date is the 23rd.[1] . . .

Be frank about your portraits. I was not in top form.

Always,

Edward

1. Weston underwent surgery to repair a hernia.

From Alfred Stieglitz

New York City

April 15, 1946

Dear Adams:

I'm delighted. If anyone ever earned the Guggenheim you did. Yes, I am very glad with you.

With warmest greetings,

Your old

Stieglitz

To Stephen Clark[1]

[Editors' note: Words within parentheses in this letter are asides typed in red by Adams on the copy he sent to the Newhalls.]

San Francisco

April 29, 1946

My Dear Mr. Clark,

It is with deepest regret that I am constrained to write you this letter. I write as an artist as well as a spectator of the arts, and also as one who has had a genuine interest in the Museum of Modern Art. My interest in photography has extended beyond the development of my own work; I have been active in promoting the awareness and understanding of creative photography. We both know that an intelligent, critical public is the strongest support of creative expression. With the establishment of the Department of Photography at the Museum of Modern Art I felt a major step forward had been taken to secure photography among the other arts as an important medium of creative expression. I have considered my modest association with the department a privilege and a pleasure, and it was gratifying to watch the department's functions and achievements grow year by year. (Yessir,

[177]

Mr. C.—if it hadn't been for you and your gang we would have continued to grow. And HOW!)

The recent turn of events is a profound shock and disappointment to me; to me it is an expression of a policy which can only undermine and defeat the basic principle on which the Museum was founded, and which reverses the directions of the formative years. (A back bellyflop and I hope it stings like Hell.)

I think it is time an evaluation of the aims and purposes of the museum be made to determine and clarify its function. Perhaps it is I who have been wrong—perhaps the Museum is not interested in *expression* as much as in *illustration*. Perhaps the museum considers the surface more important than the substance. I do not like to believe this; your great exhibitions which have made cultural history should refute my doubts. It seems strange to me that the museum which has shown Marin, Picasso, Weston, Rouault, and many other great creative spirits would at this time turn its back upon creative photography, or, at least, dilute its values. To supplant Beaumont Newhall, who has made such a great contribution to the art through his vast knowledge and sympathy for the medium, with a *regime* which is inevitably favorable to the spectacular and "popular" is indeed a body blow to the progress of creative photography. Hundreds, if not thousands of photographers have looked to the museum's Department of Photography for knowledge, guidance, and inspiration. All types—student and professional, creative and commercial— have looked to the department for the important thing that is not found elsewhere in the world to my knowledge—a distillation of the creative and imaginative elements of the art. No other art requires such penetrating evaluations as does photography; it is the prey of superficial and glamorous showmanship, and it is an "easy" art—up to the crucial level of creative expression whereupon it becomes as intense and difficult as painting and sculpture. Were this not the case there would have been no justification for the Museum of Modern Art to have sanctioned the founding of the department in the first place. (If we had only known! We would have gone to the Frick!!

O MoMA, O MoMA
Wherefore, whyfore, art thee?
If we had known how much boloney
We could have done without thee!)

The great exhibitions of war photography, while excellent representations of tremendously moving and important *subject*, were, after all, objective and illustrative—not creative or contemplative. While they undoubtedly benefited the museum in publicity and attendance I believe they would have been far more effective in Grand Central Station—where even more persons could have benefited from them. I would believe it the function of the museum to exhibit those particular photographs which contain the creative potential, for it is this potential that should permeate and strengthen everything. Mistakes have been made, of course—as in any other department of the museum—but I can see no basic criticism on any other grounds than failure to "play to the gallery" and to compromise with the sterile world of photographic salons, magazines, and manufacturers. *(and all the other lousy bastards that get in the progressive hair!)*

As I have received no notification of termination of the Advisory Committee on Photography—to which I had the honor of appointment by you—I have presumed it still exists. If so, I would be interested in knowing why the advice of this committee was not requested in this momentous decision to reverse policy. If the committee ever had a legitimate function, this was it. Of course, I am sure you will appreciate my request that my resignation from the Committee—if it exists—be effective immediately. I tender it to you with deep regret. (If this is a tender you should see the Lokomotyve!)

Let me assure you that this letter is written with no intention of praising or condemning anyone on any personal basis. My protest is purely objective. You are trading gold for brass. Believe me, I am deeply concerned for the future potency of the Museum of Modern Art. (Well, who said anything about potency??)

With sincere personal regards,
(ho hum)
Ansel Adams
(yep. compromised again!)

(needless to say the additions in red above did not appear on the original letter to the Clark Crow.) . . .

(High Ho!! Believe it or not the EASTMEN KULAK—I MEAN KODAK—CO. ARE PAYING ME 250.00 per shot for at least three 8 x 10 Kodachromes of Waterfalls mit Rainbows!—No discount if there ain't no rainbow.—Some new experimental film HUshhhhhhhhhh. So, next week I go off to that hole in the ground Yosemite and click some shutters. Wish you were along. I think of thee and your own personal May Day. Curators of the World UNITE!! . . .)

1. Stephen Clark, president and chairman of the Board of Trustees of the Museum of Modern Art.

To Beaumont Newhall

San Francisco
July 16, 1946

[Telegram]

RUMOR HAS IT STIEGLITZ DEATH. CLARIFY. LOVE.

ANSEL ADAMS

From Nancy Newhall

New York City
July 16, 1946

[Telegram]

STIEGLITZ DIED SATURDAY OF STROKE AFTER HEART ATTACK. CRE-
MATED SUNDAY. O'KEEFFE HERE. LETTER ON WAY. LOVE.

NANCY

From Nancy Newhall

New York City
Monday, July 15, 1946

Dear Ansel,

A strange week. It's one thing to realize that a Stieglitz may die at any minute, and another to come into the Place one Saturday afternoon and find him alone with a heart attack. He had called the doctor himself. No one responsible near—nobody at all, until we came. We wanted him to be quiet, but he wanted to talk, in pain, and with a racing pulse. We stayed until the girl O'Keeffe left in charge happened in. I went back later. The Place was darkened as much as the light would let it. He was worriedly dictating letters. Sunday we went over, with roses for him, but felt we had better not respond to his invitation to talk. Then, on Wednesday, as we were sitting at dinner, with the [Henri] Cartier-Bressons, and Paul and Virginia [Strand], just back from the Pacific, in walked Zoler and Melquist[1] with the news that Stieglitz had had a stroke and was unconscious in an oxygen tent at Doctors' Hospital. O'Keeffe got the telegram shopping in town, drove straight to the airfield, flew until grounded, then took a train. Dorothy[2] came down from Wood's Hole. Up there in the hospital they became reconciled, those two, and took turns in that long vigil, with Henwar[3] helping. Stieglitz never regained consciousness; died at 1:30 Saturday morning. Dorothy, watching, said he was still very beautiful, and somehow remote, with the inevitable. We did not get the news of his death till Sunday morning, deep in Long Island, having left Saturday, early, for a vagabond trip, with the news that he was doing less well. The cremation took place at eleven-thirty Sunday. Paul, who was there, said it was strange and sad. About twenty people. O'Keeffe, strained but under control. Dorothy utterly shattered, weeping, even over Steichen. Not a word was said.

This morning, back in town, I finally got hold of Dorothy. O'Keeffe had just called her, saying that it was all right for her to leave her things at the Place until she, O'K, should return in the fall, but then she wanted absolute control of the Place. As for the lease, Stieglitz had let Dorothy take care of it only because he and all his family liked making things difficult. In a little while, he would have let O'K take it. Dorothy's relation to Stieglitz she considered absolutely disgusting. That people should go on so many years wrangling! Dorothy made a few heartbroken responses, and then was quiet under this malignant whipping. Her only response can be a *Twice a Year* for everyone who cared for Stieglitz to make a statement in. Obviously, O'Keeffe will have no more of the Place as Stieglitz conceived it. She said he wanted her to send all his things to an institution. Dave called O'K, asking if he might help; she said she didn't want to see or talk to anyone just now; later in the week, maybe. Meanwhile, she had a lot to do and Steichen was helping her. I thought this all over, my sympathies utterly with Dorothy, but realizing O'K's strain and remembering that when she came, with Dave and Sally [McAlpin], to our party on May first—celebrating our leaving the museum—she looked through the door, saw Dorothy, screamed, and got back in the elevator. To make no motion toward O'K at this time would be to preclude any possibilities of working together, and close the door to the greatest photographs ever made. I went over with flowers to offer my hands and time for any service, determined that if Steichen was there, I would work alongside him at anything they set me to, quietly. The door to O'Keeffe's room was closed. The strange little terrified woman—maybe a nurse—said she would call O'K, but that she was not well. I left the flowers and my message and came away; the outbreak to Dorothy may well have been prelude to one of those breakups that happen to O'Keeffe.

Henwar comes to dinner Thursday; perhaps we shall know more then. The Place, as a Place, is dead, with Stieglitz. But what he was, what he spent his life trying to do and to say, that is greater than our little feuds. It is up to us to carry it on, each of us, with all we have to give.

And what about you? How was the trip to Yosemite, and the *Fortune* job, with the slipped vertebrae? How do you take to corsets? Hope to heaven you'll not need to spend long weeks in hospital with weights and pulleys hanging over you. Glad Minor's[4] there at the School. Give him our love. This is a letter for him too. . . .

Later

After seeing Cartier's prints—magical! He seems to pluck out of the air these plastic, very human relationships. The severe standards we set ourselves vanish; they do not apply to these. And yet Henri is as intense a purist as Edward. A guy like a crystal. Keen to have you and Minor meet/know him and see his stuff.

Dorothy called; O'K had called her again, after seeing her lawyer. The essence: hands-off after November 1 still in force, but happily a new note of dignity has been introduced. Situation not so raw as before. . . .

How's Minor feeling? Brisk again, now he can look at the Pacific?

Love to everybody. And cosset those corsetted vertebrae!

Nancy

1. Emil Zoler, painter and sometime assistant to Stieglitz; Jerome Melquist, art critic.

2. Dorothy Norman, writer, photographer, and social activist, best known for her writings on the life and works of Alfred Stieglitz. In 1932 she founded *Twice a Year*, a nonprofit journal devoted to literature, the arts, and civil liberties.

3. Henwar Rodakiewicz, cinematographer.

4. Minor White, photographer, recommended by the Newhalls, joined Adams to teach photography at the California School of Fine Arts.

San Francisco
Wednesday, July 17, 1946

My Dear Nancy,

Thanks for your wire and for the letter which came today. The rumor
was about, but I had heard nothing positive. Had a hunch and wired
you. Should be sad. Am not. Knew it was coming. Knew he was not a
happy man. Am not sad for him, but for the world. Very sad for myself;
I loved Stieglitz in a strange, remote way, and, again, I loved him in a
close personal way—not so much as a father but as a fabulous uncle! I
can't define it better, although I know it sounds thin. It will be very hard
for me when I realize I cannot write him some thought, some comment
or just a line to tell him I am thinking of him. It will be very hard when
the time comes to make a decision and know that he will not be there to
approve or disapprove.

However, perhaps he knew all along that he would always be there,
and that it makes little difference if he be in flesh or spirit.

I am subdued by the weight of our obligation. We asked for it; we
have lived towards it. I hope I will not fail you and Beau; and I am positive you will not fail all the rest. I'll help, of course, but I know the evaluations are of your domain.

The emotional pressure suggests many words; I have nothing to say.
Just like there is nothing much to say when the moon goes down or a precious letter burns. I want to write everybody—Henwar, Dorothy, Andrew, Marin. What can I say? I think I know what I can do best; I will
make a print of a small new negative I have that says many things I want
to say, and I will send copies to the closest friends. (Originals, of course.)
I am not thinking too clearly today.

But will you tell Dave, and Marin, and Andrew, and Dorothy that I
am thinking of them, just as I am thinking of you and Beaumont and
the big task ahead. And Henwar, of course.

The feuding is ridiculous—actually scandalous. I despair at the
thought of Steichen getting his claws in on the kill, as it were. I am convinced O'K is psychopathic. It's all lousy, stinko, cheap and dreadful. It
has only one thing in common: it's big—it's as big in nastiness as Stieglitz
was big in greatness. I suggest we forget it; have nothing to do with it. If
all of Stieglitz' things were destroyed Stieglitz would be just as potent,
just as inevitable.

As I write this I feel I cannot avoid writing the others too. I am imposing on you to forward the enclosed; thanks. I do not have their summer addresses.

Me, I'm OK. Minor is OK. More later. School fine. Much to say.
Here's to you and Beau and Paul!

Wish I were around to make some crepe suzettes!

Ansel

Minor is a perfectly swell egg. We talk of you often. Wish you were both
here right now. Tell C[artier]-B[resson] I want to meet him and that I
send my best wishes. How about a show of his things here at the San
Francisco Museum? I know Morley[1] would be all for it.

1. Grace Morley, director of the San Francisco Museum of Modern Art.

To Eldridge T. Spencer[1]

Yosemite National Park
[Late 1946]

Dear Ted,

Jeannette[2] arrived at our place this morning and we had a good short
visit. She gave me your note. Much appreciated.

Know how hard it is to discuss things by letter—hard enough in conversation, when it relates to emotional subjects. . . .

I think that the students do reflect my "influence," and—joking aside—
maybe I should stop fussing around and just be an "influence"! Actually
what has happened is this—by some trick of fate I developed my work
at the time of a general Renaissance of straight photography, and I
happened to be one of the very few who were articulate in writing,
teaching, and lecturing. My rationale of the exposure-development procedures [the Zone System] certainly struck a new note in mechanical
approach. I did not invent anything—just restated facts in terms of practical use. I am sure anyone with normal intelligence could have accomplished as much—but it just happened to be me who walked into the
arena at the right time.

Within twelve weeks most of the students could command basic mechanical problems; at the end of the first semester they were more ad-

vanced than I had dared to hope—mechanically and aesthetically. *Technically*—(technique—the ability to apply mechanical and aesthetic factors)—they were also quite far ahead. When I say that our class is outstanding and advanced in relation to any other photo class I can think of, I mean it in a very objective, impersonal way. I think you know me well enough to discount personal conceit. . . .

My contribution to the general advance of creative photography is second only to Stieglitz'. When I get the technical books off my chest I will have rounded out ten years' extrovertal activity which I am sure justifies my concentrating on creative work. All the time that I have been busy lecturing, teaching, writing and general propagandizing my good friend Weston (and others) have been making magnificent pictures. At the end of our respective lives I am sure the creative work has done more for photography than all the organizational preaching and teaching. I still have time to re-assert myself as a creative artist and do a bit of practicing what I preach. My own record in creative work is much thinner than it should be. . . .

Yours, with fire in the eye (not exactly bloodshot, but glittering with wrath).

Affectionately,

Ansel

me

1. Eldridge (Ted) T. Spencer, architect and president of the San Francisco Art Association, had invited Adams to set up the Department of Photography at the California School of Fine Arts.

2. Jeannette Dyer Spencer, architect and wife of Ted Spencer.

To Beaumont and Nancy Newhall

San Francisco

January 23, 1947

BEAUMONT—NANCY

I have burned many bridges behind me; commercial obligations fulfilled, most work done, start Saturday on my first Guggenheim trip. What a feeling!

Edward is here with me—not in condition to go along, but a moving spirit as always. Had a good session with the Doc here, and MAY have his final operation up here. He *must* get back in shape. Not good at all—physically and psychically. . . .

I will go to Death Valley for at least a week—then on through Joshua Tree National Monument to Phoenix and Tucson. Then on to El Paso, Big Bend, Carlsbad, and White Sands—then on to Santa Fe, Taos, Shiprock, Grand Canyon, and S.F.

The invitation to join me is more potent than ever. . . .

Have a wonderful stationwagon set-up. Plenty of room. Wonderful country.

PLEAUZE COME!

Best from us all,
Ansel

P.S. Wanted Edward to come on the trip, but he feels he must get fixed up completely soon. It was hard for him to refuse, but quite nostalgic this afternoon—his giving advice and suggestions and enthusiasms for the Death Valley area.

What a guy! Wonderful work he did for Eastman! in Kodachrome!

To Minor White

Twenty-nine Palms
California
[1947]

Dear Minor,

. . . I am a bit worried about you. First let me say that I think you are doing a grand job in every way. You are, in fact, doing too much. I know, because I am cursed with the same problem of over-production. Just figure out what the kids [at the California School of Fine Arts] are getting in relation to any other photo school! Don't squeeze it too hard. I am more interested in the quality of the work and of the thinking that will evidence itself through this project—rather than in sheer volume of work. If they miss some of the divisions of the project, don't worry. What they get and accomplish creatively will remain the important thing. Take it more easy, please. You have several years of teaching and working out your *magnum opus*—and after that you must become a creative photographer! You are too good to waste upon the academic air. . . .

[186]

As for me, I had not realized how far I had drifted from the "creative condition." But I have exposed eight dozen films and think I have some of the best stuff I have ever done. Teach, it's marvelous! Death Valley is SOMETHING! No use talking about it—it's just a tremendous nest of photographic opportunity. Interesting to recognize many of Edward's pets, and also interesting to figure how I would do them my way.

Looking back on the immediate past, I wonder how I avoided blowing up, dismembering myself emotionally and physically, with the pressure of work I brought upon myself. NEVER AGAIN! The big wide horizon seems to be actually opening up in a clear, potent way.

The earth looks very good indeed; the forms of nature—once they are integrated on the magic rectangle of the film—satisfy me completely. The fussiness of Aesthetics, of Modern, of Mode, of Non-objectivity, of the abstract, of the surrealist's pregnancies—it all seems remote, actually *outdated!* A long line of rising land is so much in itself; the hint of clear air, and the organic life of clouds—well, I guess that's for me from now on. At least—that's what I think now!

Peek in on the family once in a while,[1] and assure them they have no cause to worry about me—I am safer than ever where I am.

Give my warmest greetings to the class and assure them I am thinking of them, and very eager to see the results of the project work. We got a swell bunch—really!

Best to you and Jones,[2] et al.

Don't be too good!

As ever,
Ansel

1. White was living in Adams' home in San Francisco, next door to his parents.

2. Pirkle Jones, student of Adams and White, who worked as photographic assistant to Adams from 1951 to 1953.

To Francis Farquhar

Big Bend National Park, Texas
February 16, 1947

Dear F.P.F. et al:

Whatever you hear about Big Bend not being of National Park status, please discount it. It is one of the grandest places I have seen, and has a magical mood that, in my mind, puts it among the top really great areas. You would be nuts about it because it is undeveloped and clearly shows what a park could be if the damned predators (not wildlife) could be kept at bay. . . .

Have visited and photographed in the following areas:

1. Death Valley: most impressive, especially if you get off the usual track. Public service bad, but out of National Park Service jurisdiction. Should be bought up. . . .

2. Joshua Tree N[ational]M[onument]: Greatly under-rated area. "Wonderland of Rocks" area stupendous. Impressive mood. Have always received negative reports; why—I don't know. Think it tops. And well run by NPS [National Park Service].

3. Organ Pipe N.M.: Considerably over-rated to my mind. Not sufficiently developed to take advantage of possible high spots. As a National Park it is ridiculous. But there is lots of pressure to make it one.

4. Saguaro, N.M. Should be given back to the Indians. I got my best Saguaro pictures in Organ Pipe, N.M.

5. White Sands, N.M.: Fantastic, specific. Excellent headquarters, well operated. Publicity bad. I resent the phrase "inspirational gypsum"! That appears in the only guidebook available (excepting the NPS leaflet).

6. Carlsbad N.P. . . . Park is one of the most lucrative, and yet they cannot get enough personnel to properly operate it. THOUSANDS of people visit it. It should run on an 18 hour schedule with continuous trips. Pressure to reinstate "Rock of Ages" ceremony. I protest. Some ceremony could be developed with perhaps a passage of good music. But to tie in the hymn with the Rock is the last word of sentimentality and goo. . . .

Concession not so hot. Food so-so. Curios awful—the familiar booze bottle well in evidence, "Cool-warm-getting hotter—WOW—Carlsbad National Park!"

Approach one of the really terrible evidences of rampant resortism; Whites' city is a milestone in bad taste. Only alternative is to change entrance to by-pass this setup. Most people associate it with the Park. Big Bend N.P. just wonderful. . . .

Affectionate greetings to all,
Ansel

[188]

To Eldridge T. Spencer

Tucson
February 28, 1947

Dear Ted,

. . . A very definite change in Adams' outlook on Things in General has raised its head over the horizon and firmly planted its feet on the pillar of creative infatuation. (Block that metaphor!) In other words, the creative aspects of photography have finally triumphed, and Adams— always, as you say, a belligerent, raucous individual—has now become an extremely aggressive self-perpetuating chain-reaction (let the neutrons fall where they may)! I shall probably be extremely unpleasant to live with. But I have made up my mind that I am going to be a photographer—an artist, in the best sense of the term. I am afraid that Committees, Executives, Cooperation (such as it was) has now passed into the Age of Determination. (If you have an effective remedy for a black eye, will you tip me off?—I will probably need it soon!)

To soften the shock of this seismic self-revelation, let me assure you that I have two perfectly wonderful new jokes which I shall transmit as soon as I see you. . . .

I have every confidence in Minor White. His coming was literally a gift from Heaven! I do not think the Board realizes how few and far between photography instructors are—that is, men that will support the ideals set forth in your general program. . . .

I have been thinking a lot of late of that Thing called Art, and my thoughts in the main have not been too pleasant. Sometimes I think I have a Prophet complex, because I am constantly looking for the quality of prophecy in Art. That thing which is concerned more with life and the world in both Now and in the time to come—not just in the Now. I guess I get that to a certain extent from Stieglitz. Most of what I see seems more mere decoration than profound expression—and directed towards the most artificial and fragile elements of our culture. What I call the Natural Scene—just Nature—is a symbol of many things to me, a never-ending potential. I have associated the quality of health (not merely in the physiological or psychological sense) with the quality and moods of sun and earth and vital normal people. The face of most Art reminds me of a human face, bewildered, weak-eyed, with a skin of pallor and pimples. The relatively few authentic creators of our time possess a resonance with eternity. I think this resonance is something to fight for—and it takes tremendous energy and sacrifice. . . . Affectionate greetings to you and Jeannette and the gals.[1]

As ever,
Ansel

1. The Spencers had two daughters.

To Beaumont and Nancy Newhall

Thursday, July 17, 1947
FLASH!!!

MMA news release 47715-28——For immediate release

EDWARD STEICHEN APPOINTED HEAD OF PHOTOGRAPHY AT MUSEUM OF MODERN ART

Just got one copy of 3 p. mimeographed release. Here are the salient points.

Appointment becomes effective immediately. Rockefeller[1] says, "Museum exhibitions where photography is not the theme but the medium through which great achievements and great moments are graphically presented."

The first large exhibition—Great News Photographs. Before the end of 1948 the museum plans to present a major thematic exhibition on the order of "Road to Victory" involving the use of enormous photomurals and dramatic installation. Theme: "Photography in the Service of Science in War and Peace."

Exhibitions planned for the next 2 or 3 years—work of young American photographers who stress the documentary approach—international exhibition of new directions and tendencies which will include abstract and non-representational photography and transcendentalism in photography.

Steichen is quoted: ". . . Navy combat photographer—took photographs—marvelous photographs—of the boredom, the agony and stark tragedy of sudden death and mutilation as well as the dramatic and spectacular images of embattled machines. I hope to attain that same sense of unity through peace-time photographers so that in the end we shall have a picture of America: the warm sweetness of its homes, the greatness of its industries, the productivity of its farms, the

[190]

vastness of its natural resources, the sweep of its landscape, its big cities, its small towns, and above all the faces of the people. I stress the importance of photography as an art. It is the artist in photography who beyond his own creative achievement establishes standards, produces new influences and new uses of the medium in all human endeavor, whether it be in the service of science, education or communication."

IN SHORT EVERYTHING THAT WE FEARED***THE COMPLETE ENGULFING OF PHOTOGRAPHY AS YOU AND I AND N SEE IT AND FEEL IT INTO A VAST PICTURE ARCHIVE OF *SUBJECTS*.

Ansel

1. Nelson Rockefeller, president of the Board of Trustees, Museum of Modern Art.

From Philippe Halsman[1]

New York City
December 1, 1947

Dear Ansel,

I love your pictures and, when I met you, I started to love you too.

In this spirit of love—unhappy love naturally—I am writing you this letter. I think I owe you an explanation of what I didn't agree with at your lecture.[2]

I don't know whether you are conscious of the fact that you created the impression of belonging to the people who can be called "Holders of the Truth." It seemed to me that in your opinion there was only one kind of photography that was legitimate and meaningful: yours and that of people sharing your views. You named several great photographers. They were Weston, Strand, Dorothea Lange and once you included also Lisette Model. I agree that they and you are masters. But why only this kind of photography? Doesn't it make photography very narrow and monotonous?

How about people like Cartier-Bresson, Brassaï, Blumenfeld, Mill, Gene Smith, Kertész, Goro, Weegee, Wessel, Eisenstaedt, even Dahl-Wolfe, Hoyningen-Huené etc. Doesn't their work make photography richer and more exciting?

[191]

You have said that you have yet to see a good picture made with flash. This statement throws the entire press photography and half of the magazine photography in the waste basket.

You finished your speech by inviting the Photo League to show to people the right kind of pictures and so to educate their taste. That is quite an order. I have seen soldiers buying and reading Superman and Batman comics. Can you educate their taste by showing them pictures made by Weston or Strand? I think that, before educating their taste, one should rather work on their education purely and simply. The better taste will come then as a natural consequence.

I have discussed your lecture with other people. Some of them told me that in reality you are interested in every branch of photography. But you didn't give this impression in your lecture.

I want to repeat that your lecture was interesting and stimulating. But, Ansel, your above mentioned opinions leave me confused and bewildered.

With many kind regards and in the hope to see you when you return to New York,

Cordially,
Philippe

1. Philippe Halsman, photographer.
2. Adams lectured in New York City to The Photo League, an organization of photographers committed to the use of documentary photography for social change.

To Philippe Halsman

San Francisco
December 8, 1947

My Dear Halsman,

I am very glad you wrote me that letter; 1st, because it was good to hear from you and 2nd, I appreciate the opportunity to straighten some things out, and 3rd—I think such letters as these between us can do much to clear out the cobwebs! . . . Here goes!

It was very far from my intention that people would agree with me. Everywhere I go the whole business of photo-talks is based on "agreement." I intentionally waved a chip around just to stir up some exciting discussion. Some of it was fine, some not too helpful. Anyway, I have no illusions about pleasing the gang!

Jezuz H. Kriste! I ain't no "Holder of the Truth" but I do have very powerful convictions about the element of *expression* and beauty (there should be another term) and I feel that most contemporary photo statements suffer because they lack that intangible element of expressive quality—appropriate to the content and purpose of the statement. Believe me, I can fizzle more disastrously then anyone I know—and every time I have fizzled it was because that intangible quality was bypassed.

It is entirely my fault that I gave the impression of limited appreciation of various types of photography and photographers. I mentioned the ones you list because I do feel more sympathetic to what they do than to most photographers. But I think you will discover, if you ask about, that I think Model is one of the real tops—I like her much better than Cartier-Bresson because I think she makes no pretense of any statement other than *direct* and C-B imposes a certain sophistication and oblique approach that requires much better quality of image than he produces. I know little of Brassaï, Kertész, and Goro; some things I have seen impress me tremendously. I think Gene Smith is one of the tops—as photographer and person. I keep my tongue in my cheek about Weegee—certainly about Blumenfeld. Dahl-Wolfe and Hoyningen-Huené are slick and competent, Wessel and Eisenstaedt (especially the latter) really accomplished workers. But here is my point—it depends what you look for; do you look for photographers who expand themselves in the manner of their chosen niches—who keep repeating themselves and the client's ego and material needs—or do you look for that difficult-to-describe quality of creative force and introspection—the affirmation of life, as Stieglitz called it? Personally I am distressed at the lack of depth in most contemporary photography. On the other hand, I am perfectly willing to admit that perhaps this "lack of perceived depth" may be my own limitation—not the photographers'. But I feel the question should be posed—and let the chips fall where they may.

I think I am a bit mis-quoted about "never having seen a good picture made with flash." On the other hand, I may have made the statement, but I certainly do not mean it in the general sense. What I would like to have said was this—that I have seldom seen a flash photograph that seemed to realize the quality of the illusion of reality—the illusions of substance and light. I am usually over-conscious of the impression of flash itself—of the position of the lights, of the strange harsh luminosity and shadow-edge—of the "artificial" mood. Being a "natural" light person I am especially sensitive to artificial connotations. . . .

I certainly intended by my statement that the League should show people the right kind of pictures, to mean that the best of all creative and functional types of work should be shown. But it is not enough to merely show it—the work must be fully integrated with contemporary problems of life—sociological, technological, expressive, journalistic, etc. . . .

Perhaps I have too much faith in people, but I refuse to agree with the contemporary opinion—stressed by advertisers and publishers—that people are morons. I have had some—many, in fact—exciting proofs that almost any type of person will respond to a true, direct statement. He will not respond to a veiled, symbolic, esoteric statement—but the truth of things simply stated with emotional force gets a terrific response.

I have said, and I say again, that I feel the non-objective approach to art in any form represents nothing more than an escape of the inconsequential elite from the very consequential problems of the world. The Ben Shahn show at the Museum of Modern Art gave me more confidence in painting than I have had for years. The "expression of self" seems ridiculous in these times. But, to me, the paintings of Marin, the photography of Strand, Lange, Smith, Edward Weston, and others contain the much needed quality of "universality" and depth of meaning that is so vitally needed today. I am concentrating on the Natural Scene —the implications of the qualities of Nature. The National Parks provide the means by which millions can contact the aspects of the natural world. The effect on these millions is emotional and symbolic; it will take centuries to fully realize the potential. But that is only one phase of photography; I would be a complete damn fool to ever think there are not endless fields to explore, endless ways to advance understanding and spiritual awareness. But I can't accept the mere following of the ritual as truly representing the Messages.

Well, I hope to see you again in January! Hope the above clarifies things a bit. But I need a lot of clarifying, too!

Best to you and yours,

As ever,
Ansel Adams

To Beaumont Newhall

Yosemite National Park
March 15, 1948

Dear Beaumont:

Hope Nancy is OK now. Naturally worried about ANY operation. Edward in not-too-good state. Sometimes wonder if a strong fatalism such as his prevents any real outside help. He resents Science, Doctors, etc. A fundamentally strange contradiction. Revealing, to say the least. Distressing, to say the most. I have a strange mood of late which I can only describe as fundamental; I suddenly am aware of a deep weakness in art and its relation to humanity. The last trip to New York seemed to solidify this mood. . . . You are doing a swell job with your books. You are tops in your field. You should be making more out of it. I am tops in my particular field, and making damn little. There is something wrong somewhere. We are liberals; we try to be understanding. We build our liberalism on certain ideologies, only to find that when the ideologies are expressed in practical terms we have power politics, insincerity, domination. I am convinced that now I am heartily sick of Art for Art's sake. It seems to lead nowhere but to anesthesia. The world is in one delightful hell of a mess. . . .

Made some exciting snow details today. One beautiful storm; still not enough to relieve the drought. . . .

I started out to express myself morbidly and then work into the Steichen business, and I got side-tracked by dinner, et al, and forgot to include it.

Anyway, Steichy wires me about "post-war" photography show, and would like six of my Guggenheim pictures included.

First reaction: to Hell with it.

Second reaction, that would be rather stupid.

His wire said "ANY SIZE YOU WANT."

First impression is to pull off all the 3 x 6 foot enlargements from the walls and send them on.

Second impression is to make six swell prints and see what he does with them.

If I turn him down, he wins.

If I cooperate, he wins. . . .

WHAT DO YOU THINK I SHOULD DO? Every time I think of how lousy you were treated I get mad as hell. I thoroughly dislike the

guy. My only defense seems to be to come through with superior stuff.
JEZUZJEZUZJEZUZ K.

Whoops.
Ansel

From Beaumont Newhall

New York City
March 18, 1948

Dear Ansel,

Your concern is understandable. In these days everything seems unstable and one feels tossed about on a stormy sea which promises to become stormier still. The rattling of the saber, the thumping of the mailed fist upon the shield, the awful realization that peace is not here but an armed truce—these uncertainties strike deep, and they affect every one of us. Only by keeping integrity within one's own work can there be relief. Perhaps that is why I find it necessary to spend so many hours on the text of my book;[1] for I do not feel satisfied within myself until every fact is made secure by documentation, and until I feel that I have made the past come to life again in the perspective of the human problems and needs and drives of men. The book should have been done long ago, could have been done already and it would have been a good job. But it has to be better than that, and I can only hope that what I have put so much of myself into will meet with some kind of response. Nancy would tell you the same. Not that this is new to you, for you feel the same. We are tops, as you say: whether we will ever make out of our activities anything comparable to what goes in is another matter. So much depends not on the product, but on the ability to sell. You manage that better than either Nancy or I. Certainly art for art's sake is a dead end: art for humanity's sake is a mission which right now seems more imperative than ever, and in your photographs and in your books (I am thinking particularly of the John Muir book[2] and of the positive emotional reactions which it has evoked) you are contributing in full measure.

About Steichen's request. He asked Paul the same thing, and I will tell you as I told Paul that in my opinion the only thing to do is to let him have your best. To hold off, as you say, is his victory by default and it does nobody any good. To send him what you think he would like, only bet-

[196]

ter, is in a sense compromise. No. Send him fine prints, mounted as you would present them, with a letter specifying that the prints are to be shown the way you would like to have them shown. If he misrepresents your work, THEN you can complain. But it seems to me that he is genuinely anxious to show the work as the photographers want it shown and that he is carrying on the job really in the tradition which I established. ... If my rebellion gave Steichen pause to think and led him to this policy of showing work as is and not editing it and, so to speak, republishing it in terms of his idea of exhibition prints, then my actions bore fruit. And it is important that your prints and Paul's and Edward's should be seen today, right now, here.

Nancy is home! Came back yesterday on Saint Patrick's Day, and now is up and around, arranging the beautiful flowers that Dave and Sally[3] just sent over.

Wish you were here to celebrate! Drink meant nothing to me all last week but yesterday, with Nancy home and all, two highballs and a wonderful dinner (pardon me, for I made it) sent me to sleep in the most inhospitable way to treat a wife home after a week! More soon.

Ever,
Beau

1. Beaumont Newhall. *The History of Photography*, New York: Museum of Modern Art, 1949.
2. *Yosemite and the High Sierra*, edited by Charlotte E. Mauk with the selected words of John Muir, Boston: Houghton Mifflin Company, 1948.
3. Sally Sage McAlpin, wife of David McAlpin.

To Edward Weston

Matsonia[1]
April 10–14, 1948

Dear Edward,

I am desolated that I did not manage to see you or even to phone you before I left for Hawaii.

I think of you a lot. I wonder how I can help in any way to boost you through these particular days. I am sure you will be 100% but it is distressing to me to have you bothered with distracting things of the flesh. I had the scare of my life in NY, and I know what it means to worry about the future. Fortunately for me it was a temporary effect of too much fatigue, but I know I have to be careful in every respect. In your case, we are all anxious that you get the best possible advice, and from what I hear, much can be done to overcome the condition.[2] I ask you— we all ask you—to do everything possible for yourself, for it would be a great misfortune for our Eddie to be running on five cylinders instead of eight as usual. I think a lot about your work, and I feel that, if you care for yourself, the next ten years might well be the most profound and intense period of all. The scope and dignity of the last things I have seen are breathtaking.

I have been thinking about myself, too. But chiefly about the condition of photography. All art is in the same raft as it were, but the art we care most about is in a precarious condition. Nancy wrote me about the museum show—Steichen's latest effort—and it seems that again the method of exhibition takes precedence over what is exhibited. Just as I expected. Impact without revelation. You and I and most of our gang are devoted to the Democratic ideal. Yet, how few are doing anything about it. You and Strand are active; I am ashamed of my feeble political efforts. I think, however, that perhaps the greatest service we could make to this ideal would be to *photograph it;* not esoterically or too personally, but dynamically and with concession to wide-spread distribution of our statement. It's so easy to say it should be done, and very difficult to say just what the doing would be. . . .

My Guggenheim must be finished this year, and I will be on the road most of the time. Did I tell you I got the Guggenheim for the second time—1949—to complete the book?[3] Perhaps then I can do a little teaching, etc. but for this year it is out. I wish I was Bachrach[4] for about six months and make enough money to be Adams for six years!

I have a hunch I will not be happy in Hawaii, and will be constantly pining for Alaska and the North country. Anyway, I shall think of thee and will do my best to convalesce from Lackanookee!

Best to all.

Affectionate thoughts for you,
Ansel

Motto for the Day: O Southern Comfort Me!
　Log of a lens leer!
　No. 2 Sunday
. . . Lost 2 on the mileage pool.

Monday

Lost six dollars on everything combined.

Tuesday

Regained four dollars, lost eight dollars.

Not so good, Adams! Man at same table in dining room sunk $350.00 and still smiles about it. A great stink seems to pervade the air as we approach the Islands. It is a matter of mood. I am wondering if the place is as bad as I expect it to be?

But the ocean is perfectly beautiful. The weather has been gray most of the time, but I hope for better conditions tomorrow.

me

Wednesday AM

Finally arrived. Jeeze the ocean is big. It's been like living in the Waldorf Astoria while someone was shaking Manhattan.

1. Adams sailed aboard the steamship *Matsonia* to Hawaii, where he photographed national parks and monuments for his Guggenheim project.

2. Weston's illness had been diagnosed as Parkinson's disease, which explained the recent years of physical deterioration.

3. The photographs Adams made on his two Guggenheim Fellowships were published in a book, *My Camera in the National Parks*, Yosemite National Park: Virginia Adams, and Boston: Houghton Mifflin Company, 1950.

4. Bradford Bachrach, New York portrait photographer.

From Edward Weston

Carmel Highlands
April 1948

Dear Ansel,

Your letter meant a lot to me—they always do. But I don't like to have my friends distressed about my condition. Whatever has happened to me, I've brought upon myself, and only I can lift myself out of the abyss. You will be glad to know that I'm seeing a doctor tomorrow, armed with the literature and letters from Nancy & you.

That part of your letter devoted to photography is full of meat. Wish I could pour myself out to you in return, but alas, even this short note is a laborious effort.

[199]

Good news of the Guggenheim renewal. I hope you will do the best work of your life. I feel you will. Mine was done between the years 45–60.

Alas Lackanookee!

Love,
Edward

To Virginia Adams

Honolulu
April 1948

Dearest,

Slightly worried over not hearing from you.

Are you OK?

Still fussing around. Seeing the Supt. tonight, and will have plans made for trips to the other islands. . . .

Two trips around the island so far. Only a few pictures.

I am afraid it is, to me, a damn monotonous place. The skies are not clear blue, the clouds too many and formless, the architecture pretty lousy, the people extremely dull (with a few exceptions), and the foliage disappointing. Only the sea comes up to the brag, but the damn volcanic rock shores have little variety. The Carmel Highlands are infinitely more beautiful.

I am hoping the other islands will have more to offer. Otherwise I can't expect to get much exciting photography.

Loads of love to you and Mike and Anne. Please write soon.

Ansel

From Nancy Newhall

New York City
May 7, 1948

Ansel darling—

Jesus!

What gives?

No Anselogram in nearly three weeks!

A furrow of worry begins to appear in Newhall brows.

What have the South Seas done to you?
　—Dolce far niente?
　　—Pack trip into wilds?
　　　—Excitement?
　　　　—Depression?
　　　　　—Love?
　　　　　　—Kidnapped by brutes, rich-bitch, or other?
　　　　　　　—Jail?
　　　　　　　　—Hospital?
　　　　　　　　　—Typhoon?
　　　　　　　　　　—Earthquake, volcanic eruption, tidal wave?
　　　　　　　　CHECK ONE!
　　　　　　　or combination
　　　　　　　　or write, for heaven's sakes.
　　　　　　Especially if Newhalls can help in any way. . . .
Hope you have a crop of negatives to dream of!
Hope Hawaii has been much better than it looked at first!

Love and luck!
Nancy

From Nancy Newhall

New York City
June 18, 1948

Ansel darling—

Can you hear us shouting WISH YOU WERE HERE? (Got a red ribbon just in time!) We've been doing some celebrating by ourselves, but we really need You to do it properly. Eastman job looks really good.[1] There are drawbacks, of course, but—salary $10,000; purchase fund for books and photographs, $10,000; first year museum budget construction $400,000; yearly thereafter, $140,000! . . .

Beau did a superb job managing the lot, suggesting and persuading and changing, with great success—adding things like a print room, suggesting traveling exhibitions, . . .

And they encourage Beau to write, *and* they want him to travel—to Europe some time this year! And one just goes from London to Paris or wherever with the company arranging for hotels and paying expenses.

Well, well! Taste is the problem, of course; Mees[2] saying they don't want to set themselves up as arbiters of taste. I point out that they are whether they like it or not. And if they aren't aware of differences, why do they have an AA on the Annual Report?

. . . The potentials are very great; at the very least it seems to me we shall make it a better museum than it would have been without us and have added to Beau's career and our funds. We shall be taking the job with reservations, of course; with the line of what we know and feel must be done clearly and firmly in mind. If compromises and departures impossible to accept become crucial, we can leave and go back to books full time. . . .

Here's one for you: Harriet Tubman escaping from slavery and entering the free states: "When I found I had crossed that line, I looked at my hands to see if I was the same person. There was such a glory over everything. The sun came like gold through the trees, and I felt like I was in heaven."

Seems to me that's an Adams! The little golden soaring Aspens is near it—did I tell you Brett said he got more out of that little beauty than anything else he saw here?—but A. I will never unframe that print. B. Something with a great scope and prospect—infinite vistas of freedom and joy—as well as the gold and glory, would be even better. . . .

Oh yes, hopeful sign at Kodak: no commitments or dealings with PSA or PPA.[3] Local lights now and then maybe, but maybe, but that's all. And of course no advertising of Kodak products or slanting on anybody else's. . . .

Migod what a letter. All things should end sometime—even writing to you!

LOVE,
N

1. Beaumont Newhall had been offered the position of curator of George Eastman House, Rochester, N.Y. This new museum devoted to photography was underwritten by the Eastman Kodak Company.

2. Dr. E. C. Kenneth Mees was director of the Kodak laboratories.

3. Photographic Society of America and Professional Photographers of America.

To Beaumont and Nancy Newhall

Yosemite National Park

June 20, 1948

To B & N:

What a wonderful letter. Yep! Not much to say except cheers and again cheers and all the best things in the world for you two—who so richly deserve them.

Another feather in the cap for EK if they get Beaumont! I had a hunch things were simmering; B. made a deep impression on everybody.

If this is not coherent, the reasons are:

1st, the letter from you.

2nd, the return within the last 2 hours from the glorious Tuolumne Canyon and the Waterwheel Falls! A two day trip fraught with 40 pounds of knapsack, 18 miles of hiking, and rain in the a.m. (rain-soaked bacon and eggs, coffee so strong it etched the cup), but yesterday Oy!! such an incredible display of water going fast downhill! . . . Arrival home from Tuolumne Meadows celebrated with beer and stronger, shower, more drinks and longer; & thy letter and this answer; plus eight letters, 2 packages prepared and shipped, and a telephone call to S.F. SO! . . .

Ideas: addressed to B&N as richest friends in cosmos!

EK job of greatest importance in every way. Am all for it. Have no doubts of success.

B&N invaluable team, BUT: N must keep individuality. Strongest support to B if N proceeds with independent work. When work is accomplished in various directions, warm reflection can illuminate B at EK. But if N merely works *with* B, B gains, but not so much. . . . N must continue to write, edit, talk, and cooperate. NOTHING IS WORSE THAN A ROCHESTER WIFE. I SEEN 'EM!! I KNOW!!! B&N got the Photog. world by the tail. BUT DON'T LET ROCHESTER GET YA! . . .

I never knew two people I got more faith in—or love for !!! SO!!! . . .

Book 2[1] IS important. Wonder how many people will take the trouble to read it thoroughly? I believe in photography, but I know it is just a game to the flatulent 400,000 plus! But I take off my hat to Herc to put out books by so irritating a guy as Adams!

Well, this letter has to end, too!

Cheerio!

me

Ansel

1. *The Negative,* Hastings-on-Hudson, N.Y.: Morgan & Morgan, 1948.

From Nancy Newhall

Rochester, NY

September 8, 1948

Ansel dear—

    . . . George[1] tells us he has been mooring you to mountain tops making color panoramas of the Tetons! How does Yosemite look—or aren't you home yet? . . .

    Have even more respect for your mountains than ever, after attempting the Blue Ridge all summer. A difficult branch of the art. In only one or two Kodachromes and maybe two black and whites have I succeeded in making them rise and conveyed something of what they make you feel. Of course the Blue Ridge isn't the Sierra or the Tetons, but they do sweep and swoop until you feel like a very small bubble on a very large wave. And sometimes their distances look as fair and full of promise as Eden—your foothills from Moro Rock resemble them.

    Came across this in Edward's Daybook:[2]

    ". . . Both places were quite too beautiful, the element of possible
    discovery was lacking, that thrill which comes from finding beauty
    in the commonplace."

Earlier he speaks of Mexican churches as being an end in themselves—so beautiful that he could add nothing. Very illuminating—though Edward was still recovering from pictorialism and has been less afraid of beauty since, this still remains the basic difference between you. You, more than anyone, even Stieglitz and Paul [Strand], have consistently tackled the extraordinary problem of conveying and interpreting actual beauty. Plus its often tremendous spiritual overtones. This explains also somewhat why your interpretations of a place are so much more the place than his; he is still the sculptor—it's his use of the material that interests him. Whereas every time you photograph aspens or Mono Lake or Yosemite, you get closer both in understanding and in photographs to the thing or the place and its magic, and its many moods. And maybe it's not unrelated to approaching Bach and Beethoven again and again, seeking the whole, the essence and the subtleties, of what they have to say, and how to convey it with the utmost emotional and technical clarity.

Please conk me over the head whenever I get off the track!

Back to Brett and Edward! Both jobs[3] coming along fairly well. Plans still in flux, as you may have gathered. How are yours? How do the crop of negatives look??? Bet they are magnificent!

Love,
Nancy

1. George Waters, Jr., of Eastman Kodak commissioned Adams to make one of the first giant murals called "Coloramas" for Grand Central Station in New York City.

2. Nancy Newhall was editing Weston's diaries, published as *The Daybooks of Edward Weston*, Vol. 1, Rochester, N.Y.: George Eastman House, 1957; Vol. 2, New York: Horizon Press, 1961.

3. Besides working on Edward Weston's *Daybooks*, Nancy Newhall was also writing a foreword for Brett Weston's portfolio *White Sands*.

To Nancy Newhall

September 15, 1948

Dear Nancy,

Since your last letter I have been somewhat of a changed man. This is not the usual testimonial!! Your letter, a visit with Edward, huge forest fires, man falling off Half Dome, hot weather, old folks not well, kids away in school, impending portfolio, world conditions—WHAT a mixed parade of moods!

I think about my own work quite a lot. Never seem to get it focused. You helped to define my objectives, by comparisons. As you say, Edward reveals by sculpturing nature, I try to reveal by penetration and enlargement of experience. Actually, the note I have been trying to sound is somewhat expressed in the Beethoven song, "The Adoration of God in Nature."

I finally blew up at the Spencers the other night . . . and expressed myself in no uncertain terms about my particular reactions to non-objective art. Must have been brutal, but it came from deep within. The esoteric cliqueisms based on arbitrary symbols is indicative of the whole world viewpoint. Art, ethics, politics, and everything else seems to have no connecting, continuing thread. . . . Perhaps we must go through a real fire of some kind to re-establish a sense of reality. The serenity of the earth is the only thing left to cling to, and they are doing all they can to wreck that.

Was it not Chekov who wrote in a play, "Impressions are not enough; you don't go far with just Impressions!!" Just at this time I need more than impressions. If you have a moment to spare, please write me. About anything, just so you write. You seem to solidify things for me. I need a compass point to define the course.

As ever,
Ansel
me

To Nancy Newhall

Yosemite National Park
November 18, 1948

My Dear Nancy,

Arrived last night; too tired to drive all the way to San Francisco. All the better, as I had things to do here. Will leave today—that is, tomorrow. No, I guess I mean today; it's past midnight! Trip was wonderful in a way. Swell being with George [Waters, Jr.], but I could have dispensed with the advertising man. Thousands of dollars at stake, and no real plan; no color sequences, no thoughts of the right kind. George is a very sensitive and conscientious person. He was in a dither a good part of the time. Anyway, four days traveling, four days photographing, plus a few light-change sequences! The canyon was wonderful, clear and cold. . . . Virginia had a good time; got a little rest. But 1900 miles driving is a bit tough with a lot of photography besides! . . .

I am writing this to the Beethoven 101, and then the Beethoven 110. Wonderful records with sharp fidelity. I am torn between regret that I did not keep on with the piano—and then am more serene when I realize I am really accomplishing something in photography. I feel, however, I have only just started. But there are troubles; perhaps the structure of life is not solidly engineered without the stresses of troubles. The old folks are not well at all. We are confronted with a real problem of What to Do About It. I am sure we will solve it. At the moment I will be immersed in the portfolio[1]—for perhaps a month. . . .

The traveling spirit; the spirit that is always with us—I understand, and I bow my heart to the good fortune that such a spirit exists and is so full of presence. The sunrise at the canyon the other morning—a great surge of visual song. Before sunrise there was the comet in the clear pre-dawn sky. A beautiful thing, but also a bit terrifying to me. I know a bit too much of the cosmos to be just casual about it. To me it is a portent of the exceptional Something comes from Somewhere else, Something enormous and unexpected. Someday the earth may meet with the Exceptional. The comet in the sky, the fossils at my feet; gigantic span of distance, and gigantic span of time. At such moments I am transported to another resonance of being. At such moments I might press the keys with meaning. Releasing the shutter is not enough; the intrusion of the mechanical personality of the camera and the process distracts from the pure mood and vision. But then enters the Equivalent—the image accomplished *later;* and I am re-established as a photographer!

. . . I can't bring myself to think of comparative greatness. I have something to do, and I shall do it, I am sure. Some accomplish supremacy by ruthlessness; I can't do it that way. All the "success" is so shallow if the far-reaching inclusive spirit does not go with it. I will do my little books . . . and finish my Guggenheim, and then I may enter a new life; not a "hereafter" but a definite Here Now. I often hear that comment, "If I found a focus." I am tired of it, but not mad at it. In myself I have a focus, but I can see how others might not agree. Perhaps my lens focuses, but the plate is warped a bit. I have had the glimmer of an intense spiritual and emotional life; I know what it is. But perhaps my search is as important—or more so—than the realization. I don't know. I have learned to take nourishment from loneliness. What food shall assimilate when companionship comes to me! . . . Even the tongues of angels may be parched and swollen with heart-thirst. I used to worry about what people said and felt about my work. I do so no longer because I know I am closer to some aspects of reality than most. The responsibility lies heavy upon me. You have immeasurably lightened the burden.

Someday you will know about Stieglitz and Adams; we were both withdrawn. Several years more and we could have talked freely. Such things *cannot* be defined by the psychoanalysts.

I don't want the biography to be emasculated because of any

"thoughtfulness" for people including myself. It should be as clean and brutal as the Arizona desert; something in which one can see for enormous distances.

The fluff on the head is there, but no longer the broken toe! It was healed by strenuous kicking.

Do not all of us need to walk alone? At least, at times? But then, again, comes that thing which is the duty of human relationships and responsibilities—in which the object is for the race and the spirit. Think of me: I have been home very little, my children are growing up, Virginia is slowing up in various ways, and—while I am getting some things done—I worry if I am really accomplishing what I should. You have always a home mood around you. Beaumont is a wonderful person, with a tremendous job to do—a job which is of supreme importance to photography and to people. In comparison with me, you are on the crest of the wave. And you have accomplished a tremendous weight of good for people. You are extremely gifted. Perhaps the fact that you are somewhat surrounded by the Rochester drabness may excite and augment the inner glowings. Things will happen in direct relation to your desire to make them happen.

I listen with understanding. Think long and with humility and reverence to that which exists, and which has such a tremendous potential.

Thanks for the letter –

I wish I could write as deeply as I feel,

As ever,
Ansel

1. *Portfolio I*. San Francisco: 1948.

To Nancy Newhall

San Francisco
December 17, 1948

Dear Nancy,

 . . . PORTFOLIO ONE actually went off today. . . . One hell of a job. Total assured sales to date: 36. 8 more in the offing. And not much active promotion either.

I think you will like it. Now that it is done I can reveal to people (without seeming too sentimental or precious) that every one of the images was selected because of some appropriate relationship in mood to some aspect of Stieglitz in relation to Adams. I will be interested in what you think about it. The mood of the set as a whole is rather mournful. Next one will be light and bright and white—snow, perhaps. But I think you will like the *Oak Tree and Snowstorm*. Actually, you have seen only three of the prints. . . .

Made a perfectly gorgeous Moonrise print for George yesterday. Think the jinx is broken! Wish I had something exciting for you both for Christmas. I promised something, but I can't recall what it was! Good Gawd! Leave here on the 22nd for Yosemite, and the Big Time with the Bracebridge Dinner.[1] It's going to be *very* exciting. And there are 18 inches of snow on the floor of the Valley! . . .

Best to everyone and a ton of affectionate thinkings about you both. WHEN ARE YOU COMING WEST!! / ??

More shortly,

me

Ansel

1. The Bracebridge Dinner is an English Christmas dinner and performance given annually at the Ahwahnee Hotel in Yosemite National Park; Adams arranged and directed the music, wrote the script, and performed as the Majordomo from 1929 to 1975

From Nancy Newhall

Rochester

Christmas Day, 1948

Ansel dear—

. . . PORTFOLIO ONE came just as we were having a Christmas party for the staff of Eastman House. Just opening it up brought a gasp! It is exquisite in every detail—case, printing, mounting, the sheets between—and no matter how often one has gone through the prints each comes again with a fresh magic and a sense of further revelation. They build into a great poetic statement. In speaking of and to Stieglitz, you said a lot about Adams! I feel the connections though I can't always focus it in words as yet; fun to compare notes some day and see where we diverge. (Why couldn't you tell me what you had in mind?) Stieglitz, if he still is, must be very moved and pleased, and thanking God there is somebody in this day and age who can make something with a force and clarity and beauty uncompromised and un-surpassed. . . .

> Love and more soon—
> Nancy

What news of Edward? Thanks for postcard!

From Beaumont and Nancy Newhall

> Rochester
> December 31, 1948

[Telegram]

WE PRIZE THE MOONRISE.
WE CHEER THE MUIR.
PORTFOLIO ONE IS SURE WELL DONE.
THE NEGATIVE IS POSITIVE.
NOW ALL WE NEED IS ANSEL HERE
TO USHER IN A BRIGHT NEW YEAR.[1]

1. As Christmas gifts Adams sent the Newhalls what he considered to be the best print he had yet made of *Moonrise, Hernandez, New Mexico* and a copy of *Portfolio 1*. The telegram also refers to his latest books, *Yosemite and the Sierra Nevada* (the Muir book) and *The Negative*.

To Nancy and Beaumont Newhall

> Yosemite National Park
> January 1, 1949

Dear Nancy and Beaumont,

Your highly amusing wire evoked my muse. I only hope I find myself chipper as all get-out this AM (probably the only person in the Valley who can claim such distinction). Hate New Year's parties; went to bed at 11 PM, and snoozed under our electric blanket until 9 AM this AM. We went back on standard time today. Also have had some earthquakes! Snow, rain, etc. a good year! Sure hope all goes well with you in 1949! . . .

I have made a New Year's resolution! Yep!! It's this—I am rejecting all synthetic magic; if something does not speak to me directly in magi-cal terms I will not try to mentally force the issue. I am sure you know what I mean by "Magic." I have looked twice and thrice at a lot of art simply because others considered it worth looking at. Perplexity has been the chief outcome. Most of the Atget pictures do for me just about what the LeConte pictures did for Newhall—practically nothing! In the latter case, my interest was aroused by the subject matter and the personal connotations. Looking at them today I find myself wondering how I took so much interest in them as photographs.

Fortunately, I find many things which stir me deeply—it is not saturation which distresses me. More and more things have meanings of the deeper kind. I can't get Strand's latest prints out of my mind. (NOT the Kodak reproductions.) I think of a couple of things Nancy did at Black Mountain, and that swell New York picture that Beaumont made from the 65th St. apartment (56th?). The sequence of pictures in *Portfolio One* definitely reflects impressions of Stieglitz; I could not express them in words, but I think I got something over in the pictures themselves.

Am glad you like the *Portfolio*, the Muir, and the *Moonrise!* Can't think of any other people I would more want to be the owners thereof! Do you like the *Moonrise print?* I think that for the first time I got some feeling of tonal space. Previous prints have been too bleak and cold. Did H.[oughton] M.[ifflin] Co. send you the Muir Book? They were so ordered to do so! You were not supposed to buy it! . . .

Best from all to all,
Ansel

. . .

To Nancy Newhall

Yosemite National Park
February 8, 1949

Dear Nancy,

. . . MY CAMERA IN YOSEMITE VALLEY[1] by AA and MY CAMERA ON POINT LOBOS[2] by EW really taking shape. Edward seems vastly interested; has always wanted a book on Point Lobos. Printer is most cooperative. Think we can do these books and make a really tidy sum for EW and AA. EW needs it worse than AA; must be strapped after those operations. Will tell you more soon just as soon as I see him. Am keeping this new book idea rather on the QT because I don't want to let things out until it is sure-fire. I really feel the regional attack is well worthwhile; good photography on good subject material. Defines the subject and does not limit the photographer.

Seems funny not to exchange letters more often. But we have both been busy in the real sense of the term.

Wish I could talk to you. Need some Nancerian advice! All goes well except in the inspirational domains. . . .

I am more than gratified with the sales of *Portfolio One*—$4500.00 to date (actually 4200.00 less Weyhe's[3] discount) but that really means 45 copies. I am sure the remainder will sell within the year. PORTFOLIO TWO TAKES FORM![4] Wheeeeeeee! . . .

Understand 4000 Muir books sold to date! Reprinting in order—some better plates, too.

Crazy to see Beaumont's new book. . . .

Much love, always, as usual,
Ansel

Don't work too hard. . . . For me, I can't understand anyone worrying about "Influences"—or "getting away" from them. I am beginning to believe that self-analysis and the psychiatric approach EEEEK-EEEEEKKKKKK is about the most poisonous condiment to add to one's emotional response to the world. Fie on it all! hic!!!

GOT A GORJEZUZ NEW 8 x 10 segment of snowy forest. Will send you one when printed.

PS I still like Nature. What a Momma!

1. *My Camera in Yosemite Valley*, Yosemite National Park: Virginia Adams, and Boston: Houghton Mifflin Company, 1950.

2. Edward Weston. *My Camera on Point Lobos*, Yosemite National Park: Virginia Adams, and Boston: Houghton Mifflin Company, 1950.

3. E. Weyhe Gallery and Bookshop, New York City, sold several copies of *Portfolio I*.

4. *Portfolio II, The National Parks and Monuments*, a selection of 15 photographs, San Francisco: Sierra Club, 1950.

To Michael Adams

Yosemite National Park
February 21, 1949

Dear Mike,

Good to hear from you.　　OK

Your old man was 47 yesterday! Regretfully accepts fact that you can ski better than he can!　　OK

Herewith 25.00.　　OK

I suppose you are supposed to deposit this in the allowance fund? Anyway, don't spend any more than you have to! I am not a myllyonayre! OK?

But I do wish you luck with the skiing and don't bust any bones!

Your ma has had a slight attack of intestinal flu, but is OK. I am managing OK. Edward Weston is here for a few days, and sends his hello.

OK

OK

OK

I am sending you synonym book. There *must* be some other term but OK for everything. OK?

Love from us all,
Ansel

From Paul Strand

New York City
March 21, 1949

Dear Ansel:

. . . Rather than your getting it second hand, I want you to know that I was very disturbed by your portfolio—I do not refer to the content, (about which I would rather speak than write you) but the effect the price of it will have on the whole problem of establishing a proper value for a photograph. This arose, as you may remember, when the original suggestion of a similar folio of work of 10 photographers was raised. Either a photograph as an art work is worth something or it is worth nothing. I well remember the time when people said no water color was worth more than $100 and Stieglitz made them pay as high as $6,000 for a Marin. They did not like it then but the concept that a watercolor is inferior and of less value than an oil was broken down to a great extent. I also remember when advertisers and agencies paid $5 for a photograph and $1,000 for a painting. The commercial photographers have changed that situation, and have given photography its rightful place within the hierarchy of commercial art values—Stieglitz tried and to some extent succeeded in giving a photograph its rightful value as an art commodity. I have adhered to that principle and will continue to do so.

It seems to me that your portfolio undermines the basic concept of the value of a fine photographic print. First it says: a little over $8 apiece is a reasonable price and secondly it says that the photograph as an art work can be made in any quantity or at least quality. I don't think either is true and in the long run my feeling is that you will not increase either respect for, nor understanding of, photography as a medium of expression—I think it only fair to tell you what I think.

Our greetings to your Virginia and the very much growing up young Adamses—and to Edward if you see him—my class at the Photo League is an interesting experiment—hope for all concerned—

As always,
Paul

To Paul Strand

Yosemite National Park
March 29th, 1949

Dear Paul,

You are an honest man! I appreciate your letter very much indeed for various reasons. I know that what you say comes from the heart and from basic convictions. I don't agree with you about price, but that is a minor matter.

I have, as you know, the greatest respect and affection for you and your work. It is the only truly poetic photography in the world today. And I admire your devotion to the cause of adequate value of photographs.

I cannot agree with your logic in this respect; 1 print only from a negative may very well be worth $500.00—the photograph in itself is worth that. But, where we have *one* oil painting, *one* watercolor, *one* piece of sculpture—we also have many prints of etchings, many prints of lithographs, many prints of photographic negatives. To me the essence of the photographic process is its reproducibility. With adequate technique we can print a million duplicate prints of the same negative and each print can be as beautiful and perfect as the "master" print which, we suppose, is the expressed concept of the picture. To me, the photograph stands as an expression independent of the number of prints made from it.

In my *Portfolio One* every print is as good as if it were the final fine print I would make from the negative. The "fine" print was made; sometimes it took many hours to determine the desired perfection and feeling. Once that was done, it was a simple matter to simply repeat the exposure and development procedures. I kept accurate detailed notes and used a metronome in timing. Every 13 or 15 prints were developed at one time in 3 liters of fresh Metol-Glycin developer (6 minute developing time). What differences there are can be traced to paper differences, and to occasional failures of control. These differences are very slight. One picture—the Saguaro cactus—was intentionally printed in two ways— one slightly darker than the other. I am equally pleased with both expressions. And so on!

The price of the portfolio is fixed as a unit. The separate prints will always be priced at at least $25.00. No separate prints will be available until long after the portfolio is completely sold out—if then. If the portfolio were done in an edition of 500 copies, I would have priced it at $50.

If I could make a fine print for $1000—and distribute them to a great audience, I would be greatly pleased.

I am touched by the fact that several students have bought the Portfolio and are paying a few dollars a month. It is all they could possibly afford. $100.00 is far too much for the average person for anything. It is much more important that the people who appreciate and truly desire to have the Portfolio be given a chance to own it, than to have it placed only in the hands of the rich—who are often very unappreciative of anything but hard cash.

I can't reconcile your definitely social attitudes with your equally definite exalted financial value applied to art. Explain sometime, please!

But I DO appreciate the letter. Very much indeed! . . .

Must see you soon.

To you and V.[1] and the cat
Affectionate greetings from us all,
Ansel

. . .

1. Virginia, Strand's second wife.

To Beaumont and Nancy Newhall

Juneau, Alaska[1]
June 25, 1949

Dear B & N,

WHAT A FLIGHT TODAY! Was in Grumman Amphibian which was dropping loads of supplies to advance base of Juneau Ice Field Expedition. . . .

We crossed and re-crossed 600 square miles of glaciers and ice fields, and encircled the most incredible crags and spires I ever imagined. Bearclaw Peak rises sheer 5000 feet above the ice. We flew around it about 1000 feet distant!

Pictures will help to describe it! The rear door was open to permit dumping loads by parachute. I am full of fresh air, spray on the take-off, noise, but simply unbelievable scenery.

I am afraid Alaska is the Place for me! I am NUTS about it.

Best to you and all our friends,
Ansel

---

1. This was Adams' second trip to Alaska (his first was in 1948) to continue work on his Guggenheim project.

From Beaumont and Nancy Newhall

Rochester
[Late June 1949]

ADAMS, MOUNTAINEER
SIR!

So you're flying around in aereyplanes! What kind of maountaineering d'ye call that? . . . Now you've got the idea. Buzz them in an amphibian. Shoot them out of the side door. Hope that pilot really went down on the deck so you had to shoot upwards. There's the fun. Fun. That I'm having, thanks to O'Keefe. NOTE SPELLING!!! I wrote O'Keefe and NOT O'Keeffe. There's a difference. One makes BEER (Praise Malt!) The other makes paintings. The BEER IS EASIER TO TAKE. . . .

Ah me. Wish you were here. Cause we are going to celebrate our 14th (count 'em—fourteen) anniversary on Friday the First of July at the circus and I would like to make you unhappy with my Leica. I put Super XX in it and Paul Strand (he's a big name in photography) and Charles Sheeler (he's a ditto) draw their breath and privately shudder when I shoot WIDE OPEN AT *f*/2 at one-eighth of a second. Funny thing is: negatives are usually OVER-EXPOSED. Well that's what I'm a goin' to do on Friday and it would spoil my pleasure if there wasn't somebody there to say I'M NUTS. Which I am, else I wouldn't even under the influence of O'Keefe (note the ONE F) write to you thus. But we miss you, would rather have you here than in Alaska!! BUT WE WOULDN'T WISH YOU HERE AT THIS TIME OF THE YEAR (Rhymes!) Which reminds me. We went to visit friends. Their BELL was not working. We came in thru the door without ringing. Shouted for them. They answered. Sez I: WE WIN THE NO-BELL PRIZE (get it?)

Beau

over!
NN
Why?
BN
Favorite song of BN this month:

If I Leica you + you Leica me + we Leica both the same—UP LEICAS!

You confirm my worst suspicions about Alaska. Have always felt, sight unseen, that's where I wanted—B says the winters may be a trifle long—

Anyway—   !

N

To Beaumont Newhall

Juneau, Alaska
July 11, 1949

Dear Beaumont:

. . . The damn rain is insistent; I have made few pictures; I am disgusted; I have read everything readable in town: I have finished Book 3,[1] and work on Book 4;[2] but it still rains and RAINS AND RAINS AND RAINS AHHHHH plop!!

Anyway, I am flying to Sitka today, and will leave from there on the

National Park Service Boat for Glacier Bay on the 14th. I will be picked up on the 20th by plane and arrive in Juneau that noon. I take the PAA [Pan American Airlines] Clipper south to Seattle, arriving that evening. On the AM of the 21st, I am headed back to Kalifornia in an entirely refurbished, spit-and-polished Pontiac Station Wagon, arriving in S.F. on the 24th. Then, on the 25th, I go to Santa Cruz to work on the *Life* magazine begonia story.[3] Then, to Yosemite for a month. Then back to Santa Cruz to finish the story, and then east, and I'll be seein' Ya!

Have done some really swell black and white natural details—forest, grass, rocks, etc. But the dang weather has prevented landscape work. . . .

I did not want to mention it—you don't even tell your best friend sometimes—but I feared you were overexposing your Leica. And what particular masochistic urge prompts you to use D-76 with Super XX? Your prints will probably look like a cobble-stone pavement. My Deah Boy! Speed is but the wild oats of photography! The function of the light disturbing the halide is expressed in the following formula:

$$E_{u,y} = \lambda \cdot f_{oh}^{oh\,oh}_{cod} \sum \frac{Bang^2}{Pooh} \left(hic\right)_\bullet^p \; \mathcal{U}_\prime^\prime \mathcal{U}_\prime^{\prime\prime} \left[click\right]_{JWT^2} \times \sqrt[]{E.K.}^{-1} \times \$_\bullet$$

. . . I have much to say to both of you, and certainly wish we could have a good schmoos soon. I shall be glad when this Guggenheim Project enters its final stages. The new Yosemite book[4] is going to be a dilly— I mean good.

Am having a show at the S.F. Museum of Art.[5] Got a swell review.

Hope all goes well with you and your work. Am VERY anxious to see the History![6] . . . Maybe when Kodak sees the MY CAMERA IN YOSEMITE VALLEY book they will fall for a bunch of them. We would naturally give them a good rate on a quantity.

More soon. Affectionate greetings to all my friends and many warm thinkings about you two.

Ansel

1. *The Print*, Hastings-on-Hudson, N.Y.: Morgan & Morgan, 1950.
2. *Natural-Light Photography*, Hastings-on-Hudson, N.Y.: Morgan & Morgan, 1950.
3. A color photographic essay on begonias for *Life* magazine was never published.
4. *My Camera In Yosemite Valley*.
5. "Photographs by Ansel Adams," San Francisco Museum of Modern Art, 1949.
6. Newhall, *The History of Photography*.

To Beaumont and Nancy Newhall

San Francisco

1949

Dear Nancy and Beaumont:

Just returned from Santa Cruz and hasten to write a letter to youse guys:

1. Saw *The History* at Edward's! MAGNIFICENT WONDERFUL JOB! Am really moved. Sure did all right by Adams! A most important contribution to photography. My copy awaits me in Yosemite—where I shall be on Tuesday. Kehryste! I have been driving and photographing and I can't write on the typewriter!!

2. Also saw the *Daybook* manuscript at Edward's. Spent practically all day Saturday with him. He impressed me as being in better mood and spirits than when I saw him before. The *Daybook* is MOST impressive. I read about half of it—all I could take at one sitting. It is an astonishing piece of writing; hard to stop reading it. With the photographs it will be a knockout book. You did a grand job.

. . . He [Edward] seemed pleased and much relieved that Minor and I liked the text. Like is a feeble word—I am nuts about it! With proper build-up the book could become a real best-seller. . . .

Practically all the Alaska negatives developed: have some grand things. Did very poor in color; hope George is not disgusted with me. Mural selections completed;[1] George seems pleased. Begonia story well under way; have some good things.

Saw Brett's Portfolio. Am very much impressed with it as a whole. Find selection perfect up to six prints; then a bit repetitive. Print quality exquisite in most of subjects; a bit bleak in others. Portfolio case depressing; Gray fabric and black label out of key with subject. Printing magnificent. But entire mood damn good on the whole. I am much depressed that he has sold only eight copies! I think he agrees that his first portfolio should have stressed BRETT WESTON (representative photographs). But *White Sands* is too esoteric and unknown to arouse excitement enough to assure heavy sales. I am sure all will be sold in time, but he will have to do a more personal, extrovertal portfolio first to establish a good clientele. . . . We will all have to boost sales for him. I am going to see the San Francisco Museum of Art tomorrow in regard an exhibit for him; perhaps a small show of the portfolio now, and a big inclusive show later on. He was busy yesterday laying bricks! Such a swell guy and photographer—and laying bricks (necessity)! . . .

The History, I repeat, is MAGNIFICENT!

Love,

As usual,

me

Ansel

1. Photographs for Eastman Kodak's Grand Central Station Coloramas.

To Edward Weston

San Francisco

September 1949

Dear Edward,

Had a swell time with you and wished it might have been longer. Am hoping we can take you back to Yosemite with us and we can have a much longer gab fest.

I am slightly worried that I gave the impression of railroading you to some decision about the book [*My Camera on Point Lobos*]—at least trying to railroad you! Of course, such is not the case. It's got to be *your* book, your selections, sequences, text, et al. In trying to get over my idea of the books—singly and in series—I probably stressed the regional aspects to an extent which somewhat invaded the larger aspect of the impact of the work itself on a creative plane.

I do think the regional aspect is extremely important, hence the particular audience for the book will be somewhat different from the audience for *50 Photographs*,[1] etc. That fact may influence the selection somewhat, but never to the point where the integrity of the pictures is concerned. I think it is obvious to both of us that a selection limited to rock and tree forms would not be adequate in this case. But I think the landscapes we saw and discussed would suffice to round out the balances and tensions of the semi-abstract images.

Hence, I would say that I think it wise to include as many "landscape" or definitive environmental photographs as possible providing you are entirely satisfied with the emotional and personal content of the series. In the case of my Yosemite book, the larger part of the series will be landscapes—but new ones in which there is considerably more interpretative effects. The naturalistic details I shall use will be so dispersed in the series as to "spice it" rather than dominate it.

In your case, it is quite different. The "landscapes" will "spice up" the details! But I am sure you realize that I am unable to make any distinction in expressive quality between your semi-abstracts and your landscapes; we may have our favorites but we never find corn! I did not wish to give the impression that I leaned towards any corn in suggesting a certain emphasis on the landscapes—or, to put it better—on the definitely environmental photographs. . . .

We will work out a contract agreement which will pay the artist from the start. A rough draft is enclosed.

SEE YOU SOON. Will probably drive from Carmel to Yosemite on Wednesday.

Love—as usual,
Ansel

1. *Fifty Photographs: Edward Weston*, edited by Merle Armitage, New York: Duell, Sloan & Pearce, 1947.

From Edward Weston

Carmel Highlands
November 29, 1949

Dear Ansel,

Your long and exciting letter cheered me no end. I feel that a book on my Point Lobos will be one of *the* events of my life. I'm glad that you and Virginia are back of it. Gives me a warm glow.

I have a surprise. One fine day I thought, "Why not get down from the attic (or nooky loft) my daybook of Pt. Lobos days, see what I had to say which could be used." I found plenty! including a description of my first day with my camera, the first negative made. Also much philosophizing in re art, the camera's use & direction. I think this material could be used as excerpts from my daybook. . . .

Ansel, on acc't of my writing difficulties I can't see how to autograph any large number of books at one time. How about initialling "EW"—. . .

Abrazos & besos to all the Newhalls (which includes Euripides')
and to yourself,
Edward

1. Euripides, the Newhalls' cat.

To Edward Weston

San Francisco
January 8, 1950

Dear Edward:

Flying to L.A. this afternoon. Address the Ambassador Hotel. It's not of MY choosing!—but I gotta sleep SOMEWHERE!

Don't worry about blurb. It will be dignified. Just wanted your ideas. There has to be an announcement, and the announcement has to contain material which will encourage people to get the book. I have prepared a tentative text which will be submitted to you when good enough.

It's always the same—with you and with me and, I guess, all artists. We think our art will sell itself. It won't. It would if people could just see it. But they can't see it—hence it has to be "sold." I know it can be sold with dignity. There are to be 5,000 books which will carry your message—and it is a damned important message, too. These books will reach, in part, a new group of people. I am very happy about it.

Love from us all,
Ansel

To Nancy Newhall

Yosemite National Park
February 27, 1950
4000 ft¹ 57° X-vp burp

Dear Nancy,

I have come to a conclusion. I am not an artist. The clique of "artists" in this year of our fraud ain't my clique and I am distressed. I have figured out all the effort I have made to "get" the non-objectivists, the cubists, the whatnots and the wherewithalls—and if I applied that same effort to making a simple photograph—well—it might be a good photograph.

About 2 weeks ago I went to an opening of our local art group at the S.F. Museum; supposed to be the best yet, etc. The only thing I saw which moved me was a painting by [Morris] Graves. When I express liking for Graves I find I am immediately relegated to some passé age. It is politely insinuated that, "I don't really know what it is all about." Maybe not.

The line is being drawn so thin, so transparent (in not the good sense of the term), so attached to the old European hooks that I can't help but wonder when the big break will occur.

The other day at Edward's, after listening to a newscast, Edward said, "If we just had a big flood now it would settle everything." The very night before I had a very troublesome dream about just such a catastrophe. I have been enjoying (?) recurrent dreams of like nature—last night I was in a galvanized metal shed in the middle of a dry lake somewhere south of Inyo; there was a hell of a wind blowing and alkali dust was everywhere. I did not like the people I was with in the shed, and I tried time and again to leave—but everytime I opened the door there was such a terrible gust of wind and dust that I was forced to close the door and return to my unsavory companions! Such dreams! The same mood comes upon me at most art exhibits and concerts—dry dust, and the escapement from which only leads me to unpleasant associations; the choice is hard to make. Of course, there are always a few wonderful people and things which justify all!

. . . I guess the whole basis of "modern art" (hideous limited term) is *sensation* and not *emotion*. The racket grows upon us; just like slot machines and pinball games. I *am* distressed.

One heartening thing of late: the response to our little New Year's card.[2] The letters keep coming in—not just "thank you" letters but statements of appreciation for putting two things together and coming out with something which seems to strike many people deeply. Had quite a discussion at the Spencers' the other night: Jeannette and I were at pleasant sword's points. I stated that, to me, the Grass itself and *what it symbolized* was far more important than any photograph I could make of it; that my function as a photographer was to present this symbol with the utmost clarity and intensity at my command (of course, modified by the distillation of self). Jeannette said the grass was nothing; the only thing that mattered was the picture I made of it—the design, etc. This only intensified the keen sense of separation between the world of "art" and the world of me—rather, I should say, the world of nature which is seen by me—or by you, or by anyone.

I feel I am on the brink of a certain definite personal philosophy; I suppose it will be expressed in terms of photography—but I am not sure. I have tried hard to study response—and in so doing I have learned a lot about people and the need for some communication of real emotion and ideas—not just the parroting of the cliques. And, as time goes on, the kind of people-exploiting such as Steichen's becomes very unpleasant to me. I sense a terrific decadence, a kind of actual rot in the air. . . .

Mama very bad now. Must have nurse every night, all night, so as to give Poppa a little rest. Financial drain on AA considerable. Guess I can see it through somehow. But with 2 kids in school, and a lot of non-economic work on my hands, OW!

Michael wants to take flying lessons!!! OK in principle, but nix on the idea without proof of safe instruction and plane.

Every time I have flown of late has been in fog, rain or storm—or at night. I think I will buy a horse. . . .

I feel good—just perplexed subconsciously over the impending self-alterations and the really dismal prospects for the world at large.

More power to you with the books.

Love to you and to Beaumont and best to the gang.

Cheeriow!
Ansel

1. The altitude of Yosemite Valley.

2. For many years the Adamses sent a New Year's, rather than a Christmas, card with one of Adams' photographs reproduced on the cover; the card for 1950 reproduced *Grass in Rain, Glacier Bay National Monument, Alaska, 1948.* (See *An Autobiography,* p. 289.)

To Beaumont Newhall

San Francisco
March 23, 1950

Dear Beaumont,

. . . My mother passed away last evening—really something to be thankful for after years of misery. My father is doing far better than expected. He approaches the stature of a saint in his patience and understanding. There will be some definite changes hereabouts. We are taking my pop to Yosemite Saturday, and we have plans to reorganize the property so that he will be assured of a good income for the rest of his life. When things happen they happen fast, and always a little different than expected. In this case things are better than I had hoped for; my father was more resigned than I knew to the inevitable. . . .

Herc says Book 3 [*The Print*] is going over fine—a re-printing soon!

The Weston book announcements now in press. Edward is considerably improved, thank Gawd! But it is a pattern of ups and downs!

No other news of great import.

Love to you and Nancy
and best to all,
Ansel

To Nancy Newhall

April 18, 1951

Dear Nancy:

The spirit is willing but the so-and-so is feeble! I am pooped, peaked und pallid—batty, busted and brown—foolish, flatulent and fatigued! But like MacArthur—I shall return!! I hope HE don't return here for a long time; his visit nearly wrecked the jernt. Heil Mac! What a conceit! Me, I like Eisenhower or Joe Louis! I have done the Poppy Colorama; that is, I have made the pictures—and I hope to Gawd they like them! The conditions were absolutely antagonistic throughout. My Primeval World is letting me down! The people were OK, but the weather and the dearth of poopies! I still have the national ad to do, but I am scared to death of it as it is very hard to find anything lush hereabouts. I went well over 3000 miles looking for suitable areas. I missed one or two that were short-lived and doing their stuff while I was looking elsewhere. But it is a big state and poppies are scarce.

Virginia gets back Sunday from New Mexico—had a fine trip with Bertha Damon.[1]

I am doing some color work for *Life* in Golden Gate Park.

My letters and bills have piled up like Mont Blanc.

My bank balance is acting like an ideal peneplane,

I gotta get on a beeg deal soon or go into the ready-made clothing business.

. . . What I need right now is a good long session with you. A breakdown of all the swell letters and ideas; a plan for the future. I never felt more disorganized in my life! We have SO much to do, and here I am puttering around with necessary but wearing duties. If anyone sees a poppy field under a blue sky, with no wind blowing PLEEZE, tell me, will ya?

I shall seriously get to a worthy letter to you soon. On my neck also is Book 4 [*Natural-Light Photography*] for Herc, and 1,000,000 details. How the Hell did I get that way?

Wish I could sit down in the new house with you and B and just relax!

Love,
Ansel

1. Bertha Pope Damon, wealthy Berkeley woman who accompanied Bender and Adams on their trip to the Southwest in 1927.

To Nancy Newhall

San Francisco
July 31, 1951

Dear Nancy,

Things very bad here today. Papa very low; only a matter of a few days—even a few hours. Harry,[1] two nurses, Virginia and I here—we do all we can but there is nothing to be done. I only hope he does not linger on with pain and confusion. His mind is now veiled and he wants to get up and go to Carson City![2] But through it all the same old sweet self predominates! What a privilege just to *know* a man like Papa! It may sound trite, but I really mean it when I say he set a high level to live up to. It continues foggy outside. And slightly foggy inside! Able to postpone *Fortune* job,[3] thank goodness. Am reading over your many superb letters and getting both comfort and information! I am astonished at the grasp you have on my problems and on my work. The list of prints is magnificent!

I feel that when this is over I shall get back to creative work. I begin to doubt myself, because I have felt it so often and nothing happened! But there has been a constant psychological, unconscious strain involved and perhaps it has been a necessary stabilizing quality. As the review in *American Photography*[4] said, ". . . perhaps because of (prodigious work) Adams' prints improve . . . etc." What I want to know is—does *Adams* improve? . . .

Printing costs practically ruining Morgan! I took a cut in royalties to make Book IV [*Natural-Light Photography*] possible. I know the costs are fierce; the estimate to get the book printed out here (and bound) almost equalled the retail cost per volume! . . .

I am simply appalled at the totals of income and outgo! Endless dreams of avarice busted up by endless streams of obligations! But in some fantastic way I shall come out 3¢ ahead!

Much love and don't fuss about me. I shall get going on the prints as soon as the mood is propitious.

As ever, and, How!

Ansel

1. Harry Oye, houseman who worked for the Adams family.

2. Adams' mother's family, the Brays, were from Carson City, Nevada; it was in Carson City that Adams' father courted and married Olive Bray.

3. Adams photographed the Kennecott Copper Company's great open pit mine in Utah for *Fortune*, November 1951.

4. George Wright. "Books on Review," *American Photography*, June 1951; Wright reviewed *My Camera in the National Parks* and *The Land of Little Rain*, text by Mary Austin, with Adams' photographs, Boston: Houghton Mifflin Company, 1950.

From Beaumont Newhall

Rochester

August 4, 1951

Dear Ansel:

I wish that you had known my father. For in many ways he was like your father. He seemed so quiet and reserved, he was so gentle and so kind, and he was so wonderfully sympathetic and understanding. I came along when he was fifty; he might have been a grandfather, so far as age was concerned, but he was a real father. Like your father, he let me alone to develop my own interests, no matter how far removed they might have been from his hopes for me. I was an only child—not technically, for I had a sister much older than myself who died of typhoid while I was still an infant. I grew up alone with no real friends surrounded by my father's and mother's love of literature and music and nature. They allowed me to follow my passionate love for making things—think of it, I had a home workshop right next to the living room where I sawed and carpentered and ran my lathe. My father's praise was always modulated. Whatever I did he judged not as the work of his son, but on its own merits. And if I erred and made mistakes, they were not exaggerated. I would bring home a good report card from school, and it would be taken for granted. I would bring home failures, and nothing was said. And this cut deeper than scolding and bullyings and forced direction of my studies. I didn't really realize that I enjoyed an unusual degree of freedom until I had graduated from Harvard. I was then away, in Philadelphia, on my first job. "I think it was because I had taken up my father's profession as it seemed the easiest thing to do rather than from any real desire to become a doctor, that I determined that you should be free to follow your own course," he wrote. And he signed the letter, "Yours with much love, Herbert W. Newhall."

I didn't realize until the last years of his life that there was a tragedy, that he hated being a doctor—because he was a good doctor, a respected and loved member of the community. He never let his bitter disappointment be seen. He was happiest when his hands were in the soil, tending his wildflowers, which he collected and made to grow so that we had a living museum of the flora of New England. Towards the end, when he had given up practice except for consultations and office work, he wrote poetry. It wasn't good, but it gave him a means to express the yearning and the esthetic desires he had for so very long suppressed within himself.

The last time I saw my father was in the spring of 1933, when I left for Europe. After the disappointment of losing my job at the Metropolitan Museum I won a Carnegie Scholarship which gave me a trip abroad. Father and mother were proud that I had won this distinction. I remember that he showed more emotion at the leave taking than I had ever noticed before. Instead of the usual handshake, he embraced me.

I had spent the afternoon at a painting exhibition in Paris, when the news came to me of his death. In the same telegram mother told me not to come home, to stay as I had planned, that father would have wanted it so.

Mother told me when I came back a month or so later that it had happened very quietly. Father had a heart attack, had rallied, and seemed to be convalescing. He was in bed, unattended. He died with a lighted cigarette between his lips.

When we went through his papers, we knew that he knew that he was dying. Everything was in order, with notes written to us.

I could only wish for your father and for you so peaceful an ending. But no matter how it comes, one can never be prepared for it, one can never minimize, nor forget.

I wanted to tell you about my father because I do not know how else to tell how much I owe to him. If it had not been for deep understanding, his confidence, his belief in what lay unknown and unexpressed within me, I would not have been able to develop the way I have.

So I think I know, Ansel, how you feel about your father. To look back over the years, to measure that love, is almost too much.

Whatever I have been able to contribute is the only way I know to honor my father. I like to think that I hear him saying, "That's fine, son."

What you are doing—call it art, expression, interpretation, poetry, music, what you will as long as it is the wonderful things that so many of us so deeply appreciate—is, I feel, how best you can honor a father you love so deeply.

Yours ever,
Beaumont

To Beaumont Newhall

San Francisco
August 8, 1951

My Dear Beaumont,

Letters such as the one from you today—and from Nancy a few days ago—are among the most priceless possessions anyone could have.

The penetration of thoughts and moods through the catalyst of Other Experience seems the only way to deeply touch the heart in such situations as this. Your letter is a glowing tribute to my father, as well as to yours, and for this I am deeply grateful. The similarity of character is astonishing, and the similarity of our lives also almost unbelievable. While we are actually in dissimilar planes (obviously speaking) the basic intentions of our lives certainly coincide. We were both "only" children, we both arrived late in our parents' lives, we were both left to our own devices (but controlled by *example*—not by the rod). Both our fathers disliked their chosen (or imposed) vocations, and both turned to some creative release—your father to gardening, mine to astronomy and botany.

I am sure that your father's spirit is tremendously happy over the accomplishment of his son! As you say, accomplishment is the only real way of expressing the fundamental devotions. I am trying; someday I may round out my intentions. But what time I have wasted, what deviations of purpose have been required! I envy your clean progression to a tremendous objective!

[229]

Again, my love and thanks. And I shall try to tell Nancy what her letter meant to me, too. My father is not having an easy departure—as did yours—and it is difficult to write these days.

As ever,
Ansel

To Nancy and Beaumont Newhall

San Francisco
August 9, 1951

[Telegram]

MY FATHER PEACEFULLY PASSED AWAY TONIGHT AND SERVICES WILL BE AT 131 BUT FLOWERS OMITTED. RATHER CONTRIBUTIONS TO AS-TRONOMICAL SOCIETY OF THE PACIFIC. THE FLOWERS IN THE GARDEN ARE MORE BEAUTIFUL THAN THOSE IN THE STORES. ALL IS UNDER CONTROL HERE BUT TELL THOSE YOU KNOW WHO MIGHT WANT TO KNOW. HE WAS A GOOD MAN IN THE SIGHT OF GOD. LOVE.

ANSEL ADAMS

To Beaumont and Nancy Newhall

San Francisco
September 6, 1950ne
Late

deer folkz

wat a day I tell you I don't want another day just like it. I made many prints but in the meen tyme I saw inzuranzc man and get accident polizy which almost makes accident profitable. I tell you I have too thousand dollars for everybody in car for accident expenses and you can soo me for one hundred thousand dollarz if anything untowards heppenz. wow I dropped a martini onion in the typewriter shift and can only rite lower kaze. memo to f.b.i.; this is not code. just happyness at twelve midnite. this is the evening of my disconnection.—a new life beginz.—fanaticism is when you redouble your efforts when you have missed your aim—santayana—unquote. news for B. love A

To Edward Weston

May 22, 1952

My Dear Edward,

You are NOT finished by a damn shot! The years are bound to have certain effects—I notice my age very much when it comes to packing an 8 x 10 up-hill! Your contribution is historic and it still continues. I wonder if you have any realization of what it means just to visit you? People are vastly moved and stimulated just by your presence.

I worry sometimes that you think you are a burden to others just because you can't scramble around as you used to. Under no conditions could you ever be anything but someone deeply loved and family-close to all of us.

It seems to me that you should rest on the assurance that what you should do is what you can do—have no regrets that you cannot climb Mount Everest!

There should be some plan possible whereby under your supervision a lot of fine printing of your negatives could be done. Maybe another portfolio? The whole point would be to get it done without taxing your strength; miracles can happen under good organization.

And then there is the matter of the existing ORIGINAL prints of yours. I am sure you have enough on hand to provide you with sustenance for many years. I think they should be priced high now. The prints by Dody[1] under your supervision are worth the regular price, but the originals—they are in a different class. Perhaps institutions should acquire sets of them? This is something to talk about. . . .

I had hoped to come down over some weekends and see you. Then a job for TIME came up and every Saturday afternoon and Sunday I am busy with it as it relates to crowds of people. But I shall see thee SOON. . . .

Love to you and all,
Ansel Adams

1. When Edward Weston could no longer print because of his Parkinson's disease, both Dody Weston (Brett's wife) and Brett printed for him.

Daer Deer, Dier Dear BBB & NN

Zowie!

Adams is proud to be fit to bustin'!

Busted all the buttons off'n the vest and bent the zipper!!!

Anne GRADUATED. At last !

But what busts the buttons is that she got the highest honors

anybody ever had - all sorts of special pins, certificates, buttons, etc. and

took it all most normally.

She apparently made a real scolastic record - and in a place

where such things are hard to come by.

She also had the Class Presidency for 2 or 3 years and the

whole student body presidency last year. So, I guess it was worth it!

Where she got thebrains I don't know. But she got 'em.

Ping, goes another button !

Schedule: I go to Yosemite for a week onSaturday May 31st. Must be home on

June 7th, as O'Keeffe is get9ng an honzorary degres from Mills College

and I am invited also to the Presidents supper, etc. Can't miss that; besides

I aave a lot of work to do.

Plan to print most of tomorrow and Friday. Will get a lot

of the 150 prints for Carlson done before I leave.. Perhaps will hear from

you tomorrow or next day; at any event, you can reach me in Yosemite up

to the 6th. I have plans for a lot of new Yosemite pitchurz1 never has the

water been so good.

more soon. Love and cheeriow

ping!!!! goes another buton!

To Beaumont and Nancy Newhall

Daer Deer, Dier Dear BBB & NN,

Zowie!

Adams is proud to be fit to bustin'!

Busted all the buttons off'n the vest and bent the zipper!!!

Anne GRADUATED.[1] At last!

But what busts the buttons is that she got the highest honors anybody ever had—all sorts of special pins, certificates, buttons, etc. and took it all most normally.

She apparently made a real scholastic record—and in a place where such things are hard to come by.

She also had the class presidency for 2 or 3 years and the whole student body presidency last year. So, I guess it was worth it!

Where she got the brains I don't know. But she got 'em.

Ping, goes another button! . . .

Plan to print most of tomorrow and Friday. Will get a lot of the 150 prints for Carlson[2] done before I leave. Perhaps will hear from you tomorrow or next day; at any event, you can reach me in Yosemite up to the 6th. I have plans for a lot of new Yosemite pitchurz—never has the water been so good.

More soon. Love and cheeriow,
Ansel

ping!!!! goes another button!

1. Anne Adams graduated from Dominican High School, San Rafael, California.

2. Ray Carlson, editor of *Arizona Highways* magazine, commissioned Adams and Nancy Newhall to produce a series of photographic essays for the magazine from 1952 to 1954.

To David McAlpin

June 19, 1952

Dear Dave,

Did not intend to write you a letter or so and then "forget" about you. Have just been busy! But I do think of you a lot and wonder how things progress with you and all your activities.

I am in a quandary! Perhaps I usually am in this state, but it seems doubly potent right now. Perhaps I can get it off my chest to you, and I hope I am not imposing on you by so doing.

At various times in my career I have had "static" periods, followed by bursts of change, activity, or new channels of thought. Music-to-photography; that was a complex period. The *f*/64 period—pause—the *Making a Photograph* period—pause—the Stieglitz, McAlpin, MoMA period—pause—the war period—pause—the Guggenheim—*Basic Photo Series*—*My Camera* books—pause, etc. Now I am in a "pause" state, and it seems a long and dull one.

These periods might be interpreted in another way—a sequence of extrovertal and introvertal attitudes. All of which can be most simply described by saying that my "progress" has been intermittent, and that—like all of us—I have been subject to a variety of external forces beyond my immediate awareness.

Just at this moment I seem to have lost much respect for most modern art and photography, and seem to seek the *reasons for expression,* more than the *methods of* expression. Most "expressions" by others seem to bore me. I have no desire to be critical, but I am just not interested! The same old comments, mannerisms, apologies, formulae and "invideousnesses" circulate about the boss of "art." Some new faces, styles, methods—but no new ideas or contributions. I feel I have much more to say than I have said—or that I will be able to say in photography (as I have to practice it). I do not think this is a convenient apology for a thick attitude of mind. The economic pressure increases—and, in inverse square relationship, the creative possibilities diminish.

I have several propositions under way which, if they work out, will give the wolf catfood for awhile, but they will leave little or no time for expressive work. Without expressive work the imagination becomes desiccated. And so on!

I have done a lot of thinking of late about myself, photography, and the state of the world, and I confess I am in a mood of perplexity. I am not one to become discouraged, sour, or "revolutionary"—but I certainly can get perplexed! I have come to the conclusion that I—and perhaps many other artists in various fields—have not been orientated to reality. I am also aware that many artists, sensing this lack of orientation, have turned to Marxian concepts (which have the *illusion* of "reality" and "dedication") or have become cynical and Machiavellian.

Another type of artist has depended upon a different kind of "departure from reality"; he has become intensely personal and subjective, has built up an edifice of introspection and intellectual snobbism. He has often abandoned human responsibilities on the misconception that "nothing should interfere with his Art." The lack of human quality in such cases is usually quite apparent!

Enough about others! I have been guilty of compromise and not-too-clear thinking. I have spent too much time and energy in doing things for the good of the external cause, and not enough for my internal needs. But I do not regret it, because I think I have a certain understanding of the external world I could not have otherwise gained.

But the time is coming when my energies will no longer permit me to "spread"; in fact, that time is now. I have not been feeling myself at all, and the doctor says I appear to be in fine shape except for a chronic tiredness—and this tiredness will take quite a time to overcome (whereas ten years ago I could recuperate in a week or so). However, the need to recuperate combined with the need to increase productivity for reasons of inescapable obligations creates a kind of impasse—and this impasse together with other impasses certainly puts me in a condition of prime perplexity.

What I realize now as an important psychological burden is my sense of *incompletion:* my best work remains unprinted—many of my very best things have never been proofed! And this frustration is augmented by the piling up of *more* uncompleted—or partially completed work. Of course the commercial things get done, but I am referring to some important creative projects such as (1) continuing interpretations of Yosemite (needed because of our concession with the U.S.), (2) the various book-projects, (3) the Southwest series, etc. The ARIZONA HIGH-WAYS text-picture portfolios I am doing with Nancy are fine (bad reproductions so far, but the idea is coming along), but these are but minor expressions of a much larger idea. The chief burden on my conscience is the bulk of my creative work—the work that is the explanation and justification of Adams as photographer.

Hence, I really do not think I can conquer my problem unless I "level" myself off and bring my work "up to date." That should be my chief creative problem at the moment. When my creative work is "amortized" I will then feel free to attempt new flights—and perhaps do my best work. . . .

I have had good advice and have thought a lot about my "financial position" (if you can call it that). My parents' illness and final passing were a severe drain; the small amount of insurance my father had was quickly absorbed in paying off the loans I had to make to carry them through the last years. . . .

On the other hand, if I were able to eliminate commercial work (a pipe-dream as long as the kids are to be educated) I could settle down in Yosemite and write, make fine prints, etc. . . .

The studio in Yosemite (which I have desperately hung on to because of the security for the family which I could not provide) is now doing better and we are getting a ten-year contract from Uncle Sam with many more rights and privileges than before. The Yosemite Park and Curry Company have always been most difficult and have opposed us selling anything but films and photographic items. Virginia has plans for books and fine hand-crafts, etc., and now that we shall be permitted to sell these things we might really make a little money. Virginia got almost to the edge of financial collapse. The *My Camera* books on Yosemite and the National Parks have done all right, and will turn in a final profit of several thousand dollars. But the Weston Point Lobos book is a terrible flop (Virginia is paying off a $15,000 debt on that one)!

So, while I have much to think about, I am not implying that I am in desperate straits! But I am in a difficult state regarding the straight creative work.

There must be some way to crack this nut! I use more and more assistance, but still do not have enough work to employ a constant assistant. It is like one of those confusing mazes they use to drive mice insane; whenever I think there is a way out I find a blank wall.

I have the two final books of the BASIC PHOTO SERIES to complete. That is necessary and not bothersome. . . .

At present I have a little job for *Time,* and a possible one for *Life.* I also am starting negotiations with the telephone company[1] and Varian Associates (this latter client might also be the subject of a LIFE story).[2] I also have a Colorama for Kodak and a couple of waterfall pictures in color. Then the workshop in July—looks like I shall have to limit it to the first two week session as everyone interested desires that period.

In the fall I have further *Arizona Highways* stories, and hope to get to Aspen[3] if I am included on the panel. There is some talk of my going to Europe. I really do not want to go, and would go only if I was guaranteed a really large assignment; otherwise I could not possibly afford it.

Apart from the European trip, all of the above assignments add up to a break-even income. They sound as if they should do more; possibly the telephone and Varian clients can work into something rather large but I have no assurance at this time that this might occur. In the meantime, the creative work remains static.

I am planning PORTFOLIO THREE for this coming Christmas season. Title: YOSEMITE VALLEY.[4] This I am sure will move rather well, and it is important that I continue to produce new things on Yosemite because the National Park Service grants our concession on the explicit basis that we provide new and "artistic" photography. That is all right with me, and this portfolio can be a beautiful collection, and also make some cash. . . .

To sum up: While I do have some practical problems, and am not able to establish a nest-egg as I should, etc., I am not in serious difficulties in that direction.

But I am in increasingly serious condition regarding my creative work. I MUST catch up with myself. I can produce this creative work completion on a "break-even" basis (just as I described some of the professional assignments above).

This has been a long letter, and I certainly appreciate being able to write it to you. I hope I have not imposed on you to read it. If you have any ideas, believe me they will be appreciated!

Affectionate greetings to you and Sally and all the children.

Wish I could see you SOON,

As ever,
ANSEL ADAMS

1. American Telephone and Telegraph was interested in buying a photographic mural from Adams for their corporate offices.

2. *Life* magazine hired Adams to photograph the Varian brothers, inventors of the Klystron tube, for the article "Wizards of the Coming Wonders," *Life*, January 4, 1954, pp. 93–94. (See *An Autobiography*, p. 169.)

3. Adams attended the Aspen Photo Conference, September–October 1951, sponsored by the Aspen Institute for Humanistic Studies, Aspen, Colorado; this "think tank" on photography included Adams, Beaumont Newhall, Berenice Abbott, Dorothea Lange, and Minor White, among others.

4. *Portfolio III, Yosemite Valley,* a selection of 16 photographs, San Francisco: Sierra Club, 1960.

To Nancy Newhall

San Francisco
August 1, 1952
Friday night

Dear Nancy:

Just back from Cisco Buttes. The place has glamour because it is on the route of the early "Horizon" people; it's near Emigrant Gap, and Donner Lake is just beyond the rim-line to the east. Harry [Oye] has fixed me up; I could barely plug in the old IBM! I left at 6 AM yesterday, and have not washed since then—now 8 PM next day! It was about 110° in the foothills and about 97 where I was working. I have consumed 9 cans of fruit juices, 2 steak sandwiches, 3 quarts of milk, 6 packages of wintergreen lozenges (my lowest ebb in candy), and now I am doing my best with Harry's concoctions and a COOL hornfull fog outside!

I enclose some material which you can send back *soon* because I must answer it.

I am tired—but not in an unhealthy way.

Brought back some amazingly alive dead wood! One looks just like a duck and I honestly believe I am going "curio"; but it's suchahusky-duck!!!!!! The others look like a Weston print; WHY did that little lovable bastard tie onto *all* the amorous forms anyway?? ONLY THE BRAVE DESERVE THE FAIR!!!!!!! . . .

But it is all difficult—like youse guys, I have to make a living—and how can I afford to break away for too long on speculation? If I were alone in the world I would take all possible chances. But Mike and Anne are signed up for Stanford—and BOY! that ain't shredded wheat!! . . .

I would like to describe feebly a visual experience which I had last night:

I was sleeping on top of the Helios IV[1] which was backed against the microwave building on Cisco Buttes. If I looked up and back I saw the two 10' square "horns" which, seen in perspective, were really magnificent—I thought I could see all the separate stars of the Milky Way (of course I couldn't, but it LOOKED that way)! From deep in the valley I could hear the constant roar of the trains going over the Sierra mainline—steam, diesel, etc.—all with their particular hollow and irrefutable sounds. Across the sky above me flashed every 8 seconds the searchlight of the CAA tower. The whole thing was absolutely of the moment of our years—and yet it did not have a "camera" possibility!

[238]

I am wondering if we limit ourselves to a "chosen medium"—when we really should be in position to use ALL mediums?????? I could paint what I saw last night—*if* I could paint!!!!!

Forgive this scratchy document! It is 8:30, I can hardly see the keyboard. I have around me piles of letters, bills, etc. to be answered. I have no new jokes. I need—and am taking a shower.

More soon and a lot of it— — — — — — — — love,
Ansel
A. A.

1. Helios IV was Adams' name for his car, a 1946 black-and-white Cadillac station wagon fitted with a rooftop camera platform.

From Charles Sheeler[1]

Irvington, NY
January 9, 1953

Dear Ansel,

The photographs arrived and we are deeply stirred. The portrait of Edward [Weston]—what a masterpiece it is and what a great pleasure it is to have it. It will presently have a place of honor on the wall to share with those who have the eyes to see.

We were greatly surprised and pleased to see the results of those you made in commemoration of that occasion.[2] The conditions all seemed adverse but we evidently did not reckon with your potentialities. Three cheers for you, and three cheers again.

Also, we have noted that at last the octagonal house has been photographed. You have given it a oneness of form which none of the others did, including the Sheelers.

Last Wednesday I saw the show[3] at the MoMA. and thought your group was superlative. Devastating though—I had the impulse to go home collect my cameras and trade or sell them for some other tools. Maybe I could still make a go at something—I could try. . . .

With another three cheers for you. Musya and I wish you all good things for 1953.

Sincerely yours,
Charles Sheeler

1. Charles Sheeler, painter and photographer.

2. Adams and Nancy Newhall visited Charles and Musya Sheeler in Irvington, N.Y., one Sunday and Adams photographed them and their home. (See *An Autobiography*, p. 206.)

3. Adams' photographs were included in the exhibit "Diogenes with a Camera II," 1952–1953.

To Michael Adams

Yosemite National Park
Christmas 1953

Dear Mike—

I began this letter in San Francisco but am just finishing it up today in Yosemite. I never wrote a letter of this kind before, because I never had a son joining the Air Force before! The idea of Christmas is very strange to me at this time, but we have to keep up the illusion. I want to give you everything—but I can't think of a single thing you really need! That telephoto lens sounds good to me!

You are now a man, joining up with a very important part of our national defense. What is more important, you are taking your place in the pattern of our time (which exists whether we like it or not). I never joined up with anything; I have missed the peaks of such experience, and I envy you considerably. Now you are quite far from the little boy in *Michael and Anne in Yosemite Valley*[1]—and yet I wonder how far you can get—or really want to get—from that particular kind of reality. I doubt if you can ever realize the advantages of being raised in Yosemite—only outsiders could grasp the potentials. But such a life would have value only if it instilled in you some awareness of intangible qualities beyond the ordinary. I think it has done this for you, and that you will fully appreciate them in the future.

I have spent a good part of my life trying to understand the obligations of a parent! The conventional idea of a parent is very obnoxious to me. We gave you considerable freedom of being—it was a pet theory of ours. I think it worked out quite well; I see nothing about you that I am not proud of!

If you are man enough to join the Air Force, you are man enough to comprehend the problems surrounding us. I have never talked much about "morality" because I trusted your innate sense of values to carry you through and I distrust words written or spoken about wordless things. I have had quite a lot to do with the external world—and quite a lot with the internal world, too. I am wondering, in the afternoon of my own life, just what your day will be. It will take much effort, devotion and compassion—something beyond the thin skin of morality—to bring you to a full realization of what it is to be a man in the face of the world as it now is and in the face of a perplexing future. You cannot be misled by the obvious "easy" way—there isn't any!

When you go to Fresno on the 28th you take on a whole new world of experience—and you carry a lot of the experience of your mother and father with you—which is there to help you if you need it. You are entering a bright new world of your own. The skies are the new land— I envy you, and if I were younger I would like to be up there, too.

We cannot grasp the full meaning of your new life to you, but we would like to share just a little of it with you. Please make a special effort to write us often—to your mother especially. I don't think this is too much to ask.

Good luck—all our love!!!
Ansel

1. *Michael and Anne in Yosemite Valley*, text by Virginia Adams, photographs by Ansel Adams, London and New York: The Studio Publications, 1941.

From Brett Weston

Monterey
July 22, 1955

[Telegram]

HAVING BENEFIT SALE OF EDWARD WESTON'S GREATEST WORK. HE URGENTLY NEEDS CONTINUING DOCTORS AND NURSES CARE. GREATLY WEAKENED FROM RECENT OPERATION. CAN YOU HELP IN ANY WAY TO RAISE A SUBSTANTIAL SUM? CONTACT ME DIRECT

BRETT

To Brett Weston

San Francisco
July 22, 1955

Dear Brett—

I am deeply distressed to hear about Edward's illness. I knew nothing about it! Had I known I would have communicated with you, or would have come down to Carmel. I am always ready to do what I can to help—I am terribly fond of Edward, and find it difficult to express my feelings.

I have been thinking a lot of him of late. Had it not been for a series of problems and troubles and pressures I would have come down to see you all. But I should have written him!

Now—what can I do?? I am enclosing a small check just to help out—wish it were for ten times that amount! I have written Dr. Morley (copy of the letter enclosed) and I hope for some results there. She will be back about the 30th. . . .

I am flying east tonight with Peter Pollack [curator of photography] of the Chicago Art Institute. He will try to raise some more money for prints. Naturally, I shall see the Newhalls tomorrow, and we will get something started there. The Newhalls and I are going to New York the following Wednesday, and we will contact people there. Then I am going to Cambridge about the 3rd of August—and can do some scouting in that area.

Tell me a little about what prints will be available. I think it is good to put the appeal on a basis of recompense in terms of *prints*, rather than just contributions. I am sure Edward would prefer it that way. Now, does McAlpin know about it? If you have any suggestions on special people in the east I should see or telephone please write me. . . .

My love to you and Dody and all. I am thinking of you, as I know what these situations are! But nothing is too good for Edward! And please let me know how things progress.

And my love to him. Assure him I have not forgotten him!!! I know Virginia echoes my feelings and remarks!!!!

As ever,
Ansel

From Brett Weston

Carmel
July 25, 1955

My Dear Ansel—

Your warm wonderful letter and the check arrived—our thanks. You have three of the earlier E.W. prints due or four Print Project prints.[1] Let me know your choice. . . .

Dad's condition is slightly improved since his return from the hospital, but he is almost helpless and needs three attendants on eight hour shifts. I won't go into detail, but Dody, Bob Nash, and my ministrations, though loving, are not on the necessary professional level. We have talked of selling Wildcat Hill and having Dad move in at Garapata,[2] and this we may do shortly. However, we think it best for his morale to stay on here as long as possible, in his own place. . . .

My plan is to stay on here as head nurse until I can be free to open the portrait studio in Carmel—

Our love and thanks Ansel—
Brett

1. "Earlier" prints by Weston refers to those made by Weston himself; "Print Project" prints refers to those made by Brett Weston.

2. Brett Weston had a home in Garapata Canyon, just south of Wildcat Hill and Carmel, California.

To Edwin Land[1]

March 12, 1956

Dear Din—

I think the word we have been seeking to describe the kind of photography people like Weston, Strand and yours truly are trying to do may be —
TRANSCENDENTAL
Minor White uses it in his review of Feininger's book, *Creative Photography*[2] (which is anything but!), mentioning the fact that Feininger avoids reference to "transcendental" art, being satisfied to rest on the soft bed of Corn and Conventional stuff.

I throw this term into the pot with the hope that it might be used to clarify the ever-growing confusion in photographic semantics.

I assume that it means, actually, Art in the most penetrating sense of the term. It is the exact opposite of the "pictorial," "Human-Interest" (shallow sense) and "popular" (again shallow sense), and relates to the depths of experience and perception—with motives of quasi-religious meanings. The term "Transcendentalism" was applied to the philosophy and teaching of Emerson. We should be careful, however, to avoid any "superior" connotations.

It is distressing to be aware of the basic resistances of other artists (painters, sculptors, etc.) to the expressive aspects of photography. Even in San Francisco—noted for its photography—one cannot get into the Art Annual! The painters lean towards the Cartier-Bresson type of Observational photography—presumably believing that "distance" means "security." Or they will take interest in "non-objective" photography—but negative interest, if you know what I mean.

It is interesting to observe that the photographers of fifty to eighty years ago (and many today, too) imitate romantic, obvious painting—while today a considerable group of photographers strive to achieve the effects of non-objective painting!

Both imitations are illogical. The photographers who have followed the more-or-less clear path of straight photography clearly show that the medium has its own particular capacities for the revelation of both informational and spiritual truth!

In the selection of photographs for the proposed collection[3] I hope it will be possible to choose images which reflect all aspects of photography in their most clearly defined examples.

This further supports my contention that Polaroid—in its general presentation through the hoped-for "superior" journal—would associate itself with photography-in-entirety, rather than just glorify itself. I do not believe it will have anything to fear in any direction! It can surpass most conventional photography in many ways.

I have made enough photographs to date on Land film to be quite certain about the superior qualities of the medium. Superficially, I have been restricted by a few obvious physical short-comings and defects in cameras and materials. Once these defects are cleared up the momentum should carry us very far—and fast!

Transcendentally yours,
Ansel Adams

1. Edwin Land, founder and president of Polaroid Corporation, Cambridge, Mas-

sachusetts. In 1949, Adams became a consultant to the company and continued in that capacity until his death.

2. Minor White. "Andreas Feininger/The Creative Photographer," *Aperture*, Vol. 4, No. 1, pp. 40–41.

3. Land proposed to form a collection of photographs for Polaroid Corporation.

To Beaumont and Nancy Newhall

Poughkeepsie,[1] New York

1956

Deer Peeps,

The weather is getting me DOWN. I can't make pictures of the outside—I don't dare leave because then it would clear up—I don't like starting an inside job because then I know it would clear up outside!

Plans are for me to keep praying for sun—do the outside job, go to Cambridge, return for the inside job, etc.

In the meantime it seems perfectly ridiculous to be so near the Newhalls and not see them! . . .

U.S. Camera has asked I do a monthly column for them on Polaroid photography! Get $100 for each. Polaroid thinks it OK. Will dash off three or four a week.

1st idea. Hold the camera.
2nd " Don't drop it.
3rd " See that there is film in it.
     (Check with credit manager before buying more film.)
4th " Shake dice for the proper shutter number.
5th " ROLL DEM BONES! Click!
6th " Look, Mama! a pikture! Already with no hands, head, or feet!
Note: "It is proposed that a more accurate finder-system be considered in order to consummate a more accurate area-relationship between field and stream (pardon me, I mean *symbolic image*) so that all parts of the subjects' anatomy excepting, perhaps, the *middle* parts, will be presented within the picture area. . . ."

Anyway, I will see or write seriously, soon. Luff to Minor; will do Polaroid article. Will try to get this job done as soon as possible.

Cheeriow—and luff, . . .

Ansel

1. IBM commissioned Adams to photograph their headquarters in Poughkeepsie, New York.

To Beaumont and Nancy Newhall

Yosemite National Park
March 26, 1956

Dear Peeps—

THE WEDDING BELLS HAVE DIED AWAY[1]
  THERE'S STILL RICE IN MY BEARD,
THE CAKE IS ET, THE BILLS ARE MET,
  'TWAS BETTER THAN I FEARED!

THE BRIDE AND GROOM HAVE GONE THEIR WAY
  THE BAR IS DRAINED QUITE DRY
I DON'T KNOW HOW, BUT I HOPE THAT NOW
  TO RECUPERATE WE SHALL TRY.

This is perfectly lousy—but the Wedding was perfectly beautiful. Grand music, Anne looked wonderful. Groom swell. Pappy said all his single line OK. Mammy in resplendent new dress and hat. Oodles of people. Reception at Ahwahnee for about 400! Anne got such a pile of loot it will take three station wagon loads to get it to Menlo Park!

Sure wish you had been on hand!! Will describe details when I see you. All goes well. Hope same for you.

LUFFFFFFFFFFFFFFFF,
Ansel

1. Anne Adams married Charles Mayhew on March 24, 1956.

To Edwin Land

Yosemite National Park
July 5, 1956

Dear Din,

. . . I am working on the 4x5.[1] As I said, the holder works beautifully, and the packs function beautifully (mechanically). I suppose the surface defects and the leakage of fluid, etc. should be considered "mechanical" but I think of them as relating to the film-paper combination and not to the general structure of the pack. As soon as these defects are overcome the pack should be an accomplished project!

Now—the next step is the introduction of the 4x5 to the profession. The defects have been so severe (mostly due—apparently—from careless handling in assembly) that there is not a stock of good "pictures." I am awaiting this necessary perfection before I can make the illustrations for Book V²; I want to use the 4x5 in every possible way in this book as it will be a fine working demonstration.

I have had some enlightening and encouraging talks with Charles Sheeler. He is a wise man and a really great artist. He works slowly and with the greatest efficiency of energy. He is one of the very few artists that sell all they paint—practically before the paint is dry on the canvas! He has a great faith in the potentials of the Polaroid-Land process. He feels, as I do, that comparisons are dangerous; the process must stand on its own and contribute its own peculiar qualities to photography as a whole. He clarified a very important point that I have long been concerned with—the artist as a functioning being, working from within and with only his personal motivations, in contradistinction to the artist's work on assignments and dominated by external requirements. He feels, as I feel, that the test of art lies in its relationship to external humanity —but, also, that the artist must not neglect himself and his most subtle moods and visions. In each category, the artist must accomplish his best; the disciplines have mutual advantage. Without the deeply personal creative work the functional work can become drab and restricted.

With the Polaroid-Land process he feels the artist can learn to adapt himself to any particular quality of material—in relation to his personal expressive work, but that if the process is to function in the world of APPLIED photography certain latitudes and controls will be required. He feels we should stress "acutance"³ as much as possible. He would rather have a brilliant—even harsh—image with acutance, than a smooth, richly toned image without acutance. The VC [variable contrast] property of some of the films interests him tremendously. He is the kind of person who lets his thoughts steep a long time; I shall probably get some more good ideas from him next week! . . .

Warmest greetings to all—
Ansel Adams

1. Adams championed the creation of professional Polaroid materials and advised the company on the development of the 4x5-inch film-pack adapter.

2. *Artificial-Light Photography,* Hastings-on-Hudson: Morgan & Morgan, 1956.

3. Acutance, an objective measurement of sharpness.

From David Brower[1]

San Francisco
September 27, 1956

Dear Ansel,

. . . Last night Anne[2] and I were going over what happened in Yosemite, and Anne was especially moved by the LeConte exhibit.[3] She had seen it without benefit of music. I can only assume from what she said that if there had been music too, she could not have found words to describe her feelings, even by last night. She said, "I guess Ansel is just the greatest photographer there ever has been." She added that she was moved by Nancy's words, too, and by the way they so superbly complemented what your photographs were saying.

Let me assure you that idle praise does not pass from Anne's lips. . . .

I just thought you ought to know this and to know that Anne and I are grateful for the doors you have opened to appreciation, doors which you opened because of your genius, you bring kudos to the club which we could never afford to buy and couldn't have bought elsewhere even if we had the price.

I'll confess I was slow to grasp what *This Is The American Earth* could be and do. Your own faith in an idea made it work, inspired the initial contribution toward the material, brought Nancy's and your talents to bear, and beat the technical and human relations problems of getting it shown, and then multiplied all this by bringing the Smithsonian Institute and the State Department into the act—and now probably the book.

Through all this I, myself, have gained a new appreciation of the creative process and hope that we and our successors will find ways to administer the club in such a way that there will always be a fertile place for the seeds of ideas like yours to grow.

I'll stop right now before I get into difficulty with my figures of speech. There's more to be said, but I'll just let your imagination carry on from here.

Sincerely,
Dave

1. David Brower had become the executive director of the Sierra Club.

2. Anne Brower, wife of David.

3. Adams and Nancy Newhall organized an exhibit of photographs (by Adams and others) entitled "This Is the American Earth" for the Sierra Club to display in their Yosemite headquarters, the LeConte Memorial Lodge.

From Charles Sheeler

Birds Nest Gulch[1]
August 1, 1956

Dear Pard there ain't nothing new around here why we wouldn't know one day from another if I didn't cut another notch in my gun barrel come to think of it if this keeps up I'll have to get me a new gun there ain't hardly any more room on this here one how is it out thataway did you have a season this year when buffalos were running did you here tell of anyone striking a new vein out around Volcano just for the hell of it I am thinking of going up to get me a Kodiak bear the skin would look real pretty in front of the fireplace next winter and the Missus could wear it for a coat if it gets real cold and it would be something different from what Im not doing now. You have to keep squirming around or else your apt to mildew and that aint good.

Davy Crockett Sheeler F.I.A.L

1. The Sheelers stayed in the San Francisco home of the Adamses while they were away.

To Charles and Musya Sheeler

December 30, 1956

Dear Charles and Musya,

I have been wracking what brains I have to write you a decent telegram or letter. The mental output is in sharp contrast to the motivating spirit! However, I will begin this tome by stating that I (and all here) love you both dearly, that we miss you, that we want you back, and—just because we don't write—don't get the idea we neglect you!

It was a hectic trip east—will tell you all about it sometime! We were both terribly sorry we did not have a chance for a real visit, but it really was JAMMED.

Now I have written a little negative-positive poem, which I set forth hereon, knowing the wherewithal, poetically speaking, is lacking forthwith, but—howsomever and notwithstanding, here she be—

GREEN GROWETH THE VERDIGRIS
  RED SHINES THE BLUSH
WHO GIVES A GOOD GOD DAMN?
  PRAISE TO THE THRUSH!

[249]

TWAS THE EVE BEFORE SHOWING
   AND ALL THROUGH THE HOUSE
NOT A CRITIC WAS STIRRING
   NOT EVEN A LOUSE!

THE PICTURE IS PAINTED
   THE FRAME IS INSTALLED
THE CLIENTS ARE THRONGING
   BUT ARTIST'S APPALLED!!!

THE AUDIENCE WHISPERS –
   "HOW SHARP AND HOW BOLD"
"HOW FLUENT THE STATEMENT"
   "HOW WARM AND HOW COLD!"

THE TRUTH, MY DEAR CHILDREN,
   HAS JUST COME TO MIND:
THE THRONG IS ENTRANCED
   WITH A *VENETIAN BLIND*!!!!!!!

The above does NOT relate to the paintings of one Charles Sheeler! Exactly the Opposite!!! Now, I shall try to write one about Russian Kisses for Musya, but THAT I shall have to forward by Express or Carrier Pigeon!

I am a bit tired and non-compos-mentis. I shall go stew in my own pidity! Hayle to the New Year!!!! WOW!!!!

Loads of love from us all *ansel*
virginia
beaumont
nancy
et al
Ansel

To Beaumont Newhall

San Francisco
January 15, 1957

Dear Beaumont,

Nancy is working on the report to the USIA[1] and I am hoping she will get it done so that we can type it and send it off tonight to meet the deadline. As usual, she is doing more than is required, but there is no use trying to slow her down! After all, she is creating beauty which is exactly the reverse of what I have just come from! I went to the opening of the FAMILY OF MAN[2] at the California Palace of the Legion of Honor, Lincoln Park, San Francisco 21, California, U.S.A. SO!

It is the original exhibit as shown in that Palace of the Legion of the Dishonored [MoMA] on 53rd Street, New York City 19, N.Y., U.S.A.

I opened my mind as far as I possibly could before going. I tried to make rationalizations as to the Importance of Content, the Grand Idea, etc. I find what is, to me, the most insidious concentration of sheer ugliness, brutality, and banality I have ever imagined, much less seen.

There are some beautiful photographs (they were beautiful until they came under the Magic Fire Spell of the Great Man). There are some juxtapositions of merit. At times one gets the glimmer of another dimension. But it all goes up in the smoke of the Obvious, the Banal, and the Careless.

It is worse than I could ever have imagined it could be.

After all, the image—what one sees with the eyes—is important, just as the quality of the instrument on which music is played accentuates the quality of the music itself and makes it live in the spirit. There are some images which probably could not be any better than they are, and yet are important pictures. There are other images which have no justification for existing except in terms of the beautiful image.

In this gargantuan, crude, and brutal presentation, all good is leveled off, all sensitivity is strangled in hideous blacks and grays, spots, warps, uneven panels in big prints, bad proportions in associated prints, tricks, and bleakness.

I guess it is time for me to make a decision—or else get out of photography. The decision is simple—avoid such monkey-business like the plague and pump for what I think Stieglitz stood for, and which you people stand for—and let the chips fall where they may!

Ah Me! Ah Wilderness!

Affectionate greetings and much understanding!!!

Ansel

1. Adams and Nancy Newhall proposed that the United States Information Agency circulate the exhibit "This Is the American Earth" in Europe.

2. "The Family of Man" was an exhibit of photographs organized by Edward Steichen that enjoyed tremendous popular response.

To George Ballis

June 1, 1957

Dear George Ballis,

I shall be pleased to accept the position of vice-chairman (among others) of your Mammoth Pass Road Committee.[1]

Pressure of professional work will not permit me to be very active, except in spirit, but I shall do my best.

As the years go by I am more and more convinced that roads in the wilderness in general are the most serious single danger. The history of the past twenty years shows a sharply rising curve of use and exploitation and it is apparent to anyone who looks at the situation objectively that what we know today as wilderness may be literally non-existent in the tragically near future. What is difficult to explain to the people as a whole is that the qualities of wilderness are not to be measured in material terms; the intangible elements represent the prime cause of devotion to wilderness, and these are destroyed by what otherwise might appear as completely innocuous developments. The maximum development of secondary areas served by existing roads should become the objective. If we approach the problem of the proposed Mammoth Pass Road on the basis that while several decades ago it might have been justified as a foil to prevent the Lone Pine-Porterville Road, it is now (in the light of increasing population pressures) a major threat to the integrity of the Sierra Wilderness. We will, I am sure, accomplish more than if we merely oppose without full explanation.

Good luck, cordially,

Ansel Adams

1. The Mammoth Pass Road Committee opposed the construction of a highway that would cross the Sierra Nevada from Devil's Postpile, west of Mammoth Lakes, to the San Joaquin Valley. The road was never constructed.

To Horace Albright[1]

July 11, 1957

Dear Horace:

I have been very remiss in not writing you before this. . . .

Within my capacity for legal understanding (slight) I have attempted to take an objective view on the Wilderness Bill.[2] Emotionally, I am strongly inclined toward any means to further protect the wild places. This bill—and other important legislation over the past decades—seems to represent a kind of National Conscience—it is difficult, if not impossible, for the layman to comprehend the legal and legislative complexities, but he can (and does) respond to the underlying motivations. . . .

I came to Yosemite first in 1916 (was 14 years old). Until 1929–30 I was actively studying music—then turned to photography. My life has been largely concerned with the interpretive and expressive aspects, and I naturally have viewed the National Parks and the wilderness through the eyes of an artist rather than those of a scientist, politician, or administrator. I have been returned to the Board of Directors of the Sierra Club largely because of my "nuisance" value; certainly not because of any ability in legislative and political fields! Over the years I have seen the material values and qualities of Yosemite "improve" and the emotional, "magical," and inspirational moods regress. This is very difficult to put into words; it is frankly related to the intangibles, and can only make sense in that domain.

I have always considered that the prime objectives of the National Parks were to provide inspiration, self-discovery of spirit in the wild places, and appropriate recreation. The principal parks and monuments are set aside and protected for such human benefits—not for economic purposes. They are, in effect, vast areas devoted to the development of the spirit and for recreation in the true sense of the term. This concept places the National Parks at the highest level of an advanced civilization. With this concept as a guiding light, it is difficult to comprehend how exploitation and "development" of recent kind can be justified and it is unfortunate that the Service has become so large that it cannot dwell upon the prime problems—but must preserve its own operational momentums and *create* activities to keep afloat. What I am saying is, in effect, that the Service itself—its momentums, energies, political resources, and public relations—has become more important than what it was originally set up to serve—the parks and the park ideals and spirit. Everyone in the Service is trapped in the vast web-like machinery of operations, development, policy, and public contacts. With the best intentions the Service has, I believe, lost touch with the more subtle and fragile elements of its responsibility.

I am quite aware that there are vast legislative and operational problems which must be faced, that the increasing population pressures make the present more difficult than the past (and the future will be more difficult than the present). The parks belong to the people, but I believe it is the responsibility of the Park Service to protect and administer the parks for the people in terms of basic park and wilderness values, and not approach their responsibilities on the basis of selling the Service and the parks to the nation. . . .

I am always inclined to make comparison between the functions and administration of the National Parks and of the National Gallery of Art in Washington. Both are the property of the people of our country. The Gallery of Art exists as a most excellent depository and means of display of truly great works of art. It is there for all who *wish* to come. People are not sucked in by excessive publicity, or by extraneous activities and entertainment. Nobody is making any profit, prestige or material out of the National Gallery as far as I can judge. But many people and institutions are making profit out of the parks—operators, travel lines, peripheral business, etc.—and these exert pressures along the complex and typical pattern of influencing legislation, political and bureaucratic polity, and creating a public demand. . . .

. . . I do not believe in exclusion of anyone from the parks. But I do believe in what might be termed "natural inclusion"—the audience which is automatically attracted to the parks because of their intrinsic values—not the imposed entertainment values, or the values which are stimulated and augmented by publicity. I go to the National Gallery to see great paintings—the Gallery's function is simple and direct. But I go to Yosemite not because of the attractions of the firefall, dancing, vaudeville and popular music, urban cocktail lounges and food services, hideous curios, slick roads, and a general holiday spirit—and somewhere back of this smoke-screen of resortism the real Valley can be seen (but usually through a thick haze of campfire and incinerator smoke). One cannot point out all of the aspects of resortism and condemn them in themselves; most are quite decent and valid (excepting the Firefall and the curios) by themselves, but are simply dominant at present in terms of the Yosemite experience for, I believe, the majority of visitors. They bear little relationship to the basic values of one of the most remarkable and inspirational places on earth. . . .

That is why I support the Wilderness Bill, and why I would support ANY bill that would serve to add protection, reduce exploitation (by business OR government), and aid in securing some positive remnant of true wilderness. I appreciate the pressures which the Park and Forest

Services constantly resist, and I am thankful that so many *are* resisted, but there may come a time when the pressures might well exceed in power all the resistances we can muster under the present setup. If any legislation would serve to aid in resisting such destructive pressures it should be supported by all sympathetic people. . . .

You see, I still believe in the fairies of mood and simplicity. And I think we are straying far from the appropriate paths in our frantic "developments" of the few beautiful wild places remaining in our land.

> With warmest greetings and regards,
> Ansel Adams

1. Horace Albright, environmental leader and former director of the National Park Service.

2. The Wilderness Act, finally passed in 1964, created the national wilderness system, providing designated lands even more protection than national park status.

To Harold Bradley,[1] *Richard Leonard,*[2] *and David Brower*

> San Francisco
> July 27, 1957

Gentlemen:

My concern over the relationship of the National Park Service and the Sierra Club and allied organizations is growing, and I cannot, in all honesty, look upon this situation except with the greatest anxiety and pessimism.

I think we are in a complex position where we cannot see the forest because of the trees. I think we need to take a fresh objective view of the situation and resolve to attack the problem with all we have in reserve, and without delay.

I think we are inclined to be too gentlemanly; realistically, we are confronted with a determined, bureaucratic-organization group who have lost perspective on their proper functions and are concentrating upon the internal affairs and perpetuations of the Service.

I think the basic questions which the American People should ask the Service and Congress are:

1. Are the National Parks, in terms of their founding concepts and present need, important?

2. Are the functions of the National Park Service being properly

executed by the administrative heads in the Washington, Regional, and Park offices?

3. Is the National Park Service not guilty of criminal negligence if they permit destruction of basic values in order to achieve acclaim for "improvements" and fill an artificially inflated public "need"?

4. Is it necessary to desecrate the Lake Tenaya area by construction of a road of "highway" standards?[3] What justification can they present for such a road? How can they justify the destruction of priceless natural beauty for any reason other than urgent National security? Again, what is the fundamental *purpose* of the Parks and the wilderness areas?

I believe the above questions could be better and more vigorously framed. But what is most important is this: The Park Service MUST be thoroughly deflated and thoroughly re-organized. Heads must roll. There will be hard feelings. The American people must assert their recognition of the present danger in no uncertain terms, and a moratorium called on ALL Park "developments." Everyone is so hypnotized by the MISSION 66[4] propaganda that the lurking tragic dangers are not apparent.

I believe that we must have a strong Park Service, but I do not want to see a Service both Strong and Bad! Tenaya Lake is infinitely more important than the Park Service! I think public opinion would demand a drastic change if the facts were known.

Hence, I wish to put my opinions on record before you:

1. Immediate and vigorous action is imperative.

2. The character of this action must be relentless and severe in order to accomplish the necessary goals.

3. Whatever we do must be accompanied with maximum publicity!

4. We must pull no punches, favor not friends, and let the chips fall where they may.

5. The leading Conservation organizations should be invited to participate in this campaign. If they refuse, we must go it alone.

6. I feel that if 25 to 30 leading citizens entered Taxpayer's suits in the federal courts, accusing the Park Service of negligence and error in the fulfillment of their obligations as custodians of the people's National Parks, AND IF THESE SUITS WERE GIVEN MAXIMUM NATIONWIDE PUBLICITY, we would have placed the first wedge in the program. I do not think these suits would get anywhere from a legal viewpoint, but they might serve to awaken the public to the dire situation which now exists and threatens to worsen, rather than improve,

as time hurries on. The present Park Service personnel are, I believe, incapable of significant change of opinion. They must be frightened into constructive action. I think the recent actions of the Service, their secretive attitude, and their obvious insincerity, are evidences of a serious, if not criminal, administration of their affairs. Armed with the facts, I do not see how we can fail—unless we water down our approach to the usual innocuous and polite exchange of views. The failure of that approach is all too obvious on every hand. We gain little things and are in dire peril of losing the larger objectives.

In closing, I think we must take the attitude that—in the face of the enormous spiritual and inspirational value of the Parks and the wilderness areas—NO bureau, no plan, no established project, no road, no concessionaire, no works of man of any kind has consequential value. We must proceed as if all of these factors did not exist. They are expendable—the Parks are not. We must also wipe the slate clean of all past procedural habits, commitments, and opinions. *Our obligation is clear in only one direction.* We must admit our own errors of judgment, too.

I see no other way to save our priceless heritage.

Sincerely,
ANSEL ADAMS

1. Harold Bradley was the president of the Sierra Club.
2. Richard Leonard, a member of the Board of Directors of the Sierra Club for 36 years, was, at this time, its treasurer.
3. The National Park Service proposed the construction of a road across the Sierra Nevada through the Tioga Pass in Yosemite National Park; its specifications called for blasting and removal of part of a great granite dome on the western edge of Tenaya Lake.
4. Mission 66 was a government program to promote automobile travel in the United States and the attendant road improvements necessary for increased highway use.

To Edwin Land

January 5, 1958

Dear Din:

Edward Weston's passing[1] evokes a number of thoughts about photography. I find myself questioning a lot of directions and situations, and Weston's death closes an era and makes these questions pointed, and sometimes disturbing.

Edward represented the *artist*, and there have been very few indeed in the domain of photography. His technique was about as empirical as anything could be. His equipment severely simple. He rarely photographed anything he did not find interest in; his pictures were reflections of his inner spiritual and "unconscious" drive. Many events conspired in his favor, and yet—without conviction and energy, and an almost monk-like existence, he could not have produced the vast body of work which places him at the apex of his art.

I don't think anyone can surmise their own achievements had conditions and associations been other than they were for them. I can think up a very different life for myself had I stayed with music, had I followed Edward's direction and left the "world" as we know it or had I plunged more deeply into the world than I have done. But I have no assurance that any difference in environment, family, professionalism, etc. could have possibly given me more than I have (probably would have given less!). You made a remark once that I shall always remember (we were at Carmel). You said to me, "Edward lives in a shrine; you live in the world." I accept this as an excellent definition of the difference between Weston and myself. Of course, one could quibble about the meaning of "world," but I do have a greater extrovertal interest in things as they are than he had—he had a consuming interest in things as they *should be*. That his work has more basic esthetic quality than mine I do not doubt for an instant. But, again, the real meaning of *esthetic* is an elusive thing!

However, Edward's work remains an example of achievement-of-purpose, and as a standard of expressive quality in photography. The trends in the present world of art are, to me, distressingly "mental" and formal; there is an actual distrust of beauty, especially in photography. There is also a tendency towards "push-button" art and craft which I find discouraging. I think that for the millions of diarists who can reap such rich benefits from the Land process, for example, the "push-button" system is a helpful one. But the potentially large and growing group of serious professionals and creative people will demand appropriate controls of the medium to enable them to express their ideas, moods, and emotions in terms of photography. I am quite sure that the process lends itself to a very wide range of function and expression; I think that if Weston had been twenty years younger he would have had great interest in the process—and probably would have succeeded with it as strikingly as he did with color photography (he really knew very little about color,

[258]

and relied on intuition, taste and craft-respect). But Weston's pictures would always be Westons. They would not be standardized images any more than do Edward's color pictures look like those that come from Kodak's studios.

As I said above, Weston's technique was empirical. He actually had a great distrust of science and technology! Grades 1 to 5 in contact papers were used. He had great trouble with camera flare in his 8x10—proper printing of the edges was very difficult. He used Pyro developers simply because—after many trials—he settled thereon as the formula which gave him satisfactory whites. He cut the alkali to half (sometimes less), exposed at one-half the published speed rating of the film, used the meter as one might use a dowsing stick!—and, no matter how "off" the negative might be in relation to a "standard," he was practically always able to extract a magnificent print from it! It is interesting to observe that his exposures were based on the equivalent of 2x the integrated-brightness meter readings—and that helped him get such magnificent color exposures from the beginning.

Weston cannot be set up as a paragon of technique, but he cannot escape the summit of creativity. . . .

I am glad Weston is represented in the Polaroid collection!

Cordially,
Ansel

1. Edward Weston died in Carmel on January 1, 1958.

To Fred Seaton, Sinclair Weeks, and Conrad Wirth[1]

San Francisco
July 7, 1958

[Telegram]

AS AN INDIVIDUAL AND NOT AS A DIRECTOR OF THE SIERRA CLUB OR AS A TRUSTEE OF TRUSTEES FOR CONSERVATION I WISH TO LODGE A MOST SINCERE AND SEVERE PROTEST AGAINST THE DESECRATION OF TENAYA LAKE AND THE ADJOINING CANYON IN YOSEMITE NATIONAL PARK WHICH IS BEING PERPETRATED BY THE RUTHLESS CONSTRUCTION OF THE NEW TIOGA ROAD FOR THE NATIONAL PARK SERVICE BY THE BUREAU OF PUBLIC ROADS. THE CATASTROPHIC DAMAGE IS EN-

TIRELY UNNECESSARY AND VIOLATES THE PRINCIPLES EXPRESSED IN THE NATIONAL PARK ORGANIC ACT OF 1916 WHICH IS ACCEPTED BY OUR PEOPLE AS THE BASIS OF PROTECTION OF OUR MAGNIFICENT NATURAL SCENE FOR OUR TIME AND FOR THE TIME TO COME. I CONSIDER THIS DESECRATION AN ACT OF DISREGARD OF THESE BASIC CONSERVATION PRINCIPLES WHICH APPROACHES CRIMINAL NEGLIGENCE ON THE PART OF THE BUREAUS CONCERNED. I URGENTLY REQUEST YOU ISSUE AND ORDER IMMEDIATE CESSATION OF WORK ON THE TIOGA ROAD IN THE TENAYA LAKE AREA UNTIL A TRULY COMPETENT GROUP CAN STUDY THE PROBLEMS AND SUGGEST WAYS AND MEANS OF ACCOMPLISHING COMPLETION OF THIS PROJECT WITH MINIMUM DAMAGE. I HAVE NEVER OPPOSED APPROPRIATE IMPROVEMENT OF THE TIOGA ROAD BUT IN 40 YEARS' EXPERIENCE IN NATIONAL PARK AND WILDERNESS AREAS I HAVE NEVER WITNESSED SUCH AN INSENSITIVE DISREGARD OF PRIME NATIONAL PARK VALUES.

RESPECTFULLY

ANSEL ADAMS

1. Fred Seaton, Secretary of the Interior; Sinclair Weeks, Secretary of Commerce; Conrad Wirth, director of the National Park Service.

To Nancy Newhall

San Francisco
Saturday, July 11, 1958

Dear Nancy—

The battle is joined! My wire produced immediate and shocked action in Washington. I am leaving now for Yosemite—have a formal meeting with the regional officers and the Superintendent [of Yosemite] at Tenaya Lake tomorrow! I am DELIGHTED! The only trouble is I have now assumed an evangelical attitude (maybe I shall be the Billy Graham of the National Parks!!) and it will be a problem to follow it through effectively. But I really feel I have accomplished a lot and I shall keep you advised!¹

... All is well. LOVE to you and Beaumont and PLEASE get a rest!!

Luff,
Ansel

1. Despite valiant efforts, the Tioga Road was eventually built, dynamited directly through the Sierra's spectacular granite domes, and a large wilderness area was forever lost.

To Nancy Newhall

San Francisco
September 1, 1958

Dear Nancy—

Hope you had a GRAND vacation! I had a Hell of a trip—the worst drought in the history of the Northwest! Dust (we say the horse trails are covered with SHUST!), forest fire smoke, heat, and no snow—just nice glaciers melting furiously. I (and others) were prepared with tents, warm longies, heavy shirts, etc. There was not one cool shirt in the bunch. NO pictures worth their Hypo! Never did I carry so many pounds of cameras for such a slight result! Ah Wilderness. Better luck next time! No Colorama, of course! . . .

Have negs to develop and a pile of things to do. Will try to write a better letter soon.

LOVE!!!!!!!!
Ansel

From Nancy Newhall

Rochester
October 24, 1958

Dear Perseus

I am a woman being devoured by a poem!
—At least, Beau and Evelyn[1] think it's a poem; I didn't start out to write any poem! Just said I'll make a typethrough of the "American Earth" text[2] incorporating Dave Brower's suggestions (some of them) and new thoughts I've had or come across during the last 3 years.

Beau thinks I'm as good as MacLeish, Evelyn began with T.S. Eliot and now thinks I am Milton!

And all I do every morning is to vow I am going to get this damned new text sketched out where it can be seen. Then the typewriter and the stuff in it stares me in the face saying this is NOT all you mean or need

[261]

to say. And then the voices—your ghosts—come up with a word or a phrase. . . .

Either this is something terrific or it's just a phase of hell one NN got involved in. I warned you some time back, when I could feel this coming on, that unless restrained, I might rewrite the Creation and the Apocalypse. Well, no one gal is going to do that, but I seem propelled towards making a stab at it.

I NEED THEE! Brother and love and friend and colleague, come to me! Tell me if I got to go on like the Delphic oracle on this hot seat? Or if this is off the beam and I should, if possible, stop. . . .

This thing that's got me is either a great principle for man to live by in the future, a Bible, an Iliad, an Odyssey, or I ought to quit right now and go back to writing letters and sewing on buttons and planting bulbs.

The sooner you take a look at the dragon or archangel or flop or whatever it is, the sooner we'll all know what to do.

Love,
Andromache—I mean
Andromeda!

1. Evelyn Segal, friend of the Newhalls.

2. Nancy Newhall was writing the text for the book that grew out of the exhibit: *This Is the American Earth*, with photographs by Adams and others. San Francisco: The Sierra Club, 1960.

*To Beaumont and Nancy Newhall
and Minor White*

San Francisco
November 1, 1958
EN ROUTE FROM THE HIGH TO THE LOWELL
Munday (sick Transit)

COLLECTIVE MESSAGE FROM BEARD-IN-BEYOND
Dear Anchels—B.N.& M.

Very happy time. Magnificent food, bed and board. Reminds me *in reverse* of man who had dull weekend with friend and wrote, "Thanks for the Bed and Bored." Steak consumed at the stroke of midnight. Coffee at 6am. Gawd Bless All! Slept like a weary femme de joie. . . .

NN: Please don't think me uninterested. Simply find your writing magnificent! Once in awhile I come across some little detail where I might make a comment of fact, or flow, but all such comments are nothing but nits on a gnat's proscenium.

You are a genius in the best sense of the term. For Gawd's sake take care of yourself!

Don't think I am getting crusty or frusty, etc.—really. . . . I am really very tired. Yet I have to keep going. . . . And I really don't mind doing the shows because they are constructive—and, under your concepts— are always beautiful. So! I want to sum up the spiritual experience of Yosemite in *Portfolio III*. And I MUST get my work printed. Otherwise, one of these days something might happen and a large part of my negatives remain *in transpario:* (How's that for Platypus Latin?) As for you— well, I could go on for hours. You have a lot to do, too, and you have to save yourself for it YESSIR! YESSMAM!! More soon.

There was a time when ME was important. Then a Time when ART was important. Then a time when the World was important. Now, a time when I must do what I was designed to do—it's a kind of four-dimensional mortgage to God.

I am sure you understand. . . .

Minor White.[1] You insufferable, lovable bastard! Something good has happened to you in a year. Don't know what, but it sure has. Mood. Secure concepts. Maybe it's the Sinar?[2] Maybe the Carrymeallbacktoole-Virginny? No—those are reverberations of Larger Moods.

I was almost tearfully impressed with your "exhibit."[3] A complete integrity and beauty. Just because I don't always get the resonance between some of the words and the images does not lessen my appreciation. You put them down with complete integrity and vision. Just wait a moment, I'll be along!

I don't like the readings-into-pictures but, you see, what I *don't* like does *not* influence what I *do* like, because I trust you explicitly! Now, there are some bastards in this world who—well, you know what I mean! "Fools rush in where Minors fear to tread," etc.

We always get involved in yaks about teaching, etc. No result but agglutinations! Really—it all boils down to the fact that Those Who Have It Will Get There—maybe you can help them get there faster. Most of the others should be going in another direction in life. It is wrong to support them doing something beyond their ken. But so many schools are founded and continue on that basis. God runs his fingers along the window-sills of the words and looks for genius-dust! . . .

Luff to you all—I am quite revivified!
Whee.

Ansel

1. Minor White had moved to Rochester and was Beaumont Newhall's assistant at George Eastman House.

2. The Sinar is a fine Swiss view camera.

3. White's photographs were included in "Photographs from the Museum Collection," the Museum of Modern Art, New York City, 1958.

To Harold Bradley

San Francisco
December 22, 1958

Not for distribution!
Dear Harold—

It was wonderful to be with you all the other day, and I very much appreciate it! I wasn't too bright at the Executive Committee meeting, but I learned a lot.

First—let me extend to you and yours all best wishes for a most wonderful Christmas. Needless to say Virginia joins me in this—I go to Yosemite Tuesday.

Second—let me express a few feelings about such mundane items as the budget, etc. Of course, not having the cash myself I can be spendthrift with it!!! But, seriously—I think we have done amazingly well.

I am sure you know how and what I feel about Dave Brower. In simple terms, he is the top conservationist of our time. He is a dedicated man—and there are few of them. It bothers me to hear the little corrosions of criticism which so often attend his efforts. Of course he uses the telephone and the airplane! I, for one, would approve of his doubling the use thereof—if it would get results! I am consultant for the Polaroid Corporation; if I were to skimp on anything I would be criticized. With a big viewpoint and a generous attitude toward things in general, they have progressed in ten years to 2nd place in the American photographic industry! (2nd only to Kodak!) My budget for my own consultantship efforts is $25,000 per year. I was just asked if I needed more! Maybe I will. (I only spent $22,567.00 last year. CONFIDENTIAL!!) NOW—what I mean is this—

Dave is completely right in begging us to THINK BIG. Other organizations, not fractionally as effective as we are, think in terms of 6 and 7 figures (plus the decimal point!) We get along on peanuts, and this is too bad, because there ARE millions of $ waiting for a nest.

I respectfully suggest:

1. We do not worry about Dave doing too much. He is a creative person and lives on creation. He, alone, knows when too much is too much! It is up to us to give him the aid HE needs, WHEN he needs it!

2. I propose that we give Dave *carte blanche* (meaning sufficient funds) to go out and GET REAL MONEY. If this means extra office help— fine!!! I would gladly spend $100 to get $10,000!! I want to see Dave get 10^5 and 10^6 dollars. And I am sure he can get it!

But in the name of Him who is the great disburser—don't put our genius Dave in the position of worrying about a couple of hundred bucks Telephone Bill!!!!! My telephone bill is bigger than his and I am still solvent (partially!!!)

My best, always—
Ansel Adams

To Harold Bradley

March 24, 1959

Dear Harold,

My absence from the Wilderness Conference[1] was not entirely due to a strong antipathy to such gatherings—I have a bad "sprung" back and look like a fish hook; in fact, if you sharpened one end of me you could catch sharks! . . .

Seriously, I read the resolutions passed at the Wilderness Conference. I am impressed that nothing really new happened. The same good platitudes and expressions of noble purpose, etc.—but where are we really touching the people and exciting them? This is the great problem we have ahead, and unless we manage to accomplish it all our efforts will be useless. . . .

What is the prime purpose of wilderness preservation? I think it is mostly on the inspirational level. Conservationists as a whole—in spite of their strong personal feelings—are notoriously opaque in the expressive and esthetic domains. Someday I would like to see a conference directed to the people, in which the problems of interpretation on an esthetic and emotional level will be stressed. I just can't see the importance of national parks, etc. if they exist only on a physical, factual, and curiosity level! In fact, the entire Sierra should be one great national park and Yellowstone broken up into a group of national monuments! But such is the power of curiosity that a witch with three eyes commands more attention than a beautiful Venus with only two!!

Hope to see you soon. Best to you and the Lady—as ever,

Ansel

1. The Sierra Club and The Wilderness Society held several Wilderness Conferences to discuss the future and protection of wilderness in America.

To Nancy and Beaumont Newhall
and Minor White

San Francisco
June 16, 1959

Dear Nancy and Beaumont and Minor—

At last I have discovered the cause of my inconsolable internal itch! It was simply a kind of growing up pain. It was related to the conflict between external situations and the deep realization of reality. It is now dismissed with what may appear to be a very curt dismissal of some important things. Not so! The itch is dismissed but important things remain! All this relates to Adams; I cannot speak for the world! (The Question is, will the world speak for me?)

I wish to utter a manifesto, or man an utterfesto! To Hell with the domination of *Medium!* Art is an *attitude*. We have been talking for so many years about Painting, Sculpture, Writing, and Photography—each neatly placed according to its inherited wealth like the majority in the Social Register—and completely overlooking the Fact of Being and the relationship of the art attitude thereto, that we find ourselves awash in the great seas of doubt and grasping for whatever straw of association we can find to keep us afloat.

Appreciative as I am of the opportunity to see that film (*Day of Wrath*[1]) I find that it triggered the final explosion of conviction. It revealed to me the whole bombast of the world, the striving for effect, the reliance upon the hitching post of convention. And also the inherent nastiness of the average human approach to life. In the first place, it produced a prolonged trauma, the reciprocal of which was a surface disgust for the whole Catholic (Christian) concept of religion. In the second place, it was a weird combination of Stage and screen, imitations of old canvasses, tricks of new lenses. Excellent poignant acting, questionable moral message, unbearably slow tempo, and an unbearable promise of burning make-up.

In fact, it also supported my personal resentment of one Wm. Shakespeare, who dwelt upon human stupidity with a God-like superiority, like a trainer and his trained seals. Give me Beethoven, or give me Death (some of Beethoven, anyway)!

So, I stand alone and forlorn; unable to agree with the cultural mass, incompetent in adjustment thereto, and not at all unhappy about it! The promise of the world—the dawn wind and the smell of orchards, the inherent sweetness of simple people, the great *possibilities* of a reasonable life—these things are important and Art (except in a few instances) consistently bypasses them, concerned with introvertal investigations, opportunisms, and the phosphorescent glimmers of elegant egos! I should disclaim all relationships to art as an artist and then try to reclaim myself in the true meaning of the term (if I am justified in doing so). I have nothing going on IN my cranium and heart that is more important than the essence of what is going on in the outer world: I am but an instrument, a part of, this outer continuum. I sense a renaissance impending— a different one than we have ever had before. Who has the guts to stand out and welcome it?

Ansel

1. *Day of Wrath*, a Danish film directed by Carl Dreyer, 1943

To Nancy Newhall

Yosemite National Park
June 28, 1959

Dear Nancy,

Lookut da old letterhead![1] WHAT a day. Back quite bad. Umpty-oodles of people on hand to celebrate Virginia II[2] baptism (50 for lunch). Poe me, I want to be a Boodyst! Anyway all OK and happy. Am now sipping Mint Juleps and am in State of Euphoria (51st State).

Back has been simply raising HELL. Could hardly move this AM. Went to baptism and then to hospital. Dr. [Avery] Sturm snapped it back in place (sacroillyak this time—¾ inch out!) and I feel pretty good for the first time in ten days. First, three vertebrae askew. Then S-C. Then X-ray showed all in place. Then this AM—WOW. I limped, I creeped, I bent to Port; I creeked, I peeped, I could abort; I crawled and shuffled, clawed and grasped; my voice was harsh, my larynx rasped; Gas I did have, and bladder pressure; Pain unceasing and without measure! And then Doc Sturm did pretzel me, and once again my spine is free!!! Wheeeeeeeeee

Vell, Der truth iss—I HAVE to rest a bit. I am going to S.F. tomorrow June 29 and will launch a moderate campaign for the remainder of the year. . . .

Did you hear the story about the man who wanted to become a member of the Alaska Club? Requirements were: catch a seal bare-handed, successfully seduce an Eskimo girl, and kill a Toklat Grizzly without a gun. Vell, he comes in next day dragging a seal. OK. Next day he came in with torn clothes, bloody face, black eye, half his scalp torn off and a lost ear. "Got it boys, Did it up Right!! Now, where is that Eskimo girl you want me to kill?". . .

I will write from the Domain of Fog as soon as the fog clears!

We all send love to you and Beaumont, and beg to remind you that the years gather their goofy web, time drains the drastic residue, time is no longer (or shorter), and there is WORK to be done.

Cheeriow and LUFFFFFFFFFFFFFFFF,
Ansel

. . .

1. Adams' old letterhead read: "VIRGINIA AND ANSEL ADAMS, Operating BEST'S STUDIO Incorporated, Yosemite National Park, California—Paintings and Photographs Books Cameras and Accessories Developing, Printing and Enlarging."
2. Adams' first grandchild, Virginia, was born to Charles and Anne Adams Mayhew in 1959.

To Olaus and Margaret Murie[1]

San Francisco
July 13, 1959

Dear Friends, the Muries—

Your letter of July 10th was much appreciated!

I feel a bit like an institution! Someone—probably the same person—gave some money (unknown amount) to THE NATURE CONSERVANCY in my name!

Well, it is very touching, and very encouraging!

I just feel an increased obligation to function as thoroughly and effectively as possible. There is so much to be done. I have heard that the *Sat Eve Post* has a "hot" editorial on the Parks[2]—am anxious to see it. If we have cracked THAT citadel we have really accomplished something!!

The desecration of Yosemite has reached such heights (the new warehouse is unbelievably inappropriate) that I honestly feel something is bound to "break" in our favor. I wistfully would like to believe that the American Public will recognize what they are losing!

So, I am resolved to speak up on every possible occasion, and without regard for "protocol" or rank. I have sent a strong letter to Senator Humphrey,[3] a strong letter to Gov. [William] Quinn of Hawaii, the Director,[4] and your [Wilderness] Society (as well as to the National Park Association and the Sierra Club) on the proposed road in or around Haleakala in Maui (Hawaii), and have also written to Governor Brown[5] on the unpardonable apathy of our State Park people in their failure to acquire the Tamalpais State Park extensions (authorized by the Legislature more than a year ago).

I am thinking seriously of a very strong article on the tragedy of the Tioga Road (now more apparent than ever) and have decided to make myself as much a bother as I possibly can! It seems to be the only way to accomplish anything with the entrenched bureaucrats!

The Sierra Club people are still working in the Dream world of Compromise and "getting along"—in spite of the long history of defeat because of our mild tactics.

Perhaps a great number of sympathetic people are not in the various organizations, and are difficult to reach? I feel this is the truth; I come across many people who are just as violent on the subject as I am and yet never heard of the Sierra Club, or the other groups.

I am chafing at the bit because I have a misplaced sacroiliac and walk about with the appearance of a bent hairpin! But I am getting better and will be out and around soon with the camera. In the meantime, I can type (or can I?? This is a mussy letter!!)

My best to you and yours. Cordially,
(and thanks again for your letter)
ANSEL ADAMS

P.S. xxxxxx['d] my attending the Sierra Club Directors' meeting in Yosemite but I had a fine visit with George and Betty[6] here in San Francisco. You must come here too, one of these days—always have room!

1. Olaus Murie was a director of The Wilderness Society; Margaret was his wife and colleague.
2. *Saturday Evening Post*, July 18, 1959, p. 10.
3. Senator Hubert Humphrey of Minnesota.
4. The director of the National Park Service, Conrad Wirth.
5. The governor of California, Edmund "Pat" Brown.
6. George Marshall is a member of the governing council of The Wilderness Society and was a director of the Sierra Club. Marshall is the only person ever to have served as president of both organizations. Betty is his wife.

To Sterling Cramer[1]

January 26, 1960

Dear Sterling—

Thank you very much for your copy of the Proposal on the Minarets' acquisition.[2] I think it is very well done. I am torn between favoring a "deal" and sticking up for the principle involved. A considerable number of us feel that there should be no compromise in regards National Park areas, Wilderness areas, and ordinary recreational areas.

My personal feelings about this particular matter are based on what I believe to be the great and urgent importance to get the Minaret area back in the Park! After talking with you I did a lot of thinking: the first question that came to my mind was this: If the USA had an enlightened land-use policy there would be no question about including the Minaret area in the Yosemite National Park domain. There would also be no question of the validity of perpetuating the wild areas in the Mammoth-

San Joaquin area. The proposed road is an invasion of valuable wilderness areas. The chances are that it will be forced through, although this statement is, in effect, a bit of a threat—which I don't like. We are assuming the Fact of completion of the road, and in so doing are buying off a bit of principle. I certainly could not accept this except that it might be the saving of the supremely important Minaret area. Here I am aware that I am compromising; but it is a calculated risk in reverse—the risk that the road—as an approach road—might really protect the Minaret area. Recent developments in the National Park Service attitudes and developments do not give me very much confidence that the Parks are really safe. The Tenaya disaster should never be overlooked! It is not the individual that I am worried about, it is the National Policy. Roads have ways and means of extending themselves.

But I must fully agree with you that, if the Minaret area is subjected to proximity to a regular "through" road and remains under Forest Service domination, it is doomed.

The ideal solution would be to develop and enforce a policy of appropriate land-use whereby the Minaret area would go to the Park without any "deal" or compromise, and whereby the wilderness values of the adjacent area would also be appropriately protected.

The question is—how far off is any chance of an ideal land-use policy?

You can see I am torn between compromise and principle! The compromise you propose is a very intelligent one! I do not know if the future would curse or praise us for capitulating to the need for compromise in this matter! Irrevocable developments in National Park areas—obviously advantageous at the time of their inception—now produce emotions of regret and remorse—simply because those in charge did not look far enough into the future. Olmsted's[3] definition of National Parks still represents the supreme and logical approach. Let's think VERY carefully about our policy in this particular Minaret problem!

[Ansel Adams]

1. Sterling Cramer led the fight to include the Minarets in Yosemite National Park. Complicating the issue was the intention to complete a road from the Owens Valley to the San Joaquin Valley, the same road that had been defeated a few years earlier by the Mammoth Pass Road Committee.

2. The Minarets were part of the National Forest in the Yosemite High Sierra; they were included in the Ansel Adams Wilderness Area created in 1984.

3. Frederick Law Olmsted was a nineteenth-century landscape architect, best noted for

his design of Central Park in New York City. He was a leader in the establishment of Yosemite as a national park in 1890.

To Nancy and Beaumont Newhall

San Francisco
February 8, 1960

MEMO TO: Nancy and Beaumont Newhall

ON READING LOLITA[1] WHILE FLUED

Once upon a stormy weather
You could have floored me with a feather!
Lolita was my bedside solace;
Like a whisker's single folace
I sensed the huge diversity
Of hetero-sexual perversity!
But flu'ed I was and very flabby
(Just like Aunt Agatha's old Tabby);
I followed decadence with a bleary eye
Through every crevice of the sinful sty
And when completed, said to self –
"Those oracles that howled at Delph',
Those prophets of our causal doom, arise!!!!
Shake off your filth, disturb your flies!!!!"
But how I wished, O secret Muse
That with a nymphet *I* could fuse –
Just for a moment of illegal wonder –
Just for a memory of erotic plunder!!!

Visions and fantasies are very nifty,
But not so good on the wrong side of fifty!!!!
John Done'it!

1. Vladimir Nabokov. *Lolita*, New York: Putnam, 1958.

From Beaumont Newhall

Rochester
July 13, 1960

Dear Ansel:

We've just finished a wonderful meal, a Chinese beef and mushrooms cooked in a most beautiful wok, as the shallow curved metal pan is called by the Chinese. It is the first time that I have ever used a wok, and the efficiency with which it can be used is amazing. A dish, perfectly cooked, in four minutes!

And after the meal we sat down on the sofa and, I over a coffee (the espresso kind) plus a scotch, and Nancy with a scotch, we began to talk about some of the problems at Eastman House, and then we drifted into a discussion of *Aperture,* and an appraisal of the splendid and really moving review of the *American Earth* book[1] . . . I turned the pages of *Aperture* and came upon the back page with the amazing photograph by A.A. of the dead tree.

And then I said to Nancy, "Ansel is the greatest photographer that there has ever been."

And I looked through the magazine all over again, concentrating only on the photographs, and I allowed that Brett was a fine photographer, and I agreed that [Eugene] Meatyard deserved the presentation, and once again I came up with a start to the A.A. photograph! I know it is not one of your finest things, that it was made "on assignment," possibly as a test, and that realization made me all the more convinced of your mastery of the medium and your position in the entire history of photography. And as I spoke Nancy urged me to write what I was saying down upon paper.

But before I would do that, I reviewed with Nancy your accomplishments, beginning in 1935 when your book, *Making a Photograph,* came to me not because of my interest in photography, not at my request, but just because I happened to be reviewing books for the *American Magazine of Art.*

That book, as I know you know, changed my life.

I saw in photography something which I had never seen there before.

True, I was conditioned. I was born of a photographic mother, and I had a competent command of the technique, and hence was most receptive. I never anticipated that what you wrote would mean so much.

I have publicly stated, in your presence, the fact that your dream of a photographic museum, institute, library, collection, became my goal. I am proud of the fact that I have been able to approach your ideal closer, I think, than anybody else. I hope, and I believe, that I can attain the goal yet more closely.

It was you, in your generosity and exuberant hospitality, who introduced Nancy and me to Weston when we called you up on arriving in San Francisco. We did not know you then, but on our first meeting you asked us to look you up and we did. We were delighted when you took us under your wing, and introduced us to the West, and arranged that we should meet Weston.

There in Carmel, in the little shack and on Point Lobos, I learned more about photography than ever before. I will never forget the day when I went out, with my little 9x12 mm Avus film-pack camera, to "work" alongside Edward. He at once showed a respect for me which, as an art historian, I had never enjoyed from an artist. The experience was crucial to my career; it was he, more than anybody, who led me to adopt photography completely and to devote my life to its understanding. He showed me how to realize the ground glass image.

And it was all due to you in the first place, for without you, and your perception and generosity and concern, we might never have met Edward, the true Edward.

Since 1940, for it was twenty years ago that this experience took place, you and the Newhalls have become closer and closer. We have worked together, fought together, and we have produced much that we can be proud of. Particularly what you and Nancy have done. I've been through it all: the heartbreaks, the tensions, the glow of satisfaction, the bitter realizations that not always has our work met with understanding. We've supported one another—it was you, on the summer day in 1940 in Yosemite, on the little porch by the manzanita garden, who proposed the Department of Photography at the Museum of Modern Art, and who fought with us the fight we lost when Steichen took over.

But I'm getting beside the point. What I wanted to say three pages ago is that the experience of the workshop[2] is the most important thing that has happened to me in photography since the day you introduced me to Edward.

I've followed your working out of the Zone System[3] ever since the day that we made photographs of my bookcase in 1941 and we expanded the tonal range so that the result was amazing. I have read every word you have written, have admired your mental gymnastics, have been your loyal champion.

But until last month I never had a grasp of what you were teaching.

Suddenly a whole new vista has opened up. I take photographs now which I have always wanted to take but never could. It is not just a matter of technique: I now can SEE better than I did. For your teaching I am grateful; it is difficult for me to tell you to what extent. But every time I take a photograph and get just what I visualize, every time I "zone" a subject and it works, I am in your debt.

And what mystifies me, and maddens me, is that there ever could be any opposition to so useful, and so intelligent an approach to photography as the Zone System.

This experience, of working with you and learning to know what I have been studying for a quarter of a century, is just one of the reasons why I said to Nancy, back when I started to write you, "Ansel is the greatest."

I don't know of any photographer ever who is or was more versatile, more in command of the medium, more aware of the importance of photography, more the artist. And I include Stieglitz. You have brought to photography a dimension I find nowhere else.

Beau

1. Reviewed by Minor White, *Aperture*, Vol. 7, No. 4, 1959.

2. Beaumont Newhall assisted Adams at the Ansel Adams Yosemite Workshop in 1960; Adams held annual workshops from 1955 through 1983.

3. In 1941 Adams devised the Zone System while teaching at the Art Center School. The photographer visualizes the tonal values desired in the final print and then, using the Zone System, calculates the exposure and development of the negative needed to produce that outcome.

To Dr. Henry J. Vaux [1]

October 7, 1960

Dear Dr. Vaux:

I am appreciative of your letter of September 12th and the enclosures. I am departing for the East very soon and have been rather pressed for time and the chance to think—but I have read your material and send herewith a few ideas thereon as requested.

It seems to me that most arguments pro and con on Multiple Use of forest areas, and the other categories as well, are based on a materialistic concept rather than a concept which is inspirational, related to "mood" and to the more important aspects of the individual's existence, which, I firmly believe, are emotional rather than physical. . . .

After many years' experience with Park and Forest people, with conservationists, with the kind of "do-gooder" who tempers his principles to the wind of advantage and "financial necessity," I have come ruefully to the conclusion that very few know what they are talking about! I am distressed that so many academic people fall back on the conventional security of terms such as "management," or spice their arguments with references to "population" increases, economic travel pressures, etc. It seems to me that the whole business of wilderness preservation, National Park principles, etc., is in a desperately dangerous mess. I hope I am not entering the domain of the naive when I state that the entire problem is an extremely simple one, and that the values involved are simple values—with final and conclusive meaning.

We either have wild places or we don't. We admit the spiritual-emotional validity of wild beautiful places or we don't. We have a philosophy of simplicity of experience in these wild places or we don't. We admit an almost religious devotion to the clean exposition of the wild, natural earth, or we don't. Any management we find necessary—and may it be minimal—can be effected without impairing the wilderness aspect and moods. The cutting of trees under any circumstance would so impair the mood. The development of roads and facilities ditto. The spraying of the forests (such as the fiasco recently perpetrated in the Tuolumne Meadows area) ditto; I have seen three bug infestations in that part of the Sierra, and the forest "survives" in a natural state of change and adjustment. I hesitate to define just what the qualities of true wilderness experience are—like music and art, wilderness can be defined only on its own terms; the less "talk" the better.

The whole concept of multiple use is, to me, a shocking distortion of logic and of responsibility. "Management," unless applied with respect and devotion, is nothing but carefully calculated exploitation.

Cordially,
Ansel Adams

cc: David Brower

1. Henry J. Vaux was dean of the Department of Forestry at the University of California, Berkeley.

To Nancy Newhall

January 25, 1961

Dear Nancy,

It was seriously important to see the *American Earth* book on TV.[1] Not only was it a new "transcription" of the concept, but it seemed to have its own and different aesthetic. I had the feeling that the screen was showing what the people who read the book really see; that is, what the average spectator (to whom the book is addressed) really sees. We often lose out in that we, as "experts," look upon things such as photographs, with highly trained eyes and minds; accepting them on a somewhat different basis than the general—even enlightened—public ever can. To us, the "integrity" of the image is important—the full format, the sequence of values, etc. But it is to the spectator that the image is really addressed, and our problem is to discover what *he* sees in our images. I am not depreciating the subtleties—they are extremely important—but I am saying that our refinements augment the impact of the message—and the message remains the most important thing! That is why I believe I have a growing aversion to the highly subjective images in painting and photography, which seem only to create a "feed-back" for the artists' egos and psyches!

I believe we should do a lot of serious thinking about this medium, and work towards better esthetic and mechanical controls. The scope and size of the audience for even the little educational photography films is frightening; it is estimated that over 700,000 people in this area have seen one or more of these films. Gawd knows how many millions saw the Garroway American Earth program Tuesday!

There is a new surge of energy and purpose in Washington.[2] I think only history will tell us how far down Ike and his gang dragged us. This new surge is to be reflected in both good things and in opportunisms. It is very important to get there first with the good stuff (meaning: good ideas!).

As for me, I feel that it is very important for me to take stock of the future and realistically evaluate what I can accomplish in the remaining years. I feel pretty good (not good enough!) and I expect to be around for quite a long time to come! But the time to come cannot possibly be as productive as some of past time has been—this is a physical fact of life and cannot be denied. I sense a direct *obligation* to care for myself to the utmost degree, so that I will remain equipped to do what I have to do while I can still do it at all. In other words, I have to conserve energy, health, and peace-of-mind. I don't smoke and I am cutting down drinks to a minimum (not that I have been over-drinking; I have been a very good boy, but not really good enough!). I will undertake a program of more exercise, and will be careful not to scatter. Being gregarious, it is hard for me to pull in on all reins at once!

I think you have to do a bit of thinking along the same lines; not because I suggest it, but because it appears to be an inescapable fact that the human organism can take just so much and no more! The first disasters come from unawareness that trouble is in the offing! When the trouble arrives it is often too late. I came very close to real trouble last year, and have averted further troubles by, fortunately, anticipating them.

I think the most distressing evidence of stress, fatigue, and mismanagement is the failure of the mental functions—memory, logic, imagination, etc. These come back—at least in part—after some trauma or mistreatment, but it seems the mind never *fully* regains its elasticity and power. I find it increasingly hard to concentrate, to think a thing through without great effort, to evoke enthusiastic imagination at will. This is just a warning that I am getting down to the bottom of the well. I must allow the well to fill up again—which it can do pretty well.

I think we both have great gifts—and I don't think we have really used them too well. We have accomplished a *lot*—but there is a tremendous amount more to do. I think we have to make a choice—either we go on as we are—and enter an obvious decline—or we take hold of ourselves and regain the course. At the age of 30 or even 40 we could beat ourselves up without much apparent damage; we just can't do that now!

So, I am going to take hold of myself in a rather severe way; I won't like it too much (because I *like* coffee and candy and rich gravies and vodka) and I will resent the time involved in exercising, etc. But I feel I really HAVE to do it or—before I realize it—I will be in an irretrievably poor condition of mind and body.

And that means the end of productive accomplishment.

What an illusion life can be at this period! People come after you because of what you have done rather than what you can do! I know that I have many new contacts; requests for work, etc. comments, etc.—all very nice and heartwarming, BUT, if when I was 30 I turned out some of the work I have recently turned out there would be little on which to base a reputation! I don't say I have not improved in depth and scope and understanding—but the actual *production*—the Thing Done—needs considerable improvement!!!

So—taking a leaf out of the New Surge—let's think about ourselves in this direction! Exhibits, books, etc.—all fine. But there are new media, too; new ways of looking at things. This leads me to wonder if the Past has not been pretty well wrapped up for awhile; that our energies should be directed to new discoveries and encouragements in the arts—with some real help to artists to find their place in the Grand Stream. The sick and rotting spirit of most contemporary work is, to me, as serious as some dismal symptoms of cancer—it has no way to go but Out! But the pendulum can't swing to the other extreme with the sugary Rockwell concepts. I find that the instant I mention "health" in art, I am accused of being a reactionary! It is hard to explain what is meant. Many artists seem to *want* to live in a marsh gas world! Now we have to conserve marshes!!!!

Forgive this tirade—I have been thinking about it for a long time! Don't forget—you are a great artist and you have great obligations! I am not so poor myself, and I have similar obligations! The program is obvious!!!!

Love, always—

Ansel

1. The book *This Is the American Earth* was discussed on the "Today" show by host Dave Garroway.

2. President John F. Kennedy took office in January 1961.

From Nancy Newhall

Rochester
January 29, 1961

Dear THEE—

Wonderful letter of the 25th!

I think people do explore a photograph—how else can they really see what's in it?

If you want to make photographs round or curved or three dimensional, I am all with you!

But, for god's sake, please consider where your imitators will end up! It could be worse than Mortensen! Boy, what curves do for pornography! Funny that the first began, like Hill and Southworth and Hawes,[1] with no definite edges—their lenses being good only in the center, so it didn't matter. Then our kind come along and demand images seen exquisitely to the exact final millimeter. Then come the movies and TV, which have to move or die (they think). I am going back to an idea I had some twelve years ago: why not a frame in your room where you can see and hear a poem?—The sea around Lobos, for example, with Jeffers' text. The Sierra Nevada by you, with you and Muir; the desert by you, with Mary Austin and maybe me? ETC.!

All on tapes to be played as we now play music only. THOUGHT!

As for the future—I agree!

But *how* do we save ourselves?

I am at last, I think, beginning to be able to smile at the last 30 years—when at eleven, life becomes a deepening hell, it takes an Albert Bender plus a Cedric plus others, to bring one up again. I didn't get that kind of help until late; when you and Beau took me by the scruff of my reluctant neck to Stieglitz, that was a beginning—most humbly, most quietly, I began to learn. I can remember crying to you one night, as late as when we were in Rochester—after listening to Brahms at the Waters'—"But I can say as much as such music!" I think I have proved that now. It is—pray God for strength and time—only the beginning of what I can do.

Thanks be
For THEE and B!

Now to attain a measure of serenity. A quiet and a courage that can see but not be shaken, can act coolly and competently from an absolutely honest assay of what's involved. If I can attain these, I shall no more be crying in the dark and dying on the barricades of despair! . . .

Darling—a personal plea to thee. Really, 58 ain't much, nor 2 granddaughters[2] and other symptoms of approaching age. It's tough, this realization that the fire and energy we took for granted—and wasted—is dying down. Nearly as tough for us as the performers. But you and I can be more seriously hogtied by our emotions and despairs than by actual physical disabilities, and I am absolutely certain that once we face these squarely just as facts inescapable to this mortal condition, we won't find either them or their limitations so bad. In fact, we are quite likely to get a certain glee out of the challenge they throw at us. Marvelous and magnificent one, beloved Beard, do stop sounding as if you were eighty already!

love
LOVE
    L*O*V*E*
       and kisssessss!
         N

1. Albert Sands Southworth and Josiah Johnson Hawes, Boston daguerreotypists active in the mid–nineteenth century.
2. Adams' second grandchild, Alison, was born to Charles and Anne Adams Mayhew in 1960.

To Beaumont and Nancy Newhall

February 1961

Dear Mr. and Mrs. Newhall,

After March 20th, I will have to be addressed DOCTOR Adams,[1] if you please! I did not mention in this reply that the degree was that of Doctor of Fine Arts! It's better for photography than for me!!!!!

More soon. Things buzzing hereabouts!

Lufffff,
Ansel

Good Gawd, I am only kidding—Herr Doktor Professor will do!!!

1. The University of California at Berkeley conferred on Adams the honorary degree of Doctor of Fine Arts.

From Nancy Newhall

Rochester
February 28, 1961

Dear Beard in the Golden Hood—

JEZUZ! It's going to be an El Greco!
Tell Gerry[1] I must have a Polaroid instanter—and Virginia, please, portraits in full color!

[281]

Tell all your women to watch that beard like hawks in the days before and up to the very instant of the degree! Not a hair is to be pared without the judgment of a quorum! Do NOT give in to that ancient New England instinct to be shy and shorn; flaunt that beard in all its majesty! What the heck you think they want you up there for, anyway??? You think they want just another egghead?

I think Cedric is peering over my shoulder!

Darling, we are so delighted! All these years you have held the academic world in such awe—you whose brilliance outshines all but such undoctoral characters as Din! And now upon thee will descend like doves and Holy Ghosts a flock of doctorates—Doctor Doctor Doctor!

Why in hell doesn't the U of C give its degrees in June, like any normal university??? When you get one from Harvard,[2] we'll be there!

LOVE and CONGRATULATIONS—

N

1. Gerry Sharpe assisted Adams with special photographic projects starting in 1956.
2. Harvard University conferred on Adams the honorary degree of Doctor of Fine Arts in 1981; alumnus Beaumont Newhall attended the ceremony.

To Nancy and Beaumont Newhall

San Francisco
April 15, 1961

Dear Nancy and Beaumont—

Planned to get the prints off yesterday, but ran up against some spotting troubles! They will go today—would not arrive until Monday anyway! I am distressed that I delayed so long in getting these prints, but I have been going through a funny stage—oodles of things to do, everyone helps, general success, etc.—but I just don't seem to get anything important done! I think it is one of those periods of "adjustment" when the unconscious mind takes over and runs things. I just finished burning up about 100 old and lousy prints—NOTHING OF REAL VALUE TO N.N. OR ANYONE—just old, tired, dark, scratched, etc., prints of which I have better examples. . . .

One thing I have to discipline myself about—I should not make prints too large! The Large Print Project for Polaroid,[1] etc., has created a bit of a habit, and quality of a certain kind vanishes—to be replaced by an emotional quality of another kind. OK if appropriate! But I think I should limit myself to 8x10 for a spell.

I am sending you a variety of prints; you know the ones for George Eastman House. As for the others, they are for you, unless you feel some should be in the House—the portrait of Bob Howard, for example. The fact is, I find that my eyes are changing. I am assured that I have perfect physical eyes—but that as age progresses, the focus changes—and sometimes in "jumps." About six months ago I got a set of glasses, and within the past few weeks these are obsolete. And the ability to see perfectly is very important in photography! So—I shall have to get back to the eye-man and have a new brace of glasses made up. The gout and the fingers are better. In general, I feel no older than 20 in the heart, 30 in the mind, 40 in the psyche, 50 in the bladder, 60 in the conscience, and 70 in you-know-what!!! Ah Wilderness!!!!

Another point I must carefully study in relation to my work: in my desire to make images strong and rich I tend to make them too dark. I have been fighting this for a long time. It's not just a matter of "drying down" but it seems quite necessary to print richly and deeply. This is fine if the prints are to be seen under a STRONG light. The prints I am sending on to you are, I think, better in this respect and should look pretty well under normal lighting.

The Yosemite storm is an old negative and went through our fire;[2] the spotting is difficult! From one point of view it should not be as large, but I think size is necessary from the point of view of majesty and dramatic force. The same goes for the Mount Williamson picture[3]—terribly hard to print and not perfectly sharp as it was taken in a stiff wind. There is also a defect in the sky which is practically impossible to spot out. I have preferred to let this defect ride and do the best I can with it, rather than have anyone monkey with the negative. The Lone Pine print[4] is also best when fairly large. I hope you like the one you are getting; it seems really rich—any lighter tone in the sky seems to kill the snow values and impact. NOW—I want to be represented in the best possible way and I shall be glad to make them smaller, larger, lighter and darker—if they will work best that way in the exhibit. . . .

That's that! Hope they come in PRIME shape, and that you will be pleased. If there is anything further I can do, please Tell!!!

LUFFFF and see you Soon, thank Gawd!!!!
Ansel

Typing does not improve! I think too fast for my fingers—actually write backwards at times!!!!—and to Hell with a few lost letters!!!!

1. Edwin Land encouraged Adams to make mural-sized enlargements from his Polaroid negatives, providing further evidence of the fine quality of Polaroid film.
2. In 1937 Adams had a fire in his Yosemite darkroom. The negative referred to is probably *Clearing Winter Storm, Yosemite National Park.*
3. *Mt. Williamson, the Sierra Nevada, from Manzanar, California, 1945.*
4. *Winter Sunrise, the Sierra Nevada, from Lone Pine, California, 1944.*

To Wallace Stegner[1]

October 10, 1961

Dear Wally:

I was indeed happy to get your letter of October 4th. It sounds as if you are really established in an extremely interesting assignment.

Believe me, I regret the all too frequent disagreements between the conservation organizations and the National Park Service. I have been aware of this for a long time, and I frankly cannot absolve the organizations although I think in the main their motives are directed to the good of the National Park ideal. I'm not saying that the National Park Service does not have such a basic objective, but my own experience in the past decades has caused me to sometimes wonder if the pure and complete objective is really very clear to the Park officials at the top of the heap. I know there are hundreds of completely dedicated people in the National Park Service, but I find that as we go towards the top, political influences, status, and heaven knows what phenomena of human enterprise and conceit seem to take over and some of the actions which I have experienced certainly are most difficult to explain.

. . . I feel it is too early to praise or blame the Administration for things that happen and I am very much aware that certain Bureaus have great power. Whether or not Udall can whip reclamation into shape and whether or not he has as yet enough political power on the hill to influence Congress to keep its bond in relation to Rainbow Bridge,[2] is something which I certainly cannot anticipate at this time. I think he is doing a perfectly wonderful job and I agree with you that we should be working with him in all of the great National Park Projects and not allowing ourselves to be upset or disheartened by failures in any one domain.

However, I must say—and I say this to you without too much confidence involved, although I don't want to hurt individuals obviously, that I don't think the Park Service has been run very well under the [Conrad] Wirth administration. I have seen many examples where big operators have most obviously run the parks in which they conduct their business. I have seen serious lapses of imagination and emphasis placed on the things which I certainly think have not deserved major attention. The Park Service has been scared to death of the Forest Service and, to a certain extent, vice-versa. It may be up to the President to force the issue and bring the Bureaus of Forestry and National Parks into line. I think Ickes had a noble idea in combining all conservation agencies under one new department, which I believed he wished to call the Department of Conservation. I have a hunch Udall would approve of this, and I think that it is ridiculous for us to keep these silly administrative divisions alive with all of the internal hard feelings and political struggles for priority which seem to continue.

. . . I know that many of the things which the businessmen, the park operators, chambers of commerce, highway people, etc. believe in, are all along one direction of development and exploitation, while the serious, individual citizen, either by himself or represented by conservation organizations, is almost totally on the other side of the fence and interested in the future of our great wild areas and what it means to our people and the people to come.

I think if you really study this situation, you will find that there has been very good cause for distrust and animosity. I would prefer to have myself go on record, and the Sierra Club to go on record, as being large enough and generous enough to overlook the past and take hold of the future in a very constructive way. But this is awfully hard to do if you don't trust, and I for one do not trust the administration of the Park Service. I think it deserves the most careful examination, and frankly, the most drastic revision. Some of our conservationists who feel that way are still too timid to urge such a revolution or revision of policy and personnel, because, they say, if we weaken the Park Service then we lose more than we gain and the Forest Service will become stronger and probably will secure for all time their particular areas in question. This I do not believe. I think we could have a revision of the Park Service. We could put in a dynamic leadership. We could certainly modify the ridiculous expenditures in the remaining years of Mission 66 and we would end up with a stronger institution and a greater protection for the Parks.

Perhaps one of the great contributions you can make in your present high position in the Secretary's office, is to establish the rationale—if we can use that word—for the importance of the intangibles. If you will look at recent National Park writings and pronouncements, you will find that everything is more or less directed along the physical aspects of administration, service to people, projected service for expected people, bringing things such as roads, parking areas, accommodations, warehouses and Heaven knows what—up to very high physical standards—relating to the administration and to a certain extent the appeal of the Parks of the country at large. All of this looks very good in a material sense and undoubtedly has great political appeal, but the tragedy back of it all is the fact that the National Parks—that is, the Parks that really deserve such designation—are much more than a material resource. They exist primarily for their vast intangible value, and yet the Park Service does not have a clear concept between the terms "recreation" and "re-creation." Semantics creep in here and raise the very devil with what we feel and say—but I think that the terms "inspiration" and "re-creation" are two which should, in a sense, be the very keystone of National Park policy.

Let's be frank about it: we just don't have anybody high up in the National Park Service who has the breadth of vision, the spirit and the determination to really protect the great Park areas in the noblest sense of the term.

You and I have many friends in various positions in life, some very high in scientific, industrial, and intellectual levels, and I think we both know that not everyone is willing to accept the intangible values of wilderness as anything but a kind of euphoria, created either by an aimless leisure or as a realm of escapism. Of course, I don't believe any of this is of any importance whatsoever. Probably some people do escape and some people do not appreciate wilderness in the large social sense in which I choose to use it, but I think the fact remains that we need more support for the intangible qualities and that we can very well request this support on the basis that if we don't do something about them rather swiftly, there just won't be anything much left to preserve and to protect. I simply cannot understand how the average individual in the political and social scene can be blind to the shape of our curves of development and exploitation. To me it is so obvious, and the future is so strongly and inevitably indicated if we continue the way we are going, as to make a total mockery of everything we are doing in the National Park and wilderness areas.

Mr. Wicher, of the National Park and Conservation Association, has vastly annoyed conservatives, operators and government people by his very strong opinions rather strongly expressed. Now I think sometimes he becomes a little intolerant of the fact and I don't think he presents his point very well, but I think he is a tremendous fighter and in principle is an extremely important man in the domain of our particular branch of conservation. I think Dave Brower is an absolutely extraordinary person, who combines not only a very great sympathy and love for parks and wilderness principles, but is also a very astute and knowledgeable politician as well as having a peculiar gift of communication. I think this gift is sometimes not as explicit as it might be but that is certainly quibbling, because there is no one in my experience who has initiated more and has accomplished more—and all of this with a certain minimum amount of irritation, although of course, Mr. Wirth was certainly irritated at Dave. What probably Mr. Wirth doesn't know, is that it might well be Dave's clean-cut, objective attitude towards retaining Mr. Wirth that keeps Connie in his present position. I am frank to say that I think this was a mistake. . . .

This is quite a rambling letter, but I do want to conclude with this statement:

I believe that the magnificent country of the North Cascades is most certainly of National Park caliber[3] and that we need a man at the head of the National Parks who will recognize this and fight for it. I would like to see a man in the National Parks who could influence both the Secretary and the President to take vital action in smoothing out this most unfortunate conflict between the Forest Service and the Park Service. One marvelous tangible outcome of this new alignment would be the inclusion of the Minaret area in the Yosemite Park (of which it was originally a part). I would like to see a man in charge of the Parks who would have the imagination to see the enormous importance of making the Golden Gate environment a National Monument.[4] The Club is a little worried about stressing this at the moment. They know they have an uphill battle and they prefer to direct their energies toward objectives already initiated, but I am personally going to fight for this thing as I don't think the Park Service people will have the taste or the imagination to realize fully what a wonderful thing this project could be and how superior it would be to any possible State operation—in addition, as it is with all U.S. Government land, the costs of establishing such a Monument would be practically nothing, whereas if the State acquired it through the routine sale by the General Services Administration, many millions of dollars would be involved. Frankly, to date, the State has not shown very much imagination and push in matters of great importance. I am concerned about this because I know from many rumors and many direct statements of various people, that real estate development of the Presidio and a large part of the Marin County area[5] is very much in the works, as it were. A couple of weeks ago we were at Cedar Grove in the King's Canyon. The road is there. It is a very well built road and built to very good standards. The King's Canyon is still operating as a very modest and appropriate campsite and the only thing that alarms me is constant comments: "Well, we're going to get the road up to Paradise Valley because we want to get up into that high country"—so it's just a matter of time. The same attitude is directed toward the completion of the Mammoth Pass Road. The proponents say, "Why fight this road? It is inevitable." It irritates me to have anyone say that such a thing is inevitable—because I know perfectly well there are other values in this world which are inevitable too. (Although I must say, in this one case, I don't think the Mammoth Pass Road could do one-tenth the damage of the Tioga Pass Road, but it certainly would do 1/100th the damage that a road across the Sierra in the Mt. Whitney region would accomplish.)

This has been a long and rambling letter which I have dictated in fragments and I trust that you will not feel obliged to take it too seriously in the sense of answering it. But I do hope that some ideas may appear between the lines which might have significance to you in your new job. Above all, I think that the people need a far more intense, emotional presentation of the Parks and of the Park ideals and I would like to tell you of a proposition that I put up to Secretary Ickes many years ago when I was serving for a while as photomuralist. (Perhaps this activity was cut off by the war and has not been reopened.) The project was simply this: in every National Park there should be a gallery or exhibition room beautifully designed to present the entire National Park Service, in beautiful images, appropriate text, and all of this done in a way which would not be of the usual Museum placidity, but created with the intention of producing great excitement and pleasure and anticipation on the part of all who saw it. I feel that a very small part of our people really comprehend the enormous scope of the National Park System. Those who tour about the country and visit a dozen Parks in the summer certainly have some idea of it, but the average American citizen is confused over not only what the Parks really represent and why they are there, but is also blind to the enormous scale of the System and the enormous significance the National Park Ideal has in relation to our society.

Warmest greetings to you both[6] and believe me I certainly will look you up when I am in Washington. I don't know when it will be, but I'll be there some day.**

Good luck and love from us all.

Cordially,
ANSEL ADAMS

**My secretary says it will probably be as the leader of a MARCH ON WASHINGTON TO PROTEST THE RAPE OF THE WILDERNESS.

A.A.

1. Wallace Stegner was newly appointed as special assistant to the Secretary of the Interior, Stewart Udall.

2. Rainbow Bridge National Monument was threatened by the damming of the Upper Colorado River.

3. The North Cascades National Park, Washington, was created in 1968.

4. Established in 1972, the 72,815-acre Golden Gate National Recreation Area stretches from Marin County south through San Francisco.

5. The Presidio, spread out along the northwestern shore of the city of San Francisco, along with the Marin County headlands on the opposing shore, comprised the area known as the Golden Gate. These highly scenic lands were owned by the U.S. Army.

6. Stegner's wife, Mary Page Stegner.

To Dorothea Lange

San Francisco
May 15, 1962

Dear Dorothea,

Am in bed with a flu bug—nothing serious. It does give me a chance to write letters. Have been planning one to you for several days. Am using Nancy's lousy Hermes while she pounds away on my good Royal. Never underestimate the power of a woman. The house is almost finished. Virginia is deep in books and negatives. Nancy is deep in the texts for my exhibit.[1] I am deep in bed with the sniffles.

We DO love you even if we disagree with you documentary-wise. It is not a case of mutual influence—both Nancy and I entertain the same general thoughts about photography—although she is more catholic than I am. . . .

What bothers me is a deep-seated resentment over the one-sided direction of most documentary work. As I said, I get no *human* emotion from pictures of this type; I get only a sense of *group, mass, class condition.* As it is only a small part of the whole framework of humanity—and a damned negative one at that—I find myself entertaining an increasing tension about it.

I must say that I think I have had more experience with the seamy side than you imagine. I do not come from "wealth"; I have friends and enemies in all classes! I simply prefer the clean sidewalk to the gutter. I have sympathy for the "underprivileged," but I am not so sure that all of the "class" are of the proletariat. What I really resent is the limitation of experience evidenced by "line" emphasis. The spirit of the 30's was one of despair—the "line" psychology—often not recognized as such by the photographer himself—dominated the human scene. The camera lied and lied again—it also told some profound truths. But "revelation" finally exhausted itself, there was a crying need for a constructive approach in all art. It is childish to continue to dwell on the negative aspects of society at least to *concentrate* on them.

What about the positive potentials of America? Where are the ministers, doctors, lawyers, artists, businessmen, family people, artisans— the people with homes, professions, jobs, avocations? Where are the people that compose a large part of the nation—the ordinary, healthy, reasonably smart, reasonably aware, reasonably successful people? . . . What we really need is a revival of the Walt Whitman spirit—the acceptance of the WHOLE of humanity. Photography, when it tells the truth, is magnificent, but it can be twisted, deformed, restricted, and compromised more than any other art. Because, what is before the lens always has the illusion of reality; but what is selected and put before the lens can be as false as any totalitarian lie. While it is true that we get from pictures pretty much what we bring to them in our minds and hearts, we are still restricted by the content and the connotations of the image before us. If the picture is of a clam I don't think about flamingos! The connotations of much of documentary photography are—to me—quite rigid; proletarianism, low-level urbanism, protest, patronizing of a "class," and an ever-present aura of the "line" of psychology. On top of that is an esoteric symbolism which, too, has a questionable importance.

I resent being told that certain things have "significance"; that is for me, as spectator, to discover. I resent being manipulated into a politico-social function if it is not of value to people at large. I resent the very obvious dislike of elements of beauty; our friend Steichen has shocked me time and again by a self-conscious fear of the beautiful. Does he feel that way about a painting, about sculpture, architecture, literature, and just plain nature? He does not. I am not afraid of beauty, of poetry, of sentiment. I think it is just as important to bring to people the evidence of the beauty of the world of nature and of man as it is to give them a "document" of ugliness, squalor, and despair.

I DO think that the whole pattern of life should be subject to the photographer's interpretation—with honesty and clarity and tolerance. For every grim image of Harlem there should be some buoyant truthful image of a hopeful society and some image of the natural scene. Also, the association of texts with pictures can be dangerous to logic and truth. I have often associated texts and pictures on a basis of too much personal sentimentality. . . .

Is there no way photography can be used to suggest a better life—not just to stress the unfortunate aspects of existence or the tragic satirical viewpoint of the photographer? There must be. There is a great opportunity ahead and I think we are all muffing it.

You happen to be one of the few who has brought enough deeply human emotion into your work to make it bearable for me. I wish you would try and think of yourself as a fine artist—which you are; that is a damn sight more important to the world than being merely an extension of a sociological movement.

Love,
Ansel

1. "The Eloquent Light," an extensive one-man retrospective exhibit with photographs from 1923 to 1963, curated by Nancy Newhall for the M. H. de Young Memorial Museum, San Francisco, 1963.

To Stewart Udall

Carmel Highlands[1]
August 14, 1962

Dear Mr. Udall,

Virginia and I are very unhappy that we cannot be in Yosemite to greet you and the President [John F. Kennedy]! But prior commitments and some teaching schedules make it impossible. We are presenting the President with a copy of the now out-of-print *My Camera in Yosemite Valley*. Incidentally, do you have one of these books? If not we will try to find one for you.

The local paper (San Joaquin Valley *Fresno Bee*, I think) noted that the President would visit Yosemite, enjoy the Ahwahnee Hotel and the world-famous Firefall.[2] This is typical of the emphasis given to the artificial impositions! The Ahwahnee is an excellent hotel, but the Firefall remains, for me, a very sad concession to commercialism and mis-directed publicity. I hope the Press will note that the President *did* see the cliffs and forests, and what is left of the waterfalls at this time of year. . . .

Always appreciate your notes, and your patience with such irascible devotees of the Natural Scene, as

Yours truly –
Ansel Adams

1. In 1962 the Adamses moved to the house they had built in the Carmel Highlands.
2. Every night of the tourist season a huge bonfire made of bark was pushed over the edge of Glacier Point. As it cascaded 3,000 feet down into Yosemite Valley, it gave the effect of a fiery waterfall. The firefall was the subject of Adams' unceasing derision and complaint until it was abolished in 1968.

From Stewart Udall

Washington, DC
Tuesday

Ansel—

The President loved *your* valley—the natural beauty, I mean, not the Firefall!

Stewart

To John Szarkowski[1]

Carmel Highlands
October 14, 1962

Dear John,

Finally up and around! You didn't know it, but I was feeling rather grim the day you were here! Your presence pepped me up, and I really enjoyed it all exceedingly. But I found out the next day I was coming down with a flu bug and after fighting the Fates for the morning I gave up and went to bed. One good feature—I missed Los Angeles! I failed my friends but I probably saved myself, such as I am, from further complications. At any event, looking back on Thursday, I was not functioning under full steam. But all the others felt, as I did, that it was a great event to meet you.

You presented many excellent ideas, and I have been thinking a lot about them. One idea—about a landscape show—motivated a whole freight train of ideas, and I submit them for what they are worth:

1. I strongly feel that under your direction the department can return to its logical function—presenting photography as an art.

2. I wonder if thinking about *categories* (such as landscape) is not more related to history and criticism than to art as such?

3. We did touch upon the landscape as being either something observed (by selection) or something created as reflecting the internal events of the artist. The more I think about it, the more confused I get. It seems to me that when I do a landscape it can fall under these three divisions of the prime category:

A. A record of something important to someone (client).

B. A supplementary image—helpful to some larger project (such as many of the pictures in the *This Is the American Earth* book).

C. A creative experience, in which the fact that it *is* a landscape is incidental, perhaps accidental, and secondary in importance to the fact that from the observation and recognition thereof a subjective experience was created and expressed.

Perhaps this is something more for George Eastman House than for the Museum of Modern Art at this early stage of the "renaissance"?

The main objective should be, in my opinion, the return to expression—relating to the esthetics and other elements peculiar to the medium. The subject is absolutely secondary (as it is in most painting

[293]

and in most painting exhibitions). The subject is, really, the very personal possession of the artist. Perhaps I do not make myself clear; it is a very unclear and vague subject!! But I keep thinking of Stieglitz—he made photographs (expressions—some of which he called equivalents . . .). But a barn, a portrait, apples, a skyscraper—all these could be shown in sequence and present an amazing unity. People think only the clouds were equivalents. This is not so. Stieglitz was quite free of categories; having only one category, which was expressive photography.

The museum has, for many years, stressed *subject shows*. Even the abstract show was a subject show—abstract photography! Such, in my opinion does not exist; it is a misuse of the term (unless you want to call ALL photography abstract). I don't know what these shows prove. They are expected to prove something, and may show some relationships between the surface effects of photography and other graphic arts. But there is something missing—that is missing in a truly clear intention.

Hence, it seems to me that a demonstration of the expressive capacities of the medium could be the prime objective. No matter what subjects are involved, the pictures should be selected for that peculiar kind of magic which photography alone can provide. And by this, I don't mean just good technique in the ordinary sense of the term.

Verbalization should be at an absolute minimum. But if we can find a photojournalistic image that meets the standard, or an industrial, portrait, landscape—ANY kind of image that meets the standard—that image is worthy of display.

Perhaps the logical program would be to first have a series of exhibits which would re-define photography to the subject-sated audience, then proceed into more specific categories (but with great caution). At the same time, the one-man show (of work in the expressive domains) could always be a steady buffer to the more general and perhaps remote definitive collections.

The show now in progress is a case in point ("The Bitter Years"[2]). Naturally, I have not seen it but I venture to say I am familiar with many of the photographs included. My question would be this—how many of the photographs are photographs in the creative sense of the term? I will wager that Dorothea's, Evans', and one or two others' work will be outstanding.

How many are important in the sociological-historic domains? How MANY are just human images? All three groupings are valid and important; but I would say only the first grouping should relate to a museum of art.

You see, I am quite a rebel (as well as a hero non-worshipper)! I recall years ago being on a jury to select the best news photograph of the year—a pretentious gathering in Washington, D.C., and a tremendous number of terrible images (which had been filtered through regional juries)! Out of hundreds of images there were ten really beautiful and impressive images. But what did the jury select (2 to 1)? A picture of a smiling freckle-faced boy and a hound dawg! It was a lousy photograph, but the *subject* brought tears to 4 out of 6 eyes. Now, this image was announced and publicized as the top *photograph* of the year; Mr. and Mrs. Amurika was brainwashed into thinking it represents the art of photography. "Photography in the Fine Arts"[3] was a distressing mixmash; perhaps with Beaumont's assistance we can be assured of a constructive direction.

I have talked too much! At any event, I wish I could have the opportunity of showing you a better cross-section of my work; you saw very few things (in fact, even I have not seen more than ¼ of what I have done)! Next time, stay longer, and I shall bore you without mercy! Seriously, the perspective on work is important—not volume showings!

Good luck,
Ansel Adams

1. John Szarkowski succeeded Edward Steichen as director of the Department of Photography, Museum of Modern Art, New York City.
2. "The Bitter Years: 1935–1941 Rural America as Seen by the Photographers of the Farm Security Administration," Museum of Modern Art, New York City, 1962.
3. A series of photography exhibitions organized by Ivan Dmitri.

From John Szarkowski

New York City
October 19, 1962

Dear Ansel:

First let me say that I had a *great* time at your party. The house and the site and the day and the guests and the dinner, but most of all the host and hostess, were unalloyed pleasure. Thank you so very much.

Your large new prints were a real revelation. The one of the adobe gate under the hot noon sun has been in my mind since I saw it. I wish there had been time for me to go slowly and lovingly through your entire storage area.

Your expression of confidence is very heartening to me. Although each of us must in the last analysis depend upon his own intuitions, it is also most important that we all recognize a close relationship to each other and to our great tradition.

I think our points of view are very close; the difference probably more semantic than real. Personally I find it impossible to separate content and form—the motivation from the solution when talking about creative work. Evans and Lange are surely the most consistently powerful of the people in the FSA show, and in their work it is impossible to separate the idea from the picture. But this is not the same thing as saying that the idea is not vital—or indeed, that the particular formal and technical solution could have been conceived without the powerful motivation of the idea.

For example: would your own aesthetic and formal ideas have developed in the way they have if it had not been for your intense and personal experience of nature? Surely art is not an application of principles; it is rather the discovery of principles inherent in a new idea.

It was an act of heroism far beyond the call of duty to entertain me while you were feeling under the weather; but I must admit, with shame, that I am glad you did. I am looking forward to our next meeting, and a continuation of the very fascinating discussion of what photography is basically about.

With warm regards and deep respect,
John Szarkowski

To John Szarkowski

Carmel Highlands
October 23, 1962

Dear John,

Thank you for your very warm letter of the 19th! All I can say is—please come back, SOON!!!!

Will not burden you with long tomes, as you have a huge job to do and should not be bothered with chitchat. But I DO agree with you in that content is the reason for form. If there were nothing to say there would be no reason for saying it! I think we do agree on practically everything that is important. To me, content is both a factual and a spiritual entity. I agree that the natural scene has had a profound effect upon both my music and photography. The fact that I made photographs of it does not, however, serve as *proof* that my work is, or is not, art! I have thousands of pictures of the natural scene which neither I nor anyone else could recognize as art—just damned good records—and probably useful ones, too.

What makes Lange and Evans superior in their fields—and they certainly *are* artists—is that they have considered important subject material and given it an additional dimension of spirit and deep perception. The form achieved is not so much dependent upon the subject alone, but upon a transcendental awareness and appreciation. Gawd!! This is difficult to explain!

I am pleased that you liked the idea of the large print. I am very anxious to follow this through logically and effectively. Of course, there are many who are now trying the large print idea—and I shudder at some of the results! Also—I am happy over some; but it is a conceptual problem; not just blowing up pictures which look blow-upable!

All best, and I do hope we can meet again in the near future.

Cordially,
Ansel

Virginia sends her best, too!

To Nancy Newhall

Carmel Highlands
December 18, 1962

Deer Snookumz,

It was good to talk with you but sad to hear you have cold!!! Take care———Youse is valuable!!!!!!!!

It just ain't right that you and B have not been out here! Of all the peeps that should have celebrated our new occupancy youse is them! You have a surprise coming, because I don't think the place will look to you like you expect it to look! No one gets the correct pre-idear!! So,

[297]

please come out soon and confirm your pre-opinions!! I don't know what the place thinks about *you*—it is in for a surprise, too!

It is good news that the manuscript on the Beard is progressing. . . .

As for the artist's "best things." You pose a question. I have a few "best things" which have been repeated *ad nauseum*. I am accused of repetition, potboiling, riding a manner, etc. When I do break away and do something different, it's not my "best work." WHAT am I to do???? BOOHOOBOOHOO! I desperately want to get into some new expression but every time I do something, somebody says, "It's not what you have done, so it isn't your best work!" As for abstract expressionism—there is nothing against it providing it is sincere and contains quality and spirit. Is it not the blind following of the A-E ideas that we object to? [Aaron] Siskind made a contribution in his field; what happens to him if he tries something else? I don't think I could do a Siskind or a [Frederick] Sommer if I tried (and I don't want to try), but isn't it really the damned REPETITIONS of what they do that irks us (plus the decadence of Sommer-time putrescences)? And here I am over-repeating myself.

Well, anyway, if I feel it, I do it. I may not always be good, but I seldom stink! (I hope!!)

At any event, get over that cold!!!!

I must go on a trip around January 15th. In the meantime, will get ahead with 5 or 6 of the *Portfolio V* subjects so the slaves can be working on the mounting and spotting. . . .

All kinds of lufffffffff. I don't know WHAT I am going to do for ANYONE for Christmas! Probably catch up later!!

Ansel

From Alvin Langdon Coburn[1]

England
April 24, 1964

Dear Ansel Adams,

I am writing to say that Beaumont and Nancy have presented me with a copy of your lovely book, *The Eloquent Light,* and this is to let you know how greatly I am impressed by it.

As you probably know, I have been using a camera since 1890, so I am in a position to appreciate in some measure what you have done and are doing.

Probably you have seen my Rochester portfolio with Nancy's text?[2] And although we have never met, I seem to know you and your work very well, and am happy in what you are doing for our beloved photography.

I have a theory that there is an interior link between all those who have been deeply involved in work with the camera, that we support one another in our efforts, and build together something very real and very precious that lifts photography out of the commonplace, into its rightful place as a deeply significant art which belongs to eternity.

You have worked valiantly in this field, which forges a link between us.

Is there a possibility that you will ever come to this part of the world? If so it would be grand if we might meet!

Beaumont was here to see me in January of this year, and it was a joy to see him again. He is like a tonic with his enthusiasm for the things we mutually cherish.

I will be 83 years of age on June 11th, but I still use a camera, and my interest in Mysticism and the things of the Spirit grow with the years.

I doubt if I will ever come to America again. My dear wife Edith passed on to "the larger life" in 1957, but her presence is still very close to me. I expect you can appreciate this?

Perhaps you will reply to this letter? I hope you will.

Ever your friend and fellow worker,
Alvin Langdon Coburn

1. Adams met Alvin Langdon Coburn, English photographer, in London in 1976.

2. *A Portfolio of Sixteen Photographs by Alvin Langdon Coburn.* Text by Nancy Newhall. Rochester, N.Y.: George Eastman House, 1962.

To Alvin Langdon Coburn

Carmel Highlands
May 18, 1964

My Dear Mr. Coburn,

. . . Needless to say, I was deeply moved by your letter. Nancy Newhall did a magnificent job with the book *The Eloquent Light*—better than I, as the subject, deserve! She is a person of rare insight and imaginative capacity. It is always a privilege to work with her. And Beaumont is an equal force in his domain. I find it very difficult to imagine what my life would have been without the Newhalls!

I *have* your portfolio and am tremendously impressed with your scope and effective "seeing." Nancy—as usual—did a splendid job with the text. The power of vital "seeing" comes through any particular style; Edward Weston used to say, "I don't care if you make a print on a door mat—as long as it is a GOOD print!" All of your work that I have seen seems to stem from a deep awareness of the world, as well as a deep awareness of the potentials of photography. So much work of today seems to relate more to desecration than to elevation. I could go on for pages in this direction, but—as we really seem to feel the same in general about the world, it is not necessary!

You are quite right about the "link" between all who use the camera (with humility and devotion). I do not feel a "link" between the opportunistic professionals, and the "ash-can" sociologists; their motive seems not to be constructive. But they have their right to express themselves. I have a great love and attachment for that vague property of nature and of man which some call "beauty." I am not interested in turning over stones to find unhealthy critters proliferating, no matter what the "shock" value may turn out to be. In many ways I feel you and I have struck sparks from the same anvil!

I don't know when I might be in England; I just do not like to travel anywhere without a creative project and there is MUCH to be done in my part of the world. But a pilgrimage to you might very well be a valid and important reason for my coming over. We will see! I fear verbalizations, but your brand of mysticism I approve of! I think we would have much in common!

I do understand why you may not come to America again. I hope you have 83 more years of productivity and inspiration. My warmest greetings and regards and admirations!!

As ever,
AA

To The Sierra Club

Carmel Highlands
July 2, 1966

TO: Sierra Club
ATTENTION: George Marshall & David Brower

When I see such an approach to National Parks as evidenced in the *National Geographic*[1] I realize how our institutions have failed to truly appraise the basic values. The Firefall in Yosemite is a continuing example of how confused people can be; a man-made "event" attracts the majority of people in Yosemite every evening—becomes a "pivot" for the daily program. Out of this philosophy grows the situation shockingly revealed in that evening view from Glacier Point of the Valley Floor.

In other words, the degree of use (or exploitation) seems to be the controlling factor in Park management and development, rather than the protection of the basic values. Friends say to me, "I don't see how the lower Colorado dam can do any harm—only a handful of people see that part of the [Grand] Canyon anyway." And, "with a lake in there people can *easily* (!) see things they would never see before." I suggest we fill the Sistine Chapel about ⅔ full of water so that visitors can float around and see the ceiling paintings to better advantage!

Perhaps we should enter on a campaign to stress the basic economic value of real (natural) values! They DO have great economic significance. But people are too unimaginative to visualize what these economic values can be in time.

We had two strong arguments which helped win the Humble Oil Co. battle[2] here: One was that we were not against industry as such; this turned a lot of the opposition to our side, and, two, that the "scenic and recreational values" we were trying to preserve actually represented millions of dollars to Monterey County. When we got over these "practical facts," the opposition realized we were not just cleaning them out and they went over to our side. It was an interesting situation—those in favor of the refinery were not merely favoring a big industrial enterprise; they were supporting the industrial potential *in toto*. When they found out we were not just "nuts with sandals and knapsacks" but really were thinking of the future of the county in terms of logical growth and prosperity, they were not only astonished but changed their viewpoint. Yes, we DO want appropriate industries—non-polluting industries, laboratories, light manufacturing, food products, etc. I think it was handled

[301]

very well. The next problem is to get the land-use status at Moss Landing changed from heavy to light industry status. (We won one big battle, but not the War!!)

Hence, I plead for more sensible tactics, based on a solid, long-term strategic approach. I think getting the power plant off the Nipomo Dunes was a great achievement.[3] We cannot say there is no need for another power plant in the area; Pacific Gas & Electric would not spend many millions on a plant if they did not consider there was a need therefore. Cooperation of this kind will achieve far more than inflexible opposition.

Cordially,
Ansel Adams

1. The July 1966 issue of *National Geographic* was devoted to articles on the national parks: "The Mission Called 66: Today in our National Parks," and "Parkscape, U.S.A.: Tomorrow in our National Parks."

2. The Humble Oil Company intended to build a refinery at Moss Landing, between Carmel and Santa Cruz on the Pacific Coast.

3. In the early 1960s the Pacific Gas and Electric Company proposed the construction of a nuclear power plant on the Nipomo Dunes, one hundred miles north of Santa Barbara. Environmentalists were opposed because of the uniqueness and fragility of the dunes, and persuaded the company to select another site. Diablo Canyon, to the north, was chosen.

To David Brower

Carmel Highlands
November 9, 1966

A PERSONAL COMMUNICATION

Dear Dave,

For some reason communication between us seems to have collapsed. I am sorry about this. I sense that you think I have become fully negative to you and what you are doing, that—perhaps—I have been "taken over" by the Conservative Opposition. Such is very far from the truth! I entertain a growing distaste for the "conservative opposition" in any field. I do NOT want a return to the "Old Sierra Club" or in any way to turn back the clock. I am simply interested in keeping the clock running!!

The present situation is, I am convinced, very bad for the Club and for you. Procedures are uncertain, to say the least. You have taken upon yourself what appears to be a "dictatorship" attitude in that you seem to think it is necessary to by-pass the directives (actual and implied) of the Board, the Executive Committee, and the Publications Committee in order to achieve your objectives.

No one in their right mind can say that Dave Brower is not one of the top people in conservation history. You must surely have an objective conviction that you have been, and are, a tremendous success—and that you have done, and are doing, a tremendous service to conservation and the Sierra Club.

As I told you before; I was partially responsible for getting you into the Club (as Executive Director), and I want to do my very best to keep you there!! The way things are going now is not good at all. I think we all have to face the fact that we (and you) have been very fortunate in that situations and opportunities have been favorable to a remarkable degree. But there is no assurance that this fortunate combination will continue; a saturation point is inevitable in all affairs. There is no assurance that you or I or George [Marshall] or any of the Directors will continue. There is no assurance that we will have a continued prosperity; we might have a serious recession. This is not pessimism—I bring up these points simply because I think we should always be *prepared*. I do not think we have prepared for anyone to take your place should something happen (God forbid!). I do not consider myself as anything but an expendable person—and I have to make plans (which I have done to a certain extent) to assure continuance of some of the things I am engaged in. I am sure the Club would get along splendidly without me; I have not been very effective of late and we MUST get young people in to take the helm wisely and efficiently. We have just had a serious set-back with the election of Reagan and the defeat of Fred Farr.[1] Our problem now is the education and persuasion of the new people in power. Perhaps we have failed in the sense that we did not anticipate that this defeat might occur as it did. Returning to the main theme: I honestly believe that if you do not adjust your course to the realities of organization, you, the Book program,[2] and even the Conservation program of the Club may seriously suffer. It seems that you take criticism as final censure—opposition to any idea is basic antagonism and total defeat. I assure you this is not the case! I cannot impress strongly enough upon you the *necessity* for following directives and procedures. I am convinced that, through the proper following of directives, you will achieve more now and in the future. I am not exaggerating; you are headed for disaster on the present course. And this I would be most unhappy to see happen!

Please take a good, long, objective look at the present aspect of the Club, its finances, and its programs—and, very important, at yourself!!!

As ever,
Ansel

1. In the fall of 1966, Ronald Reagan was elected governor of California and Fred Farr was defeated in his bid for reelection to the California state senate. Farr was the first politician at the state level to make the environment a major issue.

2. The Sierra Club launched their book publishing program with *This Is the American Earth* in 1960. By 1966 Brower had published and proposed a number of exhibit-format books, by such photographers as Eliot Porter and Cedric Wright, and two more books by Adams, *The Eloquent Light* and *These We Inherit: The Parklands of America*, 1962.

To Edwin Land

Carmel Highlands
March 24, 1967

Dear Din,

We are progressing; this is the first proof of our letterhead, and I am writing the first letter about The FRIENDS[1] thereon to you.

I am convinced we have a very fine idea. It all started when Cole Weston[2]—newly appointed manager of the Sunset Center (formerly a large school and recently taken over by the City of Carmel as a cultural center), suggested that we form a group and lease available space for a photography gallery. I called a meeting of those I knew would be interested and, without delay, and with a great amount of enthusiasm, founded The Friends. We are incorporated on a non-profit basis and already have the state tax deductibility status. . . .

The Friends—while based in Carmel—intend a nation-wide service to creative photography. We anticipate that it will take a year to work out an adequate program and stabilize our effort and finances. . . . As soon as feasible we shall develop a program of exhibits, lectures, seminars, publications, and perhaps, workshops.

Our first exhibit is intentionally planned to function as a kind of introduction to creative photography—to trace the thread of creative

[304]

work from the earliest times (in photography) to the present day. This will set us up in the community as a stable organization. (There have been and are many galleries hereabouts which have concentrated on contemporary work and have not been able to survive the lack of public interest.) . . .

We would all be tremendously interested in your reactions and suggestions. What about gathering a really fine exhibit of creative Polaroid photography? . . .

Terre[3] seems fine and quite happy; the weather is beautiful now. Please come out soon!!

All best from us all,
Ansel

1. The Friends of Photography, founded in 1967.
2. Cole Weston, photographer and youngest son of Edward.
3. Helen "Terre" Land, wife of Edwin Land.

To Nancy and Beaumont Newhall

Carmel Highlands
November 9, 1967

Dear Nancy and Beaumont,

The Strand prints arrived today from San Francisco—all in good condition.[1]

They look *infinitely better* than on the walls of the corridors at the S.F. Museum! I was really distressed over their appearance and mood. You would think I could see through such things by this time—but I could not get through the depressed quality the prints had under those conditions! The last time there were Strands at S.F. we had to look at them with lighted matches!!

Our gallery has really fine lighting.

I have come to a strange conclusion! Maybe I am nuts! But it seems that, in retrospect, Weston and Strand prints take on qualities which— when you see them afresh—they do not have! I was looking through a lot of the Westons at Lane's[2]—I was impressed how soft they were in comparison to the "build-up" in my mind (which I am sure comes from recollections of their total basic "seeing," etc.). I checked with my prints here—and I got the same impression. The Strands "build up" in my mind as being of extraordinary richness—but when I see them again, they look comparatively flat and gray!! The gravures[3] seem to hold their own!!—they are VERY rich.

The Sheeler prints I saw at Lane's were also rather flat and dull—typical of an earlier age.

I wonder if I am printing too strong and tone-full!! My prints all seem to have about 2x the silver of most others I see. Brett's are quite strong, but his seem to be getting harsh. The last portfolio[4] was very poor, I thought.

This is not a critical communication, really. But I need some illumination. I know I am liable to print a bit too dark at times. But I don't think many of my prints are. It is a matter of *concept*, I guess. . . .

I have written Dave McAlpin and explained the pitiful condition of my representation at MoMA. I told him frankly that there was a lack of mutual liking and respect between AA and MoMA; my work is of another world!

I would like to discuss many future plans and ideas but the situation now is simply this:

A. I am weary.

B. I have a lot to do this next two months (exhibits, Polaroid etc.).

C. I don't know how to plan for 1968—my arthritis "gits me daown."

Hope all goes Great with youse two

LUF F F F F F F F F

Ansel

. . .

1. An exhibit of Paul Strand's photographs was shown at the San Francisco Museum of Modern Art and then at The Friends of Photography, Carmel.

2. William H. Lane of Lunenburg, Massachusetts, has a large collection of photographs by Edward Weston and Charles Sheeler.

3. Strand made both photographic prints and photogravures from his negatives.

4. Brett Weston. *Baja California*, a selection of 15 photographs, 1967.

Rochester
November 14, 1967

Dearest Beard—

The first snows are descending—uncertain, slippery, but momentarily beautiful. The kitten tree is a Chinese painting. The outside of the house is painted; new curtains are coming in; carpeting is coming for those steep stairs; an aged carpenter has been at work on all kinds of little things, and will get to work next on those damn garages. Even a little house is demanding, especially if it's old. But any rate, the bulbs are in; orange trees and chrysanthemums are blooming inside, and life ain't really so Bad!

Now—about you and print quality! My dear Adams, who do you think you are? Why do you think Newhalls and many, many others back you? Quite simply, as Beau and I see it, you were making extraordinary prints before you met Stieglitz; Strand's negatives were a help and so were Edward's prints. I remember I couldn't "see" Stieglitz's prints at first, because you were my standard of perfection. Then I learned to "see" through prints to the individual artist behind them; not everybody paints the same way! or photographs or prints! You have had an enormous effect on the whole younger generation; thank God they—most of them—now make prints where the black is BLACK and the white is WHITE. And the greys are beautiful silver. But, dear Beard, don't look back in anger and condemnation on Stieglitz and Strand and Weston. Simply praise the Lord you can do better! . . .

Love to all—and I mean ALL!
Nancy

To Board of Directors, The Sierra Club

Carmel Highlands
September 1968

TO THE BOARD OF DIRECTORS OF THE SIERRA CLUB

I left the Meeting at the Claire Tappaan Lodge[1] with a heavy heart; it was the blackest day in the history of the Sierra Club. I entertained serious thought of resigning from the Board, but reason prevailed. I wish to state that I intend to fight in every possible ethical way to regain and preserve the dignity, security, and reputation of the Sierra Club.

As a member of the Board of Directors, I cannot publicly express my thoughts; I must reluctantly support the majority decisions. But, *within* the Club, I intend to act as a *member*—a deeply concerned member—and will do all I can to protect our reputation for effective conservation and responsible leadership. Our financial situation, IF it can be managed at all, deserves most careful attention. . . .

I admired Eliot Porter's[2] statement as an ideal expression of an ideal approach to Conservation. But he, as a highly trained scientist, should surely know that without a program of logical implementation, the ideals will never bear fruit. He, Luna Leopold, Paul Brooks, Pat Goldsworthy[3] must surely realize that at this stage of the Conservation Situation, we accept the ideals, but we must also think intensely on the ways and means of putting them into effect in the fact of modern political, economic and social conditions. Cooperation is NOT compromise. I firmly believe that without cooperation we are doomed. Did anyone ever hear of militant cooperation? I believe in it! . . .

If anyone thinks I enjoy being continuously critical of management and policy I wish to dissuade them. It is extremely painful to be in opposition to an old friend. The spirit of our cause simply excludes the elements of ego, domination, self-advantage, power-play, etc. and yet in recent years these qualities have created division, confusion and material loss to the Club as a whole. . . .

The hatred which the actions and, chiefly, the attitudes of the Sierra Club have engendered in ever-widening circles in the outer world will be a long time healing. The opposition is not necessarily evil; perhaps only lacking the education and the motives for more conservation-oriented thought and action. We should first try cooperation, then persuasion; then we will have to fight. But to begin an episode with the conviction that the "other side" is evil, crooked, predatory, and dishonest is to lose half the battle to begin with. I hear sickening, vituperative, paranoid statements about the people and forces we have to deal with, and I am ashamed (and startled) with the logic and tactics involved. I am certain that if we are to be effective in the future we will have to consider the entire human "picture" and attempt some compassionate understanding of attitudes and requirements other than ours.

The question now is: when are we to resolve the internal situation and get back to work? . . . as long as the present management is in the saddle there is very little chance for its implementation. In effect, we have a "packed court" and the majority of the Board seems to be following a Leadership dogma rather than the paths of logic and leadership.

I affirm the basic principles for which we stand. I affirm the enduring magic of the world. I affirm that our prime objective is to preserve this beauty and wonder for us and for the generations to come. Please do not have any doubts of my beliefs in this domain!

But I also must affirm reality, the dominance of the predatory spirit (which we must manage), the dominance of the urge for survival of the individual and the group and their property, and the expanding problem of more and more people, more and more services, and more and more pollution, etc. These we cannot wish away, or vaporize by poetic or religious fervor. We must act and act intelligently, stop fighting windmills and ordering the waves to recede. Some of us, at least, are intelligent men. We did not give good evidence of this at the recent meeting!

Permit me to close with the re-affirmation that I believe in the Sierra Club and its objectives and that I intend to leave no stone unturned to assist in the regeneration of the Club, its effectiveness and its potentials—as well as its public image!

Sincerely,
ANSEL ADAMS

1. Claire Tappaan Lodge is the Sierra Club's lodge near Donner Summit in the northern Sierra.

2. Eliot Porter was a member of the Board of Directors of the Sierra Club.

3. Luna Leopold, Paul Brooks, and Pat Goldsworthy were elected members of the Board of Directors of the Sierra Club in April 1968 and were supporters of David Brower.

To Nancy Newhall

Carmel Highlands
September 16, 1968

Dahrlick!!

Just a line; got home at midnight after two VERY bad days at the S.C. meeting. It was a shocking and distressing affair—an unreasonable and hard to explain takeover by the Brower group, in which men like

Brooks, Porter, et al were completely Brower-washed and acted like political puppets of the crudest dictatorship. I now belong to a minority of 4! (3 in effect). But I have just begun to fight. I think we have turned the tide, however, as the membership is now rising in wrath and all hell can break loose at any time (soon). I have your letters, etc. and I promise, Sweetie-Pye, to get at them pronto!

All Luff to you and B.
Ansel

. . .

To Didi Bottemanne[1]

Carmel
January 13, 1969

Dear Miss Bottemanne,

I appreciate receiving the *Tatler* and always enjoy the news and comments. I wish I could participate in some of your activities.

I have a great respect and affection for Philip Hyde[2] and his most excellent photography. But I must answer his impassioned (and sincere) letter in the December-January issue of the *Tatler*.

His premise is incorrect. I, for one, and (more important) the majority of the Sierra Club are dedicated to the spirit of conservation and the need for the protection of all available wild and beautiful places. In this Diablo Canyon matter (unfortunately inflated beyond all reasonable importance) we did NOT "trade" one area for another; we prevailed upon the PG&E to move their nuclear plant off the Nipomo Dunes, and we did not oppose their selection of Diablo Canyon. Our prime objective was to save the Dunes which we did (and the Dunes are far more important than Diablo Canyon). There are hundreds of areas along the coast equal to or surpassing Diablo Canyon; I wish we could save ALL of them, but the realities of life prevent. We can, however, meet with Government, Highway, and Utility groups and, working with them, influence them to heed the principles of conservation to the fullest possible extent. As I have said often *Cooperation is NOT Compromise*.

It is fundamentally wrong to approach the problem by assuming that the government, highway, and utility groups are "enemies." This is a belligerent and somewhat paranoid attitude which many conservationists assume (I felt that way once, myself!). It gets us nowhere. It removes the possibility of rational discourse and cooperation. If, of course, persuasion and education fail, we must take stronger action. I am not implying we should "give in." Many grave battles are ahead!

In the case of Diablo Canyon: establishment of cooperation with PG&E was a milestone in the progress of conservation. The membership upheld the board action. I am quite sure they will uphold it again in the forthcoming election.

I wish all members of the Sierra Club could realize they live in a different world than that of John Muir! The problems are immense. An adult attitude towards all the forces of society is imperative. We must be certain the Sierra Club is governed by reason and responsibility; otherwise its effectiveness will rapidly diminish.

I, for one, most certainly do *not* feel I made a mistake when I voted not to oppose Diablo Canyon, attractive as it may be, as an alternate site to the Nipomo Dunes.

Most sincerely,
ANSEL ADAMS

1. Didi Bottemanne was the editor of *The Toiyabe Tatler*, the Reno, Nevada, Sierra Club newsletter.

2. Philip Hyde, photographer.

To the Public

Carmel Highlands
February 4, 1969

For Immediate Release

Painful as it is to prolong an unhappy controversy, it is necessary to inform the membership of the Sierra Club, as well as the general public, of the extraordinary situation facing the Club because of the irresponsible actions of the Executive Director, David Brower. The Sierra Club is a semi-public organization, and the Directors (of which I am one) are entrusted with members' funds (received through donations and dues) dedicated to the cause of conservation. Hence, as a spokesman for Concerned Members for Conservation (of the Sierra Club), I must make public statements—in stronger terms than ever before—on this most serious situation within the Club.

Ruthless arrogance and insubordination are inexcusable in any case; when they affect the orderly processes of an organization such as the Sierra Club—resulting in severe financial hazard, unethical procedures, and interruption of the prime functions of the organization—definite direct action is required. The President of the Sierra Club finally suspended David Brower from any actions relating to the making or fulfilling of financial commitments until further action can be taken at the meeting of the Board of Directors on February 8–9, 1969. Stated causes of this suspension were based on ". . . deliberate disregard of Board directives . . . and in part on the entire prior record of your [Brower's] failure to follow Board policy . . ." Mr. Brower then had the audacity to question the President's authority to suspend him! The unauthorized expenditure of $10,500 on an advertisement in the *New York Times* was the final straw precipitating the President's action.

I am not protesting the basic worth of Brower's imaginative ideas and objectives; but if they exceed the limitations of the Club's Articles of Incorporation and Bylaws and if they commit the Club to obligations far beyond its means, I, as a Director, *must* do what I can to prevent such misapplication of time, effort, and moneys, no matter how "appealing" the causes may be.

So determined is Brower that he must be in full control of the Sierra Club that he has (through his lawyers) threatened suit to those—including editors of Sierra Club chapter publications—who speak up against him and his policies. This constitutes an attack on the right of free speech. A responsible organization cannot be operated on any such dictatorial basis.

The membership must rise to save the Sierra Club. The public at large should also be concerned because organizations such as the Sierra Club are dedicated—without profit—to preserving natural beauty and man's total environment.

The present situation within the Sierra Club is unethical, irresponsible and intolerable.

ANSEL ADAMS
Member, Board of Directors
of the Sierra Club

To Dr. Edgar Wayburn[1]

April 19, 1969

Dear Ed,

I interpret the S.C. election as a mandate from the membership to clean house.[2]

With a majority of ten on the Board on the CMC side I see no way in which the Brower forces can recoup unless there are some very weak and fuzzy-thinking directors who would believe that there was a way to work with Brower, etc. . . .

At any event, waste no time on this! We are faced with a long up-hill battle to really clean up and re-establish the Sierra Club.

Cordially,
Ansel

PS . . .

BUT CHEERS FOR YOUR HEADING THE LIST IN THE ELECTION!!!!!!

And the Diablo Canyon issue victory was wonderful. *The* [San Francisco] *Chronicle* persists in the error that we *approved* Diablo Canyon; we merely did not *object*.

1. Edgar Wayburn, president of the Sierra Club.

2. In the 1969 election for the Board of Directors of the Sierra Club, Adams successfully led a group called Concerned Members for Conservation (CMC) that called for the dismissal of the executive director, David Brower.

To Nancy Newhall

1969

Dear Nancy,

I have a gorgeous picture of a Boston pavement detail—a curving Traffic Arrow—with a few autumn leaves (a Polaroid original) which is being made up for our New Year's card. I had a wonderful quote[1] for it which I have not only misplaced but forgotten!! The essence of the idea was that "You" alone, to whom the Arrow of Fate points, can save the world. It is kind of "conscience concept"; different from anything I have done. In your infinite storehouse of thoughts, concepts, ideas, and

[313]

references, does ANYTHING come to mind that might fit something like this. I might add that the Arrow curves towards you—unmistakably. My mind kept prompting me that John Donne said something exquisitely appropriate!!

Gotta think it up SOON.

LOVE,
Ansel

1. The Adamses' New Year's card for 1970 included this quote by Samuel Adams, American revolutionist, from a speech made in 1771: "Let us contemplate our fore-fathers, and posterity, and resolve to maintain the rights bequeathed to us from the former, for the sake of the latter. The necessity of the times, more than ever, calls for our utmost circumspection, deliberation, fortitude, and perseverance. Let us remember that 'if we suffer tamely a lawless attack upon our liberty, we encourage it, and involve others in our doom.' It is a very serious consideration . . . that millions yet unborn may be the miserable sharers of the event."

To Nancy Newhall

Carmel Highlands
August 26, 1970

Dear Nancy,

Just some random thoughts (I have no copy)! I have suddenly had some kind of revelation!! Photography for many decades has been considered an Art Form. ART itself has not been exactly defined; hence, how can photography be defined as art or anything else? The tastemakers (museums, galleries, dealers, etc.) have for a long time interpreted and defined this elusive human production as ART. No one really knows what it is, but they accept blindly the dictates of these "authorities." That does not mean that *knowing* is really related to *feeling*—spiritual acceptance, as it were. No evaluation of anything human can be made without this component of feeling (emotional reaction, spiritual identification, etc.). I cannot presume to be a tastemaker myself (actual or in reverse!) but I frankly see very little, read very little, and hear very little these days that has any effect on me whatever (except boredom or repulsion).

The recent production of crap and total defilement which comes through via pictures (photographs and other forms) causes me to ponder and pause to consider—WHAT AM I DOING HERE? The world seems to have taken a sudden plunge towards degeneracy. There

[314]

always has been degeneracy, evil thinking, filth, etc., but these qualities seemed to be counter-balanced and controlled by a larger sweep of culture and order. Now it seems as if the world has turned into a huge cesspool. Art seems to be doing little or nothing to elevate the spirit and clarify the problems. It seems to be reflecting a universal death wish.

However, I do not want to "die"! And I don't want you and Beaumont and some others I know to "die" either. Revolution, disaster, destruction seem just around the corner, so to speak. We represent the establishment; I do not mean the Republican, money-oriented religious establishment, but the establishment of constructive social interchange, quality and contribution. In a sense we are above politics, and yet we cannot avoid being part of the world. We are targets—physical, intellectual and creative. I do not propose to be a passing target; I shall do my best to eliminate anyone who tries to eliminate me (if I can "get them first!"). Everyone has the right to oppose me, to dislike me, to reject my work, etc. But they do not have the right to destroy me, my work, and my possible contributions. If my contributions cannot justify my existence I should, perhaps, fade away. I happen to think my contributions (and yours) more than justify our continued existence on earth and I intend to protect both the contributors and the contributions.

It is up to us to establish some pattern, some means of understanding, for photography as a communicative medium at the creative level. It is, I think, disastrous to promote photography as an eclectic expression—dedicated to a chosen few who comprehend (or believe they comprehend) what the gurus tell them to comprehend. And by guru I mean all people who set themselves up as the Ultimate Arbiters and who inflict confusions which convey mystical meanings—often with the convolutions of disordered sex (and violence).

I don't think I am paranoid. But I am in a "protective" mood!! I know that my work has appeal; people continue to buy it (even steal it). As Edward Weston said, "I don't care if photography is, or is not, considered an Art." In fact, it might be better if, for awhile, it was NOT considered an art.

I have come to the conclusion that what appeals in photography is primarily the subject; next—the way the subject is presented. Relatively few people really appreciate a mere presentation; they have to tie it to something, something real or something fashionable. In my case, observe the pictures to which people respond; all are of *something* and seem to convey some beauty and magic of seeing and execution. I think we might say the same of Edward's work, although he had a larger audience among the "appreciators" of fashionable modern art. (He didn't *want* it that way, but that is the way it turned out, I fear!) Stieglitz hit the high spots, but I do not know a single image that does not reflect some aspect of human or natural beauty. Ditto Strand (although the earlier work did stress some of the nastiness of existence). Granted that we have some obligation to point out and eliminate the bad aspects of existence; we can achieve more by passing on the aspects of beauty and the human potential.

I am not in the least ashamed that people like my pictures because of what I photograph! I am seeing my subjects in my particular way. You said once something about compassion; I honestly feel I want compassion in my images and yet it is difficult to apply that term to a mountain or a leaf! The older art forms that were definitely human (or God) oriented had this quality. Some of Stieglitz possesses it. Most contemporary art (for me) definitely does *not* possess it. The opposite—arrogance and scorn—seems to dominate.

This new portfolio[1] I am doing will confound the critics, disturb my conventional audience and perplex the "[Minor] White mystics." There will be a hell of a lot of "explaining" to do and I will not "explain" a thing!! They (the pictures) are really not too different, but most have a different emphasis. I shall not be guilty of verbalization. When I have a set I shall send it on, of course. . . .

I shall close now. Forgive this tirade. The last issues of *Infinity*[2] really set me off—along with a lot of "contemporary" images I have seen recently. Also a lot of verbalization guff from my otherwise great friend, Minor!!

LOVE — — — — — — — Beard

Ansel

1. *Portfolio V*, a selection of 10 photographs, New York: Parasol Press, 1970.
2. Journal of the American Society of Magazine Photographers.

From Nancy Newhall

Rochester

September 1970

. . . I think we agree almost to a blade of grass about most things. Such as most of *Camera Work* being pretty dim stuff! And that you are making great equivalents out of the natural scene—most of your clients have no idea what a miracle you've performed!—all they know is what is done to them by your images! For God's sake, darling, never apologize! What we did in the *American Earth* looked like Jeremiah to many people. "Hell we are building here on earth . . ." Ask them now.

What positive note is possible? We have the technical knowhow to solve our problems, but legally it's the bow wow. Kodak may have had a trout in its purified effluents but it's still the major polluter of the Genesee. Cash, man, cash. Nice speeches about preserving the environment, and so what????

Certainly there is a deathwish. Who can read the papers without one? Beau urges me to get with it. Why should I? I think of your description of Stieglitz as the mad figurehead on the Flying Dutchman. I'm mad too.

I agree about simpler living. Check the *American Earth* again. "Can we not walk in peace with Eden's angels? . . . How lightly could the earth bear man forever . . ." Good luck with the AIA speech![1] If anybody can do it and make the headlines, it's AA!

I got arthritis too and am supposed to get X-rayed and all that. But the lumps are going down and why hospitals unless you have to be carted there?

LOVE
N

1. Adams addressed the American Institute of Architects at the Ahwahnee Hotel in Yosemite Valley in 1970.

To Nancy Newhall

Carmel Highlands
October 2, 1970

Dear Nancy,

Here are the ten proof prints of *Portfolio V.*[1] . . .

What am I trying to say through them? You know me, I refuse to verbalize on the emotional content of a picture. But these pictures do seem to sum up for me certain qualities and feelings I have not clarified before. Some comments:

1 BLACK SUN Purely fantastic, hinting on non-visual worlds.

2   LADY AND SCREEN DOOR A past, almost ghostly mood. Toned intentionally in the "period" style.

3   FOREST Originally planned to be rather soft. No-go!! It is taken at dusk and I think has a stylized feeling and mood. It also has a good (I think) compositional tension.

4   LONE PINE PEAK Total (almost) desolation; emphasis on white sky and small pattern. Very non-romantic!

5   MUDHILLS Total desolation. Like it, but can't yak about it!

6   ALABAMA HILLS Intentional telescoping of planes. Relates to LONE PINE PEAK in all-over textural effect.

7   WHITE STUMP This remains monumental.

8   CLOUDS A kind of natural never-never land with gorgeous swoops and the ubiquitous moon!

9   PETROGLYPHS An extreme stylization of a very soft subject.

10 PIPES Something different from the usual Adams! It has a tortuous effect. Most people like this best of all the prints!

I also enclose copies of the printed matter layout (very rough). Adrian[2] is doing it. Let me know your ideas of the sequence as soon as you can. We are mounting and must start signing soon (and numbering!!).

LUFF to youse both,
Ansel

1. All images in *Portfolio V* (and the other Portfolios I–VII) are reproduced in *The Portfolios of Ansel Adams,* Boston: New York Graphic Society, 1977.
2. Adrian Wilson, graphic designer.

To the Trustees of The Friends of Photography

Yosemite National Park
May 12, 1971

Gentlemen,

I have a copy of the letter from Minor White to the Trustees of The Friends of Photography;[1] apparently one has been sent to Carmel but I do not know if any of you have received it as yet.

I am very appreciative of Minor's letter and his expression of interest in The Friends. He is one of the top photographers, and any and all comment from him is gratefully received.

His letter brings to the fore (as far as I am concerned) the need for a clarification of our policies and functions. I have small doubt about what they *can* be, but I think that we should now look to the future with a sharper concept of what we do and where we are going. I wish to present the following comments:

1. Minor shares a popular conception that the policies of The Friends is dictated by "tastemakers" (especially Adams and [Nancy] Newhall). This is quite incorrect; at least half the exhibits we have had have NOT been of this "tastemaker" character. I, for one, can say that they do not represent my personal interests and beliefs in photography. I cannot speak for Nancy Newhall; she has more varied interests than I do.

2. It is necessary to observe that I have tried to be as "objective" as possible and have not injected my preferences in the selection of any exhibit (except when work was of obviously inferior character). What some may think represents the "tastemaker" approach is really the general approach based on expressive and technical excellence. As I recall, the function of The Friends is simply to further creative photography in its most excellent expressions. We are not supposed to reflect any *particular* school of thought or expressive tendency. I think we have done very well in the broad spectrum of our exhibits.

3. Minor suggests we enter the "experimental" areas. This would please me very much indeed if we had the space and the staff and the finances to be so engaged. This would obviously require the facilities of an institution. A lot of what photography is "doing" does not meet with our supposed standards. "Experiment" relates more to the laboratory than to the exhibit room. We must be very careful in this direction, and continue to make most careful selection of what we display. It is interesting to note that Minor White has been extremely active in being a "tastemaker" in his own domain; he has created a potent "school" of thought and imagination, with many followers. This situation has existed since the beginnings of art. I know of few (if any) institutions that have remained as objective as we have in our presentation to the world.

4. I agree that we should make every effort to expand our search for the accomplished photographer and his valid statement. Again, as an institution of proper staff and financing (and, at least, a quasi-academic

program) we could (and should) engage in the search for new directions. But The Friends cannot spend its slender resources in such a program.

5. *Our function in relation to our audience.* With a few exceptions, our audience is "local"—mostly from the Monterey area with some visits from the San Francisco area (and a few from Los Angeles). Our audience must be expanded: this involves:

A. Greatly expanded publicity

B. More illustrative announcements

C. Publications on exhibits where justified

D. Circulation of exhibits

All this will take additional funds. I hope we are approaching a period where such funds will be available.

6. *Publications:* The portfolios[2] have been successful in terms of creative quality. Their sale and distribution must be expanded. So far, we have produced two expressive items, each quite different in character, and both have evoked considerable favorable praise. Obviously, subsequent portfolios must be *different*, yet equally valid. I would favor the new portfolio to relate to "new" work of high quality. I do not think we are in position to experiment with "experiment" unless it has attained high quality—then it would not be "experiment"! Being in the domain of "what's *new*" does not imply "what's good."

7. *Activities:* I have favored more member exhibits and "events." I think this is VERY important. Apart from the promotion of these events, they are self-supporting (or should be). Here we need the services of a staff. (As we do with our other activities!)

8. *Exhibits:* On the assumption that we shall continue to stress quality (in any field of work) and maturity of expression, it is important that we seek exhibit material with renewed vigor. We have done well on the volunteer basis. We need professional attention to this problem. We need the suggestions of members and advisors (and staff). I am grateful to Minor White's suggestions of two exhibits which seem to reflect "what's new" as well as "what's good." I am confident there are a vast number of potentially fine exhibits which relate to our function and capacity.

Returning to Minor White's comment on the new and younger worker he implies that a facility for the display of new and experimental work would serve to spot inspired and creative work therein. As we are not equipped to serve as an experimental center, we should take best advantage of what these centers have done and—when a real talent is revealed—consider exhibiting it. I wish to make it clear that I am in favor of such an approach and in favor of promoting *new work* of fine quality. I wish this to be clearly understood by all.

9. *The Ferguson Grant:*[3] We must begin to think about this; the grant should be given at the close of the fund's fiscal year (when a year's interest has accrued). The terms of the fund clearly imply the recipient as a gifted individual; obviously, we cannot "experiment" here; we must have proof of ability, quality, and purpose.

10. We are at the turning point; we must now expand membership and general activities. This will require the services of at least one person. The raising of funds is imperative. Please note: I have heard that the Oliver Foundation (New York) is favorable to photography.

Greetings to all,
Sincerely,
Ansel Adams
President

1. This letter has not been found.
2. The Friends of Photography published two portfolios of fine photographic reproductions: *Portfolio I: The Persistence of Beauty,* 1969; *Portfolio II: Discovery: Inner and Outer Worlds,* 1970.
3. The Ferguson Grant, established in 1972, is awarded to an emerging photographer who has demonstrated excellence in and commitment to creative photography.

To Judge Raymond Sherwin, President, Sierra Club

Carmel Highlands
September 13, 1971

Dear Ray:

With deep regret, but with firm conviction that my action is correct and for the general good of the Sierra Club, I herewith present my resignation as a member of the Board of Directors (a position I have been honored to hold since 1934). My resignation should take effect immediately—at least before the forth-coming meeting in Washington, which I shall not be able to attend.

The Sierra Club has developed into a large and potent national organization. It is imperative that the governing body—the directors—be composed of experts in the important fields of law, politics, science, and finance. I do not fit in any of these categories; my contributions have been (and will continue) in the fields of creative photography and the interpretation and aesthetic appreciation of the natural scene.

I am confident that I can accomplish as much, or more off the board —as a regular member of the club. It is important that whoever takes my place on the board of directors be highly competent in the fields mentioned above, as well as sympathetic to the ideals and basic purposes of the Sierra Club, and that he as well have the youth and energy to serve with effectiveness and with high qualities of imagination and dedication.

With enduring regard and devotion to the prime purposes of our great organization, with deepest appreciation for the long years of happy association with many remarkable personalities (many of them being my closest friends) and with greetings and good wishes to you, the members of the board of directors and the host of leaders and members of the Sierra Club,

I remain,
Respectfully,
Ansel Adams

To Nancy and Beaumont Newhall

Carmel Highlands
December 9, 1971

Dear Nancy and Beaumont,

Good to talk with you yesterday. It was hard to hear you. I had some 16x20 prints in process and could not sit down for a good yak. . . .

. . . Conservation is not that simple. All factors considered, the only way to save things is to eliminate ⅔ of the world population! (And keep it that way!) IF we would do all the things we SHOULD do, we might keep things going for quite a time. But the odds are against this. Have you ever considered that the USA represents about 200,000,000 out of 3,500,000,000 biological entities; we are one of a few nations that even thinks of dieting!! All this crap against pesticides has absolutely no meaning unless we spend some of the billions we put into kicking up dust on the moon in the development of *safe* control (if there really is such a thing). The term ecology (as it is misused) is a dichotomy of the first order; the cures will prove worse than the disease. It seems that when the thinkers take their heads out of the sand they realize that the prime issue is simply 3.5×10^9 biological machines consuming fuel and extruding waste; the biosphere cannot take it! For the present, there is more waste in the USA than anywhere else, but this waste potential will spread to other areas; scarcely any part of the inhabited earth is now free from some kind of pollution and exhaustion.

What are the answers? How can art and photography and other eu-phoric expressions contribute? I think it's all we have left to interpret the truth. The sad fact is that only a minute percentage of the population can produce the creative, significant arts, and another minute percent-age can understand them. Primitive art and folk art are really introver-tal and a part of established societies. This is not art in the sense of world-wide contribution.

What are the photographers doing? There are very few who are *really* concerned. Maybe 100 at the most? (I speak of good ones, not the pale, weak, drug-dazed thousands of introverts who produce terrbill snap-shots—and are often exhibited as the "new thing.") Many young people I meet simply have one emotion: a combination of scorn and hate. They offer no solutions. It is a great and refreshing thing to find a young per-son who thinks in terms of the spirit and accepts beauty as an actuality. Thoreau's "In wildness is the Preservation of the World" is a strange in-trovertal misinterpretation. The *real* wilderness is a hell of a place! The symbolic wilderness is something else—that is the kind we are worrying about. But the prime constructive element will be a reaffirmation of beauty. Stieglitz will emerge as the real prophet. Who are his philo-sophical forebears? Has anyone traced his philosophy back to significant origins? You know, I think S. would have been a good President of the Sierra Club!!! IF—. . .

A funny thing happened (not so funny, actually)! After the mail came this a.m. and letters and packages were opened by V[irginia] and L,[1] I saw a book on the table (there are always books of some kind or another around). I leafed through it and asked, "What travel book is this?" Then I realized I was looking at the Strand book![2] (Would have recognized this had I seen some known images.) It was quite a shock; without the euphoria of the name most of the pictures were just pictures!! Immedi-ately when I realized they were Strand's a different "filter" fits before the mind!! I think this is a fine, but painful, example of the conviction I have that most photographs—even among the best—create their first impact in the domain of *subject*. Hence, what is the element of communication involved? If we could define this, we would be on much firmer ground. Just to tell someone this is great does not make it necessarily so!!!!

Another look at the Strand book: disappointed!! Layout crowded. (Nancy should have done it!!) Reproductions not too hot in my opinion; bleak whites in many cases. GREAT IMAGES come through (as usual); for the life of me I don't see why many of the later images were included—as *photographs*!! NO—I am not sour this a.m., in fact, quite buoyant!!!! I think the Strand book is evidence of too many fingers in the pie—too much self-consciousness on the part of all concerned. But he IS *A GREAT MAN! I* used to think he was greater than Stieglitz; the years have changed this opinion! In the human sense, he is certainly greater than Edward. I sincerely hope there will not be the distorting flap about Paul that there is going on now about Edward! Edward would rotate in his grave if he had one. I charge thee—if my work is worth anything (and I know SOME of it is damn good!) keep it away from the "opportunity wolves." I have the itch to get going with new stuff. But I have a lot of old stuff to wade through before I am truly free. Turnage[3] doing fine. He is very blunt and has irritated many of The Friends [of Photography] trustees by pointing out our situation and our hazy objectives. He wants to broaden it into a large and contemporary institution, with new names on the board, etc. I am in full agreement! The difficulty is escaping from the provincial attitude. He did not realize how touchy some people can be; is used to talking with equals in objectivity. I have a tough problem, but shall weather it. . . . We need names on the board who are not photographers, not family (if you know what I mean), but who have an awareness of what is going on. While I probably will not like most of what is going on it is not my job to pick and choose the course of photography! We get MUCH criticism as being a cult of Weston-Adams, West Coast, rocks, and seagull drippings, in spite of a very catholic record of exhibits, etc. We have made no pretentions of being anything more than we are; we certainly do not have the money or the man power to compete with the MoMA, GEH, etc. But we can fulfill an important function—IF we set our hearts on it. . . .

I must get to printing. Liliane is yelling that the developer is oxidizing!! And my arthritic fingers are weary!

Love to you both from us all. More soon!!!!!!!

Ansel

. . .

1. Liliane de Cock, Adams' photographic assistant from 1963 to 1971.

2. Paul Strand. *Living Egypt*, New York: Horizon, 1969.

3. William A. Turnage, Adams' business manager from 1971 to 1977, who also served as the first executive director of The Friends of Photography during 1972.

From Nancy Newhall

Albuquerque[1]
June 28, 1972

To: Ansel
Re: Moonrises from La Luz

We were waiting for it. The East terrace is fairly cool. The greening desert ran down to the deep green bosque, the lights of Albuquerque were beginning to sparkle along the foot of the Sandias, which really did look like immense glowing chunks of watermelon. And then—a shaft of light of a brilliance I associate only with sun. A huge gold fireball began humping up between the peaks. I began to wonder if this really was the moon (Zone IV?) and not a nova or some other immense celestial phenomenon. The end of the world? Beau had Bach on the hi fi: next moonrise. I asked for the Creation. Of course when it soared into the clear dark sky with a few stars coming, it was indeed the familiar moon— so close it seemed as if you could leap up to touch it. Not at all like the cold lonely ghost we saw sometimes between the clouds in Rochester.

Perhaps it will not be so spectacular when you are here in July—or it might be more so, with thunderclouds and lightning. Anyway, only you can do it.

Love again—
N—

1. In 1971 Beaumont and Nancy Newhall moved to a condominium, La Luz, in Albuquerque, New Mexico, after Beaumont was named visiting professor of art at the University of New Mexico.

From Marion Patterson[1]

Menlo Park, California
September 17, 1972

Dear Ansel and Virginia,

Greetings! I'd somehow expected to see you during the summer, but . . .

I'm teaching full-time at DeAnza College for a year, replacing George Craven who is on sabbatical. I don't know how I'll enjoy the full-time assignment, but the benefits and pay certainly are nice.

I know the students will start in again with the question I managed to evade all summer, but can't now: why on earth did Adams do that Datsun commercial?[2] Instead of my giving lame excuses, I decided to put the question directly to you and give the students *your* answer. So, why did you do it? I'm sure I don't need to repeat the students' comments!

I hope that doesn't sound too negative, but frankly, I'm sick of the whole thing and know that I'm going to get another barrage of questions. . . .

Must now get to work on planning how to teach the Zone System to Instamatic owners.

LOVE always,
Marion

1. Marion Patterson, photographer and teacher.
2. In 1972 Adams appeared in a Datsun television commercial with the slogan, "Drive a Datsun, Plant a Tree."

To Marion Patterson

Carmel Highlands
September 19, 1972

Dear Marion,

It was good to get your letter. Sounds as if you have a good program ahead! Quite some changes in Yosemite—but all for the better. . . . Mike and Jeanne[1] have taken over the responsibility of the studio; it is now known as the Ansel Adams Gallery (operated by Best's Studio, Inc.). Bill and Charlotte Turnage will be the resident managers. Bill has a very fine relationship with the N.P.S. We have many things planned, including workshops! You are always welcome—no change there!!!

I regret that you are confronted with student questions about my commercial. I can answer it adequately, I am sure. The question is—will the students understand the rejoinder? This seems to be the time of large feeling and small thinking!! However –

When I was approached on this matter we discussed it with many conservation friends. My policy for years has been realistic. We live in a technical and industrial world (for better or for worse) and nothing short of a great disaster—or a revolution in the streets can alter it overnight. The kind of life we think we would like is more euphoric than otherwise. I am not denying that there are grave injustices: wars, too many people, pollution, and too much dependence upon decadent frills and indolences. The protesters of this way of life are undoubtedly sincere but they would have a very difficult time if the basic sources were to be denied them. The problem is one of *control,* not of elimination. Hence, I have believed for years that the environmentalists MUST cooperate with industry, business, and development—and VICE-VERSA. I resent the negative attitudes of so many conservationists; they have nothing to offer in exchange. Short of genocide, the world *will* progress to doom, unless people get together on a logical, realistic basis. The huge advantages of our present technological civilization CAN be directed to the betterment of life. I remind you that our medium, photography, is a most complex and inter-related technology; I find it hard to hear a photographer blast the life-style which provides the equipment and materials on which he exists. When you go to Yosemite, do you walk? Have you turned off your electricity, your water supply? Do you weave your clothes out of grass or use animal skins? In truth, it may come to that, but what a pity!!

On the basis that business and industry should be encouraged in every way to relate to the environment, this Datsun tree-planting advertisement is a step in the right direction and I am happy to have cooperated with it. In addition, the Datsun is a small, low-pollution car.

I do not believe advertisements actually sell cars! You do not get a car unless you need it and can afford it. But the advertisements may determine your *choice* of car. As it is difficult to think of our society without cars (although I am hoping there will be more and more dependence upon rapid transit) I can anticipate (with real agreement) that there must be: smaller cars, better fuel, lower speed limits, mileage tax, and general "pooling" of cars. As for me, I certainly would prefer a small car, but I have a transportation problem; too much for a small car to carry!

Hence, on the advice of valued conservation friends I took on the TV ad. I have received a few hate letters about selling "Jap" cars. I have received a few protests from ardent environmentalists. In view of the tremendous coverage I am amazed there has been so little direct protest. Of course, I have no way of knowing what people may *think* (and not write). But the vast majority of people I know warmly approve and understand the basic motive I had for doing it.

Please come and see us SOON. LOVE to you, too,

ALWAYS,
Ansel

1. Michael Adams married Jeanne Falk in Yosemite National Park in 1962.

To Beaumont and Nancy Newhall

Carmel Highlands
September 13, 1973

Dear Beaumont and Nancy,

It is ALWAYS great to talk with you but it is distressing when I hear of troubles! We are *DISTRESSED* that Nancy had some falls. We are helpless to assist being so far away in actuality (yet always close in spirit, as you know). If there is anything we can do to help, PLEASE let us know. It is not too far by plane. I find myself trapped in a continuing schedule which interferes with the basic schedules of life! But things have to be done, and time is not as long as it used to be. Anyway, sympathies!! And take good care of yourselves; get the *best* doctor you can. Yes, a bone man is not *only* for busted bones!!

I am naturally interested in your comments on the pictures.[1] I am sorry you do not react to all of them (apparently half of them!). This is your divine privilege—just as I feel I have the right to react to others' work—pro or con as the case may be. I have no defense, these were selected and approved by the publisher and assistant and several people here (after my making up about 25 possibilities). I had chosen three others as my favorites, but I could see the reasons why the prints as selected were decided upon. Just as with *Portfolio V,* there will be a wide diversity of opinion: X likes the *Mudhills;* Y thinks it is awful. Y thinks the *Woman and Screen Door* is the best of the lot, Z thinks it is sentimental. XYZ thinks the *Black Sun* is GREAT, ABC thinks it is a "trick" (positive-negative treatment, etc.). (It IS a straight print, utilizing the reversal phenomenon.) And so on. Obviously, I like all of them, or I would not have allowed them in; but, naturally, I like some more than others. The proofs you have are mostly just that—the final prints do have a far greater richness and variety of "color." Some people think the Piazzoni picture is posed; actually it is practically a candid image (as much as one can be "candid" with an 8x10!!). The *Still Life* was typical of the photography (AA) of the 1932–33 period; we were working with such images for advertisement, etc. and this appealed to me as a fine example of style and craft. It is almost universally admired—probably more than it deserves! The proof of the winter scene is poor; the final image has (or will have) far greater mood. That seems to be the most popular one for those who have seen the set! And so on.

I hope you know that I would be the last one to ask you to write or say anything about anything that you did not like or believe in! If you feel, in any way, a reluctance to make a statement on this portfolio please act accordingly! Your statement is not a critical one in the regular meaning of the term, but it should reflect an honest reaction. I will understand perfectly—although would sorely miss your presence on the printed page![2] Liking individual images is one thing; but thinking they are poor is another. I do not like [Jerry] Uelsmann, but I admire his ventures into new fields, etc. I think Brett is a great photographer, but I think he made a poor choice in his portfolio and the prints are under par. The first thought is personal and not expected or desired to be agreed with. The second thought is just an observation based on what I know he can do in the area of craft.

In truth, I HAVE been edited all these years. Who is the editor?—ME! . . . I, myself, am responsible—and for clear reason. My interest in the Natural Scene and its needed propaganda; my association with books, etc. relating to this theme; my association with the Sierra Club; my home and relationship to Yosemite, etc. all snow-balled to fix me in a pattern. Now realizing this, it is *essential* that I strive to present the whole man; a lifetime of work and observation.

The 1963 exhibit in San Francisco and *The Eloquent Light* certainly were *great* steps in that direction. The monograph[3] (reaching more people because of size and price) and the San Francisco exhibit[4] further awakened my audience to a far larger vista of my work. But, in most people's minds I am still a nature boy. Yosemite and the Sierra and the wilderness mystique are still a dominant collective force in my life. But as I get older I tend to lean more towards the human elements (but not in the slumgrime modes!). The fact is, in going through my negatives as I am doing now I am discovering many new worlds and facets of thought and feeling which clearly indicates that, for the foreseeable future, I will be immersed in revealing my life's work (most of which has *never* been really shown—and relatively few examples even printed!!). I have done little—very little—new work for the simple reasons that (1) I "pot-boil" and (2) I have hanging over me the responsibility of catching up with fifty years' creative effort.

The only photographs in *Portfolio Six* that have been around at all are: *Edward Weston, Silverton, Piazzoni*. There are a few prints out of *Still Life* and maybe one or two of the *White Post*. The others have never really been printed before! . . .

Getting back to the main points of discussion: I look upon these portfolios as a means of "catching up with Adams" in the retrospective sense. I wish to avoid the "Theme" approach. This point should be made clear. Perhaps they should not be so restricted. Perhaps the next one can be more recent. But, in fact, most of my best work (very few exceptions) was made prior to about 1960. And, I assure you, there is an immense variety between 1920+ and 1960!!! It is interesting to me how many young people react to seeing the new/old things! I do myself!!

It is astonishing to me how intense the recollections are when I see the negatives after many years; the whole picture comes back in a flash and then—because of the time interval—the visualizations seem more intense. Of course, we have the new papers, etc. and the toning—which seems to me to add another dimension. I am getting weary of dead green-blue-brown commercial colors. Purists don't like the toning; I like a variety of toning for various images (it would be just as bad to tone all the same as it would be to avoid toning at all).

In speaking the other day about the idea that "the negative is equivalent to the composer's score—and the print is equivalent to the performance" Ted Orland[5] asked, "Is this not a fine argument NOT to destroy negatives?" Is it not possible to think of another photographer in the future making a better "performance" from one of my negatives than I could? After all, I made better prints of the Brady and Genthe negatives[6] than either of them did (but, of course, such judgments relate to the opinions of *our* times). Many of Cole's prints of Edward's negatives[7] are really better to the eye but the collector has a nostalgic reaction to the original values (which is perfectly valid and probably based on a large number of psychological factors). I feel I can make far better prints today of a 1930 negative (or a 1950 negative) than I could then—a general statement, of course! . . .

Finally—PLEASE take care of yourselves!! Have a top bone and joint man look at Nancy. Please!!!!

Can't wait to see the Emerson—it must be a grand job. . . .

Virginia sends loads of love—so do I.

Cheeriow

Ansel

ANSEL ADAMS, PhD*

*Doctor of Photography; as Albert used to say

. . .

1. Adams sent the Newhalls a set of ten proof prints from his *Portfolio VI* (New York: Parasol Press, 1974), so that they could write the introduction.

2. The Newhalls did write the introduction to *Portfolio VI.*

3. *Ansel Adams,* edited by Liliane de Cock, Hastings-on-Hudson: Morgan & Morgan, 1972.

4. "Recollected Moments," an exhibit of Adams' photographs at the San Francisco Museum of Modern Art, 1972.

5. Ted Orland, Adams' photographic assistant from 1972 to 1974.

6. In 1940 Adams printed negatives by Mathew Brady and Arnold Genthe for the Museum of Modern Art's exhibit "60 Photographs."

7. Cole Weston makes and markets prints from his father's negatives. Each is stamped identifying Cole, not Edward, as the printer.

From Nancy Newhall

Albuquerque

September 17, 1973

Dearest Full Dome—

Bless you for your offer to fly in and help us! But really, there is no need. Found another wonderful doctor, orthopedic, almost in Harry's[1] class. No broken bones. just bruises, swellings, abrasions. Time, strength and patience, and the typewriter bouncing high on a bum knee with pillows under it. . . .

But never forget that presences of Adamses is worth more than rubies or fine gold!

Curious, but though we have hundreds of friends we consider dear, and would leap to help in any emergency, there are none to whom we would entrust our lives but Ansel and Virginia Adams. Or possibly Mike and Jeanne. We must get our wills in present shape. All the more serious because we have no descendants and only distant relatives. . . .

If you two or Mike and Jeanne should become responsible for us, I hope that you will take the natural course, and with kindness let us go with God.

I didn't intend this to be a document of such consequence! . . .

Please don't consider this dismal, it is merely practical, a direction in case Beau and I don't get to make new wills. Proof of intent, at least. . . .

I keep feeling we will die together in a crash or something, but I fear that is only a hope. Beau's people usually die of heart attacks in their seventies, and I could wish no better or easier death for him—alive one moment and dead the next. Mine, alas, usually live on into their eighties, to die of stroke or cancer, or now and then on into the nineties, to die, somewhat senile, in their sleep.

If Beau goes first, I shall be in extreme misery. I would have to work out a whole new way of life, which is not easy. If I go first, I would not worry about Beau; he will always be beloved, as he deserves. He will miss me, of course, but some good girl, God bless her, will soon be looking after him. And as long as nothing disabling happens to his mind or speech, he will always go on working.

Will check on local lawyers. We have one, of course, but this kind of thing may not be his specialty.

Love again—
N

1. Dr. Harry Segal, the Newhalls' doctor in Rochester.

To Beaumont and Nancy Newhall

Carmel Highlands
November 4, 1973

Dear Beaumont and Nancy,

Good to yak with you this morning. Delighted that the Brett-Edward lectures, etc. are going over well. I completely agree—it is time that Brett gets a good—really good—presentation of his work because of a rigid adherence to his feeling about selections, etc. His pictures of the "Scene" are indeed spectacular. His "abstracts"—largely because they are so stressed—can become monotonous. This is just the same thing that happens to me—the apparent emphasis on the Natural Scene creates boredom for many who are "art" conscious. It is a thing to watch out for—but by the time one is aware of it one is too damned old to do much about it.

True evaluation of any creative work probably needs 3 or 4 centuries' wait to separate the viewer-critic from the actualities of the time and the fashions and the psychology when the image was made. The history of music supports this. Was not the greatest Renaissance art of a temporary nature: festivals, occasional design, etc.? What comes down to us is probably only some ashes from the great fire. Bach was in eclipse (never was very popular in his time) until Mendelssohn "discovered" him nearly two centuries after his death. I am quite sure Edward Weston will have a quite different response a century from now. He may be trapped by the purists and instigate a new cult. He may be considered a classic influence—like Telemann. In two hundred years he may take on the Bach stature. Who knows? It is historians like Beaumont who have the tremendous opportunity to make definitive clarifications AHEAD of time; not many artists and musicians of the past have had such an advantage! I am weary unto death of the "IN" psychology and the incredible crap that passes for creative art today. But I do recognize that there ARE great innovators and—while they might bother me muchly at times I cannot reject them. However, how can I be SURE of *my* opinions and convictions? As Edward said (and almost every other great artist I ever knew said), "You do what you have to do," or words to that effect. I think Edward's and Brett's (and my prints) will "last" physically; I have little hope for Stieglitz, Strand, etc. because, in their time, not much was known about "2-hypo baths," toning, etc. I THINK ONE OF THE GREAT THINGS WE COULD DO FOR THE

[333]

FUTURE WOULD BE TO HAVE HANDSOME FACSIMILE
REPRODUCTIONS MADE OF THE GREAT IMAGES:
ARCHIVAL INKS AND PAPERS (from the original prints).

Negative = Score and Print = Performance IS OK, but the idea that
others might perform a negative opens a whole new perspective on the
creative aspects of photography; it would be easier to make a good duplicate negative than try to make a *duplicate* print! . . .

. . . I am getting a bit weary and there is no one in sight around here
who would hold up the banner. I fear for what may occur should I (and
a few others) pass out of the picture. . . .

Cheeriow, luff, and all that. More soon,

Ansel

To Beaumont and Nancy Newhall

Carmel Highlands
March 11, 1974

Dear Beaumont and Nancy,

Here I am with a semi-mild case of sniffles at my self-correcting IBM
recuperating from practical completion of the Tucson and the Met. Exhibition[1] and preparing my corpus and cerebellum for the Big Book,[2]
etc. I confess I am tired, a bit flat, distressed over the world (especially
that oaf [President Richard] Nixon) and a bit bewildered about Art (or
whatever the strange phenomenon is).

The bright factor in my present existence is that Nancy is on the
mend and in the name of ALL the saints may she remain so—to the
benefit of the world, now and to come! I know it is not easy for an ebul-
lient spirit to be considerate of self—but she *has* to be considerate of a
multitude beyond herself! We all have responsibilities which the "average" man has no concept of at all; he looks to "retirement" (oblivion) at
65±. Ours seems to build up *after* retirement age. I must admit I am a bit
weary, but I'll be damned if I will slow up until I see the red light and
the whistle blow its final peep!!

At any event, I have tried to be as compassionate as possible in regards to art, creativity, sex (all types!), egos, selfishness, conceits, stupidities, and, of course, photography! I am finding it difficult to put together
a[n expression] of concomitant conditions and situations. We all must

live and compete, but the civilized man allows for living AND competition. But the stringent note today in art (for example) is insecurity; non-belief in self and visions dependent on the "IN" complex. Several comments I wish to make:

The last issue of *Untitled*[3] (I don't mind that title as much as Beaumont does, only it does not live up to it!)—Thompson's and Webb's articles simply in-house confusion. Corrigan's article very erudite, difficult and should have been in the *Journal of Art Criticism and Aesthetics*.

Comment: The photographer (the creative artist) lives in a very different world than the critic or the aesthetician (I think he should). Most of the photographers I know just want to express themselves. Brett is a prime example (and he does a great job of it). Photographers, in general, do not comprehend the post-mortem efforts of the aestheticians. Creative photo-history is something else (*ipso-facto* in regards past creativity). ASIDE: It is interesting to me that I get a great response from showing a few slides of blue-sensitive emulsion images;[4] another kind of world appears to the student.

Historically, WHEN did the art of photography become associated with academic complexities? Does the academic complexity serve to create artists—or teachers? What are students studying for? I understand that in England a teacher can only teach if he has had five years' practical experience in the field. (This is at a more technical-commercial level than purely creative, I admit.)

I am not depreciating the essential value of "culture"; I am sure my piano was better because I studied a lot of other things. But is it *essential?* Edward and Brett were, and are, not intellectual. Wynn Bullock[5] is a very well-read man. BUT. . . .

JEEZ, I did not intend this to be so long. I do not wish to worry or burden you with it. But it seems to me that the situation represents a very important decision as to just what Education in Photography really represents: are we training creative photographers, teachers (what do they teach?), aestheticians, critics, or WHAT? All are important, but some more than others. I think this is a MAJOR problem. A gal came today and showed me a perfectly beautiful image (all the others were blah). But the one was not "accidental"; it was thought and felt out. She has no training. Where does she belong??

I shall read this over and find many boo-boos I could have corrected on the IBM. I have at least ten more pages to spout, but I shall spare you. I remain perplexed, doubtful, slightly distrustful, and rather unhappy about what is called "art." I have no doubts about what I call LOVE which is extended to both—with cheers, exaltations, fireworks, and glory!

As ever, thine's
Ansel

. . . Virginia is in Tucson; I go Friday and back Monday. It is a gray day and trying to rain. I MUST make prints and I do not feel a bit like it! Would rather write you! . . .

Have a meeting Thursday F.O.P.; a special one primarily for a vote of confidence on the way things are going, etc. I had a good talk with Heinecken[6] on the phone this AM; he is a very objective, agreeable gent, and I think he fully understands the problem. We agreed that it was healthy to promote the extremes, but I do not have to make pictures as he does and vice-versa!!

Had a thought about various photographers and their work. This may sound really fey, but I can think of both Edward's and Brett's work as epigrammatic! My favorite epigram—"Wherever I go in my mind I find Plato coming back"—seems in some way to relate, especially to Edward's work (not in fact, but in spirit). Incidentally, be sure you make it clear to Brett that *you* are putting together his exhibit;[7] as I said before, you may have difficulties in this area!

This is the final line (for this letter).

LUFFFFFF
Ansel

1. "Little Known Images," a solo exhibition of Adams' photographs, opened at the University Art Museum, University of Arizona in Tucson, in March 1974; "Photographs by Ansel Adams," a major retrospective, opened at the Metropolitan Museum of Art, New York, in April 1974.

2. *Ansel Adams: Images 1923–1974*, Boston: New York Graphic Society, 1974.

3. *Untitled* is the journal of The Friends of Photography. *Untitled 6*, 1973: Robert W. Corrigan, "The Transformation of the Avant-Garde"; Peter Hunt Thompson, "The Juried Exhibition"; William Webb, "A Prolegomenon to the Creative Experience Workshop #3."

4. Adams often included slides of work of other photographers in his lectures. The nineteenth-century photographer Timothy O'Sullivan was a particular favorite. O'Sullivan used the blue-sensitive emulsions of the period, causing the characteristic white skies without detail.

5. Wynn Bullock, photographer and one of the cofounders of The Friends of Photography (FOP).

6. Robert Heinecken, photographer and professor at UCLA, was a member of the Board of Trustees of The Friends of Photography.

7. Beaumont and Nancy Newhall curated an exhibit of Brett Weston's photographs that opened at the University Art Museum, University of New Mexico, Albuquerque, March 1975.

From Nancy Newhall

Albuquerque
May 16, 1974

Dear Ansel—

Thank you for sending us a Xerox of the article for UNTITLED.[1] Much of it we utterly agree with—the "In" group, for instance—and thank you for giving them utterance. Which could be even stronger, calling perhaps for a separate article and more complete statement.

But how wrong can YOU be about *You???* And other artists! The vast majority of major artists change and grow throughout their creative lives. Sometimes the change is so sudden it comes like an explosion! There are, I regret to say, influences, but with major artists they do not last beyond student days when the individual is groping for clues to his own expression.

This was the attitude I always took when young photographers bring me their work: regard the influences as indicating latent characteristics and seek out what nobody else has done before—the individual speaking for himself. At a stage a little further on, when the individual is really developing on his own, a small show, alone or with a group in a similar stage, is very helpful: the individual can see himself objectively. A reaction from a great artist may be of enormous power for catalyzation, but what the critics say seldom matters much. It just filters down through layers of consciousness to what, if anything, is significant to the unconscious and the intuitive.

This is the usual pattern. Remember I had studied the work of Stieglitz, Strand, and Weston intensely, from their first attempts to their major statements in different periods, before I began to study you.

I got the shock of a lifetime! YOU have always been YOU, from the first things your parents snatched from your baby fingers! There is a lit-

[337]

tle watercolor, of the Marin Hills, I think, done when you were possibly six, that is completely Ansel Adams. You have not had periods, no changes, suffered no influences—even looking over Strand's shoulder at his Taos negatives was a revelation of where you were trying to go; the "Annunciation" was its completion.

You are unique! The only parallel I can think of was Mozart; he is said to have composed, at three, a little phrase or tune that was completely himself.

Compare, for instance, Beethoven: some of his first things are hard to distinguish from the later Mozart. Or Delacroix, copying Rubens for his marvelous color and cumulous composition, yet these early sketches already have Delacroix's torque on them. Nobody's influence is on you, not Weston's, nor Strand's not even Stieglitz'. (I regard the "Equivalent" in *Singular Images*[2] as pure show-off on your part, a Me Too in the Polaroid medium.)

As for "working within one's time," which is inescapable except for those who, like Michelangelo, *create* their time, and even he, of course, was the result of previous huge thrusts and changes, the main criticism leveled against your creative work has always been that you stand *outside* your time!

Thank heaven they no longer label you as 19th century because you do landscapes! and because your greatest work is of nature and deals with the eternal, you are accused of being "Inhuman," "not interested in humanity," "oblivious to the GREAT issues of Today." They don't realize that what takes their breath away when they look at your work is your profound expression of human emotion. That you touch the innermost spirit as few artists in any medium ever have.

Amusing how Edwin Land, with his physicist mind, works around to understand this! And that his greatest praise is that it is "abstract"!

As for titles, I agree with you completely; even identifying titles are a little absurd. How many *El Capitans* or *Half Domes* have you made since 1916? Even "moon" or "fresh snow" or similar details don't help much. I should like someday to put up a little show of one such subject, maybe 20 prints of just Half Dome—perhaps even from just one viewpoint— done over many years. They would show how much—and how little!— subject matter, no matter how unusual in itself, has to do with statement, message, mood, spirit. It would be invidious to put up such a show on the same subject even by twenty good photographers.

Verbalization I also dislike intensely, and avoid it when I can. But sometimes a clue is necessary. To crack a barrier of ignorance or opinion so that it falls away and the observer can see for himself. How many people have bypassed your work because "landscape" and "nature" are out of date, not "modern." Or Weston's because it was "theatrical," or Stigelitz's cloud *Equivalents* as the vaporings of an old man. Even Paul Strand thinks that! I want to break down the walls people build around themselves—or permit to be built by their time. Myself I want to look at any work by anyone of any age directly, without prejudice—just me and the work together, alone.

It's not easy. Stieglitz came very close to it. But even he missed occasionally—for instance, on Weston's mature work. And it is very hard to see beyond personal dislikes.

SELAH! End of sermon! . . .

Can't stop!

I don't think you ever *invented* anything (who, in the last analysis, ever has?). The idea for Polaroid was around for twenty years or more before Din picked it up and made it a revolution! If the Lyric Closeup had not been around, you might have invented that—had to!

But what you have done is to achieve standards so high they were considered impossible. That's something to be proud of!

Love anyway—

N

1. Ansel Adams. "Change Relates (Presumably) to Progress," *Untitled 7/8,* 1974.

2. *Singular Images*, Hastings-on-Hudson, N.Y.: Morgan & Morgan, 1974.

To Beaumont and Nancy Newhall

Carmel Highlands

May 25, 1974

Dear Beaumont and Nancy

Here I am in a slightly bewildering state of poop. As time goes on all the problems seem to accumulate. My main regret—(although I LIKE problems) is that I do not have time to write decent letters and keep in touch. Do not think I neglect you intentionally or carelessly!! It's just a pile-up. . . .

I guess I did not make myself clear. I firmly believe that a human being is born with innate capacities and characteristics: all he can do is to add some strength and dimensions. HIS GREATNESS (IF ANY) COMES FROM A REVELATION OF THESE BASIC CHARAC- TERISTICS. EDWARD WESTON'S FIRST EARLY PICTURES HAVE ALL THE SEEDS OF HIS LATER WORK. The differences are very apparent in a superficial sense. But are they real differences? Many artists are of course, influenced, but many receive confirmation instead of influence. You will note that the students of Minor White are mostly profoundly influenced by him; you will also note that the major- ity of them are NOT his peers (and are perhaps not capable of being forces in their own right). I think you might agree that a truly forceful artist will achieve a real creative success *in spite* of everything that may, or may not, happen to him. I think we may be all confused over the ac- tual *number* of artists (or those professing to be artists) and think there are more really great ones than there are. Everything is now so slick and easy, and individuality seems to be rarer and rarer as time goes on.

Your paragraph three is very good indeed; an excellent explanation! But I can't follow you. In fact, we are entering the double-domain of be- haviorism and psychiatry, and explanations are fiercely difficult.

I was trained as a pianist—and not one of my good teachers ever played a note for me! (Two-piano teaching can be catastrophic as it can create an imitative style, with loss of individuality.) When people show me their work I go through it very quickly at first, just getting implant impressions of all-over quality, etc. I then think (or feel) as follows:

A. What did they "see"?

B. How did they "see" it?

C. How did they execute it?

On that basis I can talk with them and try to make helpful comments. But I always make it very clear that *they* are important; not necessarily their *prints*. *Their* importance may lurk behind the lousiest print—and simply because they do not have the capabilities to express themselves. Maybe they never will. Maybe it isn't worth it. Maybe they uncon- sciously create imitative images (imitating some photographer I am not familiar with).

In paragraph 5 you seem to support my contentions! You say, "You have always been You." I don't try to imitate Stieglitz's *Equivalent* images: I just approve of the "equivalent" approach. I don't understand your sentence in ( ). I thought I made it reasonably clear; please inform how you think I did not! I thirst for truth, t r u t h, T R U T H ! ! ! ! ! even more————

I am not concerned how I am labeled—if labeled at all! The *NY Times* reviews are better than expected. Obviously Kramer does not like Nature and Thornton does not understand it.[1] No matter. Both of them did not see the entire show—not enough time. I guess! For Kramer to say, "O'Keeffe's face is worth all the Yosemites" (or words to that effect) simply expresses his subject preferences—not any concept of their interpretations. I am convinced you can't win in NY unless you are at the Diane Arbus[2] end of the spectrum. . . .

. . . The whole publishing business is more and more complex and costly as the days progress. I guess this Big Book[3] will be one of the last dinosaurs! The advance sales and interest in it indicated that 30,000 copies will be printed! JEEZ!!!!!

It IS difficult to hold the particular *kind* of value-relationships I have in my prints. But we shall overcome!!!

Send everything you want to us here. Will return pm of June 2nd. It will be GREAT to see you both. CAN'T do another page; will close.

LOVE
Ansel

1. Hilton Kramer, "Ansel Adams: Trophies from Eden," and Gene Thornton, "Avedon's Father, Adams' Nature, Siskind's Homage," both the *New York Times*, May 12, 1974.

2. Diane Arbus was known for her controversial photographic portraits.

3. *Ansel Adams: Images 1923–1974* measures 17 x 13 ¾ inches.

To Nancy and Beaumont Newhall

Carmel Highlands
June 30, 1974

Dear Nancy and Beaumont,

What a dismal quirk of Nature! As I put in the telegram—it was an awful way for a spruce tree to treat a Nature Girl! It is one of the strangest and almost impossible accidents I ever heard of![1]

My heart-felt question now is—what can I do? We all feel the same way—what can we do? Mike and Jeanne and the kids[2] are here, and Bill Turnage called in. I phoned Brett; he was very unhappy about it. I called Minor and he will get in touch with Mike Hoffman[3]—I could not reach Mike directly. Minor was tearful.

I felt these people should know. They would be upset if they did not, because they, too, would like to help.

Of course, we understand there is little to do in the physical sense; she is undoubtedly in good care. But it is good therapy to know your dear friends are with you in spirit.

WE SURE ARE!!! . . .

The IMPORTANT thing, however, is to get Nancy well and bouncy again! Let us keep in touch. When a nice plant would be pleasing to her, please get one for us. In the meantime, love from ALL. More soon,

Ansel

We love you! Wish we could help!

Virginia

1. On a trip down the Snake River in Grand Teton National Park, Wyoming, a tree fell on the raft carrying the Newhalls, critically injuring Nancy.

2. Michael and Jeanne Adams are the parents of Sarah, born in 1965, and Matthew, born in 1967.

3. Michael Hoffman, publisher/editor of *Aperture*.

From Beaumont Newhall

Wyoming

July 1, 1974

[Picture Postcard]

This could have been the float, so peacefully did the trip start.*

X could have been the tree that fell instantly and exactly.

N. *much* better today. Even celebrated our 38th [anniversary] with an allowed drink. Thanks for your calls. B

*Note no life jackets. I have made a full report at NPS request, recommending mandatory life jackets, life lines, radio disaster signal in each float, and a rescue boat.

To Nancy Newhall

Dear Nancy,

Here I am in S.F. eagle-eyeing the press sheets.[1] Things are coming along well, but it is a struggle. I go to Yosemite this afternoon and return to S.F. Sunday pm. Here Monday; returning to Carmel that pm. Leave Thursday for Arles.[2] Back in Carmel about the 22nd. Fast trip! I will be interested to see how my anticipations relate to the reality. I have an open cranium!!

I talk with Beaumont often and am happy you are progressing. We all are pulling for you! Mama Nature pulled a lousy trick on you. If the Grand Teton fell on you—that would have some nobility!! But you are worth more than the Grand Teton—*you* might fall on *it!!* SHUDDER, CRACK, AVALANCHE, CRUMBLE. I can see you standing on the pile of rubble like the Statue of Liberty—Genius Triumphant!!! But to get swatted by a vagrant tree—it ain't fair!!! . . .

Get well soon. Vol II beckons[3]—but you must take care of yourself. I know Virginia sends love as do we all here. Cheeriow to you both.

Ansel

1. Adams was overseeing the printing of *Ansel Adams: Images 1923–1974* at George Waters, San Francisco.

2. On Adams' first trip to Europe, he taught at the Rencontres Internationales de la Photographie in Arles, France.

3. Nancy Newhall never finished the second volume of her biography of Adams.

To Beaumont Newhall

Dear Beaumont,

As I said in my wire—"Words fail—love abides."[1] Hence, I do not think there are any words we need exchange in the face of the sad reality. After all these years I believe our feelings, thoughts, and dreams are pretty well understood; it is very hard for me to realize what my life would have been without you both.

The future holds an enormous potential for you. I know it may not be easy. But you stand at the very top of your field. Nancy—all of us—knew this. I was amazed, gratified, and very humble at the sound of your voice last night on the phone. You were a person in command of fate and of yourself. My admiration knows no bounds for you and your spirit.

So, let us proceed from this moment in time—as I am sure Nancy would want it this way. She is now beyond sidereal time and I am sure there are many "times" and many realities. I cannot recall who it was that said, "The problem of the Universe is not *what* it is but *why?*" This is not accurate in words, but the idea is simulated. The *why* of events is beyond our experience.

Virginia (not a verbal person but one of deep feeling) and I are truly touched by your thought of having an appropriate memorial service at our home. She will return in early August and we are both anxious that this event be—in every way—a truly rich recollection of Nancy.

And we wish to do something "In Memoriam" in the form of an image of deep personal significance. Let us think about this. I will be back in San Francisco on the 23rd and will hopefully come to Carmel on the 24th. The Book [*Images*] will take many days attendance in San Francisco for about a month. It is going well, but a bit arduous. George [Waters] and Adrian [Wilson] send their love; Adrian was especially moved because of the many past associations. Anne, Mike and Jeanne know that you know they are deeply concerned and thinking very much of you.

Love from us all,
As ever,
Ansel

1. Nancy Newhall died unexpectedly on July 7, 1974.

To Beaumont Newhall

Carmel Highlands
August 18, 1974

Dear Beaumont,

I was thinking today at the beach of many things. I could not express them verbally. As the sea claimed the offering I was aware of the reality of nature and of the unrealities of time.[1]

I had no sense of termination—only of continuation. The beauty and spiritual power Nancy contributed to the world is truly everlasting. Rather than brood over her transition I rejoice that our lives coincided. You and Nancy mean more to me than you will ever know.

Hence, if Virginia and I seem less than eloquent in expressing our feelings it is because they are really inexpressible.

We wish to do something directly in memory of Nancy, but we feel it must be something that has real meaning to you, too. There is no haste involved in this; a greater perspective in time will clarify just what it should be.

We all hold a great love for you—always.

Ansel

. . .

1. The Adamses held a memorial service for Nancy Newhall at their home. Her ashes were spread on the ocean at nearby Spindrift Cove.

To John Schaefer [1]

Carmel Highlands
March 23, 1975

Dear John,

I think it is a good idea to put down some of the thoughts expressed in our chat Saturday:

1. I very much like the title AMERICAN CENTER OF (FOR) CREATIVE PHOTOGRAPHY.[2] "FOR" implies progression; "OF" is more static. This is a "forward" title. ARCHIVES implies the backward look.

2. The emphasis today seems to lie in INSTRUCTION (at a very high subjective level and not enough at the basic "tool" level) and at the HISTORICAL level (which is excellent if it is presented at the "living" level, such as Beaumont Newhall is capable of doing).

To me, there is a "middle level" which relates to a balance between significant history and a broad creative intention. I find this hard to put into words; I guess I have been thinking too much about it in symbols and "examples"!

3. I feel that a constant "aliveness" is essential; seminars, exhibits, lec-

tures, etc.—all with national publicity. The title (as in 1 above) suggests a national scope.

4. Education of photography at Arizona can take two directions: (a) the basic training, and (b) advanced graduate studies, in which students would be rigorously selected for quality of work and ability to progress. For this group, I suggest one "director" and a series of "artists in residence" (for periods of 1 month to 1 year). Many artists exhaust their potential of interest and idea-expression in a relatively short time; others have a continuing aliveness. I see this as a working group, in which technique is assumed to be adequate and therefore not stressed except when directly related to expression. Not only actual creative work, but discussion and critiques of work accomplished or in progress, interchange of concepts and ideas, single or group projects, study of book production (from concept through design and production) and constant contact with the artist in residence who would be working creatively himself.

With the backlog of a fine collection and extensive archives, the possibilities of such a program are very great, indeed. *As far as I know,* there is nothing like it in any college or university.

5. An important element in advanced instruction would be experience in curatorship and systems of display. I have yet to see a really good gallery of photography! Yours (in the art department) a possible exception—in that the lighting and environmental illumination was, in the main, rewarding.

6. The collection should aim for inclusiveness, but highly selective as to quality. Just because something is "new" is not sufficient for impulsive acquisition. On the other hand, we cannot act as "censors" or adhere to specific patterns and concepts of expression. I think it important that we make every effort to have a representative Edward Weston collection (both prints and archives). . . .

7. Among the names that come to mind for the collection are:

CHARLES SHEELER* FREDERICK SOMMER*
AARON SISKIND ALFRED STIEGLITZ* (hopefully, something)
PAUL STRAND* BRETT WESTON
GEORGE TICE IMOGEN CUNNINGHAM*
MINOR WHITE* DORIS ULMANN*
HARRY CALLAHAN PAUL CAPONIGRO (SEE 9 BELOW)

Those with an * I think should have first consideration. I know I have omitted names, but they will come to mind in time! I am sure there are—like the "rustic Milton"—MANY really fine young people who will, or are to soon, emerge on the scene.

8. I have always believed in the "project" approach. Scattered subject material is fine for the advanced and "secure" artist, but the continuing discipline of a "project" is of invaluable assistance to the development of "command" of the medium. Such projects do not imply only social or historical subjects; an interpretation of a purely personal theme can be very important if reality is established; the isolated image may have fortuitous birth—an only child, so to speak. In Los Angeles and San Francisco I concentrated in my teaching on projects of wide variety; for examples, one was to create a series of wave and shore situations; another to poetically interpret a day with a family; another was to do a series of compositions of details of a power plant. In Yosemite, we would "do" a small town such as Hornitos, or a series of old gravestone carvings (not as a mere record but in relation to mood situations—sometimes with portraits). The emphasis was always on *feeling*, and it was amazing how this approach was grasped and developed by the students. It really refers to exploring the world in depth—not just responding to an occasional perceptive event. In Tucson and environs you have a great reservoir of exciting (but not too easy!) subject material.

9. Even if works are not purchased right away the suggestive groundwork could be initiated that (without commitment) the work and archives of various photographers, if worthy, might be acquired in the future. This might stimulate some to improve. Certainly the existence of the Center will stimulate more awareness of the art, just as did (and does) George Eastman House and MoMA.

Cordially,
Ansel Adams

1. Dr. John P. Schaefer was president of the University of Arizona, Tucson.

2. The Center for Creative Photography, the University of Arizona, was the idea of Schaefer and Adams. Founded in 1975, the Center is the most important academic archive for photographers' negatives, fine and proof prints, papers, and memorabilia.

To John Schaefer

Carmel Highlands
May 19, 1975

Dear John,

Following my rushed letter of yesterday which did, in a way, express my great enthusiasm, etc., I have given further thought to the problems at hand, and I submit these ideas for what they are worth:

1. The fact that you are starting with the largest single acquisition in the history of photography is in itself a powerful news item and should be amplified.[1]

2. My comment about "soft-pedaling" my name is not false modesty. I know I am well-known and I am entirely happy whenever my name can be helpfully used. But the word must not get about that the Center is dominated by a "father-figure." It is a matter of balance and your publicity people should be appropriately briefed on this. The gift of our collection[2] does have great value in *motivation;* it, too, needs proper presentation. However, it would not be good for the project to have it related in the public mind with a single personality or point of view.

3. If [Harry] Callahan can and will take a year's leave of absence from Rhode Island [School of Design] and come to Tucson it would be a *great* advantage to the image of the Center. I do not know how you justify costs and income from special projects, but I am sure that the response to a Callahan "Artist in Residence" program should pay for itself—financially and otherwise.

4. However, a single Artist in Residence does not have the publicity impact that a number of such would over a given period of time. I would feel that, in addition to Callahan, you could have three or four Artists in Residence during a year, and that the promotion thereof be most carefully considered. . . . The kind of teaching that I feel most effective is, as I said, related to the "music conservatory" approach. Before we have a "plant" we can still converse with students, discuss their work, and evoke their support for the future when there will be adequate facilities.

5. I think the Workshop in November can be a very important one. . . . As we have no plant (labs) it would be futile to try an actual *production* program. I have always thought of workshops more as "idea factories" than "production lines." *Demonstration* is very important, but until we get some adequate laboratories such demonstrations must be limited to "field operations." Most important of all is logical use of Polaroid 4x5

materials. I do not anticipate any trouble in getting Polaroid's support in this area. Equally important is the study of "seeing" through the works of other photographers—"What did they see, how did they see it, and how did they execute it?" I have found it extremely appealing to present quite ordinary factual images to students, request them "imagine" the reality of the subject and then have them "revisualize" an expressive concept on an assumed reality.

6. . . . The encouragement of confidence in each individual to express his "equivalent" is of the greatest importance.

In fact this first workshop might well be dedicated to the concept of the "equivalent," observing history as a frontal plane—a living reality from 1839[3] to the present. You now have some very adequate material to achieve this and I hope much more can be secured in the coming months. But I warn against excessive "subjectiveness" and a domination of "history." There must be some magical domain between these extremes which introduce photography both as a fine art and as an expressive "release."

7. The most satisfactory Workshops I have experienced are those in which we "played the program by ear" and the participants left in a condition of both encouragement and excitement. We assumed they would continue on their own after copious exposure to new ideas. Our darkroom in Yosemite was designed as a *demonstration* darkroom—not as a "school" laboratory where students would actually spend time developing and printing. It is obvious that there are so many variants in teaching approaches that it will be hard to precisely define an all-inclusive laboratory.

8. Before we can define any laboratory we must first define the scope of the teaching program. Again, you will meet with strong variations of opinion. The decisions should be (my personal opinion) based on the level at which you should begin instruction. I have some strong opinions on this, expressed as follows:

a. There should be a tough beginners' class which would convey the basic techniques. There is to my knowledge NO school in the country that makes such demands. We accomplished our objectives at the California School of Fine Arts and at the Art Center School in from six to eight weeks! The facility achieved certainly "paid off" exceedingly well when the students essayed creative (or professional) work. It has always seemed to me to be the most efficient approach. Perhaps because it was the approach demanded of me in music. "Floundering" in photography can be very harmful.

b. Once a person knows enough to control his medium he is free to choose from many fields or simply to rest upon a "photo-appreciation" level. It has been my sad experience to see portfolios which show the maker to have great sensitivity and a fine "eye"—yet are so severely incompetent in basic techniques that nothing comes through. I think it is very inefficient to turn students loose in the Elysian Fields of imagination without substance to back up their visualizations and desires. . . .

c. There is something both emotional and mystical (in the best sense) in a teaching environment of utmost simplicity. Perhaps it may be apocryphal, but the classic image of the instructor communicating with his students under an olive tree (perhaps a cactus in our case) surrounded with thoughts and "vibes" may be the best solution to the immediate problem. But the instructor must be GOOD and the students COMPETENT and DEDICATED. *I am sure* that we can make "history" in this area of education in photography.

d. Your advisory committee (and it may be a wise decision to keep me off of it) should (as I said) be helpful to the Director. I also said (and affirm) that a good Director should welcome a serious advisory committee. Of late (perhaps within ten years) Directors—even Curators—act as if they wish to appoint Trustees and even Chairmen and Presidents! This represents to me an attitude of "take-over" which is ridiculous simply because they assume they are fully capable of being a dictator without regard for experience in all of the fiscal, political and human problems any institution faces. A *good* Director (or President) usually gets what he wants anyway, but should represent *many* viewpoints on photography—and the burden is on them to justify and render balanced and functional advice and counsel. To quote a (here) anonymous author, ". . . It is our pride that makes another's criticism rankle, our self-will that makes another's deed offensive, our egotism that feels hurt by another's self assertion . . ." Unfortunately, the art world really needs this basic philosophy and—perhaps—photography most of all! I bring this up simply because I know you are—or will be—faced with the eternal problem. You are doing a *magnificent* job and understand the meaning of "compassionate courage."

I cannot tell you how rewarding and gratifying it is for me to partake of this new and vital concept and work with a person of such strength of character and understanding as you are constantly revealing as this great project develops.

All best,
Ansel Adams

1. The Center's first acquisitions were the archives of Ansel Adams, Wynn Bullock, Aaron Siskind, Frederick Sommer, and Harry Callahan.
2. Adams donated his collection of photographs by others.
3. In 1839 Louis Jacques Mandé Daguerre publicly announced the important early photographic process, the daguerreotype.

To John Szarkowski

Carmel Highlands
June 22, 1976

Dear John,

I was pleased to hear you are favorable to receiving *Portfolio VII*[1] in honor of Dave McAlpin. It is a small gesture of appreciation for all he has done for photography—and for us in photography. I hope you and all will like it. My prints require a lot of light and those of VII are no exception. As I get older I get more "stimmung," "Dunder" und "Blitzen"!

I hope it will come in perfect condition. It is a lettered copy; the numbered copies only are for sale: 1 to 100, A to O.

Bill Turnage brought me the copy of the Eggleston book[2] and I am most appreciative of your thoughtfulness. It is a rather handsome production; the reproductions are, for me, far more agreeable to the eye than the originals I have seen. A fair comparison could be made only by seeing the originals along with the plates.

I sincerely try to keep an open mind about art in all forms and of all periods. I well remember the furor Group *f*/64 created! Believe it or not, I saw the first exhibit of "futurist" art in San Francisco at the 1915 Exposition;[3] I was naturally perplexed, but also thrilled. Even at the age of 13 the power and conviction of many of those creations made a lasting impression on me. My contact with Stieglitz confirmed the qualities of strength and integrity (which are not dependent on style, subject, or medium used). I feel the really important art—that which the artist must be aware of—is the art of the Now and of the Future. Both are, of course, built upon the Past but if there were no Now and Future what good would the Past have been?

The honest individual reacts to everything that happens around him, seeing the world as he is built to "see" (independent of education, associations, etc.). Unfortunately many are now influenced by what I call the "*in* syndrome"; they see and create at an "in" level, gaining security through association and dedication with a group flow of thought. I prefer to believe most are honest and sincere but there are charlatans at the highest levels! I know photographers who view the world through a 1-inch pipe with a mirror at the end!

While I have my personal reaction and "seeing" capabilities and limitations I can honestly say I have leaned far from my own creative axis to accept, appreciate, and sponsor all creative work that seems to me to have spirit, depth, and craft. To say I "enjoy" it would be shallow and have no particular meaning, except that one can "enjoy" simple craft for its own sake without emotional, aesthetic, or social overtones. And one can be moved by the latter qualities even if the craft leaves something to be desired. However, there is a great truth in the statement that "craft can exist without art, but art cannot exist without craft." As the years pass I am increasingly aware of the profound effect the arduous work with music had upon me. Without competent facility one cannot play!

After considerable thought I believe that what disturbs me about Eggleston's work is that, to me, it represents a bit of "put-on." I do NOT impute evil intent on the part of the artist; I feel the artist does not realize consciously that it *is* a "put-on." Nor do the audiences who are seeking pasture in new fields (even in dry seasons!).

Speaking largely for myself, I have gone through periods of "sublime motivation," utter confusion, and centrifugal effort. I have witnessed— and on several occasions participated in—periods of bitter "social awareness." At some time in the past 20–30 years art may have passed a peak in the best non-objective painting (I am not sure of the "peak" in photography). Following the cultural "sine-wave" I think it is now ready for a re-emergence, but I honestly believe some great social or natural upheaval will be required to produce effective motivations. At present (again in my opinion) we are in the "trough" of small purpose and centripetal subjective indulgences. (Note that I say "my opinion"; I do not wish to preach any "gospel" or spout any dogma.)

Substance cannot be overlooked (but the term invites semantic confusions). I have seriously examined the Eggleston photographs (mainly in the book). I have wiped my mind's slate as clean as I can of prejudice. I find little "substance." For me, they appear to be "observations," floating on the sea of his consciousness. A few images are agreeable and convey connotations of both reality and experience. But, for me, most draw a blank. I find his "seeing" incomprehensibly shallow and imperfect: shapes, planes, and textures are confused. The "reason for being" and the "reason for doing" escapes me. Just because something or some event exists is not sufficient reason for perpetuating it unless it, in some way, contains "magic"—and, of course, it is the artist's responsibility to create the "enlargement of experience."

Please remember that I do not wish to make pronouncements. But I must express my personal reactions as honestly as I can. I may be completely incapable of understanding this photographic "language."

At any event, your thoughtfulness *is* appreciated. I assure you, I will "take another look."

Warmest greetings and regards, always!

As ever,
ANSEL ADAMS

1. *Portfolio VII*, a selection of 12 photographs, New York: Parasol Press, 1976.
2. *William Eggleston's Guide*, New York: Museum of Modern Art, 1976.
3. The Panama-Pacific International Exposition which Adams attended daily: his parents' substitute for attendance at school that year.

From John Szarkowski

New York City
June 28, 1976

Dear Ansel:

They let me out of jury duty early last week, and I came back to the Department to find that *Portfolio VII* had arrived. It is simply magnificent. Most of the pictures I knew, of course, but among the ones new to me I think that *El Capitan, Sunrise, Winter* is glorious—really one of your very best! *Half Dome, Blowing Snow* is also new to me, and very fine. And some of the old friends are better than ever in these prints. I don't think I have ever seen such a beautiful print of the *Horizontal Aspens*.[1] It is simply radiant. This is also one of my all-time favorites; I find it even more moving than the great vertical aspens.

I do not know how to tell you how enormously pleased and grateful we are to have this great work for our collection.

Everything that you say about your response to Bill Eggleston's work seems to me so reasonable, honest, and sound that it makes me feel almost guilty for not sharing your estimate of his work. I certainly have no way of proving that the work has quality; in the end I suppose the most I can say in defense of my opinion is that the pictures have remained both memorable and challenging to me over the several years that I have known them. It seems to me that they do have a coherence of style and feeling which fits their content perfectly. That content, it seems to me, bears on the quality and flavor of everyday American life in a way that is both searching and sympathetic. This work is not just another pastiche of stylized, synthetic reportage, aiming at irony; it is I think the precisely described observation of an original and very interesting sensibility.

The last word, as always, will be had by young photographers who are still in the process of defining their own positions; they will either find the work boring, and ignore it, or find something in it that they can adopt, adapt, transpose, improve—somehow make use of for their own ends.

If all of us in the field consistently agreed as to what new work had vitality in it, and what work only had good manners, the excitement of following the life line of our remarkable medium would surely be diminished. Knowing that one might be wrong certainly does add zest to the day.

Your thoughts and your pictures also add zest to my days, for which I am very grateful.

With affectionate best wishes,
John Szarkowski

1. *Aspens, Northern New Mexico, 1958* (horizontal).

From Beaumont Newhall

Santa Fe
March 23, 1977

Dear Ansel and Virginia:

I am absolutely overwhelmed by your generosity and thoughtfulness in establishing the Newhall Fellowship at the Museum of Modern Art.[1] It is an inspired idea and a unique one: to assure the continuation of the work which Nancy and I began at the Museum and especially to give young people the opportunity to learn and believe that actual work teaches more than any amount of classroom work. I certainly know that it was so in the careers of both Nancy and myself. And above all of that is the magnificent support that your gift gives to the art that we all love so well, photography.

I have a fantasy! Were I but young enough and bright enough and un-informed enough and bearing another name, I can think of nothing I would more desire than to be a Newhall Fellow! For it would give that fictitious character exactly the training I received at the Museum—and which has made me so loyal to the Museum over all these years, despite the bitter disappointments that all of us met up with in our association with the Museum.

Dear Ansel and Virginia: I can only say that what you have done is noble. And that you chose to establish the fellowship in the name of Nancy and myself is deeply moving to me, and for that gesture my heartfelt, deep thanks. The love expressed by it is radiant: it filled your living room when Ansel made the announcement and now it is warming the hearts and spirits of so many people everywhere—and I know that it has reached Nancy and filled her with comfort and satisfaction.

Thank you for sending me the documents. They are a part of history —in the full sense of that word—for to my knowledge this Fellowship is unique in the field of photography. And I know that from the opportunities that you have offered young people will become the continuation of what you and Nancy and I worked so hard for and with such passion and devotion.

All my love,
Beaumont

1. The Beaumont and Nancy Newhall Curatorial Fellowship in Photography.

To Bill Brandt[1]

Carmel Highlands
September 3, 1977

Dear Bill Brandt,

I have been looking at your book[2] (which you so kindly sent me) and have been thinking about your work and its impact on photography.

[355]

Our concepts of "print quality" are very different, but each seems to be logically related to our statements. I cannot imagine your images with my print-style or mine in yours! That is as it should be! Imagine the catastrophe if all images were the same, bound by a fixed convention of values, etc. (This *has* happened in some forms of art, and today there are some unfortunate dominations of style and approach.)

You have established a definitely personal print style and "color" which to me is breath-taking in its power and simplicity. My only negative comment on the book is that it shows we can't match the quality of silver with the quality of ink (and vice-versa). It is possible to *simulate* print-quality, but not duplicate it, on the press. As I must have told you, Harry Lunn[3] presented me with your wonderful *Seated Nude* (the figure with the bed and candle in the distance). It is magnificent; the book does not capture the very elusive simplicity and tonal strength of the original. However, your vision is so strong that it can triumph over reproductions! When my prints are poorly reproduced I feel as if I were hearing a piano that had not been tuned for a decade!

I hope people know that I am not a prude or object to anything called "explicit" if the elusive quality of art remains. I have a profound resistance to a lot of photography of the times because of the very crass and shallow dependence upon "shock" and the pandering to fashionable "porn." For me, your work is absolutely "clean" and for this I thank you! Your nudes are very powerful in form and substance; even when you treat them as sharp black-and-whites, avoiding realistic texture, they still breathe flesh and vitality and beauty. My *Seated Nude* (your photograph!) and #134 in *Shadow of Light* are among the most beautiful images ever made. And for years I have been showing slides of your *Coal Searcher* (#39) and I have always remarked on the exceedingly personal quality of your prints.

At the age of 75+ I respond to your work with excitement and the urge to go out into the world and see new things in new ways.

Needless to say—if you ever come this way we shall welcome you with open arms.

As ever,
Ansel Adams

1. Bill Brandt, English photographer, whom Adams met in London in 1976.
2. Bill Brandt. *Shadow of Light,* New York: Da Capo, 1977.
3. Harry Lunn, one of the principal dealers in Adams' photographs.

From Bill Brandt

London, England
September 15, 1977

Dear Ansel,

Thank you so much for your letter. Everything you say is of great interest to me. It shows how deeply you have studied the book. I almost feel you know my pictures better than I do. I will keep the letter and read it again and again.

As you are a great traveler I hope you will come once more to London. We should be delighted to see you here.

With thanks and all my best wishes,

Yours,
Bill Brandt

To John Szarkowski

Carmel Highlands
April 30, 1978

Dear John,

It was actually a bit lonesome around here today! We really enjoyed your visit and we hope there will be other occasions of similar kind![1]

The Yosemite experience will be rewarding for you in many ways; I feel it will help you understand Adams and his vagrant ways! Sorry your family cannot come, but it is understandable:

Implacable
Rape of
Serenity

I was deeply interested in your approach to my work. You helped me see some things in proofs that I had not observed. Of course, many of the elements of "unsatisfactory" photographs relate to the expectations of the photographer! A committee can be composed of 2 or more members!

There will never be—or should there be—total agreement in matters of art. The amount of *sincere disagreement* is very important in such matters as planning exhibitions. I feel you are sympathetic to part of my work and your presentation will have high integrity. I warn you—I will

[357]

probably wonder WHY certain images will be included, and will wonder WHY I thought of them in the first place! But I feel quite secure in having you do the exhibit as I know it will have an *integrity*. After all you are, in a way, "performing" my work in a very large concert hall and before a very large audience. I always DID respect good conductors!!

To paraphrase an old cliche: "Artistic battles are won on the Playing Fields of Ego."

Andrea[2] and I will begin immediately to go through the prints you set aside and relate them to the book whenever possible. Books invite even more dissension than exhibits; perhaps because books are more permanent? . . .

Affectionate greetings to you and all,
Ansel

1. John Szarkowski visited Adams to do research for the exhibit "Ansel Adams and the West," at the Museum of Modern Art, 1979.

2. Andrea Gray Stillman, Adams' assistant from 1974 to 1980.

To John Szarkowski

Carmel Highlands
November 24, 1978

Dear John,

I have been remiss indeed in not replying to your letter before this. But, as usual, everything pops at once (like balloons at a birthday party)!

Appreciate information of exhibition dates. The 5th September for the special opening and the public opening on the 6th sound great. The time-span of the exhibit sounds good to me; the prints might start to fade if they were up longer! (Note for the record: this is a joke!) The festivities are thrilling in their potentials!

I hope I can have my valve job[1] *soon* and get it over with. It is not fun losing weight and otherwise restricting my dietary and libational instincts. And because the present valve is not doing a good job I do not have all the energy I would like. So—the sooner the better!

The book[2] progresses well; all the prints are made for reproduction and all the text, etc., is in order. Now, I must prepare the exhibit for you. Naturally, I want this to be tops. There is a good chance that the new Ilford paper will be available after the 1st of the year. At any event, they will have to be GOOD prints and I am sure we can manage to please you.

The *Portfolio III* prints are not the best I have made. It is interesting that the early print pleases you more. I think I would agree with you. There was more silver in those early prints. On the other hand, I was always trying to make them stronger and more "direct." As I look back on some of those early prints I find they distress me because of both "softness" and print color. I have a special negative thing about weak positives!! . . .

As I look back at myself (in one of those trick mirrors) I seem to be a kind of photographic Rock of Gibraltar (like the one the Prudential Insurance Co. uses in their ads). What I mean is that I remain the same old rock, taking pictures of the same old rocks which has now turned into a rock-a-buy baby phenomenon. I seem to have changed least of all the photographers I know—at least after 1932.

Being Nature Boy for 45 years, it was quite a shock for people to note I took pictures of people! Really interesting how much comment there was over the little exhibit of portraits[3] I had here in Carmel (and which is going to Stanford).

You were most assiduous in pouring over all those Sierra pictures. The fact remains I have numberless negatives of OTHER THINGS. I simply have to have these proofed so that I will know "where I stand." (Or where I tumble!) . . .

When do you think you will be here? The sooner the better of course, but I would like to have more images put together for you.

I am seeing my doctor on the 5th. I think that then he will be able to find a surgeon (who would dare carve me!) and set a date. The sooner the better. After 2 or 3 weeks I am supposed to regain pep (which I do not have now) and then I can forge ahead with everything at once. CRASH !!!!!

Virginia says, Kiss you, too!!! Same to yours!!

Good luck with [Bill] Lane!!

ALL BEST, ALWAYS
Ansel

1. Adams' doctors proposed that he undergo open heart surgery.

2. *Yosemite and the Range of Light,* Boston: New York Graphic Society, 1979.

3. "Ansel Adams: 50 Years of Portraits," curated by James Alinder and exhibited at The Friends of Photography, Carmel, 1978, and at the Stanford University Museum of Art, 1979.

From John Szarkowski

New York City
[Early March, 1979]

Dear Ansel:

On one of my recent calls to Carmel, Victoria[1] told me that you had been asking for your dictating machine. I must say that this is very improper behavior; the redeeming virtue of going to the hospital[2] (in addition to the fact that they repair our mechanical failures) is that we can there temporarily forget the Puritan Work Ethic, and simply rest and be waited on, and read books that are not useful to us, or intellectually enlarging. Certainly some reward is deserved, to compensate for that post-operative conviction that one has been run over, lengthwise by a steamroller. And my experience in these matters is limited to simple plumbing—or even less, simple carpentry.

If you should wonder where, when, & how I came to share in the burden of the Puritan Work Ethic, I must confess that I don't know, and can only protest that it was a mistake made by some earlier generation of my family, for which I should not be held responsible.

Considering the handicaps—which are of course those imposed by my own limited intelligence, latent energy, and competence—things are going well here. I repeat, with confidence, my guarantee that *A.A. and the West* will be so beautiful that it will move even stock brokers to tears.

Please do not try to set a new record for getting back into high gear, or even into second gear. You have already set more than your share of records, and the next one you aim for should be something really important, such as All-Time Longevity. I do not have the *Guinness Book of Records* at hand, but I think the current champion is Methuselah, at 969 years.

Please remember also that you have promised me another show after the big one—of new pictures made between Labor Day, 1979, and Labor Day, 1980. So by next September I expect you to be honed to a fine competitive edge.

With love to you and Virginia,
John Sz.

1. Victoria Bell Sexton, Adams' business assistant from 1977 to 1981.

2. On February 14, 1979, Adams underwent open heart surgery for the replacement of a valve and a triple coronary bypass.

To John Szarkowski

Carmel Highlands
March 7, 1979

Dear Puritan Work Ethic,

I enjoyed your erudite, exalted and encouraging communication more than I can tell you. One valve and three by-passes is not like removing a splinter! If anybody asks who I am, I shall say "I am Thor," but the heart beats with a resolute reiteration. And if I am well enough to be dictating this letter to Andrea while sitting at Point Lobos regarding the ocean pounding the rocks near Weston Beach, then I must be getting rapidly better!

The book is almost ready for the press. The prints for the deluxe edition[1] are all finished. I will plan to make prints for you in April and May—I should be in pretty good shape by April.

Here's to September[2] and the next 50 years!

Will keep in touch—warmest greetings to you and yours from us all,

AA

1. Besides the trade edition, *Yosemite and the Range of Light* was also published in a deluxe edition of 250, each with an original photograph by Adams.
2. "Ansel Adams and the West" was to open at the Museum of Modern Art in September.

From John Szarkowski

New York City
March 10, 1979

Dear Ansel:

If you're ever tempted to get a little tired of printing *Moonrise* or *Winter Storm*, think of poor old Timothy O'Sullivan, grinding out the *Canyon de Chelly* for nine cents a print.

It was good to hear your voice. You sound as big as ever,

Love,
John

To Philip Burton[1]

Carmel Highlands
March 10, 1979

My Dear Mr. Burton,

Bill Turnage[2] told me he had a most rewarding visit with you on the plane to Washington recently. I am pleased about this for two reasons: (1) he is on the way to be one of the top conservation leaders and possesses a remarkable logical and negotiating ability and a deep love for wilderness and all that it involves and (2) he can clarify specific problems such as Big Sur (locally) and the larger complexities of Alaska and the National Parks in general.

I had open-heart surgery less than a month ago and am feeling a bit "inconsequential"—if you know what I mean. I expect in a few weeks to be back in the groove. The operation was a great success; they tell me the next 25 years will be the most promising. But I am not too sparkling at the moment.

At any event, I wanted very much to write you to affirm my interest in all you are doing and express my wish that I might be of more tangible use to the Cause. You have done such an outstanding job in so many directions that one is hard put to comprehend the achievement. But you have proven that devotion to principle pays off!

The region known as "Big Sur" (specifically, the Pacific Coast from Carmel to San Simeon) is of undoubted magnificence; certainly unique in this hemisphere. It is a mix-mash of Government and private land, plagued by many "agencies" and highly vulnerable to development in spite of Coastal Plans, Zoning, etc. It is experiencing a perpetual "nibble"; in a few years we will go there and ask "what happened?" *It needs attention and without delay.* I am sure Bill filled you with some of the practical facts and we try to recognize the political realities. But the handwriting is on the wall, and little time remains for the political amenities. The Big Sur Foundation[3] can accomplish a lot if it has adequate funds and support.

I join with many who firmly believe the entire region should come under some management such as the Cape Cod National Seashore. Ranchers, long-time residents (artists, writers, etc.) are part of the "scene"; arrangements should be made to protect them in appropriate ways. The rumors have it, of course, that "if the NPS gets in we will all be thrown out without mercy." This whole approach has to be clarified.

The opposition is now working to *incorporate* the "City of Big Sur." Applications for numerous developments—motels and homes—are increasingly appearing. The once-magnificent coast—certainly an area of *National* Importance—will be desecrated and, as I said, we will wonder in a few years, "What happened?"

I do not know if you have visited this area. You should.[4] You will find it not a "recreational" area such as Point Reyes. It is a tremendous visual experience, a unique conjunction of ocean and mountain. Placing roads and structures on this land is certain desecration. The opposition (developers) are quite ruthless, yet one hope is that the old families who own large tracts of land, now passing to younger generations, have set up some attitude of consideration for the land and its significance.

I believe this is beyond politics. If something is not done and SOON —it will be lost for ever. Development moves with exponential tempo.

My best wishes and renewed congratulations on your extraordinary accomplishments in conservation.

Cordially,
Ansel Adams

1. Philip Burton, U.S. Congressman from San Francisco, was one of the most powerful leaders in the House and one of its most effective environmental legislators.

2. Turnage became the executive director of The Wilderness Society in 1978.

3. The Big Sur Foundation was a local group led by California architect Will V. Shaw, with strong support from Adams. Its objective was the preservation of the Big Sur coast.

4. Later that year, Adams escorted Burton and his wife, Sala, on a tour of the region.

To William Whalen[1]

Carmel Highlands
July 15, 1979

Dear Bill,

I take pleasure in sending you my thoughts and comments on the current Yosemite Master Plan.[2] These are the culmination of considerations formed over a near-lifetime of close contact with Yosemite and the Sierra Nevada. I first came to Yosemite in 1916 and have visited the Park every year since then, including a number of years as a permanent resident (in the 1930s and 1940s). My professional work (which could not be practiced in a National Park) obliged me to return to San Francisco in the late 1940s. We moved to Carmel in 1962 but our interest and contact with Yosemite has been maintained over all these years.

Also, I have visited and worked (photographically) in almost every National Park and many of the National Monuments as well. This includes Hawaii and Alaska. I feel it is important to approach any Master Plan for Yosemite with consideration for the objectives of the National Park concept in entirety. I am aware of the variations of quality and function of the different areas but the basic purpose of the National Park concept is *appropriate* protection and use; I am sure that the recreational functions of the Cape Cod National Seashore are, in most citizens' minds, quite different from the heroic natural values of Yosemite, Glacier Bay, or the Grand Canyon.

While Yosemite is perhaps the most beautiful and dramatic area of all, fresh thought and inspiration on the future of all the reserved areas is much to be desired. However, the purpose of this letter relates to Yosemite and I shall concentrate thereon. But I cannot avoid concern that any plan for Yosemite should reflect not the *status quo* of the old established Parks but definitely introduce contemporary concepts such as are being applied to most recently established areas. This means that Yosemite should be "returned" to a condition and use of an earlier day— a more pristine situation of emphasis on a higher standard of appreciation of the Natural Scene and a lesser emphasis on "expansion" and quasi-urban development. I am not urging a reduced *quality* but a simpler and more appropriate approach. . . .

I do not trust random opinion and advice that is not based on superior training and experience. Every citizen has a right to express his opinion, but this opinion must be concerned with the realities of the larger scene. If the function of the National Park Service is protecting the National Parks for future generations it seems that decisions thereon should be formulated by true experts in the various fields involved. I know many young people who would close the Parks to all uses except those related to foot travel! Some areas justify this rigorous restriction; certainly not Yosemite, which is a National Shrine. That does not mean it may be exploited or used in any way that would impair its essential values. Limitation of visitation is an essential reality! I often use the simile of the opera house; all seats are sold and some standing room as well. That is the limit; we do not sell lap-room! If we accepted more people than space would permit, the performance would be ruined for all. It is encouraging—and a moving experience—to stand at the Wawona Tunnel esplanade and look into Yosemite Valley; *no* evidence of man can be seen (except part of the distant 4-mile trail to Glacier Point, built in the 1870s, I recall). Or, standing at Glacier Point and looking eastward; no evidence of man is visible (without a telescope). However, looking down from Glacier Point into Yosemite reveals a shocking complex of poor planning and development, (especially at night when the Valley floor blazes with light like a rural community). However, in spite of all this development, the Valley itself is more beautiful than when I first came; it is clean, well-managed by the Service, free from the dust of earlier days, and the services are certainly superior. It should be made clear that what has been done—inappropriate as much of it is—has been done quite well. No matter how good the mechanics may be, the question remains—to what degree should they have been introduced in the first place, if at all? This question is addressed to all who bear responsibility for the protection of Yosemite—and this includes the citizens as well as the administrators, the ecologists, and the planners.

I do not feel that adequate expertise has been involved in the formulation of the Plan(s). We should seek an [Frederick Law] Olmsted among the many gifted individuals working in the areas of planning today. However, another force than the planners is required; I recall an old Irish legend that the early Kings of Erin held court with a General on one hand and a Poet on the other. This may be apocryphal, but a good suggestion! The planners must have basic sympathy for the environment and an understanding of its potential appropriate benefits to all our people. I believe that the problem is not difficult conceptually, but it is quite difficult in implementation, demanding a high order of technical and aesthetic capabilities. . . .

In closing, I wish to make an appeal to most seriously consider the vital importance of taking truly strong action to initiate planning of forceful consequence. We have been too hesitant, too cautious, too politically "safe," too unimaginative, and too careless of the erosions of time and the grave dangers of delay. In spite of all the good things that have occurred in the recent past the National Park principles are more vulnerable than ever before.

Most sincerely,
Ansel Adams

1. William Whalen, director of the National Park Service.

2. Master plans for the development of Yosemite National Park were prepared several times in the 1970s. None was implemented.

To Beaumont Newhall

Carmel Highlands
August 27, 1979

Dear Beaumont:

Getting in shape for the trip to New York.[1] Too many things are happening at once! I had no idea of the scope of the *Time* splurge.[2] Of course, it is not certain until tonight; if Carter elopes with Martha Graham THAT would become the prime story and little ole me would be junked or postponed. Little did we know in 1940—! It will be GREAT to see you. Hope all goes well in all ways! We both send love to you both[3] and long for a sniff of pinon!

As ever,
Ansel

1. Adams visited New York in September 1979 for the opening of "Ansel Adams and the West." Newhall also traveled to New York for the event.

2. *Time* magazine planned a cover story on Adams for the September 3 issue.

3. Newhall had remarried.

To President Jimmy Carter

Carmel Highlands
November 8, 1979

My Dear Mr. President,

I wish to express my appreciation for the cheerful cooperation I received from you and your staff in the rather complex assignment of making your portrait on Tuesday.[1] I have every reason to believe they were successful. The black-and-white photographs will be processed by me as soon as I return to Carmel on Thursday.

It was a delightful personal experience and a very special honor to meet the President of the United States as well as a man who has taken such bold stands in the domains of conservation. I am always surprised when I realize I have had close associations for more than sixty years with the great expressions of Nature that our country affords. I have observed both very good and very bad happenings in our Natural Scene; many wise and foolish decisions, devotions and exploitations. But, on the whole, we are progressing! Your incredibly bold actions on Alaska, the continuing enlargement of Wilderness areas, and the general concern for the wild, rural, and urban environment are indeed heartening. I confess to impatience at times, wishing for everything to happen at once! But wisdom gradually prevails, and I have concluded that my best service lies in creative imagery in my chosen medium and a gentle but persistent pressure on all concerned to protect all that we have that deserves protection—yet not lose sight of the realities of our resources, logically assigned, enhanced and applied, to the progress of our American civilization.

I wish to add that I looked forward to making your portrait with a certain amount of trepidation, simply because of the awesome implications of your high office and the serious national and international problems with which you constantly contend. I feared that I might not be able to overcome some evidence of serious concern in my photographs. However, I was amazed at the impression of relaxation, warmth, and self-possession you gave at all times and which was so gratifyingly revealed in the portraits. The feeling of confidence you expressed was extraordinary and this feeling was infectious; I left the White House with a conviction of security and grateful awareness of your intelligence and compassion. I have met many of our country's leaders and creative forces in the past half-century. I hope I can say to you, Mr. President—without seeming to fawn—that few if any have given me the warm and direct sense of inner peace and dignity that I found in our brief, hectic encounter. It was, indeed, one of the most significant experiences of my life.

I was deeply touched by your most kind invitation to spend Thanksgiving with you and your family in Georgia. My wife, son, and daughter and our five collective grandchildren[2] have been scheduled for more than a month to join close friends and their children for a Thanksgiving celebration, and it would be quite difficult to alter these plans.

However, some day I shall come to Georgia. I know it is an area of great natural beauty. I hope, too, that we shall have time for quieter, more philosophical conversation—we have so many mutual concerns that affect our country and our children and their children.

Again, my appreciation and warmest greetings to you and your charming wife. I look forward to your response to my notes on Alaska and Big Sur, and to our next meeting.

Cordially,
Ansel Adams

[367]

1. Adams made official portraits of President and Mrs. Jimmy Carter in black-and-white and color, using Polaroid materials.

2. Anne Adams Mayhew's third child, Sylvia, was born in 1963. In 1966, Charles Mayhew died tragically in an accident. In 1971, Anne married Ken Helms, a Unitarian minister.

From President Jimmy Carter

The White House
November 9, 1979

To Ansel Adams

I really enjoyed being with you & look forward to seeing the result of your work. The book and photograph[1] will be my prized possessions for life.

I met with leaders of the key environmental groups the day after your visit and discussed your letters with them and with my staff. All of us consider the protection of Alaskan lands the top environmental issue of our time which we can address in an incisive & substantive way.

It's good to have you as a friend and partner.
With gratitude & admiration—Jimmy Carter

1. Adams presented President Carter with a copy of his book, *Yosemite and the Range of Light,* and an original photograph, *Mt. McKinley and Wonder Lake, Denali National Park, Alaska, 1948* (see *An Autobiography,* p. 284).

From President Jimmy Carter

Washington, DC
February 15, 1980

To Ansel Adams,

Rosalynn and I are delighted by the photographs—as we knew we would be. We especially like the one taken in the doorway of the East Room.[1]

Thank you once again for the generous gift of your talents. Our warmest best wishes to you and Mrs. Adams.

Sincerely,
Jimmy Carter

P.S. Many people share our pleasure & gratitude.
P.P.S. This week we added 40 million acres of Alaskan land.

1. See *An Autobiography*, p. 305.

To Edgar Wayburn

Carmel Highlands
April 27, 1980

Dear Ed,

Just got home. For the moment can't find your new address! I must have it somewhere, but I do need your Bolinas [California] address! It was good to see you both at the Grapestake Gallery![1] *Cheers* for *Grandparenthood!!!!*

I am *personally* sorry about Whalen; such changes can be distressing.[2] . . . However, Yosemite is more important than any of us!

I was bitterly disappointed over the failure of the Service to initiate a truly strong [master] plan. The last plan is a *little* better than the previous one, but does nothing valid to remove cars from the Valley and establish appropriate staging areas. They have moved a few things around (no one knows how long it will take to effect those few things!) But there is no clean-cut plan to reduce services and accommodations within the Valley itself. The hint of a number of new rooms (ostensibly to replace tents) merely promises greater difficulty in the ultimate goal of simplification. There is a frightening lack of imagination. The morale of the Service is low. Some of the bureaucratic departments are being extremely difficult.

The new superintendent[3] is an exceptionally nice person, but apparently powerless. I can discuss details when I see you. I think the principal reason for this decision about Whalen has been coming for a long time.

I pleaded for securing a Director from "outside." After all, we do not appoint a symphony conductor from the orchestra; a rather intense search is made—often world-wide for the best person. The bureaucrats resent this as they want to maintain the bureau system.

I have learned a lot in the past several years. I talked with the Sierra Club Treasurer at Dulles Airport. I am glad that the Club is apparently prospering. I am glad to say the Ventana Chapter[4] is taking some action on Big Sur (and I hope the Main Office will follow suit).

The Cranston Bill[5] is excellent. (I can see where a few minor amendments will clarify it.) Senator [S. I.] Hayakawa [California] is *impossible*— and an embarrassment! I am worried that [Congressman Leon] Panetta [California] is waffling a bit; I think he has been brainwashed by the very aggressive opponents of the idea. . . .

I have been pleased to support The Wilderness Society because it is truly active and aggressive. I have never regained excitement about the Sierra Club (and I am sorry I must say this). However, as I do not know details I keep such opinions to myself. I AM weary of the "Holy War" in the energy area. I am convinced (have been for quite a time) that the threat of coal pollution and of acid rain vastly exceeds that of a well-managed nuclear program. The disaster in the Southwest[6] must be apparent to all—and it is only the beginning! I think we are all in for some very tough times, and a logical approach is essential. Not many members of the "Church" agree with me and I anticipate excommunication at any time!

When I became a grandparent, the realities of the future seemed more alarming than ever. Let us try to really protect Yosemite, Alaska, and the Big Sur with resolution and minimum delay! The dangers are increasing exponentially! ACHTUNG!!!!!!

All Best to All,
Ansel
Forgive Typing.

1. On April 26, Adams hosted a fund-raising reception at the Grapestake Gallery, San Francisco, to benefit Alan Cranston's 1980 campaign for reelection to the U.S. Senate.

2. Whalen had been relieved as director of the National Park Service.

3. Robert Binnewies was the superintendent of Yosemite National Park.

4. The Ventana Chapter of the Sierra Club encompasses the areas of Santa Cruz, south through Monterey County, and includes the Big Sur coast.

5. The Cranston bill provided federal protection for the magnificent Big Sur coast. It was blocked by the opposition of California Senator S. I. Hayakawa with the support of the Republican-controlled Senate.

6. Pollution from the Four Corners power plant was affecting the air quality of the surrounding national parks and monuments.

To President Jimmy Carter

Carmel Highlands
July 16, 1980

Dear President Carter:

I most strongly approve of your attitude towards the protection of the Alaskan natural scene. I am at a loss to know what to do other than to express my support. My record in conservation is longer than I sometimes realize: since 1919 I have, in many ways, been involved. However, I fully realize that the actual achievements have been accomplished by the professional conservationist and the sympathetic President and members of Congress. Hence, I stand ready to do what I can, well-knowing that what I represent is an idealistic stance. . . .

I am well aware of the political problems involved in the Alaska situation. We can become believers in greed, selfishness, and lack of concern, as representing the opposition, while belief in nature, disinterest in the profit-motive and a quasi-religious sacrificial attitude justifies the environmental approach. It is not that simple! Harold Ickes ordered that the term "values" not be used in description of National Park qualities. He felt the concept of parks, wilderness, preservation, and protection were not matters of "values" but of dedication to ideal concepts relating to the general, ultimate good of mankind. This philosophy has been important to me; I think I understand it.

In the struggle we have had for the Big Sur National Scenic Area, I find that many people living there love the place and would not wish to harm it; they would not build a road or a house, but *they demand the right to do so.* Their egos are disturbed, not necessarily their ethic. They become very vocal; they oppose the "Feds" as a matter of principle. They have no concept of how helpful the "Feds" (in various forms) have, and will, be. Mistakes have been made—sometimes serious ones—but in the end, we are a Federalist nation and it is ridiculous to think of our existing without respect and confidence in our federal institutions.

Nobody today is "sparking" this concept. When the Elephant Enterprise in Detroit[1] is over, you and the Democratic Party have a great chance. You can make potent statements, express basic facts, address the nation at a most dynamic level.

The threat of the Soviet (Marxist-Leninist) philosophy is very real. As I have often asked, "How many people in Congress or other levels of government have read the basic Marxian philosophy and studied the variations of the Leninist, Trotskyist, and Maoist approaches?" The Afghanistan episode is "just as expected." Iran will be next, West Germany, and the NATO countries could follow.

Who is going to first press the fatal button?

Why should we worry about Alaska or any idealistic concepts of the natural scene and wilderness if we are engulfed with such world threats? Perhaps, in a very few years, all such adventures of the human soul and mind may have come to naught. However, perhaps these idealistic concepts (just as devotion to the arts and sciences) will serve as the restraining influence against total destruction. People should be reminded in no uncertain terms that all they have been trained to live for and believe in might be extinguished in a moment of time. I do not think people are aware of the true situation. It should be built into the consciousness of everyone in the world that a nuclear war would extinguish all peoples and all cultures.

The preservation of Alaska is *symbolic* of hope for their future. The preservation of all resources, tangible and intangible, in all continents, is obviously essential for the future. Wilderness is but one facet of the jewel of civilization. It can be tied in with the benefits of a functioning society; it has the advantage of relating to visible and tangible experiences.

You, as our President, have the great—and quite possibly—the *only* chance to clarify this enormous problem.

May God go with you.

Most respectfully,
Ansel Adams

1. The Republican national convention.

From President Jimmy Carter

Washington, DC
August 25, 1980

To Ansel Adams,

I appreciated your congratulations & your compliments, & am determined to defeat Reagan. Our environmental commitments could be undone by him (& especially his supporters & advisors).

We need your help in the House on The Alaska Lands bill. My belief is that if it has to go back to the Senate it will be dead. Environmental issues—with this foremost—will be important in the campaign. We'll keep the issues alive.

It helps me to have your encouragement & advice.

Your friend,
Jimmy Carter

To William Turnage

Carmel Highlands
October 18, 1980

Dear Bill,

Things are moving at such a pace that there is a space-time contraction, as this letter shows! . . .

Am really worried about Reagan. The threat of his troglodytisms can put the cause back for decades. I have not seen much of anything put forth to express the real concerns. Are the conservationists doing what they COULD do if they really set out to do it?

The God-Damned fundamentalist crooks are making dire hay while the Actor shines.

Well, I shall get back to my private space-time in my darkroom and pour a libation of glacial acetic acid to R.R. (NOT Rolls-Royce!!!). May his grin freeze and his hair fall out, etc.!

A daughter comes to her mother and says—"Mom, I gotta tell you— I'm PREGNANT!" "OY!" says mother, "Is it YOURS????"

Luffff from all, More soon!
Ansel

To President and Mrs. Jimmy Carter

Carmel Highlands
November 6, 1980

Dear President and Mrs. Carter:

I was deeply disappointed at the outcome of the election. The democratic process is a strange and unpredictable phenomenon. My sympathy for you is shared by anguished concern for the country. I am hoping that the inherent forces, the checks and balances of the government, will protect the future of America and the world.

I have always been unhappy with the lame duck syndrome. The next two months could be productive and exciting. I am sure you will continue to achieve as many good works as possible. Alaska,[1] Energy, Big Sur, etc.—all are worthy of supreme effort. I only wish Congress could be counted on for similar commitment and determination!

I must tell you what a fine experience it is to know you and have the opportunity to share in some memorable moments. I trust it will be possible for us all to meet again in the future and renew this friendship which I prize most highly. It would be wonderful to welcome you at our Carmel Highlands home!

Be assured history will not overlook your great accomplishments in the areas of human rights and peace. May the next administration see the light—at least a small part of it.

Your friend,
Ansel Adams

1. The Alaska National Interest Lands Conservation Act was signed into law by President Carter in December of 1980. With this one action, 104.3 million acres of Alaskan wilderness were protected.

To Senator and Mrs. Alan Cranston

Carmel Highlands
November 6, 1980

Dear Alan and Norma,

Our congratulations! If you had not won I think it would be safe to say the country was a candidate for the Cosmic Nut-house. I sometimes think it would be a logical resolution anyways. Knowing you are still there is the one healing fact of this political catastrophe. Thank God for that!

Bill [Turnage] was here today, a very depressed man. I do not entirely blame him as I know that so many projects dear to his heart are imperilled. I perhaps sounded a bit pompous when I told him he should embrace the clinical approach. If one allows emotional reactions to take over in times of stress, one becomes increasingly on the defensive. I remember Nixon; that election was MUCH worse in impact and portent. We lived through it. We will live through this change. I do not think Reagan is dishonest, he is just not too bright. I would go to the White House to talk with him (pretentious me!) with the hope that I might get at least a sincere rejection of ideas. I would *never* go to Nixon for any reason whatever. I expressed myself to Bill as follows:

1. It IS a discouraging turn of affairs. I think the country is strong enough to survive (in the conventional sense) but I believe all of us should accept the turn of events as a *challenge,* probably one of the most severe we have ever had. This should vitalize, rather than defeat us.

2. It is interesting that the local political contestants who supported the Big Sur bill were all elected. I had come to the sad conclusion that anyone of them who supported the bill was doomed. You may have some idea of the hatred, vituperation, and scorn of the local right wing groups and individuals. . . .

3. I think we have to *intensify* our efforts. I am sure The Wilderness Society will rise to the occasion. I do not know what the Sierra Club will do—if anything—but irritate. This is a time for superb statesmanship. Let's get going!!

4. When I think six more years of Cranston I am cheered! Do not forget that you have a great reputation for total integrity and courage. I am sure there are an enormous number of people who can be of real help. We have the senatorial campaign of 1982 ahead and something must be done about Sleeping Sam.[1] We have 1984 ahead and THAT must be started without delay. I feel good about our local situation, but am really tearful over you being obliged to move from that nice old Capitol office.

5. I told Bill I felt it a GRAVE error for the President and Congress to give in to the Limping Duck syndrome. I am just naive enough to think that if we supplied force and conviction we might be able to succeed with many items before January. Of course, all the above has probably been thought about by a myriad of others by now.

Virginia and I send our most affectionate thoughts to both of you. It has been a grueling campaign and you deserve rest. Please remember that our house is your house and you both are ALWAYS welcome here.

As ever,
Ansel Adams

1. The descriptive nickname awarded Senator S. I. Hayakawa.

To Mary Alinder[1]

Carmel Highlands
March 1981

Dear Mary,

On 3-1-81 I wrote a memo saying I was deeply concerned with my health. I still am. . . .

I MUST get the work done—prints, books, etc.[2] I think it important that we have a conference—anticipating the inevitable. I would like it to be 20 years away (or more). But I am resigned to the fact that it might well be only a year or two or three.

I find that I am much more bothered with extraneous pressures and conflicts; . . . the workshop; the stupidities of the National Park Service; the pressures of "business" which Bill—with all good intentions—keeps very much alive. The "poetic moment" is rare these days, I can assure you. Things become more and more complex—word processors, heart seminars, local oppositions, endless letters (which you do a wonderful job replying to), requests for information, etc., etc., which you ditto. . . . I am not against word-processors, typewriters, Cadillacs and such—but I do not know of a truly creative person who works under the pressures I do. Instead of reserving energy for the "magical moments" of imagination I am confronted with continuous involvement. I am amazed that I have done so well so far—but I must tell you that the breaking-point may not be far off. I feel it coming—I do not want it to come—I want to do everything. But I know I can't continue as I am with the various pressures pressing the creative life out of me.

You are not initiating pressures—you are *managing* them (and for this I give deep thanks).

I have invited my own condition. I wanted to show that a creative person could live in the world, and not in a shrine. This worked fine to a point—but the point is very close to when it won't work.

. . . I am perplexed; and I do not have much time to de-perplex myself!

Cheeriow and *THANKS UNLIMITED*!!!! Lufffffffffff!

Ansel

1. Mary Street Alinder, Adams' executive assistant from 1979 to 1984 and collaborator on Adams' *An Autobiography*.

2. Adams' projects included finishing the new edition of *The Negative* (Boston: New York Graphic Society [NYGS], 1981); beginning work on the revision of *The Print* (NYGS, 1983); writing *Examples: The Making of 40 Photographs* (NYGS, 1983), and *Ansel Adams: An Autobiography* (NYGS, 1985); and making large sets of photographs (The Museum Sets) to be placed in museum collections, reproduced as the book: *Ansel Adams: Classic Images* (NYGS, 1985).

To William Turnage

Carmel Highlands
1981

Dear Bill,

Saints, sinners and politicians have a kind of "enlightened" urge to pick up the sword of righteousness and decapitate the dragons of exploitation, etc. I am looking around for an effective Excalibur which will spill the poisonous guts of the present Interior Department over the Mall so that all can see and smell!

I HEREBY DECLARE TOTAL IDEOLOGICAL WAR ON SECRETARY WATT[1] *AND HIS COHORTS*

You may distribute this challenge to all our friends and I am sure you will seek recruits, and find them.

I am sad that I cannot extend myself as far as I would like because of health, but I am sure there are *millions* who would pick up the needed arms for this conflict. The Wattites are determined to assassinate the concept of Wilderness and National Parks that we have worked so hard for over nearly a century (with some aspects for *more* than a century)!

The losses can be appalling. Time is short. Are we doing what we should and with the energy and determination the situation demands?

Perhaps Turnage could be the Winston Churchill of the Environment?

I have several thoughts on the procedures that could assist the concept.

1. Nationwide petitions, instigated and supported by the hundreds of regional groups. Divided up in this way, the cost and effort would not be large for each supporting unit.
   A. One petition based on the concepts and actions of Watt, *et al*, to date (within the *near* future).
   B. Other petitions to follow as occasions and threats demand.

2. A nationwide television program, put together with competence and artistry, that would clarify the threats facing [us].
3. A march on Washington by representatives of the environmental groups, carefully planned, dignified and effective.
THERE IS LITTLE TIME TO LOSE. THE DRAGONS ARE LOOSE!

With confidence,
Ansel Adams

1. James Watt was appointed Secretary of the Interior by President Ronald Reagan, following his election in 1980.

To the San Jose Mercury News [1]

Carmel Highlands
April 28, 1981

Letter for Opinion Page
Dear Fellow Citizen:

I have spent a good part of more than 60 years working with many others on the problems of conservation and the environment, beginning in 1919 as the summer custodian of the Sierra Club's center in Yosemite. I do not intend, at the age of 79, to now stand back and observe the destruction of our environment and all that has been accomplished to appropriately preserve and manage the resources of the earth—the physical, recreational, and aesthetic qualities of the world in which we live.

Our environment embraces the resources and activities of Man: the basic resources of mining, lumbering, agricultural products, oil, etc., the bounty as well as the beauty of the world for now and for the far distant future.

Under good management these resources—many renewable—should last indefinitely. Nearly 80 years ago President Theodore Roosevelt and Gifford Pinchot established the U.S. Forest Service and lumbering was put under well-considered controls. Otherwise, we might well have exhausted our timber many years ago.

The present administration's endorsement of free exploitation of our basic resources will have tragic consequences for the well-being of our people and the amenities of continued life on this earth. These dangerous new policies are expressed through Secretary of the Interior James

Watt. I address my critical remarks directly to him as the spokesman of these dire policies.

The impact of the fearful concepts and intentions expressed by Watt is not fully realized, except by a few experienced conservationists. I invite you who care deeply about our air, lands, and water to enter an all-out ideological war on Secretary Watt and his supporters; I am just getting started—join me! As I said at our local public demonstration against oil drilling in our coastal waters, "We must keep our cool and our dignity and fight like hell!"

My opinions are naturally intense on the general subject; I will outline a few here.

1. Coastal Oil Drilling/Exploration. Watt stands back of this "for the national interest." I remind him that there are several "national interests:" the fishing industry, the tourist industry, and the beauty of our coastal shores and waters. The potential pollution from this project is immense. I ask you to imagine oil derricks up and down our coastline. Think of oil spills. Think of our gray whales, sea lions and otters. How do you feel about this?

2. National Parks, Wilderness, and Recreational Areas. These public lands are now threatened in many deadly ways. Invasion of these lands for oil, timber, and mining, reduction of their financial support and the concept of "multiple use" of wilderness areas all have implications of most serious consequence. It appears that there are plans to turn over the management and, perhaps, the control, of our National Parks to private business. I have heard of plans to drain part of the Everglades National Park, and to open our parks to snowmobiles. I think of the High Country of Yosemite National Park in winter, the peace and quiet of the winter wilderness, to be spoiled for the growing numbers of cross-country skiers by the harsh sounds and fumes of those machines. Watt is also against urban National Parks and Recreational Areas. Of course the cities do not have the monies to maintain the parks if they revert to them. Is our land only to be experienced by those with the wealth to travel? How wonderful it is to have recreational parks where the access is close and quick, where transportation is inexpensive and people in our diverse regional areas can directly benefit.

Indeed, Mr. Watt acts ignorant about the park system that he now controls. He continues to confuse the Gateway Recreational Area in New York (one of his endangered species of urban parks) with the Golden Gate National Recreational Area north of San Francisco which is one of the most beautiful areas of our state. This Area combines several areas which are recreational and cultural with a remarkable scenic component, such as parts of the south shore of the Golden Gate and unique Point Reyes. Watt can do great damage just through ignorance of the facts of what our public lands represent.

3. The man, himself. It is common knowledge that Watt is a religious fundamentalist. He has his right to embrace any religion or creed he desires, but he has no right to impose his religious philosophy on the management of his department and the future of the American people. I have heard that he justifies his program of using our land and resources now without regard for the future by saying, in effect, there will be very little future; the Second Coming is due any time now. To me, as things seem to be going now the Second Coming will be preceded by the First Coming of the hydrogen bomb!

4. A summation of the consequences of Mr. Watt's actions and promises:

a. We are dipping disastrously deep into our resource capital.

b. The overwhelming problems of the economy and defense have taken precedence over consideration for our natural and cultural resources. I sympathize with the President in his difficult economic and political decisions. I implore him to recognize the important fact that if we lose the essential qualities of our environment no political philosophy and no effort for defense will have validity. Secretary Watt's values appear restricted to the material, immediate, and profit-oriented mentality of a two-dimensional group with little wisdom or conscience.

c. Action. We are fighting for our life and the future of our descendents. We must stand up and be counted! As a citizen I urge each of us to take on responsibility: write members of Congress, Secretary of the Interior Watt, and President Reagan; write or phone people you know and urge them to do the same. Impress on everyone you can that this is not just an "opinion" problem but the most intense threat we have ever faced to the integrity and future of our land.

I intend to fight this complex "Pearl Harbor" of our American earth to the limit of my abilities. I invite all to join with me to oppose Mr. Watt and his intended rampage. We can work together with clarity, truth, and dignity to protect our irreplaceable heritage.

"A letter a day (from a million people) might keep Watt away!"

Most sincerely,
Ansel Adams

1. This letter was published in the Sunday editorial section of the *San Jose Mercury News,* May 3, 1981.

From Arthur H. Thornhill, Jr.[1]

Boston

June 3, 1981

Dear Ansel,

As you know, I regret very much my inability to attend the ceremony at Harvard,[2] as well as your dinner party. Nevertheless, I will be with you in spirit and thought.

During this visit, I have recalled many fond memories of our association, including our recent visit to Carmel. Certainly, one of the most enjoyable took place a little over four years ago when I had the privilege of participating in the Symposium conducted in celebration of The Friends of Photography's Tenth Anniversary and in celebration of your seventy-fifth birthday.

The discussions during the day were very stimulating and candid—it was really the first time I had met with so many "stars" from the world of photography.

Of course, the evening was highlighted by your announcement of your and Virginia's establishment of the Beaumont and Nancy Newhall Curatorial Fellowship in Photography at the Museum of Modern Art.

Later at the scrumptious, festive dinner . . . I had the honor to be selected as one of five to present a birthday toast to you. As you know, Beaumont Newhall, Dave McAlpin, Jim Enyeart[3] and John Schaefer were the others.

I remember expressing pride and pleasure in being your publisher, and I concluded by toasting our future together and said I thought the best was yet to be.

Ansel, since then, we have published many of your fine books successfully and, as I said yesterday, I don't know of any author or artist who has consistently contributed as much to our list. Again, I will say I toast our future together for I still think the best is yet to be.

With best wishes.

Sincerely,

Arthur

1. Thornhill was chairman and president of Little, Brown and Company, the exclusive publisher of Adams' work since 1976.

2. At its annual commencement, Harvard University conferred on Adams the honorary degree of Doctor of Fine Arts.

3. James Enyeart was then the executive director of The Friends of Photography.

To Arthur H. Thornhill, Jr.

Carmel Highlands
June 7, 1981

Dear Arthur,

I was deeply touched by your very warm letter of June 3rd. The Harvard Commencement is, indeed, something to remember! You must have attended many of these in your lifetime. Virginia and I wish we could have shared it again with you. But you were there in spirit, as your letter so well attests. The little dinner party we had for our friends was very pleasant indeed. The "Old Firm" was well represented but we missed our Leader!

Your reminiscences of our mutual careers in the august domains of publishing and conviviality will be cherished by both of us for all the time to come.

We are having, have had, and will have a most splendid relationship— it seems to get better as time goes on—(if such is possible!). Your entire staff encourages and supports the highest levels of professional and personal ethics and quality. I am honored to be a part of your creative complex!

Thank you again for all the amenities and the achievements. Virginia joins me in warmest thoughts for you and yours. We both hope you will be able to repeat that delightful visit we had with you earlier this year.

Again, appreciation and greetings!
Ansel

P.S. Alas, this was *not* done on the Word Processor.

From Garry Trudeau[1]

New York City
September 3, 1981

Dear Ansel Adams:

My meeting with Bill has indeed borne fruit (I hope). I enclose my efforts to date in case you missed them. Also, a few new books. (None of my friends ever buys my books, so I get my publisher to send me lots of copies to give them. They don't deserve such largess, but it's a way of staying in touch.)

Anyway, the fight goes on. Washington right now reminds me of Paris in the spring of '41; the Huns are in place, the Democrats have been transformed into a docile Vichy, and out in the countryside, a few pockets of resistance hold out. You are one such pocket. I'd love to come visit—perhaps we can work it out this fall.

Until then, please stay mad. And by the way, thank you for your huge talent. Try to take comfort in the certain knowledge that your vision of the American wilderness will be admired years after we have all forgotten Mr. Watt's.

Cheers,
Garry Trudeau

1. Garry Trudeau, creator of the "Doonesbury" comic strip.

Cartoon presented to Ansel Adams by Garry Trudeau

[383]

To Garry Trudeau

Carmel Highlands
September 10, 1981

Dear Garry Trudeau:

On receipt of your letter, and the most generous enclosures with their glittering inscriptions, my spirits were elevated, my worries minimized and my faith in humanity enhanced. WOW!!

You are unique in a field of great uniqueness. I have some of your books—and have seen others—generously distributed in the world at large. I follow your daily contributions with the intensity of a monk telling his beads. (I'm telling you!!!)

Your description of Washington at the present time is hilarious—and accurate! I think there are more pockets of resistance than you might admit. People greatly admire your "Stand." Quite often I get phone-calls: "Did you see Doonesbury this morning WOW, WOW!!!" One man hereabouts said he thought you were an *Irreverent Communist!* You are making real dents in the fenders of the "Ruling Class." KEEP IT UP—WITHOUT STINT, WITHOUT FEAR AND WITH THE JOY OF ENVIABLE ACCOMPLISHMENT!!! That's right!!

The whole damn environment is at stake. I hope I live long enough to see the last dribble of WATTer over the Dam of History. Did I mention to you my idea of a true 1981 Washington breakfast?—Reagan and Haigs, Funny Side UP!!

. . . You are both[1] invited here whenever you can make it! I will be in the East around the 1st of November (for a week or so). Otherwise— HERE!

Warmest greetings, as ever,
Ansel Adams

My typing is not to be considered TYPING! Forgive?

---

1. Trudeau's wife, "Today" show host Jane Pauley.

To the Honorable Alan Cranston
the Honorable Edward Kennedy
the Honorable Paul Tsongas
the Honorable Howard Metzenbaum
the Honorable Leon Panetta
the Honorable Philip Burton
the Honorable John Seiberling

Carmel Highlands
February 16, 1982

Esteemed Gentlemen:

As I am entering my eightieth year, I am, as a citizen of the United States and a liberal and reasonable individual, constrained to express my opinions on the future of our country and our people.

I believe the Reagan administration to be the most potentially disastrous in our history. I am joined by most of my friends—liberal and conservative, Democratic and Republican—in this opinion. We are alarmed and bewildered. There is no anchor to depend upon, the rudder steers us towards deprivation for the less privileged, gross destruction of our wildlands, a ruined economy, and careless threats of war and extinction.

I know far more than I did at forty, but if I were forty again I would have the necessary strength and energy to assert myself in the preservation of our society. Recognizing that I am in the evening of my efforts, I ask of you, what can I, as an individual American, do to help you to resolve this dire situation?

I suggest that without delay we seek the support of our citizens to stop the fatal descent to oblivion our present administration promises. With great firmness and without violence or bigotry we must assert ourselves in the strongest possible ways and work for the preservation of the United States and the ideals it represents.

You are our best leaders. You are our best hope. I am ready to assist within the limits of my physical capabilities in any ways that you choose. We cannot postpone direct action.

Warm regards,
Ansel Adams

[385]

From Edwin Land

ON ANSEL EASTON ADAMS

Who makes mountains into metaphors
And metaphors into mountains
We, the University of his Friends
Confer the Degree

DOCTOR OF PRINTABLE PERFECTION

(As well as unprintable imperfections)
And invite him into permanent residence
Of loving, admiring and devoted friends
By the authority vested in me by them

EDWIN LAND

1. Adams' eightieth birthday.

To Steve Griffith[1]

Carmel Highlands
May 23, 1982

Dear Steve Griffith:

Sorry to be late with these remarks; I agree with the statement you sent me, but I don't think I wrote it. However, this expresses what I feel; you can edit or shorten it as you see fit.

It has been said that the influences surrounding the first three or four years of life command the future directions of the child in his years to come. Had I been raised in bleak and bitter urban surroundings I am certain my life would have been vastly different than it has been. From my earliest years I was surrounded by the sand dunes, shores, and hills of the Golden Gate and breathed the clean air of San Francisco of those days. As I grew up I experienced the wild areas of Puget Sound and the Santa Cruz Mountains and, after 14, Yosemite Valley and the High Sierra.

I realize I was very fortunate. Not many children have such advantages in their youth. All children deserve contact with Nature as part of their heritage. There are, of course, many exceptions—creative genius emerging from the poverty and terror of the slums and building worlds of beauty and achievement. This is not, unfortunately, the general pattern of civilization; untold millions of our people, no matter what their inherent capabilities might be, are doomed to lives of squalor and insufficiency because of our failure to realize the importance of experience with the natural world for all people.

The population in general should be given maximum opportunity for education, cultural experience, and relationship to the world of wonder and beauty—what is left of it—during their formative years. The fangs of structures rising into polluted air, the bedlam and ferocity of the streets, the weary rituals of what passes for education, and the remote horizons of smog and sameness must prey upon all but those of the most resolute spirit (and having constructive family relationships).

The present Administration typifies the short-sighted stupidities that erode the standards and opportunities of life as it might develop in our country. The experiences essential to making lives worthy of living are shunted aside for the opportunities of making money and, probably, war. Generations to come (as important, at least, as our generation) will suffer for our embezzlement of resources, practical and spiritual, that were their heritage. The more our children see and know of the natural world around them, the better equipped they will be to face the basic realities of life and realize the noble potentials of existence this planet has to offer. . . .

Cordially,
Ansel Adams

1. Steve Griffith, national coordinator of the Sierra Club's Inner City Outings.

To Howard Simon,[1] *the* Washington Post

Carmel Highlands
July 22, 1982

Dear Howard:

The announcement by Secretary of the Interior James Watt to open all of our American coasts to oil leasing is disastrous. He made his decision painfully clear to the American public on July 21st during a televised interview on the excellent MacNeil/Lehrer show on PBS. Mr. Watt never spoke of the spiritual values we gain from our environment, but he did speak strongly of the immediate material gain. He has no consideration of the future conditions under which our children and their children will be obliged to live if the greed for development and quick profit, that he champions, is not controlled in our time.

Mr. Watt is glib, clever and evasive. His continuing statements clearly reveal the catastrophe he is inviting on our country: squandering our resources, and in the process, polluting the oceans and beaches, smogging the air and stripping the land.

It is imperative that we, the citizens, gather for concerted political action and not allow the destruction of our American earth. We should all ponder John Muir's immortal statement, "Everything in the Universe is hitched to everything else." James Watt is hitched to an evil star.

Sincerely,
Ansel Adams

1. Howard Simon, managing editor.

From Peter Griffin

Fall River, Mass.
May 1983

Dear Mr. Adams:

I thought you said some awfully good, awfully true things in your *Playboy* interview (May, 1983) about the environment of course, but also about art. Ironically you seem to have quite an Emersonian view of aesthetics though apparently you don't care for Emerson's work.

There is, however, something which strikes me as incongruous about your appearance (and the appearance of your work) in *Playboy*. No one would doubt your belief in photography as art; no one should question your belief in art as life-enhancing, as a civilizing experience. Why then would you appear, and allow your work to appear, in a magazine which is essentially barbaric? . . .

I'm not a fairy or a prig, Mr. Adams. But it seems to me that there's something wrong here. I'm sure there's a lot I don't understand. Could you explain?

Yours truly,
Peter Griffin

To Peter Griffin

Carmel Highlands
May 16, 1983

Dear Peter Griffin,

I found your letter very appealing and I wish to reply with as logical explanation as I can muster.

I gave most careful thought to the proposal that I grant an interview to *Playboy*. It is a strange magazine, containing much trash. It also has produced some of the best Interviews in current journalism.

It has a *large* audience; probably 12,000,000 readers will have seen this issue. I have certain opinions I feel are necessary to express—chiefly those relating to the environment and the dismal Administration now in control. I do not like the "babes" any more than you do. I and my family and friends agree that the audience of *Playboy* was different from other publications and offered a fresh "receiving group" for the ideas expressed.

The response has been overwhelmingly favorable (as far as the letters I have received indicate). I do not know about unexpressed opinions! It is the best interview I have ever had; the interviewer did his homework well and the text is accurate and well balanced. Some concepts and facts did not "get through" the editorial office, but on the whole I am greatly pleased.

"Overlook the frame and observe the picture." I do not refer to the silly pictures which, I agree, are travesties of reality.

My best wishes,
Appreciatively,
Ansel Adams

To Senator Alan Cranston[1]

Carmel Highlands
June 25, 1983

Dear Alan,

It is heart-warming to read about your success with the state polls as well as your remarks in the press.

Royalties are down, but I was pleased to send a small check for the Cranston Cause.

I am discouraged, not only with the Administration, but with the political apathy I sense in so many areas.

Sala Burton won, thank God, but the election had a small turnout. I think people are a bit stunned by the general situation. Reagan is increasing in menace. Watt beams with apparent gloat over his "successes." Ruckelshaus seems uninspired and weak. The E[nvironmental] P[rotection] A[gency] scandal should be brought into full view. Everybody seems to be pussyfooting about.

"Political language" so far grinds along with dull fact and opinion, and no fire or passionate conviction. I have often wondered if the basic approach is wrong; to attempt to be "objective" and as passionate as a checker game. The evil people in history depend upon charisma— Hitler, for example, and the despicable Senator McCarthy. Reagan's modulated voice could make a vitamin tablet attractive. Spare us from the Fundamentalist thumpings—but millions heed. Fal(thee)well!!!!

Glenn sounds "Ole Boy." Mondale is not inspiring (and looks very tired). You are giving the impression of great honesty and seriousness.

We need fire, not glowing embers! We do not need hyperbole or bantering. I am waiting for a bit of wrath and outrage, expressed in the consistent mood of dignity and concern, impact and compassion. Like a full orchestra, not just a string quartet!

A sense of compassion is extremely important. It's what Reagan ain't got! He has "jollyfication." When severe, he reminds me of a school teacher I had, or the leading man in rehearsal of a righteous play.

Especially of late, it seems obvious that he is reading his speeches; he has a rather gifted writer who can string words together with a mellifluous intention—and not much else.

I wish I were forty again. I would respond with joy and energy to a "LET'S GO!" syndrome with all I've got. Maybe that would be a good punch-line?

Virginia and I send our affectionate greetings to you and Norma,

LET'S GO!!!
Ansel

1. Senator Cranston was a candidate in the 1984 presidential campaign.

Washington, DC
June 28, 1983

Dear Ansel,

Many, many thanks for your very interesting note. You raise some excellent points and I'm going to keep them in mind in the weeks and months to come.

Your check is appreciated very much. Thanks for sending it along. You are wonderful!

O.K. Ansel, "LET'S GO!" You're NEVER too old to respond with joy and energy. Keep up the good work.

Love to Virginia,

Affectionately
Alan

I'll be hiking in Aspen this Saturday with Bill Turnage. A 3 hours respite along the campaign trail.

To Otis Chandler[1]

Carmel Highlands
July 5, 1983

Dear Mr. Chandler,

You may have heard of my meeting (at his request) with President Reagan on June 30, 1983. *The Washington Post* interviewed me by phone later and published a fairly long piece thereon.[2] The meeting was in Los Angeles in the Beverly Wilshire Hotel.

Michael Deaver[3] phoned to say, "The President would like to meet you and discuss why you dislike him so much." I did my best. I was supposed to have 15 minutes; the meeting stretched to 50 minutes. He was charming, amiable, and persuasive, but I was inoculated against charm and was not influenced in any way. He talked quite a bit about himself and his ideas. With the 15 minute limit I feared I would not get anything in edgewise, and struggled for my priorities.

I covered the themes of the environment in general and Watt as one of the specifics. I was very rough on Watt. I frankly told him (Reagan) that he was seriously misinformed. I mentioned the damage being done within the National Park Service by switching about valued people in that branch of Interior. I stressed the seriously low morale of the National Park Service. The only thing we agreed upon was nuclear power. He could not comprehend the "juvenile protestors." I said I recognized the grave dangers attending nuclear power, but that I thought the potential damage that fossil fuel could produce would be equally lethal. I suggested that if he takes ten or twenty billions from his defense budget and applies it to a crash program for Fusion Power that our energy troubles could be over. He raised an eyebrow at that. I spoke of the basic resources as being the real capital—all property, interest, etc., was merely the "interest" on this capital and, as the New Englanders would say, "We are desperately dipping into capital." I expressed the wish that the environment could be considered a bi-partisan problem and reminded him that many factors of conservation were warmly supported by staunch Republicans in the past.

I told him that I deeply resented Watt's statement that there are only two classes of citizens: Americans and liberals. I, along with millions, consider this a prime insult.

My impression at the close of the meeting was that the vacuum had hit the fan. Michael Deaver was with us, but said nothing. I have the impression that Deaver could be approachable; he might be able to present the President with ideas that he would not accept directly from citizens or groups.

I am told that I am the first environmentalist that has met with the President (this from one of his staff).

I felt free to say what I pleased (although, because of the uncertainty of available time, I mixed my priorities and missed a few important points). After the session I felt as if I were in a "recovery room." I was trying to understand the opacity of his personality. I sensed no "aura" of the Presidency (as I did with [Presidents] Johnson, Ford, and Carter). I felt I was addressing a stone wall. He never initiated an idea or a challenge. He has his rigid conviction. He stated only well-worn facts and listed his achievements as Governor and as President. He claimed that we had much in common—that he was really an environmentalist!

I castigated Watt as the most dangerous man in his Administration (I did *not* say "except you!") and I could not understand how he (Reagan) could retain him. I said Watt was doing grave damage to the image of the Administration, not only in the present time, but historically.

The responses were bland (chiefly raising an eyebrow or assuming an expression of small-fractional interest).

It was quite an experience! And frustrating!

My best wishes,

Cordially,
Ansel Adams

P.S. The 1984 elections may well be the most important in our history. We must leave no stone unturned to defeat Reagan and his philosophies. What can the "single citizen" do???

P.S.S. I repeated what I said in the *Playboy* interview: "It is horrifying that we have to fight our own Government to save our environment."

1. Otis Chandler, publisher of the *Los Angeles Times*.

2. Adams met with President Reagan in Los Angeles on June 30, 1983 to discuss environmental issues. The meeting was front page news: *Washington Post*, July 3, 1983.

3. Michael Deaver, deputy chief of staff for President Reagan.

To Senator Alan Cranston

Carmel Highlands
August 26, 1983

Dear Alan:

As a citizen in these troubled times I await evidence of environmental enlightenment and responsibility from those who aspire to the Presidential candidacy in the coming 1984 election. There is obviously no hope whatever from the present Administration in this regard. All they aspire to is money and the opportunities for development and profit. The President agrees with the Calvin Coolidge pronouncement, "The business of America is business."

Is our country to be governed within the crass limits of such materialism for another four years? Unless a new wave of intelligence and compassion arises among our people I fear we shall repeat the disastrous errors of the immediate past and guide ourselves into oblivion.

Avoidance of war is the first priority. We agree that the causes of war lie not only in social tensions and the complexities of our arrogant and competitive society but in the neglect of the ultimate reality, the Environment. This neglect, unfortunately, is international but we could well be the first nation to reverse it. We can accomplish this only by the positive thrust of the people and I believe that the Democratic Party should undertake firm leadership in this area.

The environment, as considered by ecologists, humanitarians, and philosophical realists, comprises our basic capital, the source and resource of life and civilization. What we call "Capital"—property, dividends and security—are merely the benefits and "income" from the prime resource which is the environment, the Earth itself.

As Jeremy Rifkin wrote, "The ultimate balancing of budgets is not within society, but between society and nature."

In earlier days conservation related to National Parks and Wilderness; we now must consider the whole environment—the air, water and earth—and in the exacting terms of the future, not merely for the euphoric present. Our arena represents both the tangible and intangible resources and the battle lines are fast being drawn.

I regret that I hear little emphasis on the environment in the copious words addressed by the candidates to the nation. The Reagan Administration does not recognize the meaning of the term; experience indicates that the environmental protection efforts of over a hundred years are being intentionally eroded by the present groups in power. It seems as if all parties consider the environment to be politically too dangerous to discuss, let alone establish as an important plank in their platforms. We are faced with the most serious situations in the history of our country. Our attitudes towards war, education, the economy, and the environment are comparable to the Four Horsemen of the Apocalypse; the latter may be the most devastating.

Because of the bounty of the Earth we have become wealthy "beyond all dreams of avarice." Few realize that the bounty is approaching exhaustion. In the process of blind exploitation the destruction of the environment is exacerbated by pollution and the scarring of the Earth. I cannot conceive of a more important plank in the Democratic Platform than *concern for the Environment and determination that it shall be protected—no matter what the immediate cost*—for the millennia to come.

I support you for President because I believe that you possess the most balanced mind, the most compassionate spirit, and the most comprehensive experience in public affairs of all the Democratic candidates. You would indeed be a *great* President. Alan, I urge you to aggressively consider in work and deed and in profound depth, the fateful subject of the Environment and the future of our world.

With warmest regards for you and Norma,

Ansel Adams

To Edwin Land

Carmel Highlands

September 22–27, 1983

(Oct. 2!)

Dear Din,

I started to write you a letter on my trusty old Herpes (I mean HER-MES) while in bed,[1] but it was awful. Poking out mechanical keys with a bit of finger arthritis is unrewarding. I appreciated your call and I am sending a letter as promised. I have some ideas to unload:

My meeting with Reagan remains a sour experience. He is disarmingly cordial but seems to be a viscous sponge from the neck up. My impression of the meeting was like "when the Vacuum Hit the Fan." It is alarming to realize the power that lies in his hands. I think the Administration is leading us into international trouble. Their attitude is one of uncompromised belligerency. It is easy to say, "They know more about things than we do," but they give no assurance that they *do* know anything—or would know what to do with the knowledge if they had it. Many of Reagan's statements have been ridiculous and of simple bad taste and judgement. James Watt is impossible; we all feel he is resigning soon. It is difficult to imagine the damage he has done. . . .

I believe the Administration thinks war all the time (as perhaps does a large segment of the population), is tuned towards belligerence and has no consideration for the future. The Radical-Liberals (as Watt called the environmentalists) are deeply concerned about the future and the conservative use of our resources. What kind of world are my grandchildren and yours—and their children going to find awaiting them? Is it to be only the wreckage of slums as well as country club euphoric existence? The field of education is a disgraceful mess. Our Reagan-clone Governor [George Deukmajian] is a catastrophe. The San Jose School District (one of the largest in the State) was forced into bankruptcy. Our Community College has deep budget problems. And California is only

[395]

one of fifty states! Where is the leadership we so desperately need? The essential enticements for high talent are lacking.

One thing that was impressive for me relating to my visit with Reagan: I, as a citizen, was able to sit on the same couch with him and express in no uncertain terms what was on my mind. However, I do not clearly understand just why I found myself in that position. I have had some experience in environmental work but I am not eloquent—especially in conversation—and have had no direct governmental contact or function. So much for politics!

. . . All of the above has been set down since the 22nd of September and is finished October 2nd! It is a mix-mash of ideas and you are under no obligation to read it. (This statement should be on the first page.)

As I am now back on my feet (literally) I shall stop writing about my paranoid and euphoric ideas. . . .

We had a wonderful visit with Terre and her friend. It has been too long a time since we have seen you both. I wish to clarify a quip by Adlai Stevenson I recalled for Terre, "The Republicans stroke a platitude until it glows like an epigram."

Am delighted to hear that all goes well in all directions. We were *impressed* with the photographs of your Grandson!

With cheers and affection,
Ansel Adams

1. Following leg surgery to remove a cancer, Adams was confined to bed for four weeks.

To Vladimir Ashkenazy [1]

Carmel Highlands
October 11, 1983

Dear Friend Ashkenazy,

I must apologize for my abject failure to keep in touch with you and thank you for the records of the *106* and the "Pictures . . ."[2] I have been immobilized for a month; I had a chronic infection in my leg requiring surgery. . . .

I am writing not to dwell on my incapacitation but to tell you how pleased I am with the record covers. Before my illness I saw the proofs. I had no thought of their being used in this way, but when the decision was made I was greatly pleased. Believe it or not, just today I saw the records for the first time! They apparently came while I was in the hospital. Several times while I was immobile I wondered when the records would come—*and they were here all the time!* Our appreciation is vast—and my apology for not writing is *very* abject! The recordings are, of course, MAGNIFICENT!

We have all kept you and your family very much in mind. The thought of your having a home here remains a real satisfaction.[3] I have talked with several people who have attended your concerts—chiefly when you were conducting—and the comments were all enthusiastic.

Everything else goes along about the same. My book, *The Print,* is out. So are the new posters and the 1984 calendar. My book *Examples* (a collection of 40 images, each with a short text) will be out in a week or so. I want you to have copies of the calendar and *Examples;* where should I send them within the next few weeks?

I wish I could have done a better job with the portraits of your charming wife [Dody], but, as I wrote you, I was not happy with them. I could make good prints of one or two but I did not catch the spirit. I am usually poor when I rush; your pictures were the exception. I like the breezy one of the "Pictures" especially.[4]

We *all* send love and warmest greetings to you and yours. When will you next be with us in Carmel?

As ever,
Ansel Adams

1. Vladimir Ashkenazy, pianist, and Adams first met when Ashkenazy arrived as a surprise eightieth-birthday present and performed a concert in Adams' home.

2. Adams' portraits of Ashkenazy appeared in 1983 on the cover of two of his recordings for London Records: Mussorgsky's "Pictures at an Exhibition" and Beethoven's Sonata No. 29 in B Flat Major, Opus 106, "Hammerklavier."

3. Much to Adams' delight, the Ashkenazy family purchased a home just up the hill from his own in the Carmel Highlands.

4. See *An Autobiography,* p. 379.

To William Turnage

Carmel Highlands
October 14, 1983

Dear Bill and all,

. . . I am worried—and about the President. He is extremely danger-ous to the world. We MUST consider the whole world—the total envi-ronment—and the people, now and to come. I woke up last night with a chill, I was thinking of the power that the conservatives have to destroy us—and the power the Soviets have to do likewise—and there seems to be no human wisdom in control.

It is to be the biggest fight we have had. I wish I was fifty years younger! But my armor still fits, I can get a fresh plume for my helmet and what blood of Mars I have is still flowing!

LET'S GO !!!!!!!!
A.A.

To Everyone

Carmel Highlands
October 15, 1983

Abortion of Shakespeare by Adams

HARK! HARK! THE CLARK AT CONFIRMATION SINGS
   AND RONNIE GIVES SURPRISE,
HIS THOUGHTS WILL NOW POLLUTE THOSE SPRINGS
   WHERE THE IMPERIL'D FLOWER LIES:
AND STEAMING SULPHUR CLOUDS BEGIN
   TO STING OUR TRUSTING EYES:
WITH EVERYTHING THAT PRETTY WAS
   THE WORLD MAY SOON DEMISE!

Commemorating the appointment by President Reagan of the ques-tionable William Clark to replace the despicable James Watt as Secre-tary of the Interior.

May the Ghost of the Bard forgive me!
Ansel

From Vladimir Ashkenazy

Luzern, Switzerland
October 19, 1983

Dear Mr. Adams,

Thank you for your letter of Oct. 11th. I am delighted your work was used on my records and although I have not seen the finished product yet I am sure it looks great. I am sorry you have not been well and glad you're coming out of it. I very much hope to find you in good health next April. Would you like me to do an afternoon recital on April 22?[1] How about 2 or 2:30? It probably will be Schubert/Schumann. No compensation required—it will be just a pleasure to play for you and your friends. (I have a concert on April 23rd in L.A. so will have to leave you soon after the concert.)

I will phone you and we can discuss this but think about it in the meantime. Oh, sorry! I would love to have the calendar and *Examples*— many thanks for the offer. Can you send them to Switzerland?

Love to you and Virginia and to everybody, Mary, Jim[2] and all!

Yours as always,
Vova Ashkenazy

p.s. Could I have just one photo of Dody for my collection? You see I love her and your standards for photos are a bit higher than mine. I am sure I will enjoy having it—please!

1. Ashkenazy performed a concert in Adams' home on April 22, 1984.

2. Jim Alinder, photographer and executive director of The Friends of Photography.

To Mary Alinder

Carmel Highlands
January 24–25, 1984

AUTOBIOGRAPHY

Dear Mary,

I am sorry I am a bit slow and late in thinking about pictures. I HAVE been thinking a lot about them and regret that my present standard of energy has discouraged my getting my teeth into the project as

I should have done. The truth of the matter is I feel LOUSY and I am sure I need a check-over at a different angle.

I go through the motions of getting up in the morning, shower, etc. and then I find I do not have a "focus" or program. I KNOW all the things I should be doing but for some reason I find it hard to channel my energies into them. I must pull myself together and start afresh! Hence, I should now go through *all* the selected proofs that are put aside for my attention (and yours). I suppose I should go all through the ones I rejected, too—just to be sure. ARE THEY ALL AVAILABLE, or have they been put away? First order of business is to get them out and sit me down and threaten me with some kind of clobbering if I do not perform!

The TEXT is going beautifully. But I really think I should find a time *and place* when I could read it all without interruption from the worldly pressures. I am immensely pleased with what you have done, but there are still a few places where I am not speaking my own piece, if you know what I mean. I sense the pressures on the book and on the calendars, etc. and on the prints I HAVE NOT made. My schedule is haywire, I am drifting like a piece of avocado on a thick salad dressing! I am like a cloud in a volcanic crater that cannot rise enough to slip over the rim. I am the dowager stuck in Bloomingdale's, or the food-stamp character lost in the Four Seasons! Aye, Oye, Ugggh! Throw me a rope!!

Do you realize I have not had an electrocardiogram for a long time? I do not like the heart sensations and the feeling of weakness. Also the disturbance of sleep.

ARRAGUGGH!!!

Anyway, do not think I do not appreciate you!!!!

But I gotta do SOMETHING to get back on track!

Love,
Ansel

To the New York Times [1]

Carmel Highlands
February 25, 1984

Dear Sir,

Most of the contestants for the 1984 Democratic Presidential Candidacy are good men and would do a vastly better job than the present incumbent. But why do they prevaricate and—with one exception—avoid the prime issue of our time—nuclear war? They mention it among "other things" but why do they not give us confidence in revealing that they *know* it is the most urgent, the most fateful subject in all history?

Nuclear war would obliterate all government, all culture, and possibly all human life on earth. The endless chatter on the economy, the promises of jobs, welfare continuance, defense, justice and other aspects of our existence—including concern for the environment—is meaningless in the face of the universal catastrophe.

There are two ways to minimize the threat of nuclear war. One, to assure a resounding defeat of the Reagan Administration; and two, for the new President to give *absolute priority* to the reduction and elimination of nuclear arms.

This appears simplistic and perhaps naive. Has anyone a better solution? When will the candidates awake to reality?

Ansel Adams

1. This letter was published in the *New York Times*, March 4, 1984.

ANSEL ADAMS DIED APRIL 22, 1984.

Chronology

꧁ ꧂

1902
Born Ansel Easton Adams on February 20, at 114 Maple Street, San Francisco; the only child of Olive Bray and Charles Hitchcock Adams. The family home is completed the next year at 129 Twenty-fourth Avenue, in the sand dune area overlooking the Golden Gate.

1906
Family survives the great San Francisco earthquake, although Adams falls during an aftershock and breaks his nose.

1907
Grandfather William Adams dies and family lumbering business fails. Charles Hitchcock Adams spends much of the rest of his life attempting to repay the debts of the failed business.

1908
An enormously curious and gifted child, Adams begins a precarious and unsuccessful journey through the rigid structure of the school system. Grandfather Bray and Aunt Mary Bray come to live with his family.

1914
Teaches himself to play the piano and excels at serious music study.

1915
Despises the regimentation of a regular education, and is taken out of school. For that year, his father buys him a season pass to the Panama-Pacific Exposition, which he visits almost every day. Private tutors provide further instruction.

1916
Persuades parents to take family vacation in Yosemite National Park. Begins to photograph there using his first camera and develops an enthusiastic interest in both photography and the national park. Returns to Yosemite every year for the rest of his life.

1917
Receives grammar school diploma from the Mrs. Kate M. Wilkins Private School, San Francisco. Though largely self-taught in photography, he works that year and the next at Frank Dittman's photo-finishing business.

1920
Spends the first of four summers as the custodian of the Sierra Club headquarters in Yosemite. Photography becomes more than a hobby as he begins to articulate his ideas about the creative potentials of the medium. Continues piano studies with professional ambitions, studying with Frederick Zech.

1921
Finds a piano to practice on during second entire summer in Yosemite at Best's Studio, a Yosemite concession selling paintings, photographs, books, and gifts. Meets Harry Best's daughter, Virginia. Takes first high-country trip into the Sierra with Francis "Uncle Frank" Holman.

1922
Publishes first illustrated article, on the Lyell Fork of the Merced River, in the Sierra Club *Bulletin.*

1925
Decides to become a concert pianist and purchases a Mason and Hamlin grand piano. Explores Kings River Canyon with the LeConte family. Takes a similar trip the following summer.

1926
Takes first trip to Carmel with Albert Bender, who becomes his patron; meets Robinson Jeffers there.

1927
Makes the photograph *Monolith, The Face of Half Dome.* He considers this image to be his first "visualization," using the term to describe the photographer's pre-exposure determination of the visual and emotional qualities of the finished print. Publishes initial portfolio, *Parmelian Prints of the High Sierras* [sic] (San Francisco: Jean Chambers Moore). Goes on first Sierra Club outing. Travels with Bender in California and New Mexico, where he meets Mary Austin.

1928
Marries Virginia Best in Yosemite. First one-man exhibition held at the Sierra Club, San Francisco. His photographs will be included in more than five hundred exhibitions during his lifetime.

1929
In Taos, meets Georgia O'Keeffe and John Marin at Mabel Dodge Luhan's estate.

1930
Meets Paul Strand in Taos, becomes committed to a full-time career in photography after understanding Strand's total dedication to creative photography and seeing his negatives. Builds home in San Francisco, where he begins seeking commercial photography assignments. Publishes *Taos Pueblo,* containing twelve original photographs with text by Mary Austin.

1931
Writes photography column for *The Fortnightly;* reviews Eugène Atget and Edward Weston exhibitions at San Francisco's M. H. de Young Memorial Museum. Exhibition of sixty prints at the Smithsonian Institution.

1932
With Edward Weston, Imogen Cunningham, and other proponents of pure photography, founds Group *f*/64, and is a part of the renowned Group *f*/64 exhibition at the de Young; also has one-man show there.

1933
Son Michael born. Meets Alfred Stieglitz at his gallery, An American Place, in New York City. Opens Ansel Adams Gallery at 166 Geary Street, San Francisco, after return. First New York City exhibition at Delphic Studios.

1934
Elected to the Board of Directors of the Sierra Club.

1935
Daughter Anne born. Publishes *Making a Photograph: An Introduction to Photography* (London: The Studio Publications).

1936
One-man exhibition at An American Place. Lobbies congressmen in Washington, D.C. on behalf of the Sierra Club for the establishment of Kings Canyon National Park. Virginia inherits Best's Studio after her father's death.

1937
They move to Yosemite in the spring, where they take over the proprictorship of Best's Studio. His Yosemite darkroom burns, destroying twenty percent of his negatives. He continues to work and maintain his professional studio in San Francisco. Takes photography treks with Edward Weston through the High Sierra and with Georgia O'Keeffe and David McAlpin through the Southwest. Photographs included in first historical survey of the medium at the Museum of Modern Art, New York City.

1938
Takes O'Keeffe and McAlpin through Yosemite and on High Sierra explorations. Photographs with Edward Weston in the Owens Valley. Publishes *Sierra Nevada: The John Muir Trail* (Berkeley: Archetype Press).

1939
Meets Beaumont and Nancy Newhall in New York. Has major exhibition at the San Francisco Museum of Modern Art.

1940
Teaches first workshop in Yosemite, the U.S. Camera Photographic Forum, with Edward Weston. Organizes the exhibition and edits the catalogue for "The Pageant of Photography" for the Golden Gate Exposition, held at the Palace of Fine Arts, San Francisco. Helps to found the Department of Photography at the Museum of Modern Art, New York, with Newhall and McAlpin.

1941
Develops his Zone System technique of exposure and development control while teaching at Art Center School in Los Angeles. In 1941 and 1942 photographs national parks and monuments for the Department of Interior; project ends in June 1942 because of World War II. Publishes *Michael and Anne in Yosemite Valley*, text by Virginia Adams (The Studio Publications).

1943
Photographs at Manzanar Reloca-
tion Center, begins *Born Free and
Equal* photo-essay on the loyal
Japanese-Americans interned there.

1944
Publishes *Born Free and Equal* (New
York: U.S. Camera).

1946
Receives John Simon Guggenheim
Memorial Foundation Fellowship to
photograph the national parks and
monuments. Founds Department of
Photography at the California
School of Fine Arts in San Fran-
cisco, later renamed the San Fran-
cisco Art Institute. Hires Minor
White to teach with him. Publishes
Illustrated Guide to Yosemite Valley, with
Virginia Adams (San Francisco:
H. S. Crocker).

1947
Photographs extensively for Guggenheim Fellowship in the national
parks and monuments during 1947,
1948, and 1949.

1948
Guggenhcim Fellowship renewed.
Begins lifelong friendship with Dr.
Edwin Land. Publishes *Basic Photo
Series 1: Camera and Lens,* and *2: The
Negative* (Hastings-on-Hudson, New
York: Morgan & Morgan) and
Yosemite and the Sierra Nevada, edited by
Charlotte E. Mauk with the selected
words of John Muir (Boston:
Houghton Mifflin Company). Issues
Portfolio I in an edition of 75.

1949
Becomes consultant for newly
founded Polaroid Corporation.

1950
Publishes *Basic Photo Series 3: The Print*
(Morgan & Morgan), *My Camera in
Yosemite Valley* (Yosemite: Virginia
Adams and Boston: Houghton Mif-
flin Company), and a reprint of the
1903 title, with his photographs, *The
Land of Little Rain,* text by Mary
Austin (Houghton Mifflin Com-
pany). Issues *Portfolio II, The National
Parks and Monuments* in an edition of
105. His mother, Olive, dies.

1951
His father, Charles, dies.

1952
Publishes *Basic Photo Series 4:
Natural-Light Photography* (Morgan &
Morgan). Exhibition at the George
Eastman House, Rochester. Helps
found *Aperture,* a journal of creative
photography, with the Newhalls, Mi-
nor White, and others.

1953
Does *Life* photo-essay with Dorothea
Lange on the Mormons in Utah.

1954
Publishes *Death Valley* (Palo Alto:
5 Associates), *Mission San Xavier del
Bac* (5 Associates), and *The Pageant of
History in Northern California* (San
Francisco: American Trust Co.).
Nancy Newhall contributes the text
for all three books.

1955
The Ansel Adams Yosemite Workshop, an intense short-term creative photography learning experience, begins as an annual event.

1956
Organizes with Nancy Newhall the exhibition "This Is The American Earth" for circulation by the United States Information Service. Publishes *Basic Photo Series 5: Artificial-Light Photography* (Morgan & Morgan).

1958
Receives third Guggenheim Fellowship. Publishes *The Islands of Hawaii*, text by Edward Joesting (Honolulu: Bishop National Bank of Hawaii).

1959
Publishes *Yosemite Valley*, edited by Nancy Newhall (5 Associates).

1960
Publishes *This Is The American Earth*, text by Nancy Newhall (Sierra Club). Issues *Portfolio III, Yosemite Valley* in an edition of 208.

1962
Builds a home and studio overlooking the Pacific Ocean in Carmel Highlands, California. Over the next two decades, he produces in the spacious darkroom most of the fine prints made during his career. Publishes *Death Valley and the Creek Called Furnace*, text by Edwin Corle (Los Angeles: Ward Ritchie) and *These We Inherit: The Parklands of America* (Sierra Club).

1963
The Eloquent Light, a retrospective exhibition with prints from 1923 to 1963, shown at the de Young Museum. Publishes *Polaroid Land Photography Manual* (Morgan & Morgan) and first volume of a biography, *Ansel Adams: Volume 1, The Eloquent Light*, text by Nancy Newhall (Sierra Club). The planned subsequent volumes were not completed. Publishes revised edition of *Illustrated Guide to Yosemite Valley* (Sierra Club). Issues *Portfolio IV, What Majestic Word* in an edition of 260.

1964
Publishes *An Introduction to Hawaii*, text by Edward Joesting (5 Associates).

1965
Joins President Johnson's environmental task force; photographs published in the president's report, *A More Beautiful America . . .* (New York: American Conservation Association).

1966
Elected a fellow of the American Academy of Arts and Sciences.

1967
Founder, president, and, later, chairman of the Board of Trustees of The Friends of Photography, Carmel. Publishes *Fiat Lux: The University of California*, text by Nancy Newhall (New York: McGraw-Hill).

1970
Publishes *The Tetons and the Yellowstone,* text by Nancy Newhall (5 Associates) and revised edition *of Basic Photo Series 1: Camera and Lens* (Morgan & Morgan). Issues *Portfolio V* in an edition of 110.

1971
Following 37 years of service, resigns position as a director of the Sierra Club.

1972
Publishes a monograph *Ansel Adams,* edited by Liliane De Cock (Morgan & Morgan).

1974
First trip to Europe, where he teaches at the Arles, France, photography festival. Major exhibition, "Photographs by Ansel Adams," initiated and circulated by the Metropolitan Museum of Art. Publishes *Singular Images* (Morgan & Morgan) and *Images: 1923–1974* (Boston: New York Graphic Society [NYGS]). Issues *Portfolio VI* in an edition of 110.

1975
Helps found the Center for Creative Photography at the University of Arizona, Tucson, where his archive is established.

1976
Begins exclusive publishing agreement with NYGS, a division of Little, Brown and Company. Publishes *Photographs of the Southwest* (NYGS). Issues *Portfolio VII* in an edition of

115. Attends the opening of his major exhibition at the Victoria and Albert Museum, London.

1977
Publishes *The Portfolios of Ansel Adams* (NYGS) and a facsimile edition of the book *Taos Pueblo* (NYGS). With Virginia, endows curatorial fellowship at the Museum of Modern Art in honor of Beaumont and Nancy Newhall. Begins complete revision of his technical books with the collaboration of Robert Baker.

1978
Publishes *Polaroid Land Photography* (NYGS) and *Ansel Adams: 50 Years of Portraits,* by James Alinder (Carmel: The Friends of Photography). Elected honorary vice-president of the Sierra Club.

1979
Major retrospective exhibition, "Ansel Adams and the West," held at the Museum of Modern Art. Publishes *Yosemite and the Range of Light* (NYGS) and is the subject of a *Time* magazine cover story. Begins writing his autobiography with Mary Street Alinder and printing his Museum Sets, 75 prints representative of his life's work.

1980
Receives the Presidential Medal of Freedom, the nation's highest civilian honor, from President Jimmy Carter. Publishes *The Camera/The New Ansel Adams Photography Series, Book 1* (NYGS).

1981
Publishes *The Negative/Book 2* (NYGS).

1983
Publishes *Examples, The Making of 40 Photographs* (NYGS) and *The Print/Book 3* (NYGS). Ansel Adams Day proclaimed by the California State Legislature.

1984
Dies April 22nd. California Senators Alan Cranston and Pete Wilson sponsor legislation to create an Ansel Adams Wilderness Area of more than 200,000 acres between Yosemite National Park and the John Muir Wilderness Area. The Friends of Photography publish memorial book, *Ansel Adams, 1902–1984*.

1985
Mt. Ansel Adams, an 11,760-foot peak located at the head of the Lyell Fork of the Merced River on the southeast boundary of Yosemite National Park, officially named on the first anniversary of his death. Ansel Adams Publishing Rights Trust (AAPRT) releases *Ansel Adams: An Autobiography*, with Mary Street Alinder (NYGS). Major exhibition, "Ansel Adams: Classic Images," at the National Gallery of Art, Washington.

1986
AAPRT releases *Ansel Adams: Classic Images*, text by James Alinder and John Szarkowski (NYGS).

1987
Major exhibition, "Ansel Adams: One With Beauty," at M. H. de Young Memorial Museum, San Francisco.

1988
AAPRT releases *Ansel Adams: Letters and Images 1916–1984*, edited by Mary Street Alinder and Andrea Gray Stillman (NYGS).

BY JAMES ALINDER

Acknowledgments

❧ ☙

We deeply appreciate the permission from those listed below to reproduce these letters and photographs.

LETTERS

From Virginia Adams: Christmas 1926; August 2, 1933. Courtesy of Virginia Adams.

From Vladimir Ashkenazy: October 19, 1983. Courtesy of Vladimir Ashkenazy.

From Bill Brandt: September 15, 1977. Permission from the estate of Bill Brandt. Courtesy of Noya Brandt.

From David Brower: September 27, 1956. Courtesy of David R. Brower.

From President Jimmy Carter: November 9, 1979; February 15, 1980; August 25, 1980. Courtesy of the Jimmy Carter Library, Atlanta, Georgia.

From Senator Alan Cranston: June 28, 1983. Courtesy of Alan Cranston.

From Peter Griffin: May 1983. Courtesy of Peter Griffin.

From Philippe Halsman: December 1, 1947. Courtesy of Yvonne Halsman.

From Edwin Land: February 20, 1982. Courtesy of Edwin Land.

From David McAlpin: September 7, 1940. Courtesy of David Hunter McAlpin.

From Beaumont Newhall: February 7, 1939; September 17, 1940; New Year's Day, 1941; June 3, 1942; February 27, 1944; March 7, 1946; March 18, 1948; March 4, 1951; August 4, 1951; July 13, 1960; July 1, 1974; March 23, 1977. Copyright © 1985 by Beaumont Newhall. Courtesy of Beaumont Newhall.

From Beaumont and Nancy Newhall: December 31, 1948; Late June, 1949. Copyright © 1985 by Beaumont Newhall and the estate of Nancy Newhall. Courtesy of Beaumont Newhall and the estate of Nancy Newhall.

From Nancy Newhall: July 15, 1946; July 16, 1946; May 7, 1948; June 18, 1948; September 8, 1948; Christmas Day, 1948; October 24, 1958; January 29, 1961; February 28, 1961; November 14, 1967; September 1970; June 28, 1972; September 17, 1973; May 17, 1974. Copyright © 1985 by the estate of Nancy Newhall. Courtesy of Beaumont Newhall.

From Nancy Newhall and Ansel Adams: June 11, 1944. Copyright © 1985 by the estate of Nancy Newhall and by the Trustees of the Ansel Adams Publishing Rights Trust. Courtesy of the estate of Nancy Newhall and the Trustees of the Ansel Adams Publishing Rights Trust.

From Marion Patterson: September

[409]

17, 1972. Courtesy of Marion Patterson.

From Alfred Stieglitz: June 28, 1933;
October 20, 1933; December 7,
1933; June 9, 1934; May 13, 1935;
July 30, 1936; December 16, 1936;
December 1937; December 21,
1938; July 25, 1940; August 8, 1943;
November 5, 1943; July 4, 1944;
July 23, 1945; April 15, 1946. By
permission of the Stieglitz-
O'Keeffe Archive, Collection of
American Literature, Beinecke
Rare Book and Manuscript
Library, Yale University.

From Paul Strand: October 14, 1933;
March 21, 1949. Courtesy of
Aperture Foundation, Inc., Paul
Strand Archive.

From John Szarkowski: October 19,
1962; June 28, 1976; Early March
1979; March 10, 1979. Courtesy of
John Szarkowski.

From Arthur Thornhill, Jr.: June 3,
1981. Courtesy of Arthur Thornhill, Jr.

From Garry Trudeau: September 3,
1981. Courtesy of Garry Trudeau.

From Brett Weston: 1940; July 22,
1955; July 25, 1955. Courtesy of
Brett Weston.

From Edward Weston: January 28,
1932; December 3, 1934; Late
May or early June 1937; 1937; January 9, 1945; September 1945;
October 1945; November 1945;
December 1, 1945; March or April
1946; April 12, 1946; April 1948;
November 29, 1949. Courtesy of
the Ansel Adams Archive, Center
for Creative Photography, University of Arizona.

ILLUSTRATIONS

John Sexton: *Ansel and Virginia Adams
at the exhibition "Ansel Adams and the
West," Museum of Modern Art, 1979.*
Copyright © 1979 by John Sexton.

Garry Trudeau: Cartoon of Ansel
Adams in Yosemite. Courtesy of
Garry Trudeau.

Edward Weston: *Ansel Adams, Wildcat
Hill, Carmel Highlands, California,
1943.* Photograph by Edward Weston. Copyright © 1981 by the
Arizona Board of Regents, Center
for Creative Photography, University of Arizona.

Cedric Wright: *Ansel Adams cooking on
the tailgate of Helios IV, June 1949.*
Courtesy of the Cedric Wright
family.

Scans of photographs on insert pages
2 (top), 4, 5 (bottom), 6, and 8
(top) courtesy of CORBIS.

Index

◦ᛃ ᛃ◦

Heinecken, Robert, 336
Helms, Ken, 368n
Hill, David Octavius, 74, 126, 280
History of Photography (Newhall), 218, 219, 220
Hoffman, Michael, 341
Holman, Francis ("Uncle Frank"), 5n, 11n, 27
Howard, Robert Boardman, 283
Hoyningen-Huené, George, 191, 193
Humphrey, Hubert, 269
Hyde, Philip, 310

IBM, 238
Ickes, Harold, 285, 288, 371; letter from, 116
Illustrated Guide to Yosemite Valley (Adams and Adams), 148n
Infinity magazine, 316
Interior, U.S. Department of, 116, 289n; commissions from, 137n, 140n, 146; policy protested, 378–380, 387–396, 398

Jackson, William Henry, 132, 139
Jeffers, Robinson, 35, 92–93, 94, 164, 280
Johnson, Hiram, 83
Johnson, Lyndon B., 392
Jones, Pirkle, 187
Julien Levy Gallery, 54n, 71
J. Walter Thompson Co., 91

Katherine Kuh Gallery, 90n
Kennedy, Edward, letter to, 385
Kennedy, John F., 279n, 292
Kertész, André, 191, 193
Kings Canyon National Park, 25n, 30n, 82, 83, 116, 288
Kirstein, Lincoln, 113
Kodak. *See* Eastman Kodak
Korona view camera, 46n, 61
Kramer, Hilton, 341

Land, Edwin, 284n, 338, 339; letters to and from, 243–244, 246–247, 257–259, 304–305, 386, 395–396
Land of Little Rain, The (Adams), 227n
Lane, William H., 305–306, 359
Lange, Dorothea, 76, 146, 155, 237n;

letter to, 289–291; photos by, 80, 113–114, 158, 194; work admired, 132, 191, 294, 296, 297
LeConte, Joseph, and LeConte family, 6n, 25n, 30n, 211
LeConte Memorial Lodge, 6n, 10n, 248n
Leonard, Richard, letter to, 255–257
Leopold, Luna, 308
LeSecq, Henri, 126
Levy, Julien, 52, 71
Life magazine, 218, 225, 236

Little Galleries of the Photo Secession ("291"), 64, 72–73
"Little Known Images" (Adams exhibit), 336n
Luhan, Mabel Dodge, 42n, 43n, 47, 57
Luhan, Tony, 43
Lunn, Harry, 356

McAlpin, David Hunter, 102, 110–111, 125, 151, 181, 242, 351, 381; as benefactor, 91, 93, 100, (and MoMA) 116, 117, 122–125, 174, 175, 306; letters to and from, 122–124, 127–133, 144–145, 161–162, 233–237
McAlpin, Sally Sage, 181, 197
Magazine of Art, 132
Making a Photograph (Adams), 79–81, 164, 234, 273
Maloney, Thomas J., 172
Mammoth Pass Road, 252, 271n, 288
Manship, Paul, 50
Manzanar Relocation Center, 146, 158
Marin, John: Adams on, 47, 57, 68, 70, 150, 164, 194; *Letters of*, 53; works shown, 73, 149, 152, 159, (at MoMA) 85, 87, 178, (price of) 213
Marshall, Betty, 270
Marshall, George, 270, 303; letter to, 301–302
Mayhew, Alison, 281n
Mayhew, Anne Adams. *See* Adams, Anne (daughter)
Mayhew, Charles, 246n, 268n, 281n, 368n
Mayhew, Sylvia, 368n
Mayhew, Virginia, 267